BEFORE YOU KNOW IT

THE UNCONSCIOUS REASONS WE DO WHAT WE DO

John Bargh, PhD

ATRIA PAPERBACK

New York   London   Toronto   Sydney   New Delhi

ATRIA
PAPERBACK

An Imprint of Simon & Schuster, Inc.
1230 Avenue of the Americas
New York, NY 10020

This Atria Paperback edition February 2019

ATRIA PAPERBACK and colophon are registered trademarks of Simon & Schuster, Inc.

For information about special discounts for bulk purchases,
please contact Simon & Schuster Special Sales at 1-866-506-1949
or business@simonandschuster.com.

The Simon & Schuster Speakers Bureau can bring authors to your live event.
For more information or to book an event, contact the Simon & Schuster Speakers Bureau
at 866-248-3049 or visit our website at www.simonspeakers.com.

Interior design by Erich Hobbing

Manufactured in the United States of America

10   9   8   7   6   5   4   3   2

The Library of Congress has catalogued the hardcover edition as follows:

Names: Bargh, John A., author.
Title: Before you know it : the unconscious reasons we do what we do / John Bargh, Ph.D.
Description: New York : Touchstone, [2017]
Identifiers: LCCN 2017008149 (print) | LCCN 2017026005 (ebook) |
  ISBN 9781501101236 (eBook) | ISBN 9781501101212 (hardcover) |
  ISBN 9781501101229 (pbk.)
Subjects: LCSH: Subconsciousness. | Cognition. | Motivation (Psychology) | Human behavior.
  Classification: LCC BF315 (ebook) | LCC BF315 .B37 2017 (print) |
  DDC 154.2--dc23
LC record available at https://lccn.loc.gov/2017008149

ISBN 978-1-5011-0121-2
ISBN 978-1-5011-0122-9 (pbk)
ISBN 978-1-5011-0123-6 (ebook)

To Danielle,
my superhero

Contents

Let's Do the Time Warp Again

The distinction between past, present, and future is only a stubbornly persistent illusion.

—Albert Einstein

In college, I majored in psychology and minored in Led Zeppelin. Or maybe it was the other way around.

This was the mid-1970s, and I was an undergraduate at the University of Illinois in Champaign-Urbana. When I wasn't working at a research lab in the Psychology Department, I spent my time hanging out at the student-run FM radio station, WPGU, where I was the nighttime disc jockey. Spinning records requires more than mere technique, and this was especially true back in the pre-digital, vinyl days. It's an art that involves both intuition and expertise, and it took me quite a few on-air mishaps before I finally felt relaxed in my soundproof, windowed box at the station. To drop a new song in properly, you have to match its rhythm and even its musical key with those of the song you're fading out. Like two people meeting in the doorway of a restaurant as one leaves while the other arrives, the two songs overlap for several seconds, and this creates a pleasing sense of continuity. One of the things I loved most about Led Zeppelin was how the often strange and drawn-out ends to their songs spurred me to be more creative in the transitions I engineered. As "Ramble On" drifted away with Robert Plant's "Mah baby, mah baby, mah baby" growing softer and softer, I would overlay the thunder and rain that opens the Doors' "Riders on the Storm."

1

As a midwestern kid who was just beginning to figure out what he wanted to do with his life, I was drawn to psychology because it promised a future of explanations: why humans did what they did, both good and bad; what the components of our minds were that determined our thoughts and feelings; and, most intriguing of all, how we might use this deepening well of knowledge to reshape ourselves and our world. In contrast, the reason I was so obsessed with music was that it *defied* explanation. Why did I like the bands that I did? Why did some songs make the hair on my arms stand up or cause me to involuntarily bounce, while others provoked absolute indifference? Why did music have such a powerful effect on my emotions? It spoke to some hidden reservoir of myself that I didn't understand, but which clearly existed and was important. In 1978, after I moved to Ann Arbor, Michigan, to work on my PhD, my advisor, Robert Zajonc, would call me into his office, hold up two museum postcards with modern art paintings on them, then ask me which one I liked better. He did this for maybe four or five sets of paintings. Each time I knew right away which one I liked more, but I always fumbled for the reasons why.

Bob smiled and nodded at my discomfort. "Exactly," he said.

Psychologists were starting to realize that there were hidden, underlying mechanisms that guided or even created our thoughts and actions, but we were only just beginning to understand what they were and how they worked. In other words, an important part of what makes us who we are was still beyond explanation, yet it was the source of a key part of our experience.

Around this same time, in the late 1970s, a man named Michael Gazzaniga was driving around New England in a twenty-six-foot GMC motor home. One of the fathers of modern neuroscience, Gazzaniga wasn't just taking a road trip for fun. The purpose of his travels was to visit "split-brain" patients—people who'd had their corpus callosum, the band of fibers linking the right and left hemispheres of the brain, severed in order to reduce epileptic seizures. Gazzaniga hoped to learn new things about how different regions of the brain interacted. He would pull up in his motor home and seat the patient in front of a visual display that could present some stimuli to his right brain hemisphere and other information to his left hemisphere. Typically the patient was not aware of what was presented to the right side of his or her brain, only what was presented to the left side.

In some studies, the researchers would present visual commands such as "walk" to the right brain hemisphere, and the patient would immediately push his chair back from the computer table and start to leave the testing room. Asked where he was going, he'd say something like "Going to my house to get a soda." The explanations sounded reasonable but were completely wrong. Gazzaniga was struck by how quickly and easily his patients were able to interpret and give reasonable explanations for behaviors they did not consciously intend or initiate on their own.

The breakthrough insight that Gazzaniga took away from his experiments was that the impulses that drive many of our daily, moment-to-moment behaviors originate in brain processes that are outside of our awareness, even if we are quick to understand them otherwise. We all feel the subjective experience of will, but this feeling is not valid evidence of having willed ourselves to behave a certain way. We can be induced to make movements without willing them, as Dr. Wilder Penfield showed with brain surgery patients at Montreal's McGill University in the 1950s. He would stimulate an area of the motor cortex, and the person's arm would move. He would then warn the patient this was going to happen, and the patient would even try to stop it with his left arm, but it moved nonetheless. Conscious will was certainly not necessary for the arm movement; conscious will could not even prevent it. Gazzaniga argued that the conscious mind makes sense of our unconsciously generated behaviors after the fact, creating a positive, plausible narrative about what we are doing and why. Obviously, there is no guarantee that these after-the-fact accounts are accurate. Gazzaniga's insight put the Delphic adage "Know thyself" in a startling new light and raised new questions about the notion of free will.

On any given day, how much of what we say, feel, and do *is* under our conscious control? More important, how much is not? And most crucial of all: If we understood how our unconscious worked—*if we knew why we do what we do*—could we finally, fundamentally know ourselves? Could insights into our hidden drivers unlock different ways of thinking, feeling, and acting? What might this mean for our lives?

Before You Know It examines these questions, as well as dozens of others that are just as complex and urgent. To begin, though, we need to look at *why* human experience works this way. Once we acquire the right frame for understanding the interplay between the conscious and unconscious operations of our mind, new opportunities open up to us. We can learn to heal wounds, break habits, overcome prejudices, rebuild relationships, and unearth dormant capabilities. This, to invoke two more Led Zeppelin songs, is when transformative possibilities stop being "Over the Hills and Far Away" and begin to appear "In the Light."

We Know What We Don't Know

My brother-in-law Pete is a rocket scientist. Literally. He and I grew up in small-town Champaign together, and then he, my sister, and I all did our undergraduate work together at the University of Illinois. When I went on to the University of Michigan for my postgraduate work, he joined the navy and became an expert in antenna-guided missile systems. He's very smart.

I had been teaching at New York University for a few years in the 1980s when I went to spend a couple of weeks with my family at our little cabin in Leelanau County, Michigan, popularly called the "Little Finger" of the state. In the winter, this part of the country is a cold, forbidding expanse of snow-covered fields and gray skies, but during the summer it is twinkling lakes with Caribbean-colored waters, sand dunes rolling with happy kids, and smoky barbecues and fish boils set against sunsets over emphatically green trees. My dad bought our little unheated cabin when we were kids and we spent our entire summers there for many very special years.

On one particular day, the lake's surface was calm except for the occasional ripples that came from silent, unfelt winds. It was the perfect respite from noisy New York City, where I spent the other fifty weeks of the year. My brother-in-law and I were both early risers, so we sat in the screened-in living room having coffee, taking in the morning light.

"So tell me about the latest and greatest findings in your lab," he said.

I explained how we were finding that conscious awareness and intention were not always the source of our reactions to the world around us. "For example," I said, "there's this thing called the Cocktail Party Effect. Say you're at a party, and you suddenly hear someone saying your name over on the other side of the room. You didn't hear anything she said *before* she said your name, and you might not even have known she was at the party. Amidst all the noise, you were filtering out everything but what the person talking to you was saying, yet still your name managed to get through the filter. Why your name but nothing else? That was the first study we did, showing that we automatically process our name and other important things about our self-concept, without even knowing it."

My brother-in-law looked at me blankly. I figured I hadn't been clear, so I continued. I explained how our opinions of other people—for example, our first impressions—could be influenced unconsciously, even manipulated, by our experiences right before meeting. I had seen this firsthand in experiments my lab had conducted, and it was quite startling. "Basically," I said, "what we keep finding is that much of how the mind operates is hidden to us, and that it shapes our experience and behavior in ways that we're not the least bit aware of. The exciting part is that through our experiments, we're beginning to detect these unconscious mechanisms, to *see* these invisible patterns in our mind."

At this point Pete interrupted me, shaking his head. "That just can't be, John," he blurted. "I can't remember one time when I was influenced unconsciously!"

Exactly, I thought. That's the whole point, isn't it? You can't remember any, because you were never aware of them in the first place.

My rocket-scientist brother-in-law couldn't shake his strong belief—based on his lifelong personal experience—that everything he did was a product of his conscious choice. This is totally understandable. Our experience is by definition limited to what we are aware of. On top of this, it's bizarre and even slightly terrifying to entertain the possibility that we aren't as firmly in control of our thoughts and actions as our consciousness leads us to believe. It's hard to accept that there are forces moving the ship of self besides the conscious captain at the helm.

To truly understand the way unconscious influences operate within us every moment of every day, we must acknowledge that there is a major disconnect between what we are aware of at any given moment and what else is going on in the mind at the same time. There is so much more going on than we are aware of. It is like those graphs of electromagnetic wavelengths in physics, from smallest to largest—we can only see a small fraction of those wavelengths, called the visible spectrum. That doesn't mean all the other wavelengths aren't there—just that they are invisible to us: infrared, ultraviolet, radio, X-rays, and many more. Though we can't see those invisible wavelengths of energy with the naked eye, we do now have devices and technology to detect them and measure their effects. It is the same with our unseen mental processes: we may not be aware of them directly but science is now able to detect them, and we can learn to detect them, too—and by learning to see what is hidden, we acquire a new set of eyes. Or maybe just a new pair of prescription glasses we hadn't realized we'd needed. ("Look at everything I've been missing!") What's more, you don't have to be a rocket scientist to use them.

The Three Time Zones

Until recently, it was not possible to systematically and rigorously test how the unconscious affects our thoughts and actions. Scientists only had theories, case studies from clinical patients, and patchy experimental evidence, which naturally fueled an ongoing debate. The idea of unconscious parts of the mind, mental processes operating without our awareness, existed long before Freud. Darwin, for example, used it repeatedly in his 1859 magnum opus, *On the Origin of Species,* to refer to how the farmers and breeders of his day unconsciously used the principles of natural selection to grow larger ears of corn and breed fatter cows and woollier sheep. He meant that the farmers and breeders were not aware of the reason why what they did worked or of the underlying mechanism behind it—and they were especially unaware of the larger implications of the natural selection mechanism in regard to religious beliefs about the supernatural creation of the world, including all its animals and plants. Later in the nineteenth century, Eduard von Hartmann published a book called the *Philosophy of the Unconscious,* which amounted to nothing more than rampant speculation about the mind and its inner workings, with no data and a scarcity of logic and common sense to boot. This book became very popular and had already been republished nine times by 1884. William James, one of the fathers of modern psychology, disliked Von Hartmann's completely unscientific account of the unconscious regions of the mind, so much so that it provoked his famous dismissal of the unconscious as "a tumbling ground for whimsies." Yet twenty years later, after meeting Sigmund Freud for the first time and hearing him give a talk on the meaning of dreams, James was favorably impressed with the medical approach to the unconscious mind and told

Freud his work was the future of psychology. James appreciated Freud's efforts to move beyond easy armchair speculations to close clinical observations and interventions to alleviate his patients' distress and symptoms.

But then, just a few years after this first and only meeting between these two titans of psychology, James and Freud, came a seismic reaction from the scientific establishment of the time against the study of the mind. The conscious reports by participants in psychology studies about their internal experience, called *introspection,* were not considered reliable sources of evidence, because the same person would report different things at different times when faced with the same circumstances. (Indeed, one of the themes of this book is our human lack of accurate introspective access and knowledge about how our mind works—yet the scientists of the time were relying on their study participants to be able to report accurately on how their minds worked.) In 1913, John B. Watson famously stated that scientific psychology should therefore not attempt to study thought and conscious experience at all. The consequence of this was catastrophic. As Arthur Koestler wrote in his devastating 1967 critique of behaviorism, *The Ghost in the Machine,* Watson and the behaviorists had made a colossal logical error that caused the study of the mind—whether conscious or unconscious—to be excluded from scientific psychology for the next fifty years. As Koestler notes, this was a time when the other sciences, in stark contrast, were making tremendous advances. The dominant "behaviorist" school of psychology as founded by Watson argued vehemently that we were entirely the product of our environment. What we saw, heard, and touched—and little else—determined the things we did. We went through life much like rats that could learn to press a bar in order to get food. Consciousness was an illusion, an *epiphenomenon* that might seem real to us but played no active role in our lives. This extreme view was, of course, wrong. In the 1960s, a new paradigm came into vogue—cognitive psychology. Cognitive psychologists sought to debunk the notion that we were nothing more than sophisticated lab rats and argued that our conscious choices did matter. In giving free will back to us, however, and in fighting so hard against the powerful, entrenched behaviorist establishment, cognitive psychologists swung to the other extreme. They argued that our behavior is almost always under intentional and conscious control and rarely if ever triggered by environmental cues. This different extreme position is also wrong. The truth resides somewhere between these two poles, and can only be understood after we consider the most basic condition of existence for all life on our planet—*time*.

The overarching premise of this book is that the mind—just as Einstein argued was true of the entire universe—exists simultaneously in the past, the present, and the future. Our conscious experience is the sum of these three parts as they interact inside one individual brain. What constitutes the mind's coexisting time zones, however, is less straightforward than it might seem. Or rather, one layer is quite easy to identify, while the others are not.

The *un*hidden past, present, and future are right there in our daily experience. At any moment, we can voluntarily pluck memories from the immense archive warehoused in the brain, some of which retain an extraordinary vividness. Memories also occasionally seek us out, triggered by some association that springs the past on us as if a movie screen had unfurled in front of the mind's eye. And if we take the time to reflect—or have an inquisitive partner or go into therapy—we are capable of uncovering the ways the past shapes our present thoughts and actions. Meanwhile, we remain aware of the ever-continuing present. Every waking second, we experience life as it meets our five senses—sights, smells, tastes, sounds, textures. The human brain evolved so that we could respond usefully to the things that happen around us, *as they happen* in the present. So we devote a tremendous amount of neural resources to making smart behavioral decisions in a shifting world that we can't control. Eons of evolution shaped the gray matter between our ears into a staggeringly sophisticated command center. Think about it: the human brain constitutes on average 2 percent of a person's total body weight but consumes about 20 percent of the energy we use while awake. (Now that you've thought about it, you might want to get something to eat.)

Our imagined futures, however, we can control. We actively pursue ambitions, desires, and milestones—that prized promotion, that dream vacation, that home for our family. These thoughts at play in our minds aren't any more hidden than the past or present. How could they be? We came up with them ourselves.

It is indisputable, then, that our conscious awareness feeds us a substantial, meaningful meal of experience. But much, much more is happening in the mind than is immediately visible in these three time zones. We also have a hidden past, a hidden present, and a hidden future, all influencing us before we know it.

The human organism evolved with the mandate to stay alive and thereby keep reproducing. Everything else—religion, civilization, 1970s progressive rock—came after. The hard-won lessons of our species' survival constitute our hidden past, endowing us with automatic "protocols" that persist today, though we naturally have no personal memory of the immense ancestral history that produced such traits. For example, if a bus is coming at you, you know to jump out of the way, and your nervous system helps you do so without your having to order it to start pumping the adrenaline. Similarly, if someone you're attracted to leans in to kiss you, you know to meet that kiss. Half a century ago, Princeton professor George Miller pointed out that if we had to do everything consciously, we'd never be able to get out of bed in the morning. (That's often hard enough as it is.) If you had to painstakingly decide which muscle to move, and do so in the correct order, you would be overwhelmed. In the helter-skelter hustle of each day, we don't have the luxury to reflect carefully on the best response in each and every moment, so our unconsciously operating evolutionary past provides a streamlined system that saves us time and energy. As we will soon explore, however, it also guides our behavior in other important, less obvious ways—for instance, in such things as dating and immigration policy.

The present as it exists in the mind also contains much more than what we consciously perceive as we commute to work, spend time with our families, or stare at our smartphones (and sometimes as we do all three at once, though I don't advise this). My research over the years, as well as that of my colleagues, has revealed that there is a hidden present that affects nearly everything we do: the products we buy (and how many) while grocery shopping, our facial expressions and gestures when getting to know new people, our performance in tests and job interviews. Though it may seem otherwise, what we think and do in such situations is not entirely under our conscious control. Depending on the hidden forces acting on our mind's present at any given moment, we buy different products (and in different quantities), interact with others in different ways, and perform differently. We also have our trusty hunches, instincts, and gut reactions that Malcolm Gladwell wrote about in his book *Blink*. The malleability of our minds in the present means that "blink" responses are in fact considerably more fallible than many of us think. By learning how they really work in our brain, however, we can strengthen our ability to recognize good and bad hunches.

Then there is the hidden future. We have hopes, dreams, and goals toward which we orient our minds and lives, as well as fears, anxieties, and worries about the future that we sometimes can't banish from our thoughts. These ideas coursing through our neural pathways exert a remarkable, invisible sway over us. What we want and need strongly determine what we like and don't like. For example, one notable experiment showed that when women are prompted to think about finding a mate to settle down with, their disapproval of tanning salons and diet pills (ostensible ways to strengthen attraction) decrease. Why? Because we unconsciously see the world through goal-colored glasses. The tanning salons and diet pills are suddenly a good thing when our mind is unconsciously focused on becoming more attractive in order to find a mate. This invisible future also affects *who* we like and don't like. If you are focused on your career, you feel a greater emotional connection with people you link to your professional goals. Conversely, if you are more concerned with having fun, a different flavor of person will attract you. In other words, friends—as well as other aspects of life—are often a function of our unconscious goals, our hidden future. Examining how our desires can stealthily influence our lives allows us to better arrange our true priorities and values.

Past. Present. Future. The mind exists in all time zones at once, both its hidden operations and its visible ones. It is a kind of multidimensional time warp, even if it gives us a feeling of smooth, linear experience. None of us, not even the most adept practitioners of meditation, is ever *only* in the present. Nor would we want to be.

In essence, the mind operates much like the stereo equipment I used while deejaying at WPGU in the 1970s, except the overlays are much trickier and the sound mixers have more active inputs. It is as if three songs are always playing. The main song (the present) plays the loudest—let's say "Heartbreaker," because it's Zeppelin at their best—while the other two (past and future) are constantly fading in and out and slyly changing the overall sound. The slippery nuance is this: in the hidden depths of your mind, there are important lyrics, melodies, and backbeats that you aren't aware of. Even when they are most strongly altering the overall character of the song you're listening to, you rarely know to listen for them.

The aim of this book is to put you inside the DJ booth of your mind so that you hear better what is really going on and can start controlling the music yourself.

The New Unconscious

Humanity's long journey toward understanding the unconscious mind has taken us in a number of erroneous, if quite imaginative, directions. In the Middle Ages, when people exhibited any strange behaviors, such as talking to oneself or seeing visions, it was believed that the devil or an evil spirit possessed them. After all, religions taught that human beings were created in God's image, and God did not go around babbling to himself. Early in the seventeenth century, the philosopher René Descartes (famous for the aphorism "I think therefore I am") located the human soul—our supernatural, godlike quality—in our conscious minds. The cause of socially unacceptable behaviors, therefore, could not be the person's godlike consciousness; it would have to be an external force that took possession of a person's physical body.

Nearly three centuries later, around 1900, the scientists Pierre Janet, in Paris, and Sigmund Freud, in Vienna, independently argued that psychological maladies had natural, physical causes. Freud and Janet were the original psychiatrists. In their separate hospitals and practices, they treated patients who had psychopathologies such as split-personality disorder and tried to formulate an explanation for where these disturbances originated in the physical mind. Janet chalked up mental illness simply to abnormal functioning in the brain, whereas Freud concluded that these pathologies were produced by a separate, unconscious self that lived inside these mental patients. But then he went much further, and insisted—and quite dogmatically so—that this separate unconscious mind existed within each and every one of us, not only in mental patients. Freud demanded that his acolyte Carl Jung and others accept his theories as dogma, almost as revealed truth, and not as hypotheses to be put to scientific test (as Jung then proceeded to do anyway). And so, while his emphasis on unconscious drives was without question a ground-shaking insight, in effect Freud demonized the unconscious operations of the normal mind, claiming that each of us harbored a separate unconscious netherworld of dark, twisted urges that we could exorcise only through psychotherapy. Janet, who studied the same phenomena, strongly disagreed, but as we know, it was Freud's theories that became embedded in popular culture, where they still largely remain.

In his extensive and detailed theorizing, Freud presented the unconscious mind as a seething cauldron of maladaptive complexes bent on causing us trouble and grief, which could only be overcome through the intervention of our conscious mind (with the help of a good psychiatrist, of course). And Descartes had held that our conscious mind was our godlike quality, the physical unconscious mind representing our base, animal nature. The legacies of Descartes and Freud persist to this very day, even in some branches of scientific psychology. In short, what is conscious is *good,* and what is not conscious is *bad.* This is a convenient oversimplification that is also completely, inconveniently *wrong.*

Why do we cling to this belief and cherish it so much? I think in large part it is because we so *want* to believe it; after all, consciousness is our very own superpower that sets us apart from all the other animals of earth. Just take a moment to look at the plot and characters (Avengers, Batman, Spider-Man) in children's TV shows, or Hollywood movies, not to mention all of the TV shows for adults in which the protagonist has special mental powers or abilities. We yearn to be like those movie and television characters, to have a special advantage over others, to have these powers to right wrongs, to wreak revenge, to come to the rescue of our family and friends and the downtrodden in society. These are wonderful, satisfying escapes for us from the realities of our lives, and we spend good money and much of our valuable time to be entertained by these media fantasies on a regular basis. We want these superpowers so badly that we are understandably reluctant to give up believing in the one we *do* have (consciousness) that other animals don't.

So we are motivated to believe that our conscious mind is the source of good, and also motivated to blame the unconscious workings of the mind for what goes wrong, what is bad. When we do something others frown upon, we say "I didn't mean it" or "I didn't mean to," and come up with extenuating causes or reasons for our behavior other than "Yeah, I meant to do that, and I wish I hadn't gotten caught." One way to show yourself that you do often acknowledge other causes of your behavior besides your conscious intent is to appreciate that you invoke just these other causes when you don't want to take ownership (blame) for your actions. Suddenly, you *do* believe that your actions can be caused by something other than your conscious intentions. But if you are honest with yourself, you will recognize that this principle should be applied just as much to your positive behaviors as to the ones you'd prefer to disown.

But today, thanks mainly to the advent of cognitive science and the new methods it has made available, we have entered the era of the new unconscious. We now know that the unconscious is not a second mind within us playing by its own rules. We have scientific theories about how the mind of the average person works, and we test these hypotheses with experimental data based on the responses of average people, so we can more safely generalize about the average human mind than could Freud, who based his theories on case study evidence from a much smaller number of atypical patients who had major mental and emotional problems. Brain imaging studies have revealed that unconscious psychological processes make use of the very same brain regions and systems the conscious mind does: "The Song Remains the Same," as it were. We have a single, unified mind that operates in both conscious and unconscious modes, always using the same set of basic machinery, fine-tuned over the course of evolutionary time. The hidden mind—the mental processes operating outside our knowledge and intention—exists to help us, though it does have an array of complex effects that we will benefit from understanding. These essentially unconscious mental processes are what I have spent my forty-year career studying.

In the summer of 2003 I moved from NYU to Yale. When I arrived, my colleagues and I christened our lab the Automaticity in Cognition, Motivation, and Evaluation Lab—ACME, for short. The acronym is a telling one (though I admit I'd first wanted to name the lab ACME, for reasons soon to become clear, and only then came up with what the initials stood for). The word *acme* means "peak" or "zenith," and many of us think that our conscious mind is the high-water mark of perfection, the "Crown of Creation" (which is a Jefferson Airplane, not a Led Zeppelin, song). While it is indeed the culmination of a 3.6-billion-year evolution of life, that wasn't the real reason I wanted to name it ACME lab.

Many of you may remember the old *Road Runner* cartoons in which the rapaciously hungry Wile E. Coyote chased the innocent Road Runner down endless desert highways. The Acme Corporation was the purveyor of all of the oddly specific contraptions and explosives Wile E. used to hunt his prey. (Indeed, our lab's website includes a link to a catalog of all those fine Acme products.) In the end, however, these contraptions always managed to explode or otherwise backfire. In a certain sense, the Road Runner is our speedy and smarter-than-we-think unconscious mind, and Wile E. Coyote is our scheming and not-as-smart-as-he-thinks conscious mind. We often make Wile E. Coyote's mistake of thinking that we are so cunning and clever, and as a result our conscious plans often get blown to smithereens. The thing is, in life this is rarely as funny as it is in cartoons. Or rather, it is often funny when it happens to somebody else in real life, not so much when it happens to us.

Speaking of real life, in designing the experiments I've conducted in my lab, I have aimed to make the experimental situation as natural and realistic as possible. Being a participant in a psychology experiment is an odd experience, since you know that you are being evaluated by a *psychologist*, an expert on human thinking and behavior. (In college, I participated in a dozen psychology experiments myself, and was always expecting someone in a white lab coat to come out and stare at me after I was done, shaking his head and groaning like Lurch in *The Addams Family*.) This can make people somewhat wary, causing them to think more than usual about what they are doing, and to try to present themselves in the most favorable light. But as psychological scientists we don't want to study how people act when they are on their guard. We want to know what happens out in the real world when people aren't self-consciously modifying their behavior. So over the years, we have designed many of our studies to collect information in ways our participants don't realize are part of the actual study at all.

For example, we have studied the effects of power and powerlessness by having volunteers come into a professor's office (mine) where I casually assign them to sit in either the big leather professor's chair behind the large desk (high power), or the rickety student's chair in front of it (low power). In another study, we timed how long people took to walk down a hallway leaving an experiment, after they thought the experiment was already over. And in a third, the experimenter casually asked participants to hold his hot or iced coffee for a moment so he could reach into a folder and get a questionnaire for them to fill out: his giving them a warm or cold sensation without their noticing it was part of the actual study. In these ways, we increase what is called the "ecological validity" of the experiment, the likelihood that our findings will also occur in the real world outside the laboratory. And after decades of such research, experiment after experiment has shown that the unconscious isn't an impenetrable wall, but a door that can be opened, and to which science holds the key.

Like my brother-in-law, people who first hear about the power of unconscious influences often fear that they do not have free will or control over their lives. But ironically, refusing to believe the evidence just to maintain one's belief in free will actually reduces the true amount of free will that person has. It is those very people who deny the mechanics of suggestibility or the possibility of influences they are not aware of who are most vulnerable to being manipulated. And paradoxically, perhaps, it is through recognizing the existence of unconscious forces, and the limits to our free will, that we can actually increase the free will we do have. If I am aware, for example, how the events of my day at the office can influence how I react to my five-year-old running up to me when I come in the door at home, I can take steps to control that influence and react to this joyous if mundane occasion as I truly wish to. If I am not aware, I may well mistake my grouchy reaction as being caused by her, and soon regret how I reacted. We, as human beings, have a real and meaningful need to feel that we are the captains of our souls, and that we have control over the outcomes of our lives. If we thought we had no agency, why would we even try? The fact that there may be influences on us that we do not know about only means we have *less* intentional control than we used to believe we had, not that we have *no* control. Just think how much more control you can gain by recognizing and taking account of these influences, instead of pretending they don't exist (and so allowing them to control you).

After all, real ship captains do not have complete control over where their ship goes. They must take into account other forces, such as the ocean currents and the direction of the wind. They don't just point their bow toward a distant port and sail in a straight line. If they did so, they would crash into the rocks or drift farther out to sea. Rather, the captain adjusts and accommodates to work in concert with these powerful elements that affect the ship's course. Golfers do this all the time as well. If there is a strong crosswind they do not aim directly at the hole but take the wind into account. If you learn to adjust for the unconscious currents and crosswinds operating on you, then you will play your life better than I play golf, which is not very well at all.

This book is about discovering those currents and crosswinds. In the first section, we'll look at our hidden past, and see how we are influenced today by our ancient evolutionary history, our largely forgotten early childhood, and the culture we grew up in. This long-term past—most of which we have no memory of—affects our conscious experience of the present in startling ways. It can affect how we vote in political races, how many friends we have in grade school, and even how well we do on a math test. Our short-term past, what we did in the last hour or two, can also stealthily change what we do across diverse circumstances, causing us to spend more money than we want, eat more, or unfairly judge someone's work performance. The hidden past can even affect your future employment and the salary you're able to negotiate—all depending on what kind of drink your prospective employer is holding in his or her hand, or the type of chair they're sitting in.

In the second section, we'll look at our hidden present—the ways in which we are being influenced by our snap judgments and "thin slices." We'll learn when we can trust our gut, and when it is better to sleep on our blink responses. We'll learn why it is almost impossible to be neutral in our judgments of others (or anything), yet how this same tendency to divide the world into "good" or "bad" can be harnessed to significantly lower the relapse rate for alcoholism. Our present is shockingly supple, and we'll see how the sight of graffiti can turn an otherwise law-abiding citizen into someone who litters, and why the longer you live with your spouse or partner the more you will come to look like them. We'll also investigate how a simple status update on your part can affect the mood of your Facebook friends for up to three days, and why you might want to record the Sunday afternoon football game you watch with your kids, instead of watching it live.

In the third and last section, we'll look at the hidden effects of our future plans, and focus on the latest research on unconscious motivation. Our goals and desires exert powerful influences over us, so we do need to be careful about what we wish for, but they can also spur us on in unexpected ways. We'll see how students can be induced to perform better on verbal tests by simply thinking about their mothers. We'll also explore how to get our minds to work unconsciously to help solve problems for us (even while sleeping), and how to use our newfound knowledge of the hidden mind to help us reach elusive goals. We'll learn the art of *implementation intentions,* which have been shown to help the elderly remember to take their medication, yank people off the couch to start exercising, and motivate young men to profess their love for their fathers without embarrassment.

When I talk to nonscientists about my work, they tend to wonder which is the "real" them, their conscious or their unconscious self. Some people think that the conscious self is the true self, because it reflects a person's intentions and what he is aware of doing. Others think that the unconscious self is the real self because it reflects what the person really believes down deep, not just the version of themselves that they want to present to the world. But the real answer is "both." We need to expand our idea of who is the "I." Just like Descartes, many of us identify with our conscious mind only, as if the adaptive unconscious that serves us so well under most circumstances is some kind of alien life-form that has invaded our body. The unconscious can lead us astray if we are not aware of its influence, but remember, it evolved and exists because it helped us to survive and to thrive. (One of the big knocks on Freud's version of the unconscious is that it is very difficult to see how such a maladaptive system could have evolved through natural selection processes.) Likewise, our conscious mind also evolved as a kind of steering wheel to allow for additional, strategic control of the unconscious mechanisms. Only when we actively integrate both the conscious and unconscious workings of the mind, and listen to and make good use of both, can we avoid the pitfalls of being blind to half the mind.

In other words, it isn't a question of which is our real self, because both of them are. We can't truly know our *complete* selves without knowing the unconscious part and understanding how it shapes our feelings, our beliefs, our decisions, and our actions. The unconscious is constantly guiding our behavior—even though, like Gazzaniga's split-brain patients, we may strongly believe otherwise. Usually it helps, sometimes it hinders, but ultimately its primary purpose is to keep us safe, and to this end it never sleeps and it never rests. We can't turn off the unconscious mind, nor would we ever want to. When you come to understand the fascinating yet simple reasons behind why you do what you do, and how your past, present, and future minds influence you before you know it—well, the hidden mind is not so hidden anymore.

Robert Plant sings in one of the first Zeppelin songs, "Been dazed and confused for so long . . ." I could relate to that feeling back then, and I suppose it is why I chose the career path that I did, and the research I conduct. This is where Led Zeppelin and psychology both led me—to an appreciation of the forces that move us so profoundly, there, just below our consciousness. I sometimes still feel dazed—that's part of life—but a whole lot less confused, especially since my encounter ten years ago with a certain green-eyed alligator.

PART 1

THE HIDDEN PAST

The past is never dead. It's not even past.
—William Faulkner

CHAPTER 1

The Past
Is Always Present

Around 3200 BC, a man with brown eyes and wavy hair lay dying in a boulder-choked gully in what is now the Italian Alps, at more than ten thousand feet above sea level. The man had fallen facedown on the ground, his left arm crossed under his neck. He was five foot two, around forty-five years old, and had tattoo-like markings on his skin and a gap between his two front teeth. He had recently eaten some grains and ibex meat, and had a fractured rib. It was either spring or early summer, yet at this harsh altitude, with snowcapped peaks rising all around, the weather was unpredictable. He wore a goat-hide coat and leggings, carried a copper-bladed ax and other implements, and had a small medicinal kit with him, though it wouldn't save him.

He died, and not long after, a storm descended, sealing his body in ice.

Five thousand years later, on September 19, 1991, two German hikers were making their way down a mountain in the Ötztal Alps and decided to take a shortcut. As they left the customary path, they passed by a gully and noticed an odd shape down on its rocky floor, which was half-flooded with meltwater. They approached it for a closer look, only to discover a human corpse. Shocked, they alerted the authorities, who were eventually able to remove it from the ice in which it was still partially stuck. Soon they realized it wasn't a tragically unlucky mountaineer, as first believed, but one of the world's oldest mummies. Thanks to the ice that had covered the brown-eyed man, and the tucked-away positioning of the gully, which put it out of the path of the crushing movements of the glacier, the body was a monumental scientific find: an exceptionally well-preserved specimen of human life in the Copper Age, offering insights as well into human death.

21

In the years following the discovery of Ötzti—one of the several nick-names that the media gave to the man who met his end in that lonely ravine—scientists carefully analyzed his remains and the objects found with him. One thing they wanted to know was what had killed him. This turned out to be a less than cut-and-dried forensic task. While Ötzti had suffered a head wound on that long-ago day before the storm rolled in to freeze him, it wasn't so clear that this was the main cause of his death. For example, he had a parasitic worm (scientists found its eggs in his stomach), and a test on one of his fingernails revealed that he suffered from a chronic malady of some sort (possibly Lyme disease). The same test also revealed that his immune system had undergone periods of acute distress three times during the last four months of his life. Maybe he had just become weak from a combination of altitude and poor health, and fell off the mountain into the gully. Also, dangerous levels of arsenic were present in his blood, leading researchers to believe that he worked as metallurgist. As if this weren't enough, he also had past bone fractures and a cyst that probably was an aftereffect of frostbite.

And you thought *you* had problems.

While there were many different leads about the nature of his demise, one thing was clear: Ötzti's life was an ongoing assault from his environment. He must have been quite hardy to have made it to the age that he did. And all of this happened to a man who likely enjoyed high status in his community, as his possession of a copper ax suggests. But in the end, scientists discovered it wasn't his health that killed Ötzti, but a more intimate peril—other humans.

In 2001, X-rays revealed an object hidden beneath the skin of his left shoulder. After a detailed inspection, researchers concluded that it was a flint arrowhead, and its sharp point had punctured a blood vessel that would have caused him to bleed out in a very short time. In other words, Ötzti had been murdered, leaving behind one of the coldest cold cases in human history.

The revelation cast his demise in a new light. His head wound, it now appeared, was related to the assault that took his life. He was either bludgeoned by the same attackers who had shot him with the arrow, or he had bashed his head from a fall brought on by the heavy blood loss. Perhaps he was even shoved into the gully by his assailants. Whatever the specific sequence of events that led to his death, it was surely a ghastly scene—a fight for survival that Ötzti lost. Yet this one fateful day arguably resulted in less bodily trauma than the forty-plus years of his daily existence, which was beset with disease, painful physical damage, and a variety of hostile factors in his surroundings. Ötzti's life, just like his death, speaks to the tremendous dangers and difficulties the average human encountered throughout life during our species' long evolution. This is crucial to understand, since it was amid these same dangers and difficulties—which go back much further than the Copper Age, a relative yesterday on the timescale of human evolution—that our adaptive unconscious brain systems were shaped and honed.

The obvious yet profound thing is that, unlike the personal experiences that shape who we are in the present, *we have no memory of this past.* We have no recollections of our evolution. It is hidden from us, which is slightly unsettling considering how dramatically it influences what we think, say, and do. We are born "factory-equipped" with some very basic motivations that came into being during a very different period in human history. (We also come preassembled, of course, though we grow in size.) As Charles Darwin wrote in 1877, "May we not suspect that the vague but very real fears of children, which are quite independent of experience, are the inherited effects of real dangers and abject superstitions during ancient savage times?" Yep, we may. Humans are not a tabula rasa, or blank slate. We have two fundamental, primitive drives that subtly and unconsciously affect what we think and do: the need to survive and the need to mate. (And in the next chapter we'll focus on a third innate drive, to cooperate with each other, which is useful for both survival and reproduction.) Yet in modern life, these ancient, unremembered drives, or "effects" of the mind, often operate without our knowledge; they can cause us to be blind to the real reasons we feel or do things. By peeling back the layers on this hidden past that still affects us, and exposing the ways in which survival and reproduction are always at work in our minds, we can better understand the present.

Where's My Button?

Now, I've never had to flee murderous assailants armed with flint-tipped arrows on a mountain in the Alps, like Ötzti did. But I have—like most people—felt the same will to survive surge through my body the way it must have for him.

It was August 1981, and I had just moved to New York City to begin teaching at NYU. I was twenty-six years old, fresh out of grad school, and the only other time I'd been to the city was for my job interview a few months earlier. Right away, I was on edge. Every morning at around six o'clock, an angry man would start yelling on the street below my studio apartment. I had no air-conditioning and it was the peak of summer, so my windows were wide open. For a week or so his shouts would wake me up, and occasionally a bottle would smash close to my window. I eventually learned that then mayor Ed Koch, who was up for reelection, lived in my building, up in the penthouse, and the angry guy's projectile bottles were meant for him. Now, Angry Guy couldn't throw high enough to reach the penthouse apartment, but he sure could throw high enough to reach my studio. While knowing I was not his intended target made me feel slightly safer (only slightly), the city outside my apartment didn't.

Washington Square was a rougher neighborhood in the 1980s than it is today. (The same is true of many other parts of Manhattan.) During my first week there, two men ran right past me near the Washington Arch, the second one chasing the first one with a switchblade. Those first few months, I was too apprehensive to go anywhere but work during the day, and I *never* went outside after dark. My only furniture at that point was a wooden chair and a folding table, and every night I would double-check the four different locks on my door and wedge the top of the chair under the doorknob. Although I managed to go to sleep each night having lived another day, my flight-or-fight system was on constant high alert. I didn't yet have a sense of belonging in New York, which would only come years later. I had had a wonderful childhood in small-town America, climbing trees and playing baseball and riding my bike around with the gang of kids on my block, and then going to college in my hometown, followed by graduate school in another midwestern college town, Ann Arbor. None of this was any preparation for the multicultural, densely packed, and constantly noisy streets of New York City. It was culture shock, big-time, and I had to have my eyes wide open and attention constantly vigilant if I was going to survive in it—much less thrive in it.

Working on my degree at Michigan a year earlier, I had read an important paper by the psychologist Ellen Langer pointing out the artificiality of many of the social psychology laboratory studies of the time. This paper turned out to presage my own experiences after moving to the city, maybe because Langer based her paper on studies she ran in New York. In real life, she reminded us, the world is a fast-moving, busy place, quite unlike the quiet and calm psychology laboratory rooms where an experimenter works with her participants. Reading Langer's paper while still in Ann Arbor, I understood her argument at an intellectual level, but boy, did I really understand it on a personal one after moving to the city itself.

In many of the studies in the emerging psychology research area of "social cognition"—just starting up when I arrived at NYU—the study participants would be given a button to press when they were ready to move on to the next piece of information. They could read and think about a sentence—say, describing a particular behavior by a person in a story—as long as they wanted to, then press the button to get the next piece of information. Langer said in effect, Gee, this would be great, but in real life we do not have a magic button to press whenever we want the world to stop for a moment so we can figure out what is happening and why. We have to deal with things on the fly, in real time, and we have a whole lot of other things to do in any given instant than just form impressions of the personalities of the people we are with. Our attention has to be focused on several different tasks simultaneously, including what we need to get done at the moment, and there's not all that much attention left to ponder the world at leisure.

New York was overwhelming to me: so many people, so much traffic, so much going on to pay attention to. I wondered if I could bring impressions of the city together with Langer's point in order to create a study. One morning, I stepped out of my office building, wended my way through the crowds on the street, looking in every direction at street crossings, then suddenly came to a complete stop in the middle of the sidewalk on Washington Place. "Where's my button?" I said to myself. I wanted a button to stop the real world so I could figure it out and also navigate it safely. But of course, there is no such button. The question I soon asked myself then was, How do we do it without one?

In the history of humankind, we never had the luxury to pause what is happening around us until we figured out the right/best/safest thing to do. We needed to make sense of the world—especially the dangerous social world—quickly and efficiently, faster than our slow conscious thinking was capable of. We often needed to react to dangerous situations immediately. Not long after expressing my wish for a stop button, I benefited from these unconscious skills firsthand when I stepped off a curb on the way back to my apartment, and was nearly hit by a bicycle whizzing the wrong way down that one-way street. With no time to think, I jumped back onto the curb just in time. In fact, I found myself back on the curb before I was aware of the bicycle that had just sped past. (And I made a mental note for the next time that not everyone obeys one-way-street signs, so always look both ways.) Reflexive, automatic mechanisms (or instincts) for physical safety had protected me, bypassing slower thought processes. I thought that this faster, unconscious form of thought and behavior must be one important reason we were able to deal with the busy world on a real-time basis.

Back in the lab, we set to work to test this idea, designing a research program with the premise that there was, in addition to relatively slow conscious thought processes, a faster, automatic, and not-conscious way in which people dealt with their social worlds. This was a radical premise, because at this time much of psychology continued to assume that everything we decided and did was the result of intentional, conscious thought. Like Langer, we wanted to make our laboratory studies true to the constant onrushing of the world. After all, the point of our research was to understand what was happening out there in real life, not just what happened in quiet, simple lab environments. In one of our first experiments, we redid one of the "button" studies in which the participant could look at a piece of information we gave them as long as he or she wanted before making a judgment about a person, and only then pressing a button to continue. But we added a twist.

Seated in front of a computer screen, our participants read about Gregory, a fictitious person, and twenty-four different things that Gregory had done during the past week, one behavior at a time. In the "honest Gregory" condition, he did twelve honest things, such as "returned the lost wallet"; six dishonest things, such as "did not admit his blunder"; and six neutral things, such as "took out the day's garbage." In the "dishonest Gregory" condition, he did more dishonest things. The twenty-four behaviors of honest and dishonest Gregory were presented in a random order. We asked the participant to form an impression of Gregory while reading the behaviors. Half of the participants had a button so that they could consider each behavior as long as they wanted, before advancing to the next one. Now, so far this was just a standard social cognition experiment, the kind that Langer had criticized. The wrinkle we added was a second condition where everything was the same except the participants did *not* have a button. Instead, the behaviors were presented very quickly, with participants allowed just enough time to read each of them once before the next one came on the screen, and they had to do the best they could in "real time" in figuring this guy Gregory out.

As you might expect, having the button made a tremendous difference. With it there, with the magic ability to stop the world until they'd figured things out, participants had no problem judging Honest Gregory as more honest than Dishonest Gregory. After all, Honest Greg did twice as many honest as dishonest things, and Dishonest Greg did twice as many dishonest as honest things. But without the luxury of the stop button, the participants could not tell any difference between the two! Their impression ratings were based only on those behaviors they could later remember; they were not able to form an impression while Gregory's behaviors were coming at them rapid-fire. Without a button to stop the world for a critical moment, they could not detect even such an obvious difference between people as between Honest and Dishonest Gregory in our study. *They* couldn't, but another group of our participants could. This other group *was* able to tell the difference between Honest and Dishonest Gregory even under the rapid-fire conditions, without the stop button to help them. We had selected them for the study in advance, because we predicted they would be able to deal with the overload just fine.

Who were these special people? They are you and me. What I mean is that there was nothing particularly special about this group, except that they were especially attuned to honesty and dishonesty. How honest a person was really mattered to them, in terms of whether they liked that person or not. Honesty is of course important to all of us, but for this group it was the number one important thing about a person. It was the first personality trait that came to mind for them when asked to write down the features of a person they liked (on a questionnaire we had given to all of our potential participants several months earlier), and dishonesty came first when writing down on a blank piece of paper the characteristics of a person they disliked. They *chronically* thought first about a person's honesty when deciding whether they liked or disliked him. But each of us has our own particular sensitivities—for you it could be how generous a person is; for the person near you right now it could be how intelligent that person is. Or shy, or hostile, or conceited, or whatever. There are a wide range of personality traits we can develop these automatic antenna for; we just picked one to study as an example standing in for all the rest.

That this group with the honesty antenna was able to deal with the no-button conditions just as if they were in the button condition tells us that we are all able to develop radar to pick up the important blips of meaning in our social world, without having or needing to stop and consciously figure them out. We are able to detect aspects of another's personality and behavior that are most important to us even when our mind is very busy. We can certainly do this by the time we are adolescents and young adults—but this is not something that young children can do before they've had enough experience with the social world. It develops over time like any skill does, such as typing on my keyboard now, or driving a car—activities that are often terribly difficult and overwhelming to start with but with experience become easy and effortless.

The bigger picture our button study paints is that—just as Charles Darwin argued in his seminal book on emotions—often the same psychological process can operate in an unconscious mode as well as a conscious mode. Our participants who had the ability to automatically and unconsciously deal with honesty information formed very similar impressions of Gregory as did those who didn't have that ability but did have the button. That is, through using the button to slow the world down to a speed their conscious processes could handle, they were able to deal with the information as well as, and in the same way as, those who could do it using much faster and more efficient unconscious processes. But those participants who could not do either—who did not possess the unconscious antenna for honest behavior, and were not given a button to be able to deal with it consciously—were unable to notice the difference between the very different honest and dishonest versions of Gregory.

So now we had the beginnings of an answer to the question I first asked myself out on Washington Place, the busy New York street, that morning. Thanks to our ability to develop perceptual skills that can operate quickly, efficiently, and unconsciously under real-world conditions, quite often we don't need a button.

The Alligator of the Unconscious

Our study with Gregory and the magic button was one of the first to show that automatic, unconscious ways of dealing with our social world did exist, and that their existence within us made sense given the busy and dangerous

28

conditions—especially regarding other humans—under which we evolved. Back then (as well as today) we didn't always have time to think, so we needed to size people up quickly based on how they acted, and we also needed to be able to act and react quickly. To paraphrase the old saying, "She who hesitates has lost"—her life, a limb, her health, her child. But there is an important difference between the evolved unconscious motivations for survival and physical safety that came up in our story of poor Ötzti (to which we'll return in a moment), and our unconscious ability to detect honesty or shyness or intelligence under rapid-fire, real-world conditions.

We come factory-equipped with those basic motivations for survival and safety, but the "people radar" was a skill we had to develop out of experience and practical use. Think of it as the difference between breathing and driving. The one you were born with and never had to learn, the other you had to learn, yet both now can operate (under normal conditions) without much conscious guidance. Look a little more closely and you can see that even driving requires some evolutionary, "born this way" machinery. After all, let your dog practice driving all you want (far away from me, please) and he won't ever be any good at it. (He might approach the level of some of the drivers in my neighborhood, however.) What I'm getting at is that our ability to drive a car, which only gets up to speed (sorry) after considerable experience and practice, is like our ability to develop a "people radar" through experience and practice, as in the button study. Both depend on the ability of the human mind to create new useful unconscious "add-ons," out of our own personal experience with the world, to those we were originally born with.

When we started researching adaptive unconscious mechanisms for dealing with the busy world, back in the early 1980s, this "driving," or experience-based, unconscious process was all we social psychologists knew about. Evolutionary psychology was just getting started, thanks to Paul Ekman and other pioneers such as David Buss and Douglas Kenrick. The field of cognitive psychology had just overthrown the dominating theory of behaviorism, made famous by its most ardent advocate, B. F. Skinner. As you'll recall from the Introduction, behaviorism held that the human mind barely mattered, and conscious thinking didn't matter at all; even the complexities of human behavior—including language and speech—were said to be caused by reflexive, trained reactions to the stimuli in our immediate environment. Cognitive psychology, on the other hand, championed the role of conscious thought and assumed it was necessary for nearly all human choices and behavior. Nothing happened, according to this view, without you consciously and intentionally causing it to happen. But this wasn't right, either. (Extreme, all-or-none positions tend not to be.)

Within this "conscious-first" framework of cognitive psychology, from which my then newbie field of social-cognitive psychology took its lead, the only way an unconscious process could exist was by being conscious (and deliberate) first; then, only after considerable experience could it become streamlined and efficient enough—*automated* was the word we used—to not need much conscious guidance anymore. (Just like driving a car.) (William James had said the same thing in 1890, that "consciousness drops out of any process where it is no longer needed.") For the next twenty-five years, then, up to about the turn of the millennium, I and the rest of my field assumed that this was the only way in which unconscious mental processes came into being: starting out conscious and effortful, and only with experience and frequent use, becoming able to operate unconsciously. But I and the rest of my field were wrong, or at least holding to an incomplete picture. This was because we were not paying enough attention to the growing body of theory and research evidence from the equally new field of evolutionary psychology growing up right next to us. We were playing in our own sandbox too much, perhaps, and not looking around at the rest of the busy playground.

What caused me to finally yank my head out of the sand and look around more widely was that this "conscious-first" assumption was starting to break down. We were starting to find effects in my own lab that this assumption could not explain, but also there was a wave of exciting new findings in developmental psychology—the study of infants and toddlers who have not yet had much experience or practice in the world—showing automatic and unconscious effects in children too young to have had much conscious practice or experience doing what they were so naturally able to do. This was marvelous new evidence of just how factory-equipped we come into the world, in terms of our ability to deal with our fellow humans, and it directly contradicted the bedrock assumption that these unconscious processes only came about—in older children and adults—after a lot of conscious use and experience.

This new evidence presented me with a puzzle during my own first twenty-five years of research, a conundrum I could not stop thinking about. Finally, after many years of considering this problem, my daughter was born and I took a semester of paternity leave to be able to spend time watching and playing with her at home. And while she was crawling around and contentedly playing with her toys and stuffed animals in her playpen, I sat nearby and read, more widely than I usually did, in areas such as evolutionary biology and philosophy, trying to find the answer to my longtime puzzle. How could there be, I pondered, psychological processes—what are called higher-order mental processes dealing with evaluation, motivations, and actual behavior—that operated unconsciously but apparently without the prior extensive conscious experience and use of them that we'd long assumed was necessary for their unconscious operation?

And so I found myself, on a beautiful fall day in 2006, many years after my epiphany on the streets of New York City, up in my tree house of an attic in New Haven, Connecticut, all the windows open and watching my infant daughter crawl around on the floor in front of me. She was trying her best to make sense of the world around her, just as I was. I had a stack of books next to me, classic works on human evolution by giants such as Richard Dawkins, Ernst Mayr, and Donald Campbell. The warm afternoon sun was pouring through the windows of the nursery, and I was feeling a bit drowsy. At the time, I was getting about as much sleep as most parents of infants do—little to none. As I finally got my daughter down for a nap—as usual, quite reluctantly on her part—I spread out all my research papers and notebooks on my own bed. I knew I was still missing something, but I didn't feel I'd come any closer to what that something was. As I picked up a book and began reading, I could feel my eyes getting heavier and heavier. I fought it, until eventually I slumped over onto my notebooks and papers and fell into a deep sleep.

I was in Everglades National Park in Florida. I stood on one of those raised wooden walkways that look out over the swamp. Everything was in full color, and I could feel the humidity and denseness of the heavy air. Cypress and mangrove trees hemmed in the murky, almost black swamp water. As I stood on the walkway staring down into the swamp I saw ripples emerge, and a large and scaly alligator appeared in the murky water below. I walked ahead and the alligator swam alongside me. The alligator looked ominous, but in my dream I wasn't afraid of it. After what seemed to be maybe five or ten seconds of walking, the alligator had gotten a little ahead of me. Then it stopped and, almost in slow motion, began to roll.

It flipped completely over, exposing a long white belly that looked surprisingly tender and soft.

I awoke with a start and sat bolt upright. *That was it.* My eyes were wide open but I could still see that flipped-over alligator in front of me. I can vividly remember, even now, a decade later, the huge wave of relief that flowed over me, a tremendous release of tension. It was as if a weight I had been carrying for more than a decade just lifted away. *Of course!* I said to myself. I grabbed the pen and paper in front of me on the bed and wrote down everything I had seen in my dream, but more important, what that dream had just told me. In that moment of clarity, I finally understood how all the new unconscious effects being reported could occur without needing extensive prior conscious experience, or even any relevant experience at all, for that matter.

It's the unconscious first, the alligator—that literally flipping alligator—was telling me. *You dummy.*

I'd had it completely backward, all those years. The alligator was telling me to flip my assumptions. Sure, all the new evidence did not make sense under the seemingly unshakable assumption that extensive conscious use of the psychological process came first, before becoming capable of operating unconsciously. But the problem wasn't the evidence, it was my "conscious-first" assumption. The white belly of the alligator was the unconscious, and it was telling me that it would all make sense if I only realized that the unconscious came first, both in the course of human evolution and in the course of our individual development from infancy to childhood to adulthood. I had to flip my so ingrained assumption that for a given person, the conscious use of a process comes first, and that only after repeated use can the process then operate unconsciously, and also that over the course of human evolution, our basic human psychological and behavioral systems were originally unconscious, and they existed before the rather late appearance of language and conscious intentional use of those systems. By "systems" I mean the natural mechanisms that guided our behavior, such as approaching things (and people) we liked, and avoiding those we did not like; to naturally pay attention and notice things out in the world (like sources of food and water) that would satisfy our current needs; not to mention important survival instincts, such as the fight-or-flight response and other inborn mechanisms for avoiding danger (like our fear of the dark and becoming instantly alert after a nearby loud sound). And for each of us as infants, there are basic evolved motivations and tendencies, operating exclusively automatically up to age four, when we begin developing conscious intentional control over our minds and bodies. The alligator was telling me that not everything starts out as conscious and intentional and only after that becomes (with practice and experience) capable of unconscious operation. Mr. White Belly was saying that unconscious processes come first, not the other way around.

In retrospect, this dream was rather remarkable in another sense as well, for the dream itself was unconscious—I watched and experienced it passively, as if it were a movie on a screen. Many other scientists in the past have reported having dreams in which the solution to a problem they'd been working on for some time was revealed to them in some symbolic way. But my own scientific problem had to do with the unconscious per se, and so for perhaps the first time in human history, *the unconscious was telling someone about itself.* The answer to my decade-long quest for an answer to this fundamental question about unconscious processes had come, at last, from my own unconscious processes.

What we now know, thanks to Darwin, cultural (and cognitive) anthropology, and modern evolutionary biology and psychology, is that the human brain evolved slowly over time, first as a very basic unconscious mind, without the conscious faculties of reason and control that we possess today. It was the mind of millions of organisms that don't have or need anything like our human consciousness to act adaptively in order to survive. But the original unconscious mechanisms of our long-ago brain did not suddenly disappear when consciousness and language—again, our own very real superpowers among earthly creatures—finally emerged rather late in the evolutionary story. Consciousness wasn't a different, new kind of mind that miraculously appeared out of the blue one day. It was a wonderful add-on to the old unconscious machinery that was still there. That original machinery still exists inside each of us, but the advent of consciousness gave us new ways to meet our needs and desires, the ability to intentionally and deliberately use that old machinery from within.

So what does it mean that an unconscious mind was the foundation for the conscious version, and not the other way around? For starters, it resolves the either/or debate between the behaviorists and the cognitivists. We aren't mindless automatons at the total mercy of incoming stimuli that send us marching through life like windup dolls, but neither are we all-seeing masters of ourselves who control our each and every thought and action. Rather, there is a constant interplay between the conscious and unconscious operations of our brain, and between what is going on in the world outside of us and what is going on in our heads (our current concerns and purposes, and residual effects of our most recent experiences). The cognitive scientists and the behaviorists are both right (and both wrong, if they deny any validity to the other side of the story). On the cognitive scientists' side of the ledger, our current goals and motivations determine what we seek out and pay attention to in the world, and whether we like or dislike it (depending on whether it helps or hurts us getting what we currently want). And in the behaviorists' favor, the world itself can indeed trigger emotions, behaviors, and motivations in us—and sometimes very powerful ones—without our knowledge or control, as Darwin himself argued. As the philosopher Susan Wolf has written, anyone who thinks they are completely free from such outside influences should try to walk away from a child drowning in the ocean. Hopefully, you couldn't (and God help you if you could). There are, Wolf argues, some freedoms we just don't want to have. And many of these, naturally, relate to the number one motivation of the ancient past that formed our mind—keeping our genes alive.

Genie in a Bottle

The survival of our species was never a foregone conclusion. In fact, the odds were very much against it. After all, more than 99 percent of all species that ever existed are now extinct. As Ötzi's story vividly illustrates, human life evolved in very hazardous conditions. It is easy to forget that our "modern" brain was honed by evolution long before the comforts of modern life were even a twinkle in our visual-processing cortex. The Ötztis and Ötztettes of our past didn't have laws, antibiotics, or refrigeration; they didn't have ambulances, supermarkets, or governments; they didn't have plumbing, guardrails, or clothing stores. Fortunately for us, we don't live in Ötzi's time. But in a very real sense, our minds still do. This is a very important point to grasp.

During our species' long development, the biggest danger of all was our fellow humans. Ötzi's murder on the mountain wasn't at all remarkable, except in its fortuitous preservation of his body. Violent death at the hands of others was shockingly common among our ancestors. Analyses of human skeletons excavated from ancient cities show that about 1 out of every 3 men was murdered. And as recently as the 1970s, the murder rate for males of the Yanomami rain forest people, long isolated from modern civilization, was about 1 out of 4. Today, by comparison, the homicide rate in Europe and North America is about 1 in 100,000.

Now we seek to reduce the dangers to life and safety as much as possible. We have law enforcement, traffic lights and signals, efficient systems of exchange (money, that is) to translate our work into needed food and shelter. We also have medical science and health inspectors. So it is easy to overlook the fact that our unconscious tendencies were shaped by and adapted to this far more dangerous ancestral world, with its life-threatening natural elements such as cold and heat, drought, and starvation, and human and nonhuman organisms, such as wild animals, harmful bacteria, and poisonous plants. The fundamental drive for physical safety is a powerful legacy of our evolutionary past and it exerts a pervasive influence on the mind as it navigates and responds to modern life, often in surprising ways—like who you vote for.

In his first State of the Union address, in 1933, President Franklin Roosevelt famously said: "Let me assert my firm belief that the only thing we have to fear is fear itself—nameless, unreasoning, unjustified terror which paralyzes needed efforts to convert retreat into advance." More than eighty years later, in his final State of the Union address, in January 2016, President Barack Obama echoed Roosevelt's words: "America has been through big changes before. . . . Each time, there have been those who told us to fear the future, who claimed we could slam the brakes on change; who promised to restore past glory if we just got some group or idea that was threatening America under control. And each time, we overcame those fears."

Both FDR and Obama were referring to the effect of fear on *social change*. Roosevelt worried that the fear brought on by the Depression would interfere with making the changes to the laws and to the economy that he strongly felt were needed to begin the process of economic recovery. Obama was referring to national health care and to immigration policies. Both presidents were Democrats and on the liberal side of the political spectrum. Both were arguing against the conservative political tendency to resist social change (that's why it's called *conserv*ative). Very interestingly, both recognized that fear could cause a person to want to avoid social change—that is, to become more conservative and less liberal in his political attitudes.

Why would conservative politicians try to make voters more afraid, and liberal politicians try to make voters less afraid? It has long been known that people become more conservative and resistant to change when under threat of some kind. Research in political psychology has shown that it is much easier to get a liberal to behave like a conservative than it is to get a conservative to behave like a liberal. For example, in one set of studies, liberal college students who were asked to imagine in detail their own death then expressed attitudes regarding social issues such as capital punishment, abortion, and gay marriage that were (temporarily) the same as those of conservative college students, who had not been threatened. In contrast to the results of this fascinating experiment, however, at this time no one had yet been able to change a conservative into a liberal. Under threat or fear people are less risk-taking and they resist change, the very definition of being conservative. The study's findings led me and other scientists to think that perhaps conservative political attitudes were in the service of an unconscious motivation for physical safety and survival. But how could we test this with experiments? We looked first at the research that had already been done.

In one remarkable study, University of California researchers followed a group of four-year-old preschool children for twenty years to see what their political attitudes became when they were young adults. The researchers measured the children's level of fearfulness and inhibition at age four, then two decades years later they evaluated their political attitudes. And those who had shown greater fear and inhibition at age four were indeed more likely to hold conservative attitudes at age twenty-three.

Socially conservative adults (who tend to be against social changes such as same-sex marriage or the legalization of marijuana) participating in psychology experiments show stronger fear or startle responses in reaction to unexpected loud noises, and they also show greater physiological arousal in response to "scary," but not to pleasant, images presented to them. Other studies show that adult conservatives are more sensitive to dangerous or disgusting objects, compared to liberal adults, and that they are also more alert to potential danger and threatening events in the lab.

More recently these differences have even been found in the sizes of brain regions that are involved in emotions, especially fear. The right amygdala region—the neural headquarters of fear—is actually larger in people who self-identify as politically conservative compared to that of those who don't. During laboratory tasks involving taking risks, this fear center of the brain becomes more highly activated in self-reported Republicans than it does in self-reported Democrats.

So there does indeed seem to be a connection between the strength of the unconscious physical safety motivation and a person's political attitudes. And research had shown that you can make liberals more conservative by threatening them and making them somewhat afraid. But what if you made people feel safer instead? If the boiling water of political attitudes can be turned up (conservative) or down (liberal) by the underlying flame of physical safety needs, then making people feel (temporarily) physically safe should cause conservatives' social attitudes to become more liberal.

We conducted two experiments in which we used a powerful imagination exercise to induce feelings of complete physical safety in our participants. We had them imagine being granted a superpower by a genie in a bottle. In one condition, the superpower was to be completely safe and immune from any physical harm, no matter what you did or what happened to you; imagine Superman with bullets bouncing off him. In the control condition, the participant imagined being able to fly. We predicted that imagining being completely physically safe would temporarily satisfy and thus decrease the individual's concerns about physical safety, entirely unconsciously, and thus—if our theory was right—turn conservatives into liberals. At least temporarily.

Use a little imagination yourself and pretend to be a participant in this study. You are asked to visualize and imagine the following things happening to you:

On a shopping trip, you wander into a strange store with no sign out front. Everything is dimly lit and the shopkeeper calls you by name even though you have never seen him before. He tells you to come close and he says to you in a weird voice, "I have decided to give you a gift. Tomorrow, you will wake to find that you have a superpower. It will be an amazing ability but you must keep it absolutely secret.

If you purposely tell anyone or show off your power, you will lose it forever." That night, you have a hard time sleeping, but when you wake, you find that you indeed have a superpower.

Now the story changes depending on which experimental condition you are randomly assigned to. If you are in the *safety* condition, the passage continues:

A glass falls on the floor and without meaning to you accidentally step on the broken glass. It doesn't hurt you at all, though, and you realize that you are completely invulnerable to physical harm. Knives and bullets would bounce off you, fire won't burn your skin, a fall from a cliff wouldn't hurt at all.

But if you were in the *fly* condition, you would read instead:

You miss a step going down the stairs but instead of tumbling down, you float gently to the bottom of the banister. You try jumping from the top of the stairs again and realize that you are able to fly. You can propel yourself through the air as if you were a bird. You can travel entire distances without ever touching the ground.

After imagining having one or the other superpower, we measured the social attitudes of all the participants using a standard measure that in past studies had shown clear differences between conservatives and liberals. Then at the end, we simply asked them who they did or would have voted for in the most recent presidential election (2012), as a way to measure whether they were overall more conservative (Republican) or liberal (Democrat).

Among those who had imagined being given the superpower to fly, which was our control condition, there was the usual and expected large difference on the social attitudes measure: liberals were much less conservative on this measure than were conservatives, and imagining being able to fly didn't change that at all. However, in the "safe from physical harm" superpower condition, things were different. Not for the liberals, who were unaffected by imagining being totally safe; their attitudes were the same as in the "able to fly" condition. But expressed social attitudes of the conservative participants had become much more liberal. Feeling physically safe had indeed significantly changed the conservative participants' social attitudes to now be much more similar to those of liberals. The unconscious needs of their forgotten evolutionary past, for physical safety, had been somewhat sated by the genie imagination exercise, and this had in turn reshaped their seemingly conscious, intellectual beliefs on current social issues.

In our second experiment, everything was the same as before, except that we asked the participants questions about their openness or resistance to social change (which is the defining quality of a conservative versus a liberal political ideology). In the fly-superpower condition, there was the usual difference, conservatives being more conservative on this questionnaire than liberals. But in the safety-superpower condition, imagining being completely physically safe reduced the conservatives' resistance to social change to the level of the liberal participants. Our genie really was magical. He had done something no one had been able to do before: turn conservatives into liberals!

Again, we had predicted this effect based on the idea that our modern-day social motives and attitudes are built upon, and are ultimately in the service of, our unconscious evolutionary goals: in this case, our supremely powerful motivation to be physically safe. Satisfying that basic need for physical security through the genie imagination exercise therefore had the effect of turning off, or at least reducing in strength, the need to hold conservative social and political attitudes, much the same as turning off the gas flame under a pot of water causes the water to stop boiling.

Of Germs and Presidents

Since we did our genie study on liberals and conservatives, there has been another U.S. presidential election, in 2016. And what an election year that was! On February 9, Donald Trump won the Republican primary election in New Hampshire. From that day, with his strawberry helmet of hair and reality-TV billionaire bluster, he plowed onward to clinch his party's nomination in a series of resounding primary victories with little resistance at the polls, though with plenty—*pah-lenty*—of resistance everywhere else, even inside his own party. And then he topped it off with a stunning upset victory over Hillary Clinton, to become the forty-fifth president of the United States. With an incendiary, off-the-cuff speaking style, Trump created controversy after controversy, which the twenty-four-hour news cycle hungrily gobbled up again and again. He insulted and degraded women, made fun of a handicapped person, and bragged about his penis size and wealth. Tellingly, he also seemed obsessed with germs, and a reporter who followed his campaign and was often backstage with him described Trump as "a germaphobe who doesn't like shaking hands and will only drink soda from a sealed can or bottle. He keeps a distance from the supporters who come to his rallies."

During the campaign, Trump very often called his political rivals "disgusting"—most famously, when Hillary Clinton was seconds late getting back to the podium during a televised Democratic candidate debate with Bernie Sanders because she had to go to the restroom. As Trump told his supporters at a rally in Grand Rapids, Michigan, the next day, "I know where she went—it's disgusting, I don't want to talk about it," wrinkling his nose and giving a sour look, to the delight of his crowd. "No, it's too disgusting. Don't say it, it's disgusting." A few months later, following his own first debate with Clinton, he referred to former Miss Universe Alicia Machado as "disgusting" as well. Without rehashing the whole bizarre campaign, suffice it to say that it was one of the most memorable presidential election seasons in a long time, and according to most observers, a new low in the U.S. public dialogue.

Our physical safety is not only about avoiding physical damage. It is also very much about avoiding germs and disease. We are careful not to eat food that smells spoiled or rotten—we have evolved senses to detect—and we are squeamish about touching things that look dirty or contaminated. As Darwin argued, we are also quite sensitive to the expression of disgust by others around us, and we react strongly and automatically to those expressions by avoiding any contact with what they just ate or drank or touched and with good reason: germs and viruses have wiped out huge swaths of the human population from time to time during recorded human history.

Infection was a real killer in our ancestors' world. Getting a cut or open wound through which germs and viruses could enter the body was a very serious and potentially life-threatening situation. This was the case even as recently as the U.S. Civil War, in the 1860s, when 62 out of every 1,000 soldiers died not from being shot or stabbed, but from infections. It was only with the invention of the microscope and Louis Pasteur's discovery of microorganisms that we came to understand how diseases were transmitted. Modern-day improvements in sanitation especially have reduced the threat of plagues, widespread contamination, and spread of disease. Thanks to these advances and to our own personal knowledge regarding the importance of hygiene and protecting cuts and wounds, we are much safer from germs and diseases than we used to be. Still, viruses and bacteria are evolving just like people are. For instance, there seems to be a new strain of flu virus nearly every season.

Over the vast majority of human history, during which our mind became what it is today, there was a very real survival advantage to avoiding anything that smelled or looked as though it was full of germs or bacteria. After all, the ancient world did not feature refrigeration, or health department ratings of food found on the ground. Things that smelled "bad" to us did so for a reason. (Things that smell really bad to us probably smell really good to, say, a dung beetle.) Those of us who were put off by the odors of filthy, germ-laden material avoided them and so were less likely to be contaminated and made ill by them. Disgust and germ avoidance were thus highly adaptive components of our general motivation to remain physically safe, to protect ourselves and our families from disease.

With this in mind, now consider the modern political divide on the issue of immigration: conservatives are strongly opposed to and liberals more in favor of immigration. It was one of the central, hot-button issues in 2016 election-year politics in the United States and elsewhere, made even more prominent by the Syrian refugee crisis. One reason for conservatives' antipathy to immigration is the change it brings to one's country and culture. Social change can occur when immigrants bring in their own cultural values, practices, religions, beliefs, and politics. But given the greater concern that conservatives have with physical safety and survival, another reason to oppose immigration could be found in the frequent analogy made by conservative politicians of the past (and present) between immigrants coming to a country (the political body) and germs or viruses entering one's own physical body. Archconservative leaders of the past such as Adolf Hitler explicitly and repeatedly referred to scapegoated social out-groups as "germs" or "bacteria" that sought to invade and destroy the country from within (and who therefore must be eradicated). If immigration is unconsciously linked to germs and diseases, then anti-immigration political beliefs would effectively be in the service of that powerful evolutionary motivation—disease avoidance.

To test this possibility, we devised two studies around the time of the 2009 H1N1 flu virus outbreak, in the fall, when people are encouraged to get preventative flu shots. That year, the virus was particularly virulent, and for the first time, Yale put antibacterial disinfectant stations all over campus. We conducted our first experiment at lunchtime just outside the Commons dining hall, a large, Hogwarts-esque room with dark wooden paneling, stained-glass windows, long wooden tables, and cast-iron chandeliers hanging from a vaulted ceiling. To turn on participants' disease avoidance motive, we first reminded them about the current flu rampage, with a handout and a personal message from the experimenter about the importance of getting vaccinated. Then participants answered a survey about their attitudes toward immigration. After they had finished the survey, we asked our participants if they had already been inoculated against the flu or not.

As we'd predicted, those who had been reminded about the threat of flu at the start of the experiment but had not yet been inoculated—and so should be somewhat threatened by the flu virus—had attitudes toward immigration that were significantly more negative. But those who had already been inoculated expressed more positive attitudes about immigration. The reminder about the flu virus also reminded them that they were safe from it because of their flu shot.

We then did a follow-up study at the same campus locale. We reminded all of the participants about the ongoing flu season in the same way as before. But this time we also emphasized how washing one's hands frequently or using Purell or other antibacterial sanitizers was an effective way to avoid catching the flu. After this message, participants were randomly assigned to (a) be offered a chance to use some hand sanitizer or (b) not be given this chance. We then gave them the same political attitudes survey including items about immigration. And once again, those who had cleansed their hands after the disease-threat manipulation had more positive attitudes toward immigration, and those who had not been given this chance to wash their hands reported more negative attitudes about immigration.

As odd, or even disturbing, as it may seem, our political attitudes are profoundly influenced by our evolutionary past. Deep, primitive needs underlie our beliefs, although we are rarely, if ever, consciously aware of our reasons for holding those beliefs. Instead—myself included—we convince ourselves that our thinking emerges only from rational principles and ideologies, perhaps about rugged individualism and honor, or to fairness and generosity toward others. We are not consciously aware of the winds of our evolutionary past blowing through our attitudes and behavior, but this does not mean those influences aren't there.

But feelings of disgust affect more than our abstract political attitudes. Simone Schnall and her colleagues at the University of Virginia have shown how feelings of physical disgust, caused for example by being in a very dirty room, influence our feelings of *moral* disgust, in terms of how morally wrong we believe various behaviors are. The study participants completed morality ratings of various behaviors, such as stealing a drug you can't afford in order to save your spouse's life. If they happened to make those ratings in a dirty room, they considered those behaviors to be less moral compared to when those same behaviors were rated by other participants in a clean room.

Our primary, ultimate, deepest evolved motivation for survival and physical safety is at the root of many of our attitudes and beliefs. This need influences us largely unconsciously and usually without our understanding what is really going on. This is not a bad thing, of course. It's a matter of context. Our deep concern with physical safety and disease avoidance is, without a doubt, highly adaptive. It has become part of our genetic makeup because it helped us, as individuals as well as a species, to survive. It is such a basic and powerful influence in our lives that its reach extends well beyond the concrete, relatively simple tasks of staying alive and avoiding bodily damage. Even our moral judgments, as well as our abstract, conscious reasoning about political and social issues, can be in the service of this paramount motivation, without our realizing it.

Sharing Is Caring

Another evolved trait that helped us survive and stay physically safe is inherently social in nature—the spontaneous and involuntary emotions we experience and outwardly express to others. They were the focus of Darwin's third major book on evolution, *The Expression of Emotions in*

Man and Animals, his powerful follow-up to *On the Origin of Species* and *The Descent of Man.* This third book was all about human social life, because Darwin believed that our emotions evolved to help us communicate important information about safety and disease to each other, and that cooperation and sharing are part of our larger human nature.

Sometime at the end of the 1860s or beginning of the 1870s, Darwin invited twenty friends and acquaintances over to his house in Kent, England, to look at a series of photographic slides. Darwin had been exchanging letters with a French doctor named Guillaume-Benjamin-Amand Duchenne, who was convinced that humans exhibited sixty different emotional states through facial expressions linked to specific muscles. In slightly grotesque support of his theory, Duchenne took photographs of people to whose faces he administered mild electric shocks to engage the muscles. The sepia-tone images were strange and carnivalesque, but the radically different expressions did all look familiar as everyday emotions.

Ever an elegantly clean thinker, Darwin disagreed with Duchenne's theory. Examining the slides, he concluded that in fact human facial muscles and emotions combined to represent just six fundamental states produced by the full mosaic of facial muscles, not sixty distinct ones linked to distinct muscle groups. "Prompted by his doubts regarding the veracity of Duchenne's model," writes Peter J. Snyder, whose team of researchers discovered and in 2010 published archival evidence of this forgotten experiment, "Darwin conducted what may have been the first-ever single-blind study of the recognition of human facial expression of emotion. This single experiment was a little-known forerunner for an entire modern field of study with contemporary clinical relevance."

Darwin gave eleven of Duchenne's slides to the people he had invited to his house and asked them what emotions each slide represented. With no preconceptions or suggestions to bias them, they in effect agreed with Darwin, sorting the slides into just a handful of universal emotional states, such as fear and happiness. This seemed to confirm his theory that certain emotions come factory-equipped inside the human mind and body.

Inexplicably (and unfortunately), for almost a full century after Darwin published his book on emotions, the psychological sciences did next to nothing with his insights. Then, in 1969, Paul Ekman and his colleagues published a groundbreaking paper that both ratified and expanded on

Darwin's ideas. After collecting a staggering amount of data from every corner of the world, Ekman and Wallace V. Friesen showed that not only were basic types of emotions human universals, but so were their manifestations. In cultures across the globe—even in primitive ones that had existed in isolation from the rest of us for the last several thousands of years—we expressed *the same emotions with the same facial muscles and expressions.* Wherever these researchers went, subjects showed anger with the same bared teeth and close-knit eyebrows, and the subjects knew that others making this face were angry. The same went for happiness and other keystone emotions. Darwin was right.

As Darwin went on to theorize in his book, our species evolved to both feel and express emotions automatically and involuntarily because these two behaviors helped us to survive. Darwin crucially understood that we don't choose to have particular emotions but, rather, that they happen in us unconsciously. (We would never choose to feel anxiety and worry, yet they serve useful functions; they get us up and doing something about a problem, before it's too late.) Darwin did recognize that people can also voluntarily and consciously express emotions in several ways, and even fake them. We can try to appear pleased and happy with a gift we find disgusting (say, a joke coffee mug in the shape of a toilet), and we can mostly suppress our glee during our office rival's epic fail of a boardroom presentation. But even so, Darwin believed that our emotions were better expressed unconsciously, and that they leaked out despite our attempts to manage them. As the Eagles sang, "You can't hide your lyin' eyes."

Above all, Darwin observed, our involuntary emotional expressions serve an important communicative function to the others around us— that there is something to be afraid of, such as drinking this water or biting into this berry—and for that information to be valid the emotional expression has to be largely automatic and involuntary. This explanation of facial expressions brings us to another fundamental and innate component of the human drives to survive and reproduce that we unconsciously possess, even in early childhood, as we are building our social bonds: *cooperation* with one another.

Our emotional expressions were the original way humans shared information with each other about the state of the world. Primatologist Michael Tomasello has devoted his career to the study and comparison of humans to our closest genetic neighbors—other primates, such as apes and chimpanzees. Tomasello argues that there is an "intrinsic human desire to share emotions, experiences and activities with others." He has concluded from his decades of research that our evolved motivation to cooperate and coordinate our activities with others is no less than the crowning trait that distinguishes us from other primates. A brief glance around at human civilization (and a moment's comparison with the collective feats of any other species) will tell you just how important that single difference between us and other animals has been.

If cooperation is an evolved motivational tendency—in the ultimate service of our survival, just as eating and breathing are—then it should be present in young children even before they have sufficient life experience to develop it on their own. To test whether our cooperative tendencies are innate, Harriet Over and Malinda Carpenter, researchers at the Max Planck Institute for Evolutionary Anthropology in Leipzig, Germany, assembled sixty eighteen-month-old toddlers and had an assistant show each of them a series of eight colorful photographs of everyday household objects, such as a bright red plastic toy teakettle, a shoe, and a book. In the upper right corner of each picture were other, smaller objects, not the main event of the photograph, but off to the side. It was this smaller feature of the photograph that was designed to trigger the unconscious goal of cooperation in the young children. For one group of children, two dolls were shown in the upper right corner of each picture. These two dolls were always close to and facing each other, signaling a bond of friendship between them. Other groups of children were shown other things in the upper right corner of each picture—for some it was the same two dolls but facing away from each other, for another group it was colorful blocks. The researchers predicted that the children who were shown the two friendly dolls would cooperate with the experimenter more than the children in the other photo conditions, because the friendship between the dolls is a cue to the innate, evolved human motivation to help and cooperate. The other conditions of the experiment all lacked this key ingredient of the friendly dolls.

After an assistant showed the infant the eight color photographs, the experimenter came in to play with the child, bringing some wooden sticks, which she then pretended to accidentally drop. She then waited ten seconds to see if the child would spontaneously help on his or her own, without needing any requests for help from the experimenter. The results were quite clear: 60 percent of the children in the friend-doll-priming condition spontaneously got up to help the experimenter pick up the sticks, compared to only 20 percent in all other conditions.

This study makes several important points. First, that even children as young as eighteen months will spontaneously help, without being asked or told to do so, consistent with Darwin and Tomasello's notion that we were born to cooperate. Second, those children didn't help just anybody, but only when the idea of a personal bond of trust was active in their minds (caused by seeing the two friendly dolls). In normal life outside of the laboratory, this idea of trust and friendship would be active instead when they were with people such as family members that they love and trust. Third, both the friendship cue and the cooperation goal operate unconsciously. It was just subtly there in the background, not even the main, large feature of the photographs. Yet the presence of those two friendly dolls in the corner of the pictures was sufficient to unconsciously cue the idea of social bonds in the toddlers, and the cue of trust and friendship was the gateway to their spontaneous cooperative behavior.

Sometimes, then, an innate or evolved tendency does not manifest itself in our lives no matter what. We cooperate, yes, but only with people we feel we can trust. This makes a lot of adaptive sense, because we can certainly be taken advantage of (and many people are) if we blindly trust and cooperate with just anyone. Learning and knowing whom we can and can't trust is one of our major life tasks, and as the Over and Carpenter study of the eighteen-month-old children shows, we are already making those choices soon after birth. This leads us to the basic idea of the next chapter—that there are innate tendencies gleaned from our hidden evolutionary past that depend as well on what happens in our own very early (and equally hidden) experience as infants with our parents, siblings, and social group. We will pick up the story of how nurture interacts with nature to unconsciously influence whom we trust and help, and whom we don't, in Chapter 2. For now, though, let's turn to another facet of the forgotten evolutionary heritage lurking in our mind. Our genes certainly care a lot about our safety and survival, but with one main underlying goal—surviving long enough to have children. Random genetic improvements in our ability to survive increase our chances to mate and pass these improvements down to our offspring. This last objective, of course, is one of our other fundamental drives: to *reproduce*.

The Selfish Gene

In 2013, scientists discovered something new about Ötzti—he had children.

The murdered mummy of the Alps, it turned out, had lived on—through his genes. Researchers collected and analyzed blood samples donated by nearly four thousand people in the region of Austria near Ötzti's final resting place, and they found matches. Nineteen, to be exact. These people shared a genetic mutation that linked them to their posthumously famous ancestor. The existence of these *very* distant relatives of Ötzti cast a new light on his story. Yes, he undoubtedly failed at his number one drive, both conscious and unconscious: to stay alive. But he succeeded at the other overarching goal our brain evolved to achieve: to pass our genes down to the next generation. Or to put it more sweetly, to have kids.

Much of the early, original work in the field of evolutionary psychology focused on just this: "mating." As Richard Dawkins argued in his landmark book *The Selfish Gene,* our genes are all about getting themselves into the next generation. Think about it: without exception, each and every one of your direct ancestors had children. It was something all of them were successful at. If this hadn't been the case, you would not be here today reading this book.

As we saw with our unconscious need for physical safety, our biological mandate to reproduce can have surprising manifestations in today's world. One of the best examples comes from an Italian study conducted from August 2011 to September 2012. These researchers carried out an intriguing experiment about the effects of physical attractiveness on hiring practices, without actually putting any participants into a lab room together. They sent 11,000 résumés to 1,500 posted job openings. The disproportionate number of résumés to openings was because they sent multiple résumés to each posting. Each of the résumés had the exact same work history, and thus equal qualifications for the job. Some of the applications had photographs attached, while some didn't. (Also, of course, the names were different.) The applicant was described as being either Italian or foreign, and as male or female. Of the résumés with photographs, the applications were evenly divided up to have one attractive man and one unattractive man, and one attractive woman and one unattractive woman. (The subjects were rated on attractiveness by another group of people when the experimenters were developing the study materials.) Since the résumés were otherwise identical, different responses would have to be attributed to this variable—the photo. So the researchers were basically asking: would having an attractive photograph attached to your résumé increase your chances of being called in for an interview?

The answer was a resounding "yes." Overall, Italian applicants were favored over foreign applicants. This isn't surprising. Among the Italian applicants, however, being attractive was a definite advantage, especially for females: attractive females were far more likely to be called back than unattractive females with the same qualifications, by a whopping 54 percent to 7 percent. There was also a considerable though less dramatic advantage for attractive men over unattractive men, 47 percent to 26 percent. Based on the study's findings, you'd be better off sending in no photo at all than an unattractive one; the callback rates in the no-photo conditions were higher than in the unattractive-photo condition. The results of this study are dispiriting from an egalitarian perspective, if not shocking. This phenomenon has a name: "the beauty premium."

Like it or not, physical attractiveness is a significant predictor of career advancement and promotions. Workers of above-average looks earn 10–15 percent more than workers of below-average looks, a gap that is comparable to race and gender gaps in wages. The question is why this is so. After all, there are laws against discrimination, plus many companies have stern guides for hiring practices. Moreover, there are countless good-hearted bosses and personnel directors who passionately believe in equal opportunity and try to hire the most qualified person for the job, no matter what they look like. The point is, even these well-meaning people are prone to pander unwittingly to the beauty premium. According to the authors of this report, their unconscious mating drive is part of the reason.

You don't have to be a teenager to know that our adult conscious minds are often preoccupied by sexual thoughts and feelings, and that we all would rather look at people who are physically attractive than at those who are less attractive. (Brain imaging studies have shown that when heterosexuals are shown faces of attractive opposite-sex individuals, the reward centers of their brain become activated.) Less obvious is how these feelings invisibly influence our behavior when they really "shouldn't," since they run counter to the egalitarian, merit-based ideals most of us genuinely subscribe to. Most likely, many of the Italian hirers (who didn't know they were part of an experiment) would claim that the photo didn't affect their decision, or would be willing to reconsider their choice if it could be proved that they had been swayed by the beauty premium unconsciously.

We have this bias toward attractiveness because of our selfish-gene history: the unconscious mandate to reproduce, reproduce, reproduce, so that we as a species don't go extinct. This deep-seated urge is so strong that studies have shown that men's mating motives are triggered by the mere presence of attractive women, even when they are trying to focus on something else. One study showed, for example, that when working on a difficult, attention-demanding task in the laboratory, male participants were distracted more and had worse performance when interacting with a woman during the task (but not when interacting with a man), and even more, the more attractive the woman, the worse the male participants' performance on the task. While this may sound like science backing up familiar caricatures of unreformed male horniness, these hidden "behaviors" occur in all of us. In a certain sense, our bodies are in constant stealthy, unconscious communication.

Physical attractiveness is not the only trigger for the mating motive. Our unconscious detects hormonal signals of fertility that operate through the nose. In one of a series of fascinating studies on hormonal influences, Florida State University researchers showed that heterosexual male college students were more attracted to a female participating in the same study when she happened to be at the peak ovulation time of her cycle than when she was at the least fertile period, without the young men being aware of this influence at all. They also were more likely to unconsciously imitate and mimic the woman during her fertile than her nonfertile days; as we will see in Chapter 7, this subtle mimicry is a natural and unconscious tactic we use to bond with new acquaintances. Again, the men in these studies were completely unaware of how these subtle fertility cues, unavailable to their conscious awareness, influenced their attraction and behavior toward the women. Of course, all of this leads our species to that most universal of experiences—family.

I live in the countryside, across from a lake, and down the road is a small working farm. If you travel down my road in the springtime, you can see unconsciously operating evolutionary goals all over the place, everywhere you look. Every spring the little goslings stay very close to their mother goose and father goose, and often we have to wait patiently in our cars as they cross our road in single file—one parent in the lead, the other bringing up the rear. The baby cows wander around the large hayfields with the rest of the cows; the baby deer stay close behind their mother. They instinctively keep close to their parents and to other animals of their kind. You don't see the various baby animals—the little cows, deer, and geese— all playing together in the farmyard like in some baby-animal playschool. They stay close to their parents and siblings instead. Newborns, whether they are ducklings or humans, must depend on their parents and caretakers to keep them warm, fed, and safe from predators. It's part of their, and our, hardwired nature, and it's a matter of survival.

The little farmyard animals and their parents are bonding. They do not blindly trust other animals or even their own kind outside of their own small social circle; trust can be exploited and you can be taken advantage of, to the exploiters' benefit but your harm. This early experience is important to survival. In humans, our early experiences set the tone not only for whom we can trust as an infant and small child, but whether we feel we can trust people in general or not, for the rest of our lives. Like our long evolutionary past of survival and reproduction, which compels us to crave physical safety, to be able to deal with a fast-moving world without having to stop and think about it, to avoid contamination and disease, to share information through our emotions, and to help our friends and family, our own personal past of early experience stamps its own indelible unconscious influences on us. Yet we have few if any memories of these early years of our life, causing us to be largely unaware of how powerfully they have shaped our feelings and behaviors. Our experiences in these years constitute a second form of hidden-past influences upon us, and these are the focus of the next chapter.

CHAPTER 2

Some Assembly Required

On March 10, 1302, a forty-six-year-old politician in Italy was sentenced to death by fire in his hometown of Florence. A former soldier, he was a romantic soul who wrote poetry and moonlighted as a pharmacist, but he had gotten tangled up in a bitter local power struggle. That wasn't hard to do in fourteenth-century Florence. Three centuries earlier, a battle for control had begun between the pope and the Holy Roman emperor. A group called the Ghibellines, known as the Whites, supported the emperor, while the Guelphs, known as the Blacks, remained staunchly behind the pope. Medieval Italy was not yet a unified state, but a fractious patchwork of fiefdoms, so the imperial tensions between the pope and the emperor frequently played out in the smaller realms of cities. It was a time rife with the worst of human nature: intrigue, double-crossings, and vengeance.

In Florence, a new, crusading *podestà,* or high magistrate, had recently taken power. He was of the Blacks, and he soon brought charges of corruption against this politician, which resulted in his death sentence. The newly condemned man was away from Florence at the time of the judgment, so to avoid being burned at the stake, he began a life of exile in Tuscany and elsewhere, an exile from which he would never return. He'd chosen to bond himself with the wrong group, altering the course of his life. The politician's name was Dante Alighieri, the man we know today as the author of *The Divine Comedy.*

Around 1308, Dante began work on the poem that would secure his place in history. Using the time of his exile to explore the heights and depths of human nature, he finished *The Divine Comedy* in 1320. Over some fourteen thousand lines, he pondered the spiritual consequences of our deeds through a fictional journey to the afterlife. He divided his book into three parts corresponding to Christian theology: "Inferno," "Purgatorio," and "Paradiso." Accompanied by the poet Virgil, he descends into the underworld, where he witnesses the *contrapasso,* or poetic justice, that awaits all sinners after they die. Dante in fact introduced the idea of poetic justice; instead of the Old Testament's "eye for an eye" justice, he envisioned a deeper, more satisfying retribution that would more effectively balance the scales against the types of sins committed. He had a dark and expansive imagination, and his vision of hell is painstakingly detailed, a nightmarish guidebook that is both maplike and cinematic. His Inferno has nine "circles," each defined by the degree and substance of sin, with lawyers on Level Five and murderers on Level Seven. (No, Level Six is not Menswear.) The lowest circle of hell, where Lucifer resides, is the Ninth Circle, Cocytus, where the worst sinners of all are punished. The worst sin, according to Dante—after all, murderers are up a few floors on Level Seven—is to betray the trust of those close to you, as Dante himself had been betrayed.

Cocytus in turn is divided into four regions, which reflect the different arenas of life in which treachery and betrayal can occur: Caina, for those who commit treachery within their own family—named after Cain, its star prisoner, who slew his brother Abel. Antenora, for those who betray their country or homeland, named after a Trojan general who plotted with the Greeks to destroy Troy. Ptolemea, for those who betrayed their close friends. In this region, Dante displays his personal abhorrence of such crimes by devising an added punishment for those who betray their friends: their souls descend straight to hell upon their act of betrayal, while they are still alive, and their living bodies are possessed by demons. And the final innermost zone of Cocytus is named Judecca, after its most famous resident, Judas Iscariot, who betrayed Christ. In Judecca are the damned souls who, by betraying their benefactors, committed crimes that had great historical consequences.

At the center of the Ninth Circle is Lucifer himself, who betrayed God at the beginning of time, and for whom hell was created in the first place. Dante describes Lucifer as the "wretched emperor of hell, whose tremendous size (he dwarfs even the Giants) stands in contrast with his limited powers: his flapping wings generate the wind that keeps the lake frozen and his three mouths chew on the shade-bodies of three arch-traitors, the gore mixing with tears gushing from Lucifer's three sets of eyes." This is a fantastic, grotesque description, and yet the detail that jumped out at me when I read it was *that lake.*

Dante's Ninth Circle of Hell, reserved for the most dastardly sinners, is not the fiery, torturously hot inferno of the title. Quite the contrary—it is a large, frozen lake. Here the damned souls are completely covered by the ice—like "straw in glass," resembling hellish variations on poor Ötzti, whose bodily remains, you'll recall, were preserved in their own chilly purgatory for thousands of years. But why, in the devilish imaginarium of *The Divine Comedy,* did Dante opt to freeze betrayers "in the cold crust," instead of, say, burning them at the stake, as his enemies had tried to do to him?

Dante, like all truly great poets, had a sensitivity to human nature and could express things in words that the rest of us experience only on an intuitive level. Yet as with other great prose and poetry, once a gifted writer expresses those ideas we immediately resonate with them. In his *contrapasso* for betrayal, the poetic justice of freezing for eternity souls so coldhearted that they could betray their own friends for personal gain, Dante echoed the sentiments of St. Paul, more than a thousand years earlier. In his *Apocalypse*, written in the third century AD, St. Paul wrote of hell: "Even if the sun rose upon them, they would not be warmed because of the extreme cold in this place and the snow." We use such figures of speech today, understanding each other perfectly well when we speak of a warm friend, or a cold and distant father. Why do we employ these metaphors that mix emotional and physical sensations, and why have we done so for millennia?

What Dante could not have known—but somehow did, without the benefit of modern science—is that seven hundred years later, neuroscience would show that when a person is dealing with social coldness (like betrayal of trust), the same neural brain structures are engaged as when that person touches something cold, or feels cold all over, as when she goes outside in the wintertime without a coat. Similarly, experiencing social warmth, as when you are texting your family and friends, activates the same specific part of the brain that is stimulated when you are holding something warm in your hand. Our brain comes with these associations wired in, which is why Dante's choice to punish social treachery with eternal freezing represents the perfect balance of crime and punishment.

We are born to bond with and stay close to our parents and our family, and if all goes well that bond forms and is a very positive influence on our social relationships for the rest of our lives. But evolution cannot guarantee that our instinctive trust will be well placed, that our innate desire for closeness and bonding with our parents will be reciprocated by them. And so, remarkably early in our lives, as early as one year old, this bond is set, or it isn't—we become either securely or insecurely attached to our moms and dads, or whoever is taking care of us. This powerful effect of our very early experiences in life sets the tone for how close and stable our friendships and romantic relationships are for the rest of our lives. And yet we are not aware of this early influence on us, because we have very little memory of this time in our life. This hidden influence of our own personal past comes from our evolutionary past, and we are equally unaware of how it affects us.

Dante got this right, too: the importance of trust and its dark sibling, betrayal, both of which are central to human life. Not for nothing did he consider the betrayal of friends, one's country, one's cause as the worst sins of all, its perpetrators assigned to a lower level of hell than even murderers. Trust is the basis of all our close relationships in life, and when you come right down to it, our close relationships are the most important things in each of our lives. When we trust another person, such as a friend to whom we tell something very private, we make ourselves vulnerable, but it is a risk we are willing to take in order to make that relationship even closer. The revelation of private information, confiding in the other person, is the currency that creates close relationships in the first place, the trading chips that establish trust between two people. And the number one reason close relationships come apart is that this trust breaks down, and we feel a friend or partner no longer has our back, because he or she is doing things behind it.

Yet when we are first born, tiny helpless infants, we have no choice but to place our trust, our lives, in our parents' hands. We absolutely have to trust that they will take care of us—feed us, shelter us, keep us warm and safe—because we are unable to do these things on our own. But Mother Nature, operating through natural selection, has always appreciated Dante's lesson about betrayal—that placing our trust in others is, unfortunately, not a sure thing, not a completely safe bet. Richard Dawkins describes many animal species in which one type, called "cheaters," makes their easy living off of the trust and cooperation of the others, called "suckers." So while we as infants are certainly ready, able, and willing to trust in our parents, siblings, and neighbors, they may turn out not to be trustworthy. This is something we learn very early in life.

The nature of our bonds with our parents, when we are infants, echoes our evolutionary past. This is where nature and nurture meet, where our species' evolved predispositions and assumptions about our world that have evolved over eons are tested in the fires of actual experience, being validated or not based on our own personal reality. Can we trust people, or can we not? This question brings me back to my alligator dream.

Flipping my deeply held assumptions on their backs, that toothy, back-stroking reptile showed me how the unconscious aspects of our mind are primary in our lives; first, the compelling motivations that we are born with, and second, the earliest knowledge about people that we form from our experiences as infants and toddlers. Strikingly, after the age of five or so, we do not retain any explicit conscious memories or awareness of having formed these important impressions. Both of these foundations of our future thoughts and actions, created by our hidden past, operate the rest of our lives in the background, unconsciously, driving much of our daily behavior and shaping much of what we think, what we say, and what we do. Sometimes for the better, but other times for the worse.

Warm and Cold Monkeys

As most adults can attest, our parents, and their style of child-rearing, have a large impact on making us the people we become. This happens because of the things they consciously give to us: love, guidance, and punishment. It also happens because of the things they unconsciously give us: love, guidance, and punishment. They give these things to us consciously and intentionally, of course, but also when they don't realize it, as we are watching and learning from them even in their unguarded moments. That is, our parents shape us in ways both intended and unintended, especially when we're very young and malleable. They make deliberate parenting decisions, certainly, but in the daily bustle, much of the time they're also just busy being themselves, and having to get lots of other things done. As children, we naturally absorb and imitate their behaviors. (Our two-year-old grandson Jameson is still, a week after returning to Indiana from his visit to our house, repeatedly throwing his arms in the air and yelling

"Yaaa!" because out on our deck one day he happened to see me step bare-foot on a hot coal that had fallen out of our barbecue.)

One of the most powerful influences our parents have on us, one that lasts the rest of our lives, is whether we form a basic trust in other people. What matters greatly is our own experience with our parents and caretak-ers, our relationship with them, and whether we feel secure and safe with them or not. Researchers of child development call this our *attachment* to our parents, and we can become securely attached to them, or insecurely attached. We know or intuit we can count on them, that they will be there for us when we need them (which is fairly often when you are an infant), or not so much. Remarkably, this feeling of attachment (or the lack of it) is pretty much set by the time we are just one year old.

Current research is examining how this plays out over the life span. Jeff Simpson and his colleagues at the University of Minnesota have been fol-lowing a group of children now for more than twenty years to gain new insights into human life trajectories. When they were twelve months old, the infant participants and their mothers were given what is known as the "Strange Test," which, despite its spooky name, is the standard measure of how securely attached a child is to his or her parent. How does the child react, for instance, when the mother leaves the room? Does the child stay close to her when strange creatures (a man in a dragon suit) come into the room? Or does the child become distressed when the mother exits the room, leaving her alone with the experimenters, who are very nice and all, but still strangers? A securely attached child does not react with panic or upset to these situations as often as an insecurely attached child does, for the simple reason that a securely attached child feels more confident that her mother is coming back soon and would never leave her in a dan-gerous situation. In other words, securely attached children trust their mothers. Those who are insecurely attached, on the other hand, will cry and become distressed and even panicky in a strange situation, because in their experience the mother may not come back soon, and will not nec-essarily respond to their distress. They lack trust and confidence that the mother will "be there" for them when needed.

Now, by following this same set of children through childhood and adolescence, and into young adulthood, Simpson and his colleagues are able to see how much this early attachment with their mothers predicted how well the social lives of these children turned out. And indeed, how much these children trusted their mothers at age one as measured by the Strange Test predicted the quality and outcomes of their relationships with schoolmates in elementary school, friends in high school, and now their romantic partners. How did the one-year-old securely attached children compare to the less securely attached children as they grew up? In their early grade school years (age six), the securely attached children were rated as being more socially competent by their teachers. In high school (age sixteen), they had more close relationships with friends. And in their early twenties, they had more positive daily emotional experiences in their adult romantic relationships, were more committed to their partners, and recovered better from the normal, everyday conflicts that occur in close relationships. And these behaviors and broad-stroke life patterns had been foretold by how securely attached they had been to their mothers at twelve months of age.

When I was a brand-new father, I got some advice from a colleague who is an expert on close relationships and attachment. She told me to simply hug my daughter as much and as often as I could. I appreciated this, but, like most parents, I didn't feel I needed any outside advice on this topic, because I naturally loved my daughter more than anything in the world— also, I've always been a hugger. Later, when she was two, I brought her to my office, where there was a couch and then a bit of a gap before a hardwood coffee table with sharp edges. My colleague came by to see my daughter and observed her crawling from the couch over the gap to the coffee table and back again with reckless abandon. "Now that's a securely attached child!" she exclaimed. Knowing as I did that secure attachment would have positive consequences for the rest of my daughter's life, my coworker's summary judgment came as wonderful news to me.

Simpson and his team have shown how remarkably, even frighteningly, powerful our early experiences are in shaping our capacity to trust others, to succeed in friendship and then love. Yet *we have no memory of these early experiences.* The density of this early childhood amnesia is profound, and we all have it. We have about as much conscious memory of the first few years of our life as we do of our long evolutionary past, which in both cases is near zero. But it is a real double whammy to your ability to understand yourself when the most dramatically influential period of your life also happens to be the one you have the least conscious memory of.

Every parent knows the poignancy of losing those years of shared memories with their little ones. You remember those times so well, and sometimes remind your child of those cherished past moments when they are older, only to be met with a blank stare. When my daughter was very small, nearly every day she insisted on watching her favorite movie, *Cars*, with her hero Lightning McQueen. She rode around the house in a red toy Lightning car (No. 95, of course), sat in a Lightning McQueen chair, had a Lightning McQueen throw blanket, and on car trips would squeal and point with delight at any and all red Corvettes, thinking they were Lightning himself. (I may have played along with this, as for years she believed Lightning McQueen lived in Durham, Connecticut.) Several years later, when she was five, she wanted to watch a movie before bedtime, and I suggested *Cars*. It had been a while since we had watched it, and I reminded her how much she liked it. You can imagine my deep shock when she gave me that blank look, and told me quite firmly that she'd never seen it! (She told me this, ironically, while sitting in that same Lightning McQueen chair in front of the television.) And indeed, throughout the movie she showed no signs of remembering it at all. She was genuinely surprised by the plot turns and had no idea what was going to happen next. For her, it was as if she was seeing that movie for the first time.

As adults, insecurely attached people tend to have difficulties in friendships or romantic relationships and feel distrust toward their partners, yet it rarely occurs to them that part of the problem might reside in the hidden files of their personal history. Rather, their focus is usually on the present, on what is readily available to their conscious awareness, because after all, it is that conscious part of our mind that is trying to understand what is going on. It can only use the material it is aware of. So we think that a friend's behavior, a colleague's reactions, or maybe something else that doesn't click about a relationship is causing the problem. We do not appreciate that these feelings that we have about others may come instead from the wellspring of our early attachments with our parents. Of course, these forgotten pasts can be a blessing as well as a curse. Their effect is also there for the happy ones among us who do feel trust in their friends, who do allow others to get close to them, and who tend to have longer-lasting and happier close relationships. They believe their friends and lovers are trustworthy people, but they too lack conscious awareness of the fact that a big chunk of the reason why they feel this way comes from their experiences as an infant.

What we are discussing here in essence is *nurture,* as opposed to *nature.* In the previous chapter, we looked at nature, how we come into the world factory-equipped with the dual drives to preserve our physical safety and to reproduce. Yet the factory of evolution did leave a number of dials that could be fine-tuned, which start out in a default position but which our early experience can adjust through nurture to more accurately reflect the specific features of our home and local environments, independent of the time-distant and slow-moving forces of evolution.

The process of natural selection is very slow. Our innate genetic adaptations to our world occurred very, very long ago. There is no way that evolution can keep up with faster-moving changes, such as today's advances in technology and the social uses to which it is put. Human cultures and norms of social behavior by those around us are changing at a much, much faster rate than the snail's pace of biological evolutionary processes. This is why we have the *epigenetic* stage of adaptation, when nurture and nature come together, when experience either turns on or doesn't certain behavioral and physiological switches embedded in our genes. This formative period, when we as infants quickly fine-tune ourselves to first our caretakers and then our larger community and culture, is supremely important to our successful development as individuals. The new science of epigenetics is on the front line of understanding how this process works in our brains and bodies, and the simplest way to think of their findings is the following: we become what we become not only through our DNA or only through our environment, but through their *interaction.* This interplay between genes and experience, between our forgotten evolutionary past and our early lived past, is our personal destiny.

As an illustration of this process from elsewhere in the animal kingdom, consider the indigo bunting. This is a small, migratory bird native to the Americas, which is born with an innate ability to use the night sky, or "star maps," to navigate long distances. But here is the kicker. Evolution cannot possibly furnish these birds with a complete and accurate star map ready-made for their brains, because the pattern of the stars in the night sky is constantly, gradually changing as the universe expands. The night sky today is not the same night sky of one thousand or even five hundred years ago. So the solution nature has come up with for the indigo bunting is to give it the innate capacity to quickly absorb the pattern of the night sky stars that is accurate *for them,* during their own lifetime.

In a classic experiment conducted at a planetarium in Flint, Michigan, in the 1960s, Stephen Emlen and Robert T. Longway put indigo buntings into contraptions with an ink pad on the base, so their feet would get inked when they walked on that base. Rising upward from and surrounding the base was a paper cone, expanding outward, like a cup that is narrower at its base and wider at its top. A screen lid kept the birds in the cone, but they could see out through the screen. Where exactly they walked on the cone, to go up to look outside, was thus marked by their inky feet. Using this ingenious apparatus, Emlen and Longway could expose the birds to different star orientations on the ceiling of the otherwise dark planetarium and then the next day remove and examine the paper cones to see which direction the birds had moved and oriented themselves. The researchers could change the star patterns any way they wanted to; they could move, for example, the position of the North Star or how the stars moved in relation to each other. When Emlen and Longway shifted the position of the planetarium's stars, the birds shifted their orientation as well, as shown the next morning by their inky footprints on the paper cones. The buntings had learned a "sky map" as they watched the rotation of the stars. How did this astoundingly malleable operation occur in their bird brains? They were born with the hardware to navigate in this way, and through experience they "downloaded" the actual maps that would serve them in their given location.

As the dynamics of human attachment reveal, we too require some additional assembly and fine-tuning after we are born. When we come into the world, we have the innate tendencies, motivations, and goals that make up nature's effect, anticipating to some extent the general conditions of our life, but then nurture's effect takes over to adapt us to the actual conditions on the ground. Nature's possibilities are adapted to nurture's realities, especially during our early, memoryless years.

Many people are familiar with the famous monkey studies by Harry Harlow in the 1950s. These looked at the social problems of infant monkeys raised alone, and you may recall that each one had a maternal stand-in—a cloth mother and a wire mother. By observing the monkeys' behavior, Harlow demonstrated that softness and comfort are essential for early life, above and beyond the primary need for food. The baby monkeys preferred to be with the fake mother covered in soft carpeting, even though they were fed from a bottle protruding from the wire mother. What is less known about this experiment is that the cloth mother was also the *warm* mother. Behind that comforting piece of cloth was a 100-watt lightbulb. The general area around the wire mother was kept warm by ambient heat but not from a direct source, as with the cloth mother. The lonely infant monkeys, deprived of their actual mother's warmth, sought out a substitute and preferred being with the physically warm cloth mother. The saddest little monkeys of all were those deprived even of the source of physical warmth (and comforting cloth). To this day, I'm somewhat haunted by the movies shown in my college psychology classes of these pathetic creatures huddled in the corner of the room, alone and rocking themselves while the other monkeys ran and played with each other. The impact of whether the monkey had the cloth or the wire ersatz mother continued well beyond infancy, affecting the course of their entire adult social life.

In a way, Harlow had conducted a shortened, simian version of the longitudinal study in which Jeff Simpson and his colleagues tracked the Strange Test children over two decades. The monkeys raised alone did better later on—not great, but they could function socially—if they had had a source of physical warmth to cuddle against and become attached to, even though it came in the form of a lightbulb with a cloth torso.

Harlow's study showed that when the monkeys held on to their cloth pseudo-mother, feeling its warmth against their own skin helped to establish a level of trust of and attachment to their comfortable but curiously nonresponsive parent. That we (as well as little monkeys) so strongly associate the physical warmth of being held close by our parent with the social warmth of their being trustworthy and caring toward us is the flip side of Dante's astute and poetic connection between the physical coldness of the Ninth Circle of Hell and the social coldness of the traitors and betrayers condemned to spend eternity there. The salvation of those cloth-mother infant monkeys was that warmth helped to turn on the latent switch in their brains, connecting physical warmth (from being held close) and social warmth (I can trust this person, she cares for me and keeps me safe). That is why, compared to their wire-mother siblings, they turned out to be more socially well adjusted later on. As fellow primates, then, we have the innate potential and tendency to develop social warmth and trust toward others as long as we have a source of social warmth as infants (and interestingly, Harlow's study shows that physical warmth can be a serviceable though imperfect substitute for this).

John Bowlby, the pioneering English attachment researcher, was one of the first to note that physical feelings of warmth were linked early in life to feelings of safety and that feelings of coldness were linked to feelings of insecurity. Especially with mammals that breastfeed their infants, the experience of being fed and held and protected goes hand in glove with the physical experience of warmth and closeness. Because these two things always happen together, they naturally become associated in the mind. This simple linkage is what allows us to predict and anticipate events in our life—that a yellow traffic light means a red will soon follow, that a flash of lightning will soon be followed by a loud clap of thunder, and when Uncle Ed greets us at his door he will say (as he always does), "Well, who's this then?" Our early experience with our parents, being held close by those we trust the most, leads us to associate their physical warmth with the "social warmth" of trust and caring. Bowlby argued that this association, this co-experience of physical warmth and social warmth, was such a constant in our species for such a long period of time that it eventually became wired into our brains by evolution.

Lawrence Williams and I tested this idea in a natural, everyday situation—holding a cup of hot or iced coffee. If our unconscious has a hardwired connection between physical warmth (as when holding a hot cup of coffee) and social warmth (trusting and being generous to others), then holding something warm like a cup of hot coffee should increase our *social* warmth, too, our closeness to others. And the same with holding something cold (or feeling cold in general), like a cup of iced coffee—that should increase our feelings of social coldness and distance from others. But the strength of that association, how much the warm and cold experiences affect us as adults, should depend on our early experiences with our parents, our *attachment* to them when very little. These warm and cold effects depend not just on our long-ago hidden evolutionary past but on our own hidden infant past as well.

But first we had to test whether holding something warm or cold affected our social feelings. In our first study we replicated a classic impression-formation study by Solomon Asch, one of the early pioneers of social psychology. Asch performed a simple experiment in which he gave his participants just six personality traits that he said described a person, and participants rated how much they liked that person. Five of those traits were the same for everyone in the study, but one was different. Half of the participants saw the person described as *warm* along with the other five traits, and the other half read that the person was *cold* along with the other five traits. As you might expect, the participants liked the person who was described as *warm* and independent and sensitive, etc., to the person described as *cold* and independent and sensitive, etc.

What Lawrence and I did was quite simple: we repeated Asch's procedure, but with just the five words that were the same for everyone. No one saw the words *warm* or *cold* in descriptions of the person they read about. Instead of those, we substituted an actual warm or cold physical experience, right before they read about the person. Would it have the same effect as reading the person described as warm or cold? That would only happen if the physical warm or cold effect was associated in the subjects' minds with the social version of warm or cold, as Bowlby predicted, and St. Paul, Dante, and Harlow all intuited.

In our study the participant was greeted in the lobby of the psychology laboratory building at Yale. Then, during the elevator ride up to our lab on the fourth floor, the experimenter—who was part of our research team but was kept in the dark about the predictions of the study—casually asked the participant to hold the paper cup of coffee that was in his hand so he could reach down into his briefcase for some forms. Then he took the cup of coffee back and handed the participant the forms on a clipboard. All this took about ten seconds, but this brief holding of the coffee cup was the critical moment in our study. It was either a cup of hot coffee or of iced coffee from a nearby coffeehouse.

Once in the lab room, the participant read about a person described just as in Asch's original study. And all participants read the same, identical description. But just as we had predicted, based on Bowlby's theory, those who had briefly held the warm cup of coffee liked the person more than did those who had briefly held the cup of iced coffee. The brief physical experience of warmth or coldness had activated the analogous feelings of social warmth or coldness, which then influenced our participants' liking of the person they read about. This happened entirely unconsciously: after the experiment was over, our careful questioning of the participants showed that they had no clue that holding the coffee in the elevator had in any way influenced their opinions of the person.

Of course they didn't—would you have had any idea that whether you were holding something warm or cold in your hands could affect how you felt about someone you were meeting or reading about right then? I know for a fact I wouldn't have, because this effect happened to me in a hotel room in Philadelphia *after* we had run and published the study! It was about 9 a.m. and I was attending a conference, in my room getting dressed and just about to head down for the day of talks, when my phone rang. A science reporter was on the line, wanting to ask me about the coffee studies, which had been published a few months earlier. And she specifically wanted to ask me about Lawrence Williams, because her article was about graduate students in psychology. I remember speaking of Lawrence in enthusiastic, glowing terms, going on about what a great person he is, in so many ways. When I paused to take a breath, the reporter shocked me with a simple question:

"By any chance do you have a cup of hot coffee in your hands right at this moment?"

I looked down at my right hand, almost in disbelief. She was right. I was holding one of those paper cups of coffee from the in-room coffee machine in my right hand as my left held the telephone. "Oh my God," I said. "I do. Wow."

She laughed. "Busted!" And then she explained that while she was sure I had a very positive opinion of Lawrence, it seemed to her that I was going a bit overboard with my superlatives, and she had a hunch that the warm-coffee effect might be operating—even on me, someone who knew all about its effect, but who was not paying attention to it at the time. My experience in that Philadelphia hotel room was very similar to that of participants in a study by Dutch researchers Hans IJzerman and Gun Semin. After they briefly held a warm beverage, they reported feeling closer to people they were prompted to think about, compared to those who had just held a cold beverage.

A decade later, other psychology and neuroscience experiments have confirmed this primal association between physical and social temperature, between feeling warmth and then acting in a warm, prosocial way. In fact, brain imaging experiments have shown that the same small region of the human brain, the insula, becomes active in response to both types of warmth—when touching something warm like a heating pad, and when texting family and friends. And Yale neuroscientists Yoona Kang and Jeremy Gray, along with social psychologist Margaret Clark and myself, showed that a separate small region of the insula responds both to holding something cold and to being betrayed by another participant in an eco-nomics game. Betrayal of trust, the ultimate social coldness—I can just see Dante and St. Paul up there in the clouds, nodding their heads (and maybe John Bowlby is there, too). Today, seven hundred years after Dante wrote the *Inferno,* and nearly two thousand years after St. Paul wrote his *Apoca-lypse,* we know where their intuitions came from, why they both considered being frozen in ice the poetic justice for people who betray others. And why today we still speak so easily of a warm friend, or a cold father. We always will. Because the connection between physical and social warmth, and between physical and social coldness, is hardwired into the human brain.

Yet at the same time, we know from Jeff Simpson's (and others') attach-ment research that the ability to trust in our parents and caretakers is not automatically taken for granted by evolution; there is instead a critical period of epigenesis after birth in which this connection is set or not, based on our actual experiences. Can we trust them or not? The baby monkeys in Harlow's studies who had no source of physical warmth did not trust and could not interact with their fellows in adulthood. They hid in a corner by themselves instead of joining in the monkey fun. It was as if without any source of warmth, even physical warmth, their capacity for friendship and play had withered and died inside them.

What this suggests is that not everyone will make the connection between physical warmth and social warmth, or at least not to the same extent. We should expect securely attached children to show this connec-tion more strongly than insecurely attached children. To test this predic-tion, Hans IJzerman and his colleagues went to a Dutch day care to study the warm-cold effect in sixty children from four to six years of age. The researchers first asked the children a series of fifteen questions that deter-mined whether they were securely or insecurely attached. The children then went to do the actual experiment in either a cool room (around 60 degrees Fahrenheit) or a warm room (around 75 degrees), and which one they went to was randomly chosen for them. Then they were all given a bunch of colorful stickers. (Children love stickers. Think SpongeBob and Disney princesses.) They were then given an opportunity to share some of their stickers with another child—a friend.

The young children who were in the warm room gave more of their stickers to the other child than did those who were in the cold room, who were less willing to share their coveted stickers. Once again, feelings of physical warmth had activated feelings of social warmth and generosity. But *only* the securely attached children shared more in the warm room. The researchers found that the room temperature influenced the generosity (or stinginess) of only those children who had shown, in their answers to those questions, that they were securely attached to their parents. The warm room did not affect the degree of sharing of the insecurely attached children. Just as with Harlow's monkeys then, firmly setting the human child's brain switch to connect warmth and generosity, warmth and trust, warmth and friendliness, seems to depend on how things actually go in the home in the critical first few years of life.

We have seen how our deep and basic motivations for physical safety and survival, from our distant evolutionary past, bubble up to affect our social and political attitudes. So too does our own personal distant past as a tiny infant bubble up to affect our close relationships and basic dealings with other people. Because we have no conscious recollection of either of them, these two forms of our hidden past unconsciously influence us for the rest of our lives.

The Good, the Bad, and the Cultural

But nature has given us another set of cues about whom we can trust and cooperate with, a legacy of our long tribal past, in which, as Ötzi knew only too well, other human beings were the most dangerous creatures around. These are cues about whether other people are similar to us or not. Do they look and sound the same as those close around us, such as our parents and siblings and close neighbors? There has been a tremendous amount of research on such *in-group versus out-group* distinctions, and their consequences, in my own field of social psychology over the last fifty years. This research is showing that we are tuned to in-group/out-group distinctions starting at a very young age, indicating it is an innate tendency to do so. Even little eye movements by too-innocent-to-have-a-mean-thought infants subtly reveal preferences for members of their own group.

This preference is related to something John Bowlby noted about baby animals in general: that they have an evolved general predisposition to stay close to those who are similar to them. They don't go off and play in the farmyard or forest with the other baby animals; instead they stay close to their own kind, the animals most like them who will be the ones who take care of them, give them food, provide warmth and shelter, and, most important, don't try to eat them. As Bowlby recognized, human beings behave more or less the same way. For example, developmental psychologist David Kelly and his colleagues have shown that infants only three months old, given the choice of looking at faces of people who are the same racial-ethnic group as theirs (Caucasian) or the faces of a different racial-ethnic group (African, Middle Eastern, Asian), preferred to look at members of their own group. And just as with attachment and trust, this effect depended on the infants' early life experience, because Kelly did not find any such preference in newborns. Similar studies have shown infants to also have a preference for their native language over other languages, even though they don't yet understand a word!

The preference for those who are like us makes sense with regard to our evolutionary past. Long ago in our tribal, hunter-gatherer days, we rarely encountered strangers, and if we did, it might well have meant a threat to our survival. (Strange-looking people on horseback at the town gate was usually not good news.) It is understandable, then, that one legacy of human evolution is that we feel safer when we are with people who seem familiar, and less safe with people who are unfamiliar. But here is a glaring case where our technological advances have far outstripped the snail's pace of evolution.

We can now easily travel to far-off lands, and people living there can travel to ours. We see and hear events going on everywhere on earth almost instantaneously, thanks first to the invention of radio and television, then to satellites and now the Internet. Many modern cities are now polyglot societies in themselves, with people from cultures around the world rubbing shoulders with one another on a daily basis. In short, our social surroundings are nothing at all like the towns and villages of the Middle Ages and before. Yet inside each of us still live those evolved preferences for our own group and, to some extent, against other groups that look, sound, and act differently. This is a sad and unfortunate legacy of our long evolutionary past, because after all, for all our seeming differences, there are infinitely more things that we share—those basic human needs for safety, the longing for warmth and trust, a desire to live well and take care of the people we love.

Yet we evidently cannot help dividing our social world into *us* and *them,* no matter that the dividing factors are often arbitrary things we have no control over, like our skin color or place of origin. In his original research on the in-group/out-group bias, British social psychologist Henri Tajfel and his colleagues showed just how ridiculously minimal these "us versus them" cues could be. They had their participants draw colored balls from an urn so that some drew red balls and some drew blue ones. (The selection was entirely random.) But later, when given the chance to divide up some money, the participants gave more to those who drew the same color ball as they had, and less to the others in the room. It doesn't take much at all to snap us into thinking in terms of "our group" and the "other group" and to trigger liking and positive treatment of our own, and dislike and negative treatment toward the other. In fact, it turns out that even the very word *us* is unconsciously positive, and the word *them* is unconsciously negative—in the "automatic evaluation" experiments discussed in Chapter 5, *us* has the same automatic (immediate and unintended) positive effect on people as do words such as *cake, birthday,* and *Friday,* while *them* has the same automatic negative effect as *poison, tornado,* and *Monday.*

If a random red or blue ball is enough to trigger these "us versus them" feelings, then it is hardly surprising that group stereotypes and prejudices are inspired by more pronounced and substantive group differences, such as different languages or accents, different skin color, and different religions and cultural practices. Every culture on the planet has these stereotypes about the relatively powerless, or different-looking or -acting groups of people in their society. For a long time researchers in my field believed these developed in an individual only in late childhood or adolescence, maybe starting around age ten at the earliest. That is why many of us had such hope that the educational system could do a lot to ameliorate these negative group stereotypes in societies. Yet the recent advances in child social psychology, such as David Kelly's pioneering study of the facial preferences of young infants, are starting to paint a much more pessimistic picture: that these in-group/out-group preferences may be forming much earlier in life, well before a child starts school.

Yarrow Dunham, a developmental psychologist at Yale, has studied young children's implicit liking for their own group versus other racial and social groups. He took a standard technique for measuring unconscious, automatic biases in adults and adapted it for young children. This technique, called the Implicit Association Test, has buttons labeled Good and Bad, and kids simply press the Good button as fast as they can if a picture of something good comes on the computer screen, like a yummy piece of pie, and press the Bad button as fast as they can if something like a scary spider appears. So far, so good (and bad). Then the children are asked to do an unrelated activity. Later, the (white) children use these same buttons, but they are now labeled White and Black, and their job is to sort photos of faces of White and Black people as fast as they can.

And then comes the crucial part of the study. The children are then asked to do both tasks at the same time. So each button, the left and the right one, serves two purposes. The left one, for example, is to be used to say either White or Good, and the right one to say either Black or Bad, depending on whether a face or something else appears on the screen. Then the experiment is repeated but with one button standing for both Black and Good, and the other button for White and Bad. If a face comes on the screen, then use the White or Black button labels and press the correct button (left or right) depending on whether it is a face of a White or a Black person, but if anything else appears on the screen, then use the Good or Bad labels (of the same left and right buttons) and press the correct one. The key is whether the child is using the same (say, left side) button to indicate both Good and White, and the other (say, right side) button to indicate both Bad and Black, or, in the opposite condition, the same button for Good and Black, and the other one for Bad and White.

If the child—or any adult for that matter—associates White with Good, and Black with Bad, in their minds, even if they aren't aware of doing so, then the task is easier if the same button is used for White and Good, and the other button for Black and Bad. And it is easier the more strongly they associate White with Good, and Black with Bad. The stronger that association for them, the faster they will execute the sorting task. But they will also, for the same reason, be slower when the button labels are changed, so that now White and Bad go together on one button, and Black and Good go together on the other. The way that Dunham measured the extent of pro-White and anti-Black feelings in their White child participants was to take the difference in their response times in the one condition versus the other—the extent to which they were faster when Good and White (and Bad and Black) went together on the same button, compared to how much slower they were when Bad and White (and

Good and Black) went together. That gives a measure of their automatic or implicit racial preferences.

Notice how this experiment identifies implicit and unconscious prejudicial feelings because the children are not being asked at all what their feelings are toward Whites versus Blacks. This is only revealed indirectly by the extent to which "good" is associated with one group in their minds, and "bad" associated with the other group. Using this test, Dunham and his colleagues discovered that White six-year-old children showed the identical unconscious pro-White bias on this implicit test as do White adults. In fact, the size of this racial preference remained the same for different age groups—for six-year-olds, ten-year-olds, and adults. In contrast, an explicit measure, as on a questionnaire, of liking for Whites and disliking of Blacks showed that the preference vanished with age. We clearly do learn in society that we should not like or favor one group more than another group, and so we say this (and, it is hoped, also believe it) when giving our conscious, intentional responses to such questionnaires. But the implicit and unconscious group preferences change not a whit over the life span. The implicit or automatic racial biases inside us at age six seem to stay inside us for the rest of our lives.

Similar findings of in-group preferences in young children have now been shown for the majority group populations in the United States, Japan, and United Kingdom. These very early preferences form the foundation for lifelong tendencies to favor one's own group at the expense of other groups. If you have liked one group more since infancy, you will tend to want to spend more time with them, meaning you'll have less time and fewer interactions with those of other groups, causing these biases to further ossify. In other words, you will involuntarily de-diversify your existence beyond socioeconomic factors that inherently limit our exposure to people who are different from us.

These are discouraging findings, to be sure, but all is not lost. There is a big difference in experience between a three-month-old who tends to prefer looking at faces of people similar to her parents and siblings, and a six-year-old who shows greater unconscious liking for their own racial group compared to a different racial group. Parents often look back and say that their children grow up so quickly: one day they are starting kindergarten and the next they are off to college. But if we parents think about it for just a moment, we know all too well that each and every day, especially with very young children in the house, is a long, wonderful, but exhausting grind. And between the ages of three months and six years, there are more than two thousand of such long, grinding days. Each of these days contains a whole lot of experiences for those children, who are soaking up knowledge about their social world like sponges during this time. Two thousand of such days during which they are exposed to their town's, their country's, their region's culture—through television and other media, and neighborhood children at the playground. They learn values, notions of what is important, cultural preferences, who the good people and bad people are, and how to behave across a wide variety of situations.

This spongelike process, however, comes with built-in hazards. When children soak up culture, they absorb it in all its imperfection, including our society's ideas about what different social groups are like. They trust it all blindly; they have no idea what part of it is correct and what part of it is just ignorant bias. They have no way to tell the two apart. And what is more, this cultural knowledge doesn't just affect how they expect others to behave; it also affects what they come to expect from themselves, depending on what social groups they belong to: males or females, whites or blacks, Muslims or Christians, and so on. From the broader culture they are immersed in, then, our children unconsciously pick up ideas about what they themselves are supposed to be like, and what they personally should and should not be able to do.

We may not remember the first few years of life, but that doesn't mean nothing of significance happened to us. On the contrary, much did happen that shaped our assumptions about the world, our feelings toward other people, and our confidence in ourselves. A life is like a flower, expanding from a tightly packed bud ever outward, opening more and more to the outside world. From the arms of our parents we then move around by ourselves inside our homes and then out to the broader neighborhood and town and culture that surround us. But as we move into the wider world, as we move from childhood onward, we continue to soak up what we see and hear and are told—now by other children, and by television and the mass media—in a totally innocent, gullible, trusting way. Our culture represents the third channel through which our hidden past continues to influence us today.

CHAPTER 3

Prime Time

When we are children, around age five or six or so, our world starts to seem less confusing and intimidating. We've started to figure it out, to know right from wrong, and to be able to anticipate what is going to happen next. We feel proud to be from our town, our state, and our country. We know what is important to respect and value, what might be a funny prank to pull on a friend and what might not be so funny, what we can get away with and what we can't. We don't really think about any of these things too much; they are just the way things are. What we aren't aware of at this young age is that our ways of thinking, feeling, and acting are not the only ones possible. We have absolutely no clue that it all could so easily have been very different for us. If we had been born in a different country, with different values and beliefs than our own, then we would have become a very different person.

You can take any human infant at birth to whatever far corner of the world you choose and that child will learn the language and the culture and the ideology of that country just as if he had been born there in the first place. The obviousness of this fact doesn't subtract from its remarkableness. You would have been a very different person in many respects had you been born elsewhere, into a different culture with a different language. These days, in our highly globalized, topsy-turvy world, it's not unheard-of to find, say, a person with Asian ancestry going back thousands of years, and whose native language is Spanish. Peru, for example, has a large community of people with Japanese heritage. And then there is the strange case of two brothers born to an American father in a country that wasn't the United States. Naturally, those brothers learned the language of that country perfectly, and they also learned many other things.

73

What they absorbed from their surroundings illustrates that the hidden mind is nurtured by the cultures we live in, ranging from the culture of our own family to the culture of the entire nation.

These two sons of an American father were born and grew up in North Korea.

Communists and Protestants

In 1962, James Dresnok was an American soldier stationed in the Demilitarized Zone, or DMZ, on the border of North and South Korea. The Korean War had ended nine years earlier, and this no-man's-land dividing the Communist North from the capitalist South was part of the conflict's legacy. Back home in the United States, Dresnok's wife had recently left him. His life was in shambles.

One night, perhaps restless and lonely, or maybe just bored, Dresnok snuck off his base with forged leave papers—and got caught. Instead of waiting around for his looming court-martial, he opted for a radical solution that would rewrite the trajectory of his life: he ran across the DMZ and defected to communist North Korea. As Dresnok told a pair of British filmmakers decades later, "On August fifteenth, at noon in broad daylight when everybody was eating lunch, I hit the road. Yes, I was afraid. Am I gonna live or die? And when I stepped into the minefield and I seen it with my own eyes, I started sweating. I crossed over, looking for my new life."

In his new home, Dresnok married a Romanian woman who lived in North Korea and with whom he had two kids, Ted and James. Although the lives of the Dresnoks are cloaked in mystery for the most part, it does seem that they did relatively well in North Korea, thanks in part to the exceptionalness of their being Americans. Both the Dresnok boys and their father have acted in North Korean movies, often playing American villains. A new twist in their strange family saga occurred in May 2016, however, when the now grown-up Ted and James, slender men in their thirties, appeared in a propaganda video released on the Internet in which they attacked the United States. For what? For being like a villainous country in a movie.

"The U.S. wants to conquer the world, pursuing an anti–North Korean policy, trying to take over Asia," said Ted. An aspiring diplomat, he was dressed formally in a suit. Sitting next to Ted at the conference table was his brother James, an army captain wearing his olive-drab uniform and North Korean emblems. James echoed these sentiments and praised the North Korean leader Kim Jong-un. The video briefly raised diplomatic speculation about its meaning and made for a juicy news story for a few days.

Many Americans would feel that the Dresnok sons were brainwashed or indoctrinated by the North Korean government. But they didn't have to be—at least, not any more than you or I had to be brainwashed or indoctrinated to hold our own quite different beliefs. Imagine if their father had not taken the extreme measure of defecting to the North, and instead had returned home and eventually married a woman in the United States. His sons Ted and James would speak English, not Korean (unless he'd married a Korean), and they'd have a very different set of values and ideologies than they do today. So as children growing up in North Korea, they did what we all do—soak up the language and culture of where they happened to be born and grew up.

North Korean ideology stands out because it is so different from our own, but compared to the rest of the world, American ideology is also different from that of any other country or culture. Yet because we in the United States soak it up unquestioningly when we are very young, our beliefs seems natural and right to us, just as North Korean ideology seems natural and right to Ted and James Dresnok. To much of the rest of the world, however, there are aspects of mainstream, traditional American morality and ethics that seem rather, well, odd. I'm not talking about politics here, or about democracy versus socialism. I am talking about the legacy of the Puritans, one of the first groups to arrive in the New World nearly four hundred years ago now, and the great impact it continues to have on American culture today.

The culture we live in is like water to a fish: it is all around us and so constant and commonplace that we hardly even notice it. Longtime scholars of cultural influences on individuals, such as Dov Cohen of the University of Illinois, have sketched out the many ways in which culture permeates our daily lives, operating sotto voce in the background, a ubiquitous and powerful source of implicit influences on our values, choices, opinions, and actions. In any country, culture emerges from a shared historical past, one that we learn about in school and in books, but which we don't remember firsthand. But we began absorbing our culture before we went to school, when we were very young. Researchers have argued compellingly that the United States' famous Protestant Ethic isn't just a favored cultural trope, but a set of values most Americans carry unconsciously. Even four centuries after European settlers landed on Plymouth Rock, our puritanical origins still shape Americans' behavior regarding sex, money, and work.

The story begins back in the sixteenth century, when Protestants broke away from the Roman Catholic Church in protest over the corruption of the church establishment and its perceived deviation from the values and interdictions of the Bible. In England, the Anglican Church was established as a new Protestant church. However, a subgroup of these English Protestants—the Puritans—felt that the Anglican Church had not gone far enough when it broke away; it had not reformed as much as the Puritans believed it should. So they decided to emigrate to the New World and establish their own, new church based on the stricter values they believed in. Fervent in their religious zeal, they braved the long, dangerous voyage across the ocean to a primitive, uncharted continent, taking a leap of faith if there ever was one. They came to America in order to establish a religious utopia in what is now the United States—and in so doing became one of the first large groups of people to arrive in America in the early 1600s. And because they got here first, they exerted a disproportionate influence on the cultural values of all the people who came to inhabit the United States.

The Puritans gave us two core values, or "ethics." The main one, known as the Protestant Ethic, is that hard work earns you eternal salvation. If you work hard, you are a good person, and you go to heaven. Conversely, if you don't work hard, you are not a good person and your "idle hands" will be "the devil's playground." The other core value we call the Puritan ethic, or just Puritanism; it holds that promiscuity and overt sexuality are evil. The Puritans used this principle to guide their choices in clothing and language, and to condemn casual sex. And of course a big part of the Puritan legacy is the bedrock Christian belief in God and the Bible.

Remarkably, these religious values and basic ethics regarding work and sex that are still so strongly ingrained in American culture run against the grain of all other modern Western industrialized countries. As a general rule around the world, wealth and democracy produce secular and less traditional societies. Historically, Protestant, democratic, industrialized, and wealthy countries were the first to secularize and remove overt religious influences from their government and culture, and today they are among the least traditional societies in the world. *Except for the United States.* Despite being a mainly Protestant, democratic, and very wealthy country, the United States is one of the *most* tradition-oriented countries in the world. In the standard values survey of people all around the world, called, naturally, the World Values Survey, the United States is far above the world average on the survey's index of traditional values—such as conventional family structures, nationalism, sexual repression, moral absolutism, a clear-cut difference between good versus evil—and a tendency to reject divorce, homosexuality, abortion, euthanasia, and suicide.

While other industrialized Protestant countries have become dramatically less religious and traditional over the past seventy years, the United States is just as religious today. In the year 2000, 50 percent of Americans rated God's importance in their life as a maximum 10 on a 1–10 scale, and 60 percent said they attended church at least once a month. In 2003, the same percentage of people attended church once a week as had in March 1939—before World War II. In 1947, nearly all—94 percent—of Americans said they believed in God, and in 2001 that figure was unchanged. Except for Brazil, all other countries showed a drop in this percentage from 1947 to 2001. Finally, seven out of ten Americans say they believe in the devil, compared to three out of ten British people and two or fewer out of every ten Germans, French people, and Swedes.

Still, what makes America so exceptional in its religiosity and traditional values is not so much these values per se, but rather that it has kept these values in the face of such booming economic prosperity. If you predict from levels of economic wealth and development only, based on all the other countries in the world, only 5 percent of Americans should see religion as central to their lives. The U.S. cultural heritage is thus so powerful that it runs completely against this worldwide trend. This heritage comes from the Puritan Protestants who fled religious persecution in England—*four hundred years ago.*

When they were graduate students at Yale, Eric Uhlmann and Andy Poehlman conducted several experiments with me on the unconscious and implicit influences of this Protestant cultural and ideological legacy.

We set out to test whether this Puritan Protestant cultural ideology oper-ates unconsciously to influence judgments and behavior of modern-day Americans. Also, given that this ideology is unique to the United States, we needed to show that it did not influence the judgments and behavior of non-Americans. What were the manipulations we used to show this? In several of our studies we followed the lead of researchers in the field of cultural psychology, who have routinely used what are called *priming* methods in order to demonstrate how cultural ideologies and values oper-ate unconsciously to influence a person's judgments and behavior. These methods have been around now for more than fifty years. Typically the important information is presented in a disguised or sometimes even sub-liminal manner, so that if it affects the participant as it is predicted to, the influence is not something she was aware of. In this way the influence is shown to operate unconsciously, not consciously.

For example, in some of the original priming studies in cognitive psy-chology dating back to the 1950s, study participants were given a list of words to memorize in a first experiment; then, in a second, unrelated experiment they were asked to give the first word that came to mind for each of a second list of words. This is what we call a "free association test." What the experimenters found, to their surprise at the time, was that the words in the first experiment—for example, *stop, butterfly,* and *rough*—were more likely to be given in the second, free association experiment, in which the participants were asked to give the words that first came to mind when they heard the words *highway, animal,* and *wood.* This prim-ing effect occurred even for words from the first experiment that a par-ticipant had forgotten. The memory location of these words had been *primed,* or made temporarily more active, through the words' use in the first experiment so that these same words became more *accessible,* or ready to be used, or said, or written down, as free associates in the second exper-iment. And all without the person knowing this effect was happening, and certainly without the person intending it to happen. After all, some people couldn't even remember these words as having been on the list of words to memorize in the first experiment.

Social psychology started to use this "two unrelated experiments" tech-nique to show how impressions and other judgments about people could be affected by one's recent experience. For example, if you just saw fire-fighters rushing into a burning building, or had been reading a history of a major war, your concept of bravery and heroism would likely be primed. Just like those single words in the original priming study, that larger concept of bravery would be more active than usual. So if you then heard a news story about a person, say, trying to sail alone across the Atlantic, you'd be more likely to think of that person as very brave, maybe even heroic—and not as crazy and reckless, perhaps even suicidal, instead.

Priming effects are natural and automatic. Our everyday experiences activate ideas and desires and even ways of thinking about the world. Primes are like reminders, whether we are aware of the reminding or not. We walk through the airport on the way to our gate and the wonderful, intoxicating smell of a Cinnabon wafting by reminds us how good they taste, of how hungry we are, and how much we'd really like one. Our conscious mind was on a completely different matter at the time, that of getting to the gate on time, not thinking about Cinnabons at all. So it was the smell that did all that "priming" work. Let's say that then, a few days later, we get cut off by one too many drivers on our morning commute, and when we finally get into the office, we find ourselves thinking what a selfish jerk our coworker is because he happens to be printing out a long document on the office printer when we need to use it. As we will see in the next chapter, these common everyday experiences affect us well after they are over and we have moved on to a completely different situation. In the lab, however, researchers have made good use of the basic principles of priming and accessibility (the readiness of a mental concept to be used) to study how one kind of experience can unconsciously shape and influence what a person does or thinks next, without her knowledge or awareness of these effects. Many of the studies of the unconscious effects of one's culture, even in young children, have used these priming methods.

Now back to our experiment on the Protestant Ethic, in which we employed the priming method. We included not only American participants (for whom we expected to show effects) but also participants from other wealthy Western industrialized countries—Canada, Italy, and Germany—for whom we did not expect to show any effects. Because the Protestant Ethic holds that heaven and the afterlife are the reward for hard work in one's earthly life, we tested whether Americans did indeed strongly associate the idea of *heaven* with the idea of *working hard,* using the standard "two unrelated studies" experimental technique. Our first experiment was described to participants as a language test, and in it they constructed a series of short, four-word sentences out of scrambled-up words. For one group of participants, some of these words had to do with the afterlife. For example, *trip dormitory heaven was the* (to which the participant could write down "The trip was heaven," and less likely to a college student but also grammatically correct, "The dormitory was heaven"). In the control condition, the primes were equally positive words but not related at all to religion (for example, *trip dormitory wonderful was the*). In this way, we primed or activated the idea of heaven and the afterlife for some participants, without their being aware we were doing so, and we didn't prime the idea for other participants (in the control group).

We predicted that for Americans, priming the concept of religion and the afterlife should also prime the Protestant work ethic, because the two are so intertwined in American culture (and therefore in the minds of Americans). These "heavenly" words, we hypothesized, should cause the American participants to work harder on the subsequent task—in this case, solving anagrams. But this same priming task should not cause the Germans, Italians, or Canadians to work any harder, because the link between salvation and working hard is not part of the cultures they grew up in. Only if ideas of heaven and the afterlife are strongly but implicitly associated with working hard in one's mind should our priming of the first influence the second.

And that is what we found. Our U.S. participants primed with religious concepts did work harder and score higher on the anagram task, compared to U.S. participants in the control priming condition (with no exposure to words relating to heaven). And, as we expected, the heaven priming only affected the task performance of the Americans; it did not influence the anagram performance of the participants from the other countries. Finally, when carefully questioned after the study was over, no one in our experiment showed any awareness of the connection between the religious primes in the first task, and how hard or well they worked on the anagram task. It was a completely unconscious cultural influence on their behavior.

In our second study, we further established that these cultural influences operate unconsciously. We asked American participants to read a story about two young potato peelers who had just purchased a winning lottery ticket together. After winning the lottery, the first potato peeler retired, while the second continued to work peeling potatoes even though he was now a millionaire. We asked the participants to describe both their intuitive, gut feelings regarding each of the two potato peelers and their more conscious, deliberate judgments of them. The gut feelings were significantly more positive toward the one who continued to peel potatoes even after winning the lottery, compared to gut feelings toward the one who then retired rich and carefree. In contrast, on the deliberative, more thoughtful judgments, the two potato peelers were rated as morally the same. The Protestant Ethic at work—continuing to work after no longer needing to, financially, makes you a better person.

So now, on to the Puritan ethic. In our third study, we tested whether Americans strongly associated the Protestant and Puritan ethics with each other, as we would expect, since these ideas are pillars of the founding American ideology. We predicted that, if they are strongly associated, Americans should have more conservative attitudes about sex after they have been thinking about work! To show that this was an exclusive effect of American culture we chose a group of bicultural Asian-Americans to be our participants. This allowed us first to prime either their Asian identity or their American identity—so that within the same person, different effects of the work-related prime could occur depending on which of their two cultural identities was currently active. In other words, we were switching on different aspects of the early and now-forgotten pasts that had shaped their cultural identities.

For some participants, the Asian aspect of their identity was first primed using a questionnaire with items such as "What is your favorite Asian food?" For the other participants, their American identity was primed instead by asking "What is your favorite American food?" and with related questions about favorite movies, books, musical groups, and so on. Next, all participants completed a scrambled-sentence test, except that for one of the participants some of the words on the test were related to work—such as *office, work, job.* For the control participants, there were no words related to work on this first "language test." Then everyone read a story about a high school's proposal to make the school dress code stricter by prohibiting the wearing of revealing clothing at the school, and then answered questions about the study. We predicted that only when the American part of the Asian-Americans' identity had first been primed, activating uniquely American cultural values, would priming *work* then cause a more conservative, Puritan response to the *sex* questions. The participants would be more in favor of the stricter dress code. Sure enough, this is what we found. Those who had been assigned to the Asian-identity priming condition showed no effect of the work priming on their responses about the school dress code. The Protestant (work) and Puritan (sex) ethics do not go together in Asian culture. So our opinions about morality, the rightness or wrongness of various social behaviors, are influenced by our cultural ideology, which we absorbed so readily as young children that it has become part of our hidden, unconscious past.

Thus work and sex—the twin Protestant and Puritan ethics—appear to be strongly linked in a uniquely American set of cultural values, one rooted in the country's distant origins. Today, four hundred years later, we still see a profound effect of the founding ideology of the Puritan Protestants on the moral judgments of twenty-first-century Americans. For the most part, we are unaware and unconscious of these influences. They are the water that (many, not all) American "fish" swim in, and they generate feelings and moral values surprisingly consistent with those of our deeply religious Puritan forefathers and foremothers of the 1600s.

Costs and Benefits

As our experiment on the American values with Asian-American participants showed, we can feel and behave differently depending on which aspect of our personal identity is currently active. Our identities have multiple aspects—mother, musician, teacher, yoga enthusiast, NASCAR fan. Within each of these is stored ingrained, implicit knowledge about appropriate values and behavior, likes and dislikes. Ways of being. Children learn from their culture what it means to be a boy or girl, an Asian-American or an African-American, a child or an elderly person—how you are supposed to act, what you are supposed to be able to do, and what you are not to do. And young children can adopt these cultural beliefs so strongly that they will actually behave differently, at a stunningly young age, depending on which aspect of their identity is primed.

In 2000, I attended the first annual meeting of the Society for Personality and Social Psychology, which has since become the largest conference in my field in the world, attended by thousands of researchers, students, and professors. This yearly event basically consists of symposiums, panels, and lectures in which eager, enthusiastic scientists present their ideas and latest findings, discuss and argue about them a bit, then head straight for the evening reception and cash bar. There was great excitement that year in Nashville at the first-ever convention, and I met dozens of new colleagues, but what stands out most in my memory is a talk, in the grand ballroom of the hotel, by the late Nalini Ambady.

Ambady was a brilliant social psychologist from Kerala, India, who went to graduate school at Harvard and took seminars with the likes of B. F. Skinner. She left us much too soon, succumbing to leukemia in 2013. She was a colleague I greatly respected, and I was not alone in that. The huge ballroom in Nashville was packed to hear her present her latest research, a study she had conducted with her colleague Margaret Shih on young Asian-American girls and boys. Nearly two decades later, their findings are still some of the most compelling demonstrations of just how early in a person's life cultural influences on their motivation and behavior can begin.

Thanks to the pioneering research of Claude Steele, we have known for some time that reminders that cue or prime a person's social identity can affect their test and academic performance, usually in a negative way. Merely checking off their racial or ethnic group at the top of a standardized test causes African-Americans to do worse on that test than if they had not checked off that box. Society teaches us that our social group is good or not so good across a whole lot of life domains. For example, that blacks can't cut it academically, or that girls and women can't do math or science as well as boys and men, that elderly people are slow and have bad memories. Remember the movie *White Men Can't Jump*? Steele called this phenomenon *stereotype threat*. If you are reminded of your group status before performing a test or task, and the cultural stereotype says that your group is not very good at it, your performance will be affected. You will, consciously or unconsciously, "buy in" to that stereotype. Often this comes when the going gets tough, because when things get hard (such as more advanced math classes for girls) members of the stereotyped group start to attribute the difficulty they are facing to their group's inability ("I'm having trouble with this because I'm a girl") and stop trying. Others pick up their effort at these moments, try harder, and so do better.

There is some good news, though. The same effect can also help performance if your group is supposed to be good at the task. This is called *stereotype gain.* For example, Asian-American teens are stereotyped as nerdy, overachieving, and good at math. That this is a widespread cultural belief is perhaps best illustrated by the infamous 1987 *Time* magazine cover story with six brainy-looking Asian kids posing together, and the headline "Those Asian-American WHIZ KIDS."

So what are you supposed to believe about yourself if you happen to be an Asian-American girl? According to American culture, one part of your social identity (Asian) says you should be good at math, while another part (female) says you should be bad at math. Ambady and Shih recognized that the dilemma of Asian-American girls afforded a unique research opportunity to gauge the automatic, unconscious effects of a person's social identities on their actual behavior and performance. So in their first set of studies, they showed that high-school-age and ten-year-old girls alike did better on standardized, age-appropriate math tests if they were first instead primed with their Asian identity, so that it was the most active aspect of their identity when they worked on the test, but these girls did worse if they were instead primed beforehand with their female identity. It was disturbing that these effects showed up as early as fourth grade, but the researchers suspected that grade school teachers, from first grade on, had already gotten the message across, through different classroom treatment of boys and girls, that girls were not expected to be as good at math as boys. So, unfortunately, by fourth grade this was apparently already ingrained in the girls' heads.

In their next study, the one Ambady presented in that packed Nashville ballroom, she and Shih used an even younger group of children: five-year-old Asian-American girls who had not yet started grade school. Cleaner slates, as it were. As before, though, they also had groups of fourth graders and high school students. Their assumption was that the stereotype effects would not be present until fourth grade because they were being transmitted by the grade school teachers and the culturally biased learning environment. Their assumption would be proven when the Asian or female primes did not affect how well the kindergartners did on the math test, but did affect how well the older girls did.

Ambady and Shih and their team brought the eighty-one Asian-American girls into their lab at Harvard—71 percent had been born in the United States—and randomly divided them into three groups: Asian-identity primed, female-identity primed, and a no-identity primed control group. The five-year-olds had their Asian identity activated by coloring in a picture of a two Asian children using chopsticks to eat rice out of a bowl; a different group of five-year-olds had their female identity activated by coloring in a picture of a girl holding a doll; and the control group just colored in a neutral landscape. The identities of the older girls were primed in the same way they were in Ambady and Shih's original study. Then all the girls took a standardized math test appropriate to their age group. The identity primes for the five-year-olds would fail, right?

I will never forget the audible gasp from the audience in the crowded ballroom that afternoon when Ambady then presented the results of the study. Most of us there had placed so much hope on the educational system as the way to fix these harmful beliefs—harmful not only to girls themselves but to our society itself, in terms of wasted valuable human capital, and underdeveloped and underused abilities and talents. We never expected, and neither had Ambady or Shih, that these cultural beliefs that girls can't do math were already entrenched in the heads of five-year-olds, before they'd even *started* school. They were so entrenched that subtle priming manipulations could cue that identity and unconsciously affect their performance on a math test.

But they had. The effects of the Asian and the girl coloring book primes on the five-year-old girls were there, just as they were for the fourth- and eighth-grade girls. The "girls can't do math" belief was in the heads of all of them, even the preschool kids. When Ambady put the results up on the overhead projector, it felt like all the air had just been sucked out of the room. We in the audience just looked at each other, shaking our heads in disbelief. So much for Plan A, getting to these kids right away in first grade, nipping these false beliefs in the bud.

We now know that, for better or worse—often worse, as we've now seen—cultural stereotypes can take root even before kids start school. Yet this is not to say that they can't be further perpetuated by teachers in the classroom, as the famous 1960s "Pygmalion in the Classroom" studies by Robert Rosenthal showed. In those studies, classroom teachers were given a false set of standardized test results about their students. High or low test scores were randomly assigned to each child. They were not related at all to the child's actual abilities (and neither the children nor their parents ever saw or knew about these scores), yet at the end of the year, the students' grades and test scores corresponded to those false scores. Because only the teachers knew about those scores, and because the scores were unrelated to the child's actual ability, the only way this could have happened was through the teachers treating their students differently based on their expectations of them.

But in the case of the Asian-American five-year-olds, they showed negative effects of cultural stereotypes, that "girls can't do math," even *before* they had started school. So how did these deeply embedded early stereotypes find their way into the unconscious minds of these small children? One possibility would be that their parents were telling them that girls can't do math, but when I spoke to her recently Shih strongly discounted this explanation. "These were high-achievement-motivated parents," she said. "They had high aspirations for their daughters. Some even thought that participating in this study at Harvard would help their girl get into Harvard later on!"

It is certainly the case that American culture, at least, socializes girls quite differently than boys. One defining difference is the greater emphasis on physical attractiveness and appearance for girls than for boys. Early on in the home, getting ready for school in the morning, there is more attention to brushing and even styling the girl's hair, and to the outfit she is wearing, than to boys' appearances. And as they get older, the emphasis on physical appearance becomes more obviously about sexual attractiveness; researchers have described how girls and young women are "socialized into a culture that sexually objectifies the female body" and "the greater cultural demands placed on women to meet physical attractiveness ideals." It is almost as if women in our culture grow up to develop—at a very early age—two distinct self-identities: their body, and their mind. Society seems to say, "It is better to be pretty than smart," as if these two attributes were somehow mutually exclusive.

The nature of this subtly absorbed, unconscious past suggests that when a female's body identity is made salient—say, at the beach—her "mind" identity—her intelligence—should suffer. The beach's emphasis on the body and attractiveness triggers the cultural stereotype that a woman is to be valued and judged according to her physical looks, not her knowledge and intellectual abilities. A now-classic study at the University of Michigan by Barbara Fredrickson and her colleagues showed just this under controlled laboratory conditions. Male and female undergraduates came into the psychology lab, one at a time, for a study on "emotions and consumer behavior." They were told they would be evaluating three types of consumer products: a unisex fragrance, an article of clothing, and a food item. After the participant rated the fragrance product, he or she went into a dressing room that had a full-length mirror on the wall. They were randomly assigned to be in the swimsuit or the sweater condition. The women tried on a one-piece swimsuit, available in sizes from 4 to 14, or a sweater available in sizes S, M, or L. The men tried on either a pair of swim trunks (four sizes, from S to XL) or a sweater (sizes M, L, and XL). Over headphones they were instructed to look at themselves wearing the item of clothing, and then they completed a set of questionnaires involving how they felt about their body.

After getting dressed again, the participants came out for the next part of the study, which was a challenging math test with twenty questions taken from the GMAT (the test you take when you apply to business schools for an MBA degree). They had fifteen minutes to work on it. The instructions made clear to the participant that this was a test of their mathematical ability. The final part of the study was a taste test of Twix candy bars. The package was unwrapped and the two candy bars were placed in front of the participant on a plate, with a glass of water and a napkin nearby. The participants were told to eat as much as they wanted.

Their answers confirmed that, as you might expect, wearing the swimsuit focused the participants' identities more on their bodies than did wearing the sweater, and this was true for both men and women. As for eating the candy bars, overall the women ate less than the men, and if trying on the swimsuit had made them feel bad about their bodies, they then ate less of the candy bar than did the other participants. But the big news was about the math test performance. Recall that the participants were randomly assigned, by chance, to the swimsuit or the sweater condition. Also, the researchers controlled for important factors such as the participants' overall math ability. Yet women who tried on a swimsuit instead of a sweater then did significantly worse on the math test (an average of 2.5 correct answers versus 4). Focusing on their bodies caused them to display less intelligence. Here's the kicker: men's performance on the math test was undisturbed by whether they had tried on the swim trunks instead of the sweater. Priming their body identity didn't "harm" them in any way.

Just as with our studies of the Protestant and Puritan ethics, these results show that our various cultural beliefs are intertwined, that they are all associated with each other. After all, there is no logical reason why emphasizing physical attractiveness or increasing body consciousness should cause worse performance on a math test, *unless* both of those beliefs about women were components of the (American) cultural stereotype for women. So that when that stereotype is made salient, both of those beliefs—that women are supposed to make themselves physically attractive and are worse at math than men—are up and running in women's minds. Priming one aspect of this cultural identity by having the women try on the swimsuits activated the other aspect. Keep in mind that these were college students, undergraduates at a large Big Ten university, who were successful students with a very strong academic identity compared to other, less high-achieving people. Yet even they succumbed to this damaging cultural belief about women and math, without knowing it.

If these unconscious influences are already present in the minds of preschool children, we can't entirely blame our school systems. And physical attractiveness biases are likely not the fault of our educational system (or if so, only marginally). So where do these subtle winds blow from? What forces are constructing the hidden past of our minds? Shih said she and Ambady suspected that the girls had learned the stereotype through mass media and the general culture they had already been exposed to so much already in their young lives. There are a lot of developmental questions about children's understanding of race and gender. For gender, though, it seems clear where some of the influences come from. "Dolls and princesses," Shih said, noting the toys and models girls are given from a very early age. "Not spaceships."

Just watch a little television and peruse newsstands for the messages targeted at girls and women in our culture (and many other cultures). On the cartoon and other entertainment channels directed at children, the girls' toys advertised are often pretty dolls with hair to brush and different outfits to dress them in. Bracelets and necklaces and other forms of body adornment are routinely marketed to girls. So in their next research project, Ambady and her colleagues focused on the cultural transmission of racial biases in the United States via the mass media. They did a careful study of the content of the most popular prime-time U.S. television shows. The study was conducted in 2006 and focused on eleven shows, such as *Bones, CSI, Friday Night Lights,* and *Grey's Anatomy*, all of which had an average viewership in the United States of 9 million people. However, they chose only participants who had never watched any of these shows before. All of the TV shows selected had a white and a black character of equal status—meaning that the two characters were equally important to the show's theme and had equal job status (for example, both were police detectives). From these programs, a total of fifteen white and fifteen black characters were selected, and participants in the study were shown nine silent clips from the show featuring each character.

Now comes the twist: the featured white or black character was then edited out of the scene so that all that the participants saw was how the main show character, such as Mark Harmon or David Caruso, reacted to that character. Watching that clip, you would have no idea who the main character was interacting with at that moment. Because the audio had been digitally removed from each clip, the only information participants had was the main character's nonverbal behavior—their facial expressions, gestures, body language—toward the (off-screen) show character. The researchers wanted to know whether the show's main character was perceived to behave differently when interacting with a black or a white character on the show. Two hundred sixty-five total clips just like this were presented to each participant in a random order. After each clip, participants were asked how much the character (who was visible) liked or disliked the unseen character; they also rated the overall positivity of the interaction between the two. There was high agreement among the participants when they answered these two questions.

The results revealed that the nonverbal behavior of the main character was more positive toward the white characters in the show and more negative toward the black characters. Even though the participants who made these ratings did not know who the main character was talking to at the time, they could still detect in the main character's facial expression and body posture a more negative attitude toward the black character. Multiply these subtle differences in treatment of white and black characters by the many such interactions the main character has in each show, multiple that by the number of episodes of the show, and multiply that by the number of popular shows on TV—and then multiply all that by the millions and millions of people watching all those shows, and you can get an idea of how powerful this cultural influence is on viewers, on our positive and negative attitudes toward blacks and whites. The differences were subtle but not so subtle that they could not be picked up by the participants who viewed them—just as they would be picked up by the millions of viewers, including children, at home watching that episode of their favorite show.

The real question, of course, is whether these more negative attitudes toward the black show characters have an effect on the viewer. We may notice them at some level, but that doesn't mean they necessarily affect our racial attitudes. For example, as you watch these shows more, do your unconscious attitudes toward blacks become more negative? The news here, unfortunately, is not good.

In their next study, Ambady and colleagues examined the effect of watching these shows on the racial attitudes of viewers. A measure of each show's relative (subtle, nonverbal) negativity toward blacks was calculated by taking the difference in the main character's liking and positivity toward the unseen black character versus that toward the white unseen character. (Some shows displayed more of this negativity than others.) Then a new group of fifty-three participants were asked which of the eleven shows they watched regularly, and they were also given the adult version of the Implicit Association Test, or IAT, that uses Good-Bad and White-Black buttons to see how strongly the person unconsciously associates white with good, and black with bad. In this way the researchers could see if the more a person watched prime-time TV shows that had relatively high degrees of racial bias, the more racially biased they themselves became. And yes, this turned out to be the case. The more nonverbal bias in the shows they watched, the more negative the person's implicit attitudes toward blacks. The actors' hidden biases were unconsciously absorbed by their viewers.

So there is credible evidence for the cultural transmission of stereotypes and beliefs through the mass media; greater exposure to racial bias on prime-time television shows is linked to greater levels of personal racial bias. Such biases later shape our thoughts and actions before we know it; we aren't aware of these biases or where they came from. The mass media also conveys cultural stereotypes through the way it presents the news to us. This may be an even more insidious way in which cultural beliefs are transmitted, because we expect the news to be an accurate reporting of the real world. And so, if it inaccurately presents to us negatively biased "news" about different groups in our society, we will tend to believe it is factual—just as young children soak up everything they hear without questioning it.

Before the cable TV and Internet revolution in communications, most people got their news watching the evening broadcasts of the (then) three major networks—CBS, NBC, and ABC—and reading the newspaper and major weekly newsmagazines—*Time, Newsweek,* and *U.S. News & World Report.* Even today, tens of millions still watch these programs and read these magazines, or new outlets and media with similarly wide reach. In 1996, in the pre-Internet heyday of these news sources, Yale political scientist Martin Gilens conducted a landmark study, the first of its kind, to examine the content of both the major weekly newsmagazines and the three major television network evening news broadcasts. He focused on the visual content that these mainstream mass media outlets presented while the anchor or reporter spoke about the problem of poverty in America—what were the pictures or videos that were selected to be the backdrop to the magazine text or the television narration?

The 1990 U.S. Census showed that African-Americans made up 29 percent of the poor in the United States. So roughly 30 percent of photos of people living in poverty in the United States should have been of African-Americans, right? In reality, in the 182 newsmagazine stories on poverty that Gilens studied, from 1988 to 1992, the photographs associated with the newsmagazine stories were of blacks *62 percent of the time*—twice as frequently as they should have been. Naturally, this gave readers the strong but quite erroneous impression that the majority of poor people in the country were African-American. And Gilens found that the same thing happened in the evening news broadcasts by the three major television networks—fully 65 percent of the people shown in the TV news stories about poverty in the United States were black Americans. Such disproportionate representations affect not only people's attitudes toward poverty— that is, "most poor people are black"—but also black people's unconscious beliefs about themselves and their community.

In his report, Martin Gilens reminded us that when the journalist Walter Lippmann used the term *stereotype* in its psychological sense for the first time in the 1920s he was referring to the "pictures in our minds" that have more of an influence on our attitudes and behavior than reality does. And because we all rely heavily on the news media to get our "pictures in our mind" about the world, is it any wonder that people develop the stereotype and false belief that most of the poor people in the United States are African-American? Now, couple this belief with the Protestant Ethic,

which as we've seen is still such an important part of the U.S. cultural ideology: Gilens describes one national survey taken during the same time
period showing that 70 percent of those responding believe that "America
is the land of opportunity where everyone who works hard can get ahead."
If you hold that belief, then you would conclude that poor people just
don't work as hard, or don't want to work as hard, as other people. Meaning they are lazy, and since most poor people are black (according to what
you see in the news all the time), well then, black people must be lazy.
This quite potent and unjust cocktail of biases in the cultural and individual consciousness has its origins in the unintentional and unconscious
biases of those who control our newsfeeds.

The mass media, both the entertainment and the news sectors, exerts
tremendous power over the shaping of cultural beliefs and attitudes.
Ambady's study of negative racial attitudes in the top-rated television programs, and Gilens's study of racial bias in news media coverage of "poverty
in America" stories both show this quite clearly. But then the question
naturally arises: why is the mass media in the United States portraying
blacks in these ways? Is it that the editors and producers in charge are
racially biased? In the case of the news stories about poverty, Gilens presents evidence against that explanation, showing that the photo editors
who choose the pictorial content and the TV news editors who choose
the associated video footage are in fact generally more racially *liberal* than
most Americans; and in the case of the top-rated entertainment shows, it
seems unlikely that Mark Harmon and the other actors were intentionally
trying to convey their relative dislike for the black characters in their programs. After all, the television programs selected for Ambady's study were
the only top-rated ones that (quite intentionally) included both white
and black characters whose roles were of equal status (for example, both
detectives, both supervisors) in a deliberate attempt to present the races
in an egalitarian manner.

So if the cause was not conscious and deliberate on the part of those in
charge, it must have been unconscious and unintended. Gilens ends his
study of the mainstream news media by saying that "the consistent pattern of racial misrepresentation (along with the consistently liberal nature
of these editors' conscious beliefs about racial inequality) strongly suggests
that unconscious negative images of blacks are at work." People who work
on newsmagazines and in the TV news business are members of the same

culture as their readers and viewers; they soaked up the same culture the rest of us did. So did the actors who portray the main characters in the top-rated entertainment programs. And culture exerted an unconscious influence on their choices of photographic and video content for their news stories, and on their nonverbal facial expressions and body postures toward the black characters in their shows. Even though these behaviors and choices are likely running against the consciously held beliefs and values of people in the media, that doesn't stop their unconscious beliefs from having a very strong impact on the rest of us.

The editors and producers in charge of the content we consume may be just like the rest of us in one respect—that of having soaked up the same cultural biases as we did—but they are quite unlike us in another. They have a very powerful role in determining the "facts" the rest of us unconsciously learn from the media sources we generally (and should be able to) trust. They influence us without our realizing it and they help shape the hidden mind of early childhood. They need to use that power more responsibly than they have in the past, and efforts such as Gilens's to make them more accountable are very positive developments.

Leaving the Tunnel

Now that we have seen how cultural beliefs and values embed themselves in the hidden mind, it is useful to think of the early years of our lives as a kind of tunnel. First, in infancy, you see only what enters your narrow tube of attention: your family, your house, and other passing stimuli. This is your entire world. Then, as a toddler, as you begin walking and interacting with objects and people, that tunnel widens and becomes more like a country road. You travel down it, with your senses focused mostly on the road in front of you and the other travelers, but you do notice the landscape streaming by, the occasional building, and other roads that cross yours. This landscape includes more subtle stimuli: the layers of your culture, media, and the attitudes of others, which you absorb without noticing and without questioning. As you develop from a child into a preadolescent and then into a teen, this spatial expansion continues. Your experience becomes more of a busy highway, and you periodically get off that highway to stay in different cities and meet the inhabitants and see the sights: school, friends, trips, more media, and more things you observe and notice. No memories of that original tunnel remain, and most early memories of that country road disappear, too. You take in more and more of your surroundings and you settle into the perceptual driver's seat of a fully developed adult. By then you have arrived at your destination as a full-fledged, card-carrying representative of your culture—with all its nice features, but all its warts, too.

Our everyday experiences, such as holding a hot cup of coffee, are constantly triggering or priming our deeply ingrained cultural beliefs and values. Americans who encounter words relating to heaven and the afterlife then work harder on a task than otherwise, and become more judgmental about revealing dress and sexual behavior. People with multiple aspects to their identities, even young preschool children, can have very different attitudes and even behave differently depending on which identity is currently up and running in their minds, without having any idea of the effect these cultural identities are having. We soak up these cultural influences like crazy as children and they are all around us, in the television and other media we spend so many hours watching, and in the subtle facial expressions and nonverbal behavior of our parents and older siblings toward members of other social groups. These stereotypes and other beliefs become second nature to us, so ingrained that even well-meaning people with liberal racial attitudes, in positions of great responsibility in the mass media, nonetheless communicate—and thereby perpetuate—those stereotypes to their viewers and readers. The cultural background we inhaled so innocently in our preschool years is there in the background of our adult lives all the time, operating in our minds behind the scenes like the hidden puppet master at our fourth birthday party. In the case of the Dresnok boys, it was powerful enough to turn the sons of an American soldier into sworn enemies of the United States.

"Pay no attention to that man behind the curtain!" exclaimed the Wizard of Oz, but, like Dorothy and her crew, maybe it's prime time we did.

CHAPTER 4

Life Lingers

Zombies!

It's been forty years now, but I still remember that dark and rainy October night, because it was one of the scariest of my life. I was in college and I was walking home at about 10 p.m. from an auditorium on one side of campus to my apartment clear on the other side. I passed many people on the sidewalks going in the opposite direction—except that they were not people. They were *zombies.* Groups of them, zombie after zombie staggering toward me, wanting to devour my flesh and slurp my brain! I did everything I could to avoid them, taking side streets and sticking to the shadows, but no, they were still there, coming right at me! I finally made it home safely, sweating and shaking.

This was way before zombies became trendy and there were things like Zombie Night, as was the case at a 2016 Miami Marlins baseball game. ("Help us vote for the best-dressed Zombie!" the team tweeted during the game.) No, this was back in the mid-1970s, only a few years after George Romero's horrifying cult classic, *Night of the Living Dead,* was released, and I had just attended a screening in one of the big campus auditoriums. All the way home I was convinced that at least some of these normal-looking people all around me were actually zombies, like in the movie, and I was on high, paranoid alert.

What had happened to me? While my body had left the theater and was walking home, my mind was still in that theater, still immersed in the plot and logic and visceral horror of *Night of the Living Dead.* Clearly, something had taken place in my unconscious to fill me with a fear that I knew was irrational and childish, even as it set off the adrenaline alarms in my body.

In daily life, as we move from one context and experience to the next, our senses immediately move on and take in the information in the new situation, the new present. Yet our mind takes some time to shake off the effects of the previous moment. Our mind lingers in the recent past and only gradually moves on into the new situation. This means that the residue of the recent past can influence how one interprets a new situation, how one behaves in it, the choices one makes, and the emotions one feels. I don't really believe in zombies, but that one night, I did.

Back then in college, as I've said, I was an FM radio disc jockey on the student station. This was the era of "progressive rock," and FM radio was relatively new. Unlike commercial AM stations, we could play longer cuts of music—more music, fewer interruptions. As I mentioned in the Introduction, one of the arts of FM rock radio at this time was segueing from from one song or instrumental piece into the next, as seamlessly as possible, much as club and dance party DJs do today. I'd overlay the long, drawn-out ending of Robin Trower's "Bridge of Sighs" with the long, drawn-out opening of Savoy Brown's "Hellbound Train" (bonus points if you've heard of either one of them), "cross-fading" the one into the other. The first song lingered and carried on into the next.

Our minds, too, are constantly segueing from one situation to the next. This is crucial to understand: what is active and influential in the mind at any given moment is more than what is going on right now in the present. The vestiges of recent experience only gradually dissipate with time. What we *think* is affecting us in the new situation is what is right in front of us, available to our conscious awareness through our senses. But there is much more going on behind the scenes than we realize.

That's what this chapter is about: the *carryover effect* of one experience into the next—the very, very recent past—and how it can bleed into the occurring present.

Two consecutive experiences are often quite distinct from, and unrelated to, each other. Your mother calls you at work and just after you get off the phone your boss comes in to give you some pressing new assignment. Or someone holds the door for you as you enter the fast-food restaurant and then you head back out into heavy holiday traffic. There's no rational or logical reason why the phone call with your mother should affect how you act toward your boss, or why someone being courteous to you on the way into McDonald's should affect how you drive on Interstate 95. But they do. These thoughts, feelings, desires, goals, hopes, and motivations from Situation 1 do not vanish in a nanosecond as we exit stage right into Situation 2, as if there were some kind of on-off switch. Instead, they leave a residue that affects our subsequent experience in subtle yet powerful ways.

Motorcycles and Misattribution

Night of the Living Dead was released in 1968, but that same year also saw the release of a quite different movie—one that, in an odd way, would turn out to influence psychological science and lead to the discovery that "life lingers." In fact, you can still watch the trailer of this movie on YouTube today.

"Now you'll know the thrill of wrapping your legs around a tornado of pounding pistons!" a rakish male voice growls over images of a leather-clad woman riding a snarling motorcycle, before cutting to a man pulling at the zipper of her outfit with his teeth. "She goes as far as she wants, as fast as she wants, straddling the potency of one hundred wild horses!"

So goes the trailer for the 1968 British-French film *Girl on a Motorcycle,* also known as *Naked Under Leather,* directed by Jack Cardiff. It starred the blond-haired it-girl Marianne Faithfull, whom a writer later described as follows: "Quite simply, there was no female anywhere on the planet as cool and as sexy as she was during the 1960s. She was born with one of the most classically beautiful faces of all time and she just had *that look* which embodied the era as no other woman could." In the film, Faithfull played Rebecca, a recent newlywed who skips out on her hubby—with whom she envisions a stultifying future marriage—and rides off on her motorcycle to meet her lover (played by the classically handsome Alain Delon) and embark on a series of erotic, hallucinatory adventures (which involve leather, nakedness, and, of course, pounding pistons). The film was a hit in Britain and garnered the scandalous X rating of that era.

Midway into the next decade, in 1975, the psychologists Dolf Zillmann, Jennings Bryant, and Joanne Cantor used *Girl on a Motorcycle* in a classic experiment to demonstrate how physical activity can affect conscious, rational thoughts. All the participants in the study watched the film, but only after engaging in a workout—riding a bike of their own, in fact, albeit just an exercise bike with few if any pounding pistons. The key to the experiment was that each subject took in Marianne Faithfull's performance while in one of the three different stages of physiological arousal that follow exercising. In the first phase, right after the physical activity is over, we know that our high levels of arousal—heart pumping, maybe shortness of breath—are because of having exercised. In the second and key phase, we believe we have calmed down and are back to our normal arousal state, yet we are actually still physiologically aroused. Our arousal state lingers on for a while even after we feel that it is over and done with. In the third and final phase, arousal has actually returned to normal levels and we correctly believe that we are no longer physiologically aroused.

The question Zillmann and his colleagues asked was how the participant's state of arousal following the workout would affect how sexually aroused he became by watching the segment of *Girl on a Motorcycle*. The subjects in the first phase of the heightened physiological state resulting from the exercise, who were still fully aware of the exercise's effect on them, didn't report any greater level of sexual arousal from the movie than did a non-exercising control group. And participants in the third phase, who were no longer actually aroused from the exercise, also were not that sexually aroused by the movie. In fact, both the first and the third group reported fairly negative impressions of the film. Importantly, those were the groups that had an accurate read on their arousal levels. But then there was the second group. That is where things got interesting.

These participants did sense that they were physiologically aroused while watching the movie; even though this was really caused by the lingering effects of their exercising, they thought the effect of the exercise was over with, so they mistakenly attributed their arousal solely to Marianne Faithfull and her leather-bound adventures. They also reported liking *Girl on a Motorcycle* significantly more than did the other two groups. The lingering effect of the exercise was no longer in their conscious experience even though it was still in their bodies, so they attached their unconscious feelings instead to what they *were* aware of at the moment—the movie.

Cantor, Zillmann, and Bryant's experiment established the important concept of *excitation transfer*. They showed that physiological arousal caused by one experience (a workout, but also, for example, a frightening or violent encounter) could be misunderstood as the result of a subsequent experience. There is a time window, then, after an arousing experience, when we are prone to misunderstand the real reasons for our arousal, believing it is being caused by what happens to be going on right then in the present and not a lingering, carryover effect of the recent past.

In another famous demonstration of the same effect, men who had just crossed a rickety pedestrian bridge over a deep gorge were found to be more attracted to a woman they met while crossing that bridge. How do we know this? Because they were more likely to call that woman later on (she was one of the experimenters for the study and had given these men her number after they filled out a survey for her) than were those who met the same woman while crossing a much safer bridge. The men in this study reported that their decision to call the woman had nothing to do with their experience of crossing the scary bridge. But the experiment clearly showed they were wrong about that, because those in the scary-bridge group were more likely to call the woman than were those who had just crossed the safe bridge. You may remember Keanu Reeves's line to Sandra Bullock at the end of *Speed* as they're about to kiss after a long, traumatic day together.

"I have to warn you," his character says, "I've heard relationships based on intense experiences never work."

"Okay," Bullock's character says. "We'll have to base it on sex then."

So, hmmm, why do you suppose teenagers like scary horror movies so much? Because physiological arousal from watching, say, ax-wielding maniacs or malevolent spirits transfers into—and is misunderstood as caused by—sexual feelings and attraction to the person they're seeing the movie with (especially after leaving the theater). Maybe that's why back in the day, my own pack of teenage friends liked to tell each other ghost stories around a fire on the Lake Michigan beach well into the night.

Lingering arousal can be misinterpreted in ways other than as sexual feelings and attraction. Another experiment by Zillmann and his colleagues in 1974 focused on anger and aggression. Would the arousing effects of exercise, they wondered, cause people to think that they were angrier at another person? Strong emotions do have an active physical arousal component to them, and one very influential early theory of emotion held that often we feel the arousal and only then interpret what emotion we are feeling based on the context. When Roger Federer breaks down in tears after winning Wimbledon, we understand that he is crying tears of joy, not feeling abject sorrow; the same racking sobs and tears at a funeral we understand are not tears of joy (we hope) but the expression of a very different emotion.

Once again, the male participants in the study rode an exercise bike for ninety seconds. Then, either immediately after or following a delay, they took on the role of "teacher" in a re-creation of the notorious Milgram study on obedience. Their job was to deliver shocks to a "learner" after every wrong answer, believing they were subjects in a study of how punishment affects learning. But first, in an interesting twist to the original Milgram procedure, the "learner" was given the opportunity to shock the "teacher." The learner got to ask the teacher his opinion on twelve controversial issues of the day, and the learner could give him a shock for every one he disagreed with. It was prearranged that the teacher would get nine shocks out of the twelve opinions, so you can imagine that after getting shocked nine times the teacher participant was now pretty ticked off at the learner. Uh-oh, now it was the teacher's turn to shock the learner for every wrong answer. The teacher was given the leeway to vary the intensity of the shock from 1 (mild) to 10 (rather painful)—"whatever he felt was most appropriate."

Just as in their erotic film study, the researchers found that if the teacher gave the shocks right after exercising, there was no effect of the exercise on the intensity of the shocks given, compared to a group that did not exercise. But if the shocks were given after a few minutes' delay after exercising, now the teacher was angrier than usual at the learner and gave him more intense shocks for each error. The arousal from the exercise was still there after the delay but the teacher participant misunderstood it as being anger at the learner for giving him nine shocks, and so gave the learner more intense shocks as a result. Once again, the participants didn't feel that the exercise bike had anything to do with how strongly they shocked the learner. They were unaware of the lingering effects of exercise on how angry they had become afterward.

These *misattribution* effects are made possible by lingering influences of recent experiences that are still affecting us on an unconscious level. This isn't the long-ago evolutionary past of our species, nor the forgotten past of our infancy and early childhood, nor our past of collective biases absorbed from growing up in a given culture. It is what we experienced five hours ago, five minutes ago, five seconds ago. We remember it, yes, if asked to do so, but we don't appreciate how it might still be affecting us at a later point in time. Like the men who watched *Girl on a Motorcycle* or were crossing the rickety old bridge, we might be sexually excited for reasons other than the ones we are aware of; like the men who gave stronger electric shocks in the "learning experiment," we might be attributing how angry we feel to the present moment. Such conscious confusions and misunderstandings are happening to us *all the time.*

One very common situation in which we feel anger is on the highway. We feel road rage at the selfish, reckless behavior of the other drivers. And in the course of all the driving I've done in my life, I've noticed how this irritation at others' bad driving adds up, that I become more angry at the fifth and sixth person who cuts me off, or is going 25 miles an hour on a twisting, two-lane country road, than I am at the first or second person who does that. Now, why would I be any more upset with the fifth or sixth person than the first or second? Each of them did the "bad thing" only one time. But I react to the later offenders as if each *is the same person annoying me over and over again.* Naturally you would be angrier at the same person the fifth or sixth time she cut you off than you would be the first few times. Except, of course, many different people have annoyed you only once; intellectually, you know this very well. But each time, the anger inside builds up, more and more, so it might as well be the same person, according to the way you feel inside. Actually, William James understood this principle long before there were any cars and highways at all. He called it the "summation of stimuli," describing how the first few occurrences of annoyance aren't enough to provoke the response, but they lead to a "heightened irritability," and eventually another such (small by itself) annoyance is enough to "break the camel's back." Leading, as we all know, illogical and irrational as it may be, to our greater anger at the later culprits.

A Sunny Outlook on Life

Sexual arousal and anger are powerful emotional experiences. But it doesn't take that level of intensity for an experience to linger on and influence us without our knowledge. Even milder emotional states, the ones we call *moods,* can carry over from the events that caused them to affect us where and when we might least expect.

"Weather is a purely personal matter," wrote the Colombian poet Álvaro Mutis. In my case he was certainly right. Central Illinois, where I grew up, does not boast an enviable climate. In the winter, lucky us, we were far enough north to feel the arctic winds swooping out of Canada (the "Alberta Clipper"), and in the summer, we were far enough south to experience the hot, humid air coming up from the Gulf of Mexico. I was ten years old before we got our first air conditioner, so on the many 100-plus-degree days in the summertime we (and the rest of the town) would just live in one of the public swimming pools. As you can imagine, this climate shaped my day-to-day life back then.

The current weather is an ever-present prime in our lives, an ongoing, background moderator of our emotional state. We all know this from experience, from noticing how we often feel on a glorious, sunny day versus on a drippy, gray day. But weather can influence our moods even when our attention is not called to it, and these moods can affect our behavior in ways we well know they shouldn't, and would try to prevent if we realized what was going on. Social psychologists Norbert Schwarz and Gerald Clore uncovered this complex interaction between mind and weather when they conducted a much-cited study in none other than my hometown of Champaign.

In the late spring of 1983, a female experimenter telephoned participants either on warm and sunny days, or on rainy days. She was calling from town, from the University of Illinois campus, and she was calling local numbers randomly taken from the student phone directory. This was back in the day before caller ID or smartphones that gave information about the caller's actual location, which made it possible for the experimenter to say she was calling from the Chicago campus of the university, about 150 miles north. By telling the participants she was that far away, she could casually ask, early in the conversation, "By the way, how's the weather down there?" (She knew, of course, what the weather was like, because she was right there herself.) But she only asked half the participants about the weather, calling their attention to it, and did not ask the other half. Next, all respondents were asked four questions about how satisfied they were with their entire lives to that point. The final question of the four had to do with how happy they felt at that moment.

Let's take first the students whose attention was called to the day's weather, by the experimenter's casual "how's the weather down there?"

question at the start of the phone call. These students were in the same position as the exercise bike riders right after getting off the bike in the Zillmann arousal studies. They saw the sunny or rainy day outside and knew how it could be affecting their mood. For these student participants, then, the weather and the mood it inspired had no effect on their ratings of how well their entire lives had gone. If they felt in a happy or sad mood because of the weather, they were conscious of it, and so didn't misunderstand those feelings as being responses to the questions they were being asked by the experimenter over the phone. The carryover was neutralized.

But the students whose attention was not called to the day's weather closely resembled the participants who, a decade earlier, rode the exercise bike and, after a short delay, watched *Girl on a Motorcycle*. If it happened to be a sunny day outside, those students reported themselves as *more satisfied with their entire lives* to that point, compared to students who were called on a rainy day. They were asked the question, they consulted their inner feelings, and they took those feelings to be in response to the question that was asked—about their present situation—unaware that those feelings also came from the day's weather. That they did come from the weather was shown by answers on the final question, because as one might expect, students who were called on sunny days felt happier at that moment than those called on rainy days. We all know that whether it happens to be sunny or rainy outside right now should have no influence on whether we feel our entire life to that point has gone well or not. Yet it did—the effect of the weather carried over, lingered on to create an unconscious influence on the students.

Well, you might be thinking, those Illinois students were just answering some survey questions over the phone. Their answers were not all that important to them. When our decisions are more important, we will be more careful and won't be influenced by these extraneous and silly moods. Fair enough, but let's see about that. What about financial decisions to buy or sell stocks, decisions regarding which millions upon millions of dollars are at stake as fortunes are made and lost every second?

In 2003, University of Michigan behavioral economists David Hirshleifer and Tyler Shumway published a comprehensive study of how the day's weather affects the performance of the stock market in a particular city. Included in their analysis were weather and stock price data from twenty-six major stock markets around the world, over a period of fifteen years. They assessed the relation between morning sunshine in the city where a country's major stock exchange was located and the behavior of that stock market that day.

They first removed seasonal stock return effects on stock prices. For example, perhaps stocks just do better in the summer months (which happen to have more sunny days) than in the winter months (which happen to have more cloudy days) because of factors unrelated to the weather, such as the annual economic cycle. Yet the researchers still found that morning sunshine experienced by the stock traders on their way into the stock market or into the offices of their financial institutions was strongly and significantly associated with increases in stock prices that day, and cloudy weather that morning associated with poor stock returns that day—across the twenty-six stock exchanges and holding over the fifteen years. "Our results are difficult to reconcile with fully rational price-setting," they wrote. "There is no appealing rational explanation for why morning sunshine near a country's stock exchange should be associated with high market index returns. This evidence is, however, consistent with sunlight affecting mood, and mood affecting prices."

In other words, stock markets do better when it's sunny, even though there's no valid economic reason this should be so. The moods of the thousands upon thousands of human beings around the world in charge of buying and selling millions upon millions of dollars of stocks each day are as unconsciously vulnerable to weather as the moods of those Illinois college students. Weather can also affect public opinions and hence public policy about important social and environmental issues—such as about the weather itself. In a 2014 study published in the international science journal *Nature,* Columbia University decision scientist Elke Weber and her colleagues looked at how much a given day's weather—warm or cold—affected the public's concern over the global warming problem. To put this in perspective, global warming is perhaps the most important challenge humanity faces in preserving our species and keeping our planet habitable. Things have gotten so bad that the astrophysicist Stephen Hawking now says the human race has about one thousand years to find a new planet to live on. Yet climate change is also one of the most controversial issues that currently faces policy makers and everyday people like you and me, since some still deny it even exists, even today as coastal Georgia towns and entire Pacific islands are flooding because of rising ocean levels caused by the melting polar ice caps. What is fascinating (and sadly ironic) is how opinions regarding this issue fluctuate as a function of the very climate we're arguing about.

In general, what Weber and colleagues found was that when the current weather is hot, public opinion holds that global warming is occurring, and when the current weather is cold, public opinion is less concerned about global warming as a general threat. It is as if we use "local warming" as a proxy for "global warming." Again, this shows how prone we are to believe that what we are experiencing right now in the present is how things always are, and always will be in the future. Our focus on the present dominates our judgments and reasoning, and we are unaware of the effects of our long-term and short-term past on what we are currently feeling and thinking.

We've already seen how "local warming"—physical warmth and cold experiences—affects our feelings of trust and cooperation versus distrust and antagonism. These two types of "temperature," physical and social, are so intertwined in us that their corresponding brain regions become wired together, as long as we were able to trust our parents to be there for us when we were infants and toddlers.

What that mental association creates, though, is another pathway through which our recent experiences can carry over and affect us in the present, before we know it. Our physical warm and cold experiences can cause us to feel socially warm or cold, and our social warm and cold experiences can cause us to feel physically warm or cold. And we are completely unaware of the effect of one type of warmth/coldness on the other.

For example, we can all remember times when a group of our friends left us out of something they were doing, and the much better times when we were invited to join them instead. To study the effects of social rejection or inclusion in the laboratory, psychologist Kip Williams developed a computer simulation called Cyberball. In the game, three stick figures on the screen toss a ball to each other, and each participant is represented by one of the stick figures. About midway through, in the rejection condition, the two other players stop throwing you the ball, and just throw it to each other over and over from that point on. (In the inclusion condition, they keep throwing to you as much as they did before.) Although this is just an insignificant computer game, and you don't even know the other two players, you still feel a pang of sadness and unhappiness at being excluded. Being included is social warmth, and being excluded is social coldness.

Then comes the key measure: after the experiment, all participants were asked, along with other innocuous questions about the experimental room, to estimate the room temperature. The socially cold, excluded participants judged the room temperature as being lower (colder) than did the socially warm, "included" participants. The experience of social coldness had activated the associated feeling of physical coldness. The excluded participants assumed the room was colder, but it was actually the same temperature for all the participants.

Were their bodies actually colder, or did they just rate the room as colder (because, for example, the idea of coldness was primed in their minds)? To find out, Hans IJzerman and his colleagues conducted a further study in which they measured the participants' actual body temperature after playing Cyberball, using a very sensitive thermometer used for industrial coolers, accurate to within three-hundredths of a degree Celsius, attached to the participant's fingertip. And the study showed that being rejected in the Cyberball computer game (experiencing social coldness) did actually cause participants' skin temperature to drop, an average of .38 degrees Celsius, or .68 Fahrenheit. (This seemingly small change is actually a significant fluctuation for the body.) So no wonder the previous study's participants judged the room temperature to be colder—they were literally colder themselves, after experiencing *social* coldness.

A team of neuroscientists led by Naomi Eisenberger of the University of California, Los Angeles, replicated IJzerman's findings at a major Los Angeles hospital, with nurses taking the body temperature of participants every hour over a six-hour period using an oral thermometer. The controlled hospital setting enabled other influences on oral temperature readings, such as food, drink, and exercise, as well as the room temperature, to be held constant for everyone in the study. Along with having their temperature taken, the participants rated, every hour, how socially connected they felt at that moment to their friends and family, how much they agreed with statements such as *I feel like being around other people, I feel outgoing and friendly, I feel connected to others.* Once again, the higher the body temperature reading (within normal range), the higher the rating of social connectedness—the body warmth and social warmth measures went up and down together. Remarkably, how close and connected you feel to your family and friends affects your body's temperature—and vice versa.

What this means is that, at least to some extent, physical warmth might be able to *substitute* for social warmth missing in one's life. Recall the poor little monkeys in Harlow's studies. The ones who had access to the warm cloth mother, even though they were reared in isolation, could still socially function passably well as adults, compared to the pathetic little monkeys with no physical warmth to cling to. Because the physically warm experience is connected to feelings of social warmth in the brain, the physical warmth experience substituted to an extent for the missing mother in the infant monkeys' lives. What about times then when we are feeling socially cold, because of rejection or loneliness? Would we then seek out physical-warmth experiences as passable substitutes for the missing social warmth? Any port in a storm, right?

In the Cyberball studies, participants who had been excluded during the ball-throwing game were more likely to say that they wanted to see people who cared about them later that day. They had been rejected and wanted to feel better by being with family and friends—their social thermostat had registered social coldness and so kicked on the desire for social warmth, just like your home thermostat registers coldness and kicks on the furnace to heat up the house. But the rejected participants had another desire compared to the other (not rejected) participants when rating what they'd most like for lunch that day. They had a stronger desire for warm food and drinks than for cold food and drinks.

If physical warmth can substitute for the missing social warmth in a person's life, at least somewhat, then perhaps applications of physical warmth could be used as a cheap but effective therapy for emotional disorders, such as depression, which are often characterized by feelings of social isolation and decreased social connection (that is, social coldness). And as it turns out, depression is also characterized by a malfunctioning in the patient's body cooling system.

Putting two and two together, doctors at one mental hospital recently decided to treat sixteen of their patients diagnosed with major depressive disorder with a single two-hour session of "hyperthermia," in which a set of infrared lamps is used to warm the entire body. These researchers measured the depression levels of these patients using a standard psychiatric scale both before the treatment and then one week after the single heat lamp treatment. And they found a marked reduction in depression levels, from an average score of 30 before the treatment to under 20 a full week later. The doctors concluded that this whole-body heat treatment produced rapid and lasting relief from the symptoms of depression in their patients and likely does so by improving the functioning of brain pathways that link physical to social temperature.

This clinical study is encouraging news. As we learn more about the unconscious influences on our mind, emotions, and behavior, we can use that knowledge to make positive differences in our lives. Mental Health America, a nonprofit national public service organization, concluded in 2016 that fully 20 percent of adult Americans (more than 43 million people) have a mental health condition, and more than half of them do not receive any treatment. Psychotherapy, for example, is expensive and not readily available to many people. Might they be helped by simple interventions that are available to them? After all, it turns out that a warm bowl of chicken soup really is good for the soul, as the warmth of the soup helps replace the social warmth that may be missing from the person's life, as when we are lonely or homesick. These simple home remedies are unlikely to make big profits for the pharmaceutical and psychiatric industries, but if the goal is a broader and more general increase in public mental health, some research into their possible helpfulness could pay big dividends for individuals currently in distress, and for society as a whole.

Triple Crown, Triple Angry

Angelina Corcoran, Angelina Jolie, Angelina Dorfman, Angelina Ballerina.
Which of those names is very famous and which are not famous? You instantly recognize the familiar name and confidently report that Angelina Jolie is the most famous. That's because you've heard her name far more times than the other names. (And if you have a preschool child in the house, you might also recognize that gifted mouse, Angelina Ballerina, star of the eponymous cartoon show.) Here how easily you recognize a name is a good guide to how frequently you've seen or heard it, which is what fame is all about. This makes sense in general, because the more often something happens in our experience, the more memories we form of it and the stronger or more accessible they will be.

How easily something comes to mind is called the *availability heuristic*. It is a kind of a shortcut we all use when deciding how likely or frequent a type of event is. The availability heuristic was discovered by Daniel Kahneman and his longtime research partner Amos Tversky. These judgments of frequency matter in our daily lives because we make choices based on how often various things happen or are likely to happen. How often is a crime committed in a neighborhood we are considering moving to? How often have we had a pleasant experience at a certain park? How often have we enjoyed a meal at a particular restaurant? Decisions about where we decide to live, to go out to eat, to play are all based on these judgments.

There are other influences on how easily something comes to mind than just past frequency. Recent experience can make some of our memories easier to recall than others. This is another way that our recent past can carry over to unconsciously influence our judgments. It can mislead you when you base your judgments of past frequency on how swiftly something comes to mind. It can even cause someone to become famous overnight.

Memory researcher Larry Jacoby (famous in his own right) and his colleagues had participants come into his lab one day and study a list of nonfamous names. Then those same participants came back to the lab the next day and he gave them a new list of names. There were names of famous people on that second list, like Michael Jordan, but there were also some nonfamous names from the list the day before, like "Sebastian Weisdorf." The participants were asked which of the names were of famous people, and which were not. They were more likely than usual to say the nonfamous people were famous, too, if they had happened to have seen that name on the list the day before. This happened even when the experimenters told the participants that if they remembered having seen that name on the list from the day before, it was guaranteed to *not* be a famous name. But they still thought these names were famous. Whoever he was out there in the world, Sebastian Weisdorf had literally become famous overnight.

So this was an unconscious effect of recent experience on the participants' judgments of fame. Their recent experience of reading a name made it more available in their unconscious the next day, and they used this availability as a cue that the name was famous. They confused recent experience with long-term experience. (So if any of you parents said Angelina

Ballerina was more famous than Angelina Jolie, I'm with you. I watched enough of that show with my daughter in her preschool years for Ms. Ballerina to be the most famous Angelina of all time—in my mind, that is.)

Our memory is therefore fallible. It is not the objective video recording of reality we sometimes think it is or want it to be. It can be fooled by our recent experience, but also by the fact that we pay selective attention to some things and not to others, and what we pay attention to is what gets stored in our memories. If we paid equal and impartial attention to everything that happened then our memories would be a very accurate guide to what happens most frequently around us. But our attention isn't into equal opportunity. This can (and does) lead to some squabbles at home, like about whose turn it is to do the dishes.

Household chores were actually the topic of a 1979 study in which roommates and spouses were asked how often they took care of daily tasks such as doing the laundry, cleaning, washing the dishes, and taking out the cat litter or walking the dog. You might write down, right now, the percentage of the time you do these things compared to when others do them, then ask everyone else you live with to do the same, and see how the percentages add up. If you were all objectively correct, then of course the total should add up to 100 percent; there can't be any more than 100 percent of the chores being done. But in the 1979 roommate study the total percentage of times the two people said they did these chores averaged way over 100 percent, because each person thought they did it more than half the time. This couldn't be true, so what gives?

When you wrote down your percentages, and when the housemates in the study did so, you probably tried to remember the times you did those chores. You could likely see yourself doing them in your mind's eye. Maybe you also tried to remember when other people did those chores— but of course you wouldn't have as many memories of them because often you weren't there when they did them! It's as simple as that. You will have more memories of yourself doing something than of your spouse or housemate doing them because you are guaranteed to be there when you do the chores. This seems pretty obvious, but we all know how common those kinds of squabbles are, nonetheless. ("I am *too* the one who unloads the dishwasher! I remember doing it last week!")

We pay attention to some things and not to others. Moreover, the things we pay attention to are more important to us than other things.

When I was about twelve years old we had a big family reunion and I decided to bring a tape recorder so that we'd have a recording of our grandparents and uncles and aunts and cousins for posterity. I come from a large extended family, so it was a really noisy room. During the gathering, our grandma sat on the couch and told some great stories in the middle of all the other conversations. We listened and enjoyed all of them, and a few days after the reunion, we went back to listen to it again. What a disappointment! Just noise, noise, noise, a million people talking at once and no way to pick out her voice from all the other people talking, even though we heard her so clearly at the time. We quickly figured out that we hadn't noticed the background noise because we had been so captivated by our grandmother's stories. We'd filtered out what everyone else was saying. The actual, physical sounds in that room at the time, without the mind's built-in filters, were there on the tape recording.

But what you consider to be important can change, for example, when there is a big change in your life. These dramatic new currents that alter the flow of your experience set into motion a domino effect, changing what is important to you, which changes what you pay attention to, which changes the kinds of memories you have later, and thus your positions on important political and social issues. Yet as Richard Eibach, Lisa Libby, and Thomas Gilovich of Cornell University argued in a 2003 research article, we often unwittingly mistake—or misattribute—changes in *ourselves* for changes in the *world*.

When you have a baby, especially your first one, suddenly the very mundane things around you take on dangerous, sinister aspects—the stairs, the window blind cords, electric outlets, household cleansers under the sink, prescription medicines on the bathroom countertop—they all seem to be emitting evil laughs and are labeled with skulls and crossbones. The parent's need and responsibility to protect and keep the child safe changes the parent's view of the world, makes the parent vigilant and alert to these new potential dangers, and leads the parent to think that the world has become a more dangerous place. Aware of this tendency, Eibach and colleagues analyzed data from a representative sample of 1,800 U.S. citizens over the age of eighteen, who were asked how they thought crime rates had changed over the past eight years. If the respondent had not had a child during this period, their most common answer to this question was that crime had declined (as it in fact had). But if the respondent had a new baby during this period, their most common answer was that crime had increased during this period (as it had not).

These new parents were not aware of how having the baby had changed their attention toward safety issues, which had recast their own recent experiences and thus their body of memories concerning the likelihood of dangers out there in the world. In this fashion, the past becomes a foreign country, as the author L. P. Hartley wrote, and one that we are liable to romanticize. As Eibach and colleagues point out, almost every generation believes that art and music and the work ethic and you name it are not as good now as they used to be, the moral climate has deteriorated, children are more spoiled now than they were twenty years ago, there is more crime, et cetera, et cetera. The funny thing is, historians have noted how the belief that society is changing for the worse is a constant going back *thousands of years*. The ancient Greeks and Aztecs thought so, too. Eibach and colleagues quote the eminent jurist Robert Bork, who made the point with his legendary pith:

> To hear each generation speak of the generation coming along behind it is to learn that our culture is not only deteriorating rapidly, but always has been. . . . No doubt the elders of prehistoric tribes thought the younger generation's cave paintings were not up to the standard they had set. Given this straight-line degeneration for so many millennia, by now our culture should be not merely rubble but dust. Obviously it is not: until recently our artists did much better than the cave painters.

So if it is not objectively the case that the world is constantly changing for the worse in all these ways, what explains the persistent and prevalent belief that it is? Eibach and his research collaborators suspect that it is because each of us experience many changes as we grow up and mature. Instead of playing all day, we have to go to school; then, instead of being taken care of by our parents, we start to have chores; then as teenagers we work at a fast-food restaurant. Then comes a real job, bills to pay, a stressful commute, and, finally, kids of our own to take care of on top of everything else. We are exposed to meanness and selfishness and hatred and betrayal, from which we are largely sheltered during childhood. Then, of course, our youthful strength and vitality start to fade with age. Need I say more?

While we may not be aware of the manner in which inner transformations trick our minds into seeing outer ones, we are certainly aware, moment to moment, of our emotional state. We know without a doubt when we are happy or sad, angry or hurt, peaceful or anxious. Emotions grab hold of our attention and consciousness and don't let go. Elizabeth Phelps, an NYU psychologist specializing in emotion and memory, calls attention to the fact that most of our very long-term memories, the things that come to mind when we reminisce about our lives, involve the experience of a strong emotion. These once-recent pasts that become distant but remembered pasts remain in our minds because they so absorbed our attention at the time. They were important in some way, important enough to provoke the strong emotion in the first place.

When we are in the grip of a strong emotion, such as anger, we feel sure we are right, and that we are seeing the world and other people as they really are. That tends to spur us on to act on that belief, not at all recognizing that we are in a temporary emotional state. No clearer example of this could be given than the very public, nationally televised behavior of Steve Coburn, owner of the 2014 Kentucky Derby winner California Chrome. After his horse went on to win the Preakness Stakes, Coburn and his wife were in the owner's box at New York's Belmont Park three weeks later to cheer their horse on to victory and the coveted Triple Crown of horse racing. But another horse swept by Chrome on the backstretch and dashed Coburn's hopes. He was understandably upset, even distraught at having come so close. But he was also angry, because the horse that won the race had not taken part in the other two Triple Crown races and was more rested as a result. Coburn didn't believe this was fair, and when interviewed on TV after the race went on an angry rant about how the other horse (and owner) didn't deserve to win because they had ducked the other two races. At the very end of the tirade, his wife told him to stop, but he overruled her, saying emphatically, "No, this needs sayin'!" In the heat of the moment he certainly felt so, but after a day or so, in further interviews he expressed regret for what he'd said and chalked it up to his heated emotions at the time. Coburn's emotional state, angry then calmed down, determined what he believed to be the truth—as those emotions changed, so did the truth.

Emotions have an even more powerful carryover effect on us than the lingering memories they produce. They put different basic motivations into play, such as aggressiveness, risk-taking, and wanting to make a change in your current circumstances—as we will see in Chapter 8, "Be Careful What You Wish For." These unconscious motivational states can then exert a profound, catalytic, and even metamorphic influence on what we like, how we think, and what we do. They can change our lives, and sometimes even end them.

Hoarded Emotions

In June 2014, a postal worker in the affluent community of Cheshire, Connecticut, noticed that mail at one of the houses on the route had piled up to a worrisome extent. It had been two weeks since the owner, a sixty-six-year-old woman named Beverly Mitchell, had collected any of her mail, so the carrier called the police.

After it became evident that no one inside the house would open the door for them, officers looked for another way in. This turned out to be a less-than-simple matter. Mitchell, as many of her neighbors knew, was a hoarder. The house was so densely packed with clutter that the police weren't able to use normal entrances, like the front door. Mitchell had been amassing newspapers and other objects for years, effectively turning her home into a warehouse without easily navigable passageways. The police used a backhoe to make a hole in the side of the house and clear debris before entering. It turned out that the first floor had collapsed, requiring the assistance of the Department of Emergency Management as well as other local and national agencies. Three days after first trying to enter, the authorities discovered Mitchell's body in the basement, where she had been living. She had been crushed and asphyxiated under the debris she had spent years collecting.

I live in a small town near Cheshire, so I read about Mitchell's horrible, lonely death in the New Haven newspaper soon after it was reported. It was like an episode of the reality TV series *Hoarders* I had watched. As many people know, hoarding is a significant problem in the United States. Somewhere between 5 and 14 million people in the country are hoarders, according to *Scientific American*. As shown in the reality TV series, in many cases entire houses are filled many layers high with purchases, many of which are never even taken out of the box or used at all. In nearly every case of the dozens documented in the show, the hoarding began after a traumatic event in the hoarder's life, such as a divorce or the loss of a child or sibling or parent; very few of these cases were not precipitated by a major and quite emotional life event. In one episode, for example, the hoarding of two twin sisters began when their beloved brother, a soldier in the military, was killed in action. The compulsive purchasing and hoarding became so bad that the twins had to move out of their family home, where they grew up, because it was condemned as a health hazard by the town's public health department. And so I saw this same psychological pattern play itself out near me: in follow-up news coverage, Beverly Mitchell's relatives and neighbors recounted how she had lived in that house with her mother all of her life, and that the hoarding had started soon after her mother passed away.

Behavioral economics, the study of human financial and consumer choices, has shown how emotional states put basic motivational states such as aggression or withdrawal into action, and these states in turn change how we value objects when we make buying and selling decisions. For most of us, this applies mainly to when we go shopping. Jennifer Lerner and her colleagues were the first to show how emotions experienced in one situation, such as when watching a sad or disgusting movie scene, carried over to affect purchasing decisions in a second situation, without the person's awareness that the emotion was still influencing them. Specifically, the persistent emotional state in their unconscious changed the price they were willing to pay to buy something.

Lerner employed another one of Nobel laureate Kahneman's contributions to behavioral economics, called the "endowment effect." This phenomenon is one of the most robust and important behavioral economic tendencies in human nature. In the simplest terms, we place more value on an object if we own it than we would place on the same object if we didn't. Our ownership "endows" the object with additional value. Imagine someone coming into my office and noticing my many coffee mugs. (I have quite the collection.) If I ask that person to give the value of one of them, say my Starbucks Cleveland mug, they may respond something like "Five dollars." But now another person comes into the room, and I give her that Starbucks mug to keep, and ask her what its value is. She would tend to give a higher amount, say, "Seven dollars and fifty cents." It is the same old mug in both cases, but we all tend to endow objects with greater value if they are ours and we own them. This makes a lot of practical business sense. It helps us to buy low and sell high.

What Lerner and her colleagues showed in their experiments was that this basic endowment effect was changed and even reversed if the person recently had a certain kind of emotional experience. The emotions Lerner focused on were disgust and sadness. Disgust is a very powerful and practical emotion, from an evolutionary perspective, because it urges us to stay away from anything that might contain harmful germs. When we feel it, we want to get rid of whatever we are holding or smelling or tasting at the time. Basically we want to get away, and stay away, and fast.

Translated into economic behavior, then, disgust should compel one to want to sell what one already has at a lower price than usual, because the underlying motivation is to get rid of what you have; it should also cause a decrease in desire to buy or acquire anything new, which would lead to lower buying prices as well. The emotion of disgust should change the otherwise universal endowment effect by lowering both buying and selling prices. In other words, it should make you bad at business.

In their disgust study, Lerner and associates didn't mess around. Their participants first had to watch an infamous four-minute scene from the movie *Trainspotting,* in which a man uses an epically filthy toilet. To make this emotional experience even more powerful (as if it needed to be), they asked participants to write about how they would personally feel if they were in the same situation. Then some of them were given a highlighter as a gift. (If you ask me, they deserved new cars.) But the point of the study was how the participants valued that highlighter. Without being aware of the effect of the movie clip on their valuations, they took a lower amount of money to sell their gift back, compared to the luckier participants in the control group who did not watch the clip. Those without the highlighters offered less money than those in the control condition to buy one. Disgust equaled buy low and sell low.

The effect becomes even more interesting in the case of sadness. Sadness is an emotion that triggers the basic motivation to *change one's state.* It makes good sense that when we are sad, we want to get out of that sad state, and so we become more ready to act and do something—almost anything, really—about it. We just want to feel something else! For Lerner's experiment, participants were shown a clip taken from the movie *The Champ*—the scene in which the boy's mentor dies—and were asked to write empathetically about it. (Gee, what a wonderful experience this study must have been for the participants—spend four minutes looking at a disgusting toilet, or watching Jon Voight die. And for this just a highlighter?)

The emotion of sadness was expected to trigger the motivation-to-change emotional state. How would this affect the participants' buying price for a highlighter, or selling price if they had already been given one? The carryover effect of the emotion actually produced a *reversal* of the standard endowment effect. In service to the unconscious motivation-to-change state, the participants didn't require as much money to get rid of the highlighter (lower selling price), but they also wanted to *pay more* than usual to acquire the highlighter if they didn't already have it (higher buying price). Buy high, and sell low. You won't stay in business very long doing that. And it is certainly not a business model we would practice intentionally or deliberately. The behavior is an unconscious and unintended effect of the emotional state.

Clearly the take-home message here is that you shouldn't go shopping when you are sad. You will be quite willing to pay more to buy the same things compared to when you are not sad. But this is easier said than done, because people often use shopping to help them feel better. It's fun, like getting yourself a present, and many of us do it to cheer ourselves up. Yet we should beware of the underlying motivation-to-change state, triggered by sadness, that is driving the shopping behavior. There is evidence that compulsive shoppers tend to be depressed, and that shopping helps make them feel happier (or at least less sad). That sadness is at the root of much compulsive shopping is shown by the fact that antidepressant medications are effective in reducing such shopping. Buying new things can help us feel better for a time, but it can ultimately lead us to feel even worse when the bills come in and we have to struggle to pay them. And remember that sadness also makes us willing to pay more for things.

A year or two after the Lerner study about sadness was published, I noticed a change in the type of music being piped in over the speaker system of the supermarket I frequent. Now, it had never been the type of music I would choose to listen to on my own (I never heard any Led Zeppelin being played, for instance), but it was on the whole upbeat and cheery. Then came a sharp change. Suddenly the music was all weepy ballads, sad, minor-chord melodies, and a whole lot of James Taylor. And nothing has changed since then, except the downer songs are new, like

Tim McGraw's "Live Like You Were Dying." But the nadir came recently when my wife found me just standing there in the produce section, staring up at the ceiling. Then she heard it, too. The store was playing "If I Die Young," by the Band Perry—the melancholy chords were bad enough, but the lyrics were coming in crystal clear to all the shoppers, and they are morbid and morose, to say the least.

I've noticed similar sad music being played at Walmart, and it turns out that I'm not the only one who has. In 2015, at an annual shareholders meeting where several plans for improving business were proposed, the *Washington Post* reported, "the one that seemed to draw the most whoops from the crowd was a pledge to ditch a CD that has apparently been on loop in the stores for months and begun to drive employees crazy." What was the disc that had been playing at the stores ad nauseam? What were the employees sick of hearing? An album of songs by the notoriously weepy Celine Dion.

I confess that going into stores and noticing the relentlessly sad music being played makes me a bit angry, for two reasons. First, that the store would alter its customers' moods just to get more money out of them (talk about *cold*hearted). Second, think about the poor employees (especially the teenagers), who, unlike us shoppers—who can get the hell out of there or avoid that store in the future—have to listen to the sad music for hours upon hours each day. Their working conditions may well have a constant, long-term effect on their moods and behavior. This brings me back to the tragic case of that Cheshire woman, who died under the crushing weight of her own purchases.

Losing a loved one is a very, very sad event, of course, and one that subtly continues to affect the deceased's family and friends for many months, even years afterward. It must be even worse if you continue to live in the house where she lived with you. Every day there are reminders of her, forcing repeated acknowledgments that she is no longer there with you. The unabated sadness could cause you to buy repeatedly in order to continually change your emotional state. Not only can the recent experiences of life linger, but they can hang around a long time, like an albatross, if those recent experiences are repeatedly re-evoked and so continue to affect a person's behavior over a much longer time period. The most traumatic and emotional of these experiences can thereby precipitate dramatic changes in the individual and in the course of her life. To remedy this, the best solution isn't to alter one's temporary state (as through shopping), but to change the more permanent environment that continues to evoke the loss, with all its unconscious consequences for the person who was left behind.

R.I.P., Beverly Mitchell.

Life lingers because the brain lingers. All brain activity, emotional or not, requires chemical transmissions across nerve synapses, and chemical changes do not turn on and off instantaneously like an electric switch. They take some amount of time to settle down and return to their original state. Until they do, your brain goes on sparking and simmering with bits of the past that are not actually there in front of you anymore. Take your "mind's eye," for example.

In 1960, George Sperling performed a landmark study that demonstrated the existence of what he called the *visual buffer*. We can think of this as a kind of temporary storage unit in the mind where information persists after it is gone from the outside world. Participants in his experiments were presented a visual stimulus, but they didn't know what they would be asked to recall, so they couldn't consciously focus on any one thing, and they weren't actively rehearsing or intentionally keeping the information in mind. In addition, there were too many items to memorize. If you had been a participant in those long-ago studies, you would have seen something like this:

You would first be shown the display on the left for a few seconds, then a blank screen in order to produce a delay until the third screen appeared. On the third screen, there was a circle around one of the original display locations, and your job was to say what had appeared in that location—in this case, "8." You did not know in advance for any of the displays where that circle was going to be. By varying how long the delay screen was up, Sperling could find out just how long the original display had persisted in a participant's mind's eye. The shorter the delay, the more likely you would have been to get the right answer, because it would still be right in front of your eyes—or so it would seem to you. The participants in Sperling's experiment could respond correctly because they could still "see" the right answer in front of them, even though it really wasn't there at all, except in their own minds.

Another one of the basic judgmental biases that Kahneman discovered is a form of priming effect called *anchoring*, in which using a certain range of numbers in one context carries over to influence the range of numbers you use in a subsequent context. So, if you are first shown a series of photographs of preschool-age children and asked to estimate the age of each child, you would be using numbers in the range, say, of 2 to 5. But if you were first shown a series of photos of high school students and asked to estimate the age of each of them instead, you would be using numbers in the range of 14 to 18. Then let's say you are asked a series of questions, such as "How many U.S. presidents have died in office?" or "How many World Series have the Boston Red Sox won?" The correct answer in both cases is 8, but if you'd first focused on the preschool age range you would tend to give lower estimates than if you'd first focused on the high school age range. (This effect doesn't apply if you already knew the right answer and weren't guessing.) The range of numbers used in the first task is primed, more active and available, and is more likely to be used in the second judgment task.

As with all of the other carryover effects of recent thought and experience that we've discussed, anchoring effects operate unintentionally and unconsciously. Kahneman points out that this applies even to very weighty real-life situations involving numbers, such as in business negotiations over prices for services or supplies, determination of monetary damages to be awarded in court cases, and estimates of future earnings or sales. Even absurd numbers can stick and have their carryover influence, such as in one study in which participants first read that Mahatma Gandhi lived to be a million years old. As Kahneman puts it, you have "no control over the effect and no knowledge of it. The participants who have been exposed to random or absurd anchors . . . confidently deny that this obviously useless information could have influenced their estimate, and they are wrong."

Given this powerful effect of numerical anchors on our behavior, I can't help but wonder if, all things being equal, people tend to drive faster in general on Interstate 95 than on Interstate 40 (someone should do a study). I bring this up to give me the excuse to tell the one about the three elderly ladies stopped by the state police for going too slow on a state highway, bottling up traffic for miles behind them. "But officer," the driver counters, the speed limit sign said 20." The officer chuckles. "No, ma'am, this is *Highway* 20, the speed limit is 55." Then he looks in the backseat and sees the two passengers blanched and wide-eyed, breathing heavily and sweating profusely. "What's wrong with your friends back here, ma'am?" he asks the driver. "Oh, they're okay, officer," she says. "We just got off Highway 143."

So life lingers on in the mind well after we've moved on to something else and don't think our recent past is influencing us anymore. This applies to the arousal and emotions we feel, like anger and sadness, and how attracted we are to each other. Moods carry over as well, and can bias even our important financial decisions. The effects of our social encounters and whether we feel included or excluded by others linger on, causing us to choose a warm bowl of soup instead of our usual ham sandwich. Our recent experience can cause us to believe global warming is a real problem, or not much of a problem at all, and if the recent experience is intense enough, it can even cause us to worry that our fellow pedestrians are actually zombies. (Fortunately, not very often.)

Everything I've discussed in this chapter has related to how our recent past can interfere with our clear perception of the reality of the present. This can cause us to be more attracted to another person than we otherwise would have been, and angrier with others, as in experiences of road rage. It can alter our financial decisions and change our opinion about important world issues. The world changes faster than our minds do, and life lingers in our subjective experience more than it does in reality, making us vulnerable to making bad choices. We strongly assume that what we are thinking and feeling is driven by what's happening right now in front of us, and we hardly ever question that assumption. Yet quite often something more than what is right here and now is acting upon us. It is the past—our species' ancient past, our unique unremembered infant past, and our very recent past, just now receding in the rearview mirror of our day. All of these different yesterdays matter, because they are still affecting the most important moment in every person's life—the only moment Einstein believed actually existed—the present.

PART 2

THE HIDDEN
PRESENT

---

*Remember that man's life lies all within
this present, as t'were a hair's breadth
of time; as for the rest, the past
is gone, the future yet unseen.*
　　　　—Marcus Aurelius, *Meditations*

CHAPTER 5

Should I Stay
or Should I Go?

At the dawn of the twentieth century, around the time Sigmund Freud was publishing his landmark *Interpretation of Dreams,* the Swiss neurologist Édouard Claparède decided to play a trick on one of his patients—all in the name of science, of course.

The patient was a forty-seven-year-old woman with a brain impairment brought on by the onset of Korsakoff's syndrome, a form of amnesia. She wasn't able to retain any new memories that went back more than fifteen minutes, though her intellectual abilities remained unchanged. Her awareness of the recent past wiped itself clean again and again in an unending cycle of forgetting. Each morning she arrived at Dr. Claparède's office at the University of Geneva with no recollection of having been there before, and believing she was meeting the bearded, bespectacled doctor for the first time. Claparède always greeted her with a hearty handshake, and she always politely replied that it was nice to meet him. The young doctor happened to be a critic of Freud's demonized version of a separate unconscious mind, and he wondered if his patient's amnesia might not be as complete as it seemed. What if short-term memories persisted in some hidden recess of her mind, in lieu of those that erased themselves from her consciousness?

One day, when she arrived at his office as usual, Claparède held out his hand to shake his patient's—but with a thumbtack he had taped to his palm. When she shook his hand, she felt a sharp pain as the tack pricked her skin. Fifteen minutes later the memory of the disagreeable incident had vanished from her conscious mind, so he held out his hand to shake again. Here was the moment in which Claparède might glean new insights into how—or *if*—unconscious memory functioned when its conscious counterpart failed. And sure enough, the patient reached out toward him, but right before they clasped hands, she abruptly drew hers back.

Intrigued, Claparède asked her why she wouldn't shake his hand. "Doesn't one have the right to withdraw her hand?" she responded evasively, becoming agitated. She reverted to vague explanations, unable to explain her intuition. The knowledge of what might happen if she shook with the good doctor had appropriately guided her behavior to avoid a possible repetition of that painful pinprick, and this response operated without the involvement of any conscious intention on her part. In other words, her memory was having an implicit effect on her behavior, in the absence of her explicit memory and lack of any conscious awareness of the previous painful handshake. Her memory was unconsciously working to help keep her safe in the present, just as it had evolved to do.

The story of Dr. Claparède's slightly sadistic yet illuminating experiment was a crucial first baby step in psychology's modern understanding of unconscious effects, and contemporary research on amnesiacs has confirmed what Claparède was the first to notice. In a 1985 study of patients with Korsakoff's syndrome, Marcia Johnson and her colleagues found that the patients showed the same patterns of liking and disliking for people and objects as the normal participants did, even though they had little to no memory of those people and objects otherwise. For example, all participants were shown photographs of a "good guy" (as described in fictional biographical information) and a "bad guy." Twenty days later the Korsakoff's patients had virtually no memory of the biographical information; nonetheless, 78 percent of them liked the "good guy" in the photos better than the "bad guy." In the absence of any conscious memories of the reasons why, the amnesiacs still had appropriate unconsciously generated positive or negative feelings about people and objects that they had previously encountered.

Claparède's little prank revealed a vital and primitive unconscious function of our minds. In the ongoing present of life, in which we are continually buffeted by obstacles and tasks and things we need to confront and deal with, all of which fully occupy our conscious mind, this evaluative, "good or bad" mechanism is constantly operating in the background.

While our conscious attention is often elsewhere, this unconscious monitoring process helps us decide what to embrace and reject, when to stay and when to go.

Good. Bad.

Yes. No.

Stay. Go.

This is the ultimate, fundamental binary code of life. It embodies the primary predicament of existence—for all animals, not just human beings. All forms of animate life share this basic "stay or go" conundrum, even the most primitive. Good or bad, stay or go is the original animal reaction to the world. Eons of evolutionary time have made "stay or go" the fastest and most basic psychological reaction of the human brain to what is going on outside of it. This initial reaction colors everything that comes after it: good or bad, stay or go, like or dislike, approach or avoid. We go down one path and not down the other. Revealing how it works exactly, what causes us to immediately veer in one direction instead of the other, sheds new light on why we are doing what we are doing. Sometimes there is simplicity at the heart of complexity.

Back in the 1940s, University of Illinois psychologist Charles E. Osgood performed landmark research on, literally, the meaning of life. What are the basic ingredients we use to give our words and concepts meaning—ingredients such as how good or bad something is, how big or small, strong or weak? To get the data for his investigation, he had thousands of people make many ratings of different "attitude objects," pretty much anything you can have an attitude toward, such as *war, cities,* or *flowers.* You would rate each of them, let's say *war,* for example, as to how sweet to bitter, fair to unfair, or bright to dark it is. Not to worry if these seem strange scales to rate that object on; you just go with what feels right to you. I'd say *war,* for example, was on the bitter, unfair, and dark side of those scales. Then he used a sophisticated data technique called factor analysis to distill all those ratings down into a very small set of basic factors, the "ingredients" underlying how we feel about most things, the bases of most of our attitudes. And by doing so, Osgood found that things were actually quite simple: we used only three main factors to organize and sort out all these things in our mind, and with just these three dimensions he could account for nearly all the variability in those ratings. It all came down to E-P-A: evaluation, potency, and activity. Or in other words:

good or bad, strong or weak, and active or passive. Trees, most people would say, are good, strong, and passive (they just stand there). Trains, on the other hand, are (for most people, anyway) good, strong, and active.

Of these three main components of meaning, Osgood found that the single most important factor was the first, *evaluation*. Most of the meaning that words and concepts have for us boils down to variations on good or bad, just with different flavors. The second most important was *potency*, or strong versus weak, and the third was *activity*, or active versus passive. Think about it from our (very) old friend Ötzti's perspective: when encountering a new person it was most important to know if they were bad (an enemy); next important was how powerful they were (uh-oh), and finally how active—fast, healthy, and mobile—they were (phew, his horse is stuck in the mud).

But first and foremost, we need to know if the "something" out there is good or bad, for us or against us—and we need to know it right away. Osgood published his major book on this research in 1949. Ten years later, the director of the American Museum of Natural History in New York City, T. C. Schneirla, published an influential paper comparing all animals, from the simplest single-cell paramecium all the way through to human beings. His message was that all animals, from the simplest to the most complex, possessed basic *approach* and *withdrawal* reactions to good versus bad things. Put a source of food (some sugar) near it and the paramecium moved toward it. Put a small electric wire and tiny shock near it and it moved away. And from there all the way through the animal kingdom to human infants as well, Schneirla showed that all animals possessed these two basic response options.

If good-bad, approach-withdraw is the most basic animal reaction to the world, then it is easy to see why Osgood's research revealed evaluation, good or bad, to be the primary meaning for all of our concepts about the world. Each of us today has within us remnants of the entire evolutionary history of our species. What back then were the original, first single-cell reactions to the world's creatures are now, in every present moment, our own first reactions to our experiences. What came first in the very, very long-term past is now first in the short-term present. In spite of all of the astonishing mechanisms and systems that we eventually developed from that original, single cell, the primordial question is still there at our core.

Should I stay or should I go?

While we constantly engage in our complex modern activities such as going out with friends, keeping up with the news, and performing our jobs, we are nevertheless still reliant on this primitive, elemental division of behavior. We must decide whether to "say yes" and stay close to each stimulus (person, object, situation) we encounter, evaluating whether it is advantageous, or at least not unsafe, or "say no" and increase our distance from it.

We make these calculations both consciously and unconsciously, again and again, but often the unconscious part, like the alligator's symbolic belly in my dream, comes first. This was the case for Claparède's patient because she didn't have conscious memory to aid her decision-making, yet it is true for non-amnesiacs as well. In many cases it's the conscious mind that plays explainer afterward, trying to make sense of a judgment that we seemed to already "know" so solidly that our assessment felt like an incontrovertible fact. Earlier, I told the story about when I was in grad school and my advisor Robert Zajonc called me into his office to show me museum postcards of abstract art, to ask me which paintings I did and didn't like. I could quickly and confidently point to the one I liked (I preferred Kandinsky—he's a good cave painter!) but then, when Bob asked me why, I hesitated and sputtered something about the colors and forms and Bob just grinned at my discomfort—and my evident inability to give many truly good reasons.

As the old cliché has it, "I don't know much about art, but I know what I like."

At that time in the late 1970s, Bob was doing important work on the *mere exposure effect*, which is, basically, our tendency to like new things more, the more often we encounter them. In his studies, he repeatedly showed that we like them more just because they are shown to us more often, even if we don't consciously remember seeing them. For example, the Korsakoff amnesiacs in Marcia Johnson's study showed this preference later on for new things they were shown more often over other things they were shown less often, despite having no recall of ever seeing any of those things before.

Zajonc's research on the mere exposure effect was important for many reasons. First, it showed how we can develop likings and preferences unconsciously, without intending to, based solely on how often and how common the experience is. This makes complete adaptive sense, because the more we encounter things that do not harm us, the more we like and the more we approach (stay). The mere exposure effect is all about creating the default tendency to stay when things are okay. (And if things are not okay, and, say, a snake jumps out at us in that nice little grassy area by the stream, all bets are off, and that experience completely overrides the mere exposure effect. Note that it took just one little pin-prick to stop Claparède's patient from shaking hands with him again.)

Second, the mere exposure research showed how our likes and dislikes can be immediately provoked in the moment, independent of any conscious calculations or recollections, as shown not only by my spontaneous reactions to the art postcards in Bob's office, but also by the findings of his mere exposure studies and Johnson's demonstrations with her amnesiac patients. Much of our *affective* (or evaluative) system operates outside of consciousness. Like the dream alligator was telling me, that yes-no system came first in our evolution, before our development of a more thoughtful way to make those evaluations.

Before Zajonc's influential paper "Preferences Need No Inferences" appeared in 1980, researchers believed that all our attitudes were the result of this slower, more thoughtful process of conscious calculation. He argued instead that often we have immediate affective reactions to things like paintings and sunsets and meals and other people, without first thinking about them so carefully. His idea led to a transformation of the field of attitude research a few years later, thanks mainly to the original research on "automatic attitudes" by Russell Fazio, a young professor at Indiana University.

For a long time in the mid-twentieth century, the study of attitudes was somewhat in disarray. This was primarily because attitude research had a rather poor track record of predicting actual behavior. After all, the main reason attitudes started to be measured in the first place, back in the 1930s, was to be able to predict behavior. Yet many early studies showed that people would say one thing on an attitude questionnaire, but do something else entirely. It is easy to say on a piece of paper that you are going to donate money to a charity, for example; it is harder to get out the old pocketbook and write out the check. The important question soon became *when* would attitudes predict behavior, and when would they not?

Along came Fazio in 1986 with the idea that maybe only some attitudes predicted behavior, not all of them; some of our attitudes might be stronger and more important than others. I don't like peanut butter and I will not eat it under any circumstance; I don't like cooked carrots either but I'll eat them if they're on my plate, no big deal. And Fazio reasoned that the strong and important ones would exert a more consistent and reliable influence on our actual behaviors. So the question became, how do you tell the strong and important ones from the weaker and less important ones? Fazio reasoned that the strong attitudes would be those that came to mind immediately and automatically whenever we encountered the object of that attitude in our environment. In other words, the fact of our liking or disliking something would have more of an effect on our behavior if it reliably came to mind without our needing to stop and think. He conjectured that, just like my fast positive reaction to the Kandinsky postcard, our strong attitudes will be the ones that come to mind quickly, and our weak attitudes will be the ones that take us longer to express.

To measure how strong or weak a person's attitudes were, he just had participants press either a Good or a Bad button on the computer (computers being a new exciting research toy back in the 1980s) as fast as they could after each name of nearly a hundred mundane objects appeared on the monitor screen in front of them. For example, they would tend to say Good very fast to *birthday, kitten,* and *basketball* (the study was done in Indiana, after all, so Hoosier hardcourt fever clearly was a factor), and Bad very fast to *Hitler, poison,* and *tuna.* (I actually like tuna, so I never really understood this.) But on the whole it took them longer to say Good or Bad to more neutral, less passion-inducing words like *calendar, brick,* or *yellow.*

Fazio and his colleagues then selected the words (the "attitude objects," the scientific term for these stimuli) to which the person responded the fastest—their strong attitudes—and those to which they responded the slowest—their weak attitudes—and used them in the next part of the experiment. This next part tested whether the person's attitudes toward each of these words became active immediately and automatically as soon as the participant read that word on the screen. The attitude object word, such as *butterfly,* would be presented on the screen first, for just a quarter of a second, too fast for a person to be able to stop and consciously decide whether they liked it or not. Then a second word would be presented, an adjective such as *wonderful* or *terrible,* and all the participant had to do was to press the Good or Bad button to say whether that second word had a positive or negative meaning.

The logic of this new method Fazio introduced, called an *affective priming* paradigm, was quite elegant and simple. If the first word, such as *butterfly,* automatically triggered Good or Bad, then that response would be primed and more ready when it came time to say whether the second word, such as *wonderful,* was good or bad. If the attitude prime automatically suggested the right response to the adjective that came next (as in *butterfly-wonderful*), then those responses should be faster. And if it suggested the wrong response—say, if *cockroach* came before *wonderful*—then those responses would be slowed down, because the participant would be all primed and ready to say Bad and would have to stifle that tendency and say Good (the right answer) instead.

But this would happen only if the first attitude became active immediately and automatically. What Fazio showed was that the person's strong attitudes did just that. For example, *beer* unconsciously primed *beautiful,* and *accident* unconsciously primed *disgusting*—but the weak ones, words like *brick* and *corner,* did not become immediately active.

By sheer coincidence, the same year that Fazio's research on automatic attitudes was published, another young up-and-coming attitude researcher, Shelly Chaiken, joined the Psychology Department at NYU, where I worked. In her office one day soon after she arrived, we decided to start some research together. What should we do? we wondered. Hmmm, well, she was an attitude researcher, and I was an automaticity researcher, so (ding!) what about studying automatic attitudes? It was, you might say, a no-brainer.

Shelly and I had several interests in common besides psychology research, so when we weren't terrorizing the graduate students by playing golf in the hallways of the Psychology Building, or making Peet's coffee fresh from the beans we had delivered each month from Berkeley (where she used to live), we designed several studies to better understand the automatic attitude effect. One thing we were interested in was how general the affective priming effect was. It did happen for the strongest attitudes (that people were fastest to say good or bad to) and it didn't happen for the weakest ones (that people were the slowest to respond to), but what about all those (which were most of them) in the middle? Did the effect happen for only the few strongest ones, or did it happen for all but the very weakest? And did it happen only after people had just thought about those attitudes, as they had in the first part of Fazio's procedure? The answers to these questions would determine how often we'd expect the effect to occur in real life.

Other lines of research had given us good reasons to believe in Fazio's basic idea—Schneirla's description of the fundamental approach-avoidance response across the entire animal kingdom, Osgood's research showing the importance of the good-bad dimension to the meaning of pretty much everything, and my advisor Bob Zajonc's demonstrations of "feeling without thinking." Still, Shelly and I were concerned that the intentional, conscious evaluation aspects of Fazio's experimental procedure might have played a role in the results he got, so we expected, and predicted, that getting rid of those aspects would reduce or even eliminate the apparent unconscious effects.

Boy, were we wrong. Exactly the opposite happened. To our great surprise, over several years of trying to "get rid" of the effect, by removing things that might inadvertently influence the outcome of the procedure, what we kept finding was that the effect instead got stronger and more general than it was before. When we waited several days between the first attitude expression task (in which the subject said whether those things were good or bad as fast as she could) and the second task, which tested whether the attitudes were automatic, the effect happened for *all* of the objects, even those that inspired the weakest attitudes, as well as the strongest and everything in the middle. Then we changed the task that tested whether the attitudes were automatic, taking away the Good versus Bad buttons and asking participants to just say their second words out loud. Once again, we continued to get the automatic attitude effect, but now we got it for all of the objects, those generating both strong and weak attitudes. Amazingly, *everything*, it seemed, all the objects we used, was evaluated as good or bad under these stricter conditions, which, after all, were designed to mimic life outside the psychology laboratory more closely than did the original studies by Fazio and his colleagues. The new conditions captured more closely the *mere* effect of encountering these objects in the real world, without any conscious, intentional thought about how you felt about them at all.

The unconscious workings of our mind send us signals about when to stay and when to go not only about our passionate likes and dislikes, but also about our most lukewarm, indifferent opinions, and all those in between. If anything, in fact, the more we eliminated the conscious and intentional aspects of the tasks in our studies, the stronger and more general was the effect. Not the other way around. Now decades have passed since the original studies appeared, and since Shelly and I started our own research on the effect. Happily, twenty-five years of further research by many labs around the world have confirmed our findings, which were startling (especially to us) at the time.

My alligator friend, were he to actually exist, would be grinning and nodding his toothy green head at this conclusion. The unconscious evaluation of everything does appear to be a very old and primitive effect that existed long before we developed conscious and deliberate modes of thought. And so when we remove those conscious components of the task, as Shelly and I did in our series of studies, and leave the unconscious to its own devices, the attitude effect shows up more clearly than ever before. After all, the unconscious approach-or-withdraw response evolved to help protect us millions of years ago, before there was any such thing as conscious, deliberate thought (or any other thought, for that matter).

Push and Pull

Many years ago, a graduate student of Osgood's at Illinois, Andrew Solarz, tested the connection between evaluation of things as good or bad, and approach or withdraw arm movements in response to those things. This was back in the day before computers, and most psychology labs had a machine shop where the technical staff would create amazing pieces of apparatus to enable the psychology professors to test their theories. These often had enough wires and tubes and dials and levers to put Dr. Frankenstein to shame. They sometimes took months, even a year, to make. Solarz had the shop techs create for him a masterpiece of ingenuity in order to test his hypothesis. In his experiment, he presented words one at a time to his participants by means of a display box mounted on a response lever. A mechanical device would drop a three-by-five index card with the word printed on it in large block letters into a slot area on the box (which was on top of the lever, above where the participant was gripping the lever) so that it was now visible to the participant, and at this exact moment, an electronic timer would be started. The participants would then either push or pull the lever, depending on their instructions, as quickly as they could. It was kind of like a scientific slot machine.

Some of the participants were instructed to pull the lever toward them if they liked the object named on the card (for example, *apple, summer*), and to push the lever away from them if they did not like it (*worm, frozen*). The other participants were given the opposite instructions: to pull if they disliked, and push if they liked the object. At the end of the study, he computed the average times it took for the participants to push to indicate "good," push to indicate "bad," pull to indicate "good," and pull to indicate "bad."

What he found was that indeed, participants were faster to say "bad" by pushing the lever away than by pulling the lever toward them. And they were faster to say "good" when pulling the lever toward them than when pushing it away. Pushing the word away recalls the little paramecium moving away from the electric wire; pulling the word closer recalls the single-cell creature moving closer to the food. Solarz's participants were acting the same way, without realizing it, of course, being immediately ready to increase rather than decrease the distance between themselves and something they did not like (even though it was just a word on an index card), as well as immediately ready to decrease instead of increase the distance between them and something they liked. Their immediate feeling of liking or disliking when they saw the word also just as immediately caused their arm muscles to be more ready to make the appropriate movements. The good-versus-bad switch in their minds was literally making their muscles more ready to stay than to go.

At NYU more than thirty years later, Mark Chen and I set out to repeat the Solarz study but with the technological help of computerized displays and timing. We still had to get our machine shop people to make the response lever, though, to be like the one Solarz used—a three-foot-long Plexiglas rod connected to an electronic switch at the base, which was then wired into a computer input port. Our first experiment was a replication of the Solarz study, and we found exactly what he had found. But as in his original experiment, our participants were consciously and intentionally classifying each of the objects, because that is what they were instructed to do. Would the push-pull effect happen even when the participants were not consciously thinking about likes and dislikes at all?

So, in the second experiment Mark and I ran, we just had the participants move the lever as fast as they could each time a word appeared in the middle of the screen, like in one of those early rinky-dink computer games (think Pong). Every time a word came on the screen, the participant just knocked it off the screen as fast as he or she could by moving the lever. Sometimes they pushed the lever to do this, and other times they pulled the lever. And once again, they were faster to push for bad things and pull for good things, not the other way around, even though they were not trying to evaluate anything at all.

The logical next step is to assume that we are likely to have those basic, primitive approach and withdrawal reactions to people, the most important "attitude objects" there are. Michael Slepian, Nalini Ambady, and their colleagues showed just that. They used the push-pull lever design and had their participants push or pull the lever to respond as quickly as possible to photographs shown on the computer screen in front of them. The participants were told their job was to move the lever one way if they saw a picture of a house, and to move it the other direction if they saw a picture of a face. So they believed their task was to classify the photographs in terms of faces versus houses—they were not thinking in terms of whether they liked the face or not. The trick of the study was that the faces varied in terms of how trustworthy they were—they had been separately rated by other people, so that the faces shown to participants ranged from appearing untrustworthy to appearing trustworthy. (We will describe the remarkable power of faces in more detail below.) And indeed, participants made faster approach (pull) movements to the trustworthy faces, and faster avoid (push) movements to the untrustworthy faces, all accomplished unconsciously because the participants' conscious task was not about judging the faces at all.

Today this basic approach or avoidance effect is being used to help make positive changes in people's lives—to change negative behavioral tendencies, such as racist attitudes and cravings for alcohol and addictive drugs. Canadian psychologist Kerry Kawakami and her colleagues had white participants make pull (approach) joystick movements when they saw a black face on the computer screen, and push (avoid) movements when they saw a white face, and they did this for several hundred faces. Afterward, the participants' automatic or implicit attitudes toward blacks as measured by the IAT procedure were more positive. Moving their arms in one direction instead of the other had actually changed their unconscious racial attitudes. And in another study, Kawakami and colleagues showed how making approach arm movements could change not only racial attitudes but also actual behavior toward blacks as well. After making the approach movements in response to a series of subliminal black faces the participants never even consciously saw, they then sat closer to a black person in a waiting room than did participants who had not just made those approach movements. This may not seem a very practical way to reduce racism in everyday life, but it does show the potential power of our ancient unconscious evaluation system over our modern-day social attitudes and behavior—and intriguingly, how our innate, evolved unconscious tendencies can be used to override our acquired cultural unconscious tendencies.

Another positive way this approach-avoid system has been deployed is to help alcoholics stop drinking. Reinout Wiers of the University of Amsterdam has developed such a therapy to combat alcoholism and other addictions. He had patients who wanted to stop drinking come in to his lab each day over a two-week period. There they would perform a simple computer task, taking about an hour, in which they classified photographs on the screen as either in landscape (wider) or portrait (taller) format. The critical part of the training was whether they pushed or pulled a lever to make their responses. The set of photographs was prearranged so that the patients always happened to push the lever when photographs of alcohol-related objects such as bottles, corkscrews, mugs, and wineglasses appeared. (There was also a control condition in which a different group of patients did the same task but without any alcohol-related photos being shown.)

This "pushing away" of alcohol-related objects was intended to increase the avoidance motivation toward alcohol in these patients. It was remarkably successful. Two weeks of pushing away the photos of the alcohol-related objects changed the patients' unconscious attitudes toward drinking from positive to negative, as measured by the IAT test. And even more remarkably, follow-ups on these patients one year later showed a significantly lower relapse rate (46 percent) than for those in the control condition who had not pushed away the alcohol-related photographs (59 percent). Not perfect, not zero, but remember that the difference between those two percentages represents real people with real families and real jobs who did not relapse and start drinking again, *when they otherwise would have.* Wiers and his team used our scientific knowledge about unconscious mechanisms to give practical help to people wanting to make important changes in their lives that they were having difficulty accomplishing through good intentions alone.

What's in a Name?

I've always loved to drive, and have driven across the United States a total of six times. The only state of the lower forty-eight I haven't driven through in my own car is North Dakota, and doing so someday is high on my bucket list. I am also a lifelong fan of car racing. Like many people of my generation, I grew up listening on the radio to the Indianapolis 500 every Memorial Day. My dad and I used to listen to it on a transistor radio while we worked on the house or in the yard all day. It's no surprise then that I later became a stock car racing fan. Ever since he was a rookie in 2002, my favorite driver has been the great Jimmie Johnson, a seven-time champion. My wife, Monica, on the other hand, roots for Danica Patrick, a world-class driver and bold shatterer of the glass ceilings of stock car racing (and Indy car racing before that) who is more successful than any other female racer in history.

While we can both present convincing, completely rational reasons for why these drivers are our favorites, please take note of our names and their names. **John** likes **J**immie **John**son (and he liked Junior **John**son before that). **Mo**nica likes **Da**nica. Our names share sounds and initial letters, and the magnetism begins there. (My wife has a much better excuse because Danica is the only female driver—still, that's a similarity, too.) This is called the *name-letter effect,* a phenomenon discovered in the 1980s that reveals another important unconscious source of preferences. We tend to embrace people who are "like" us, even if the source of that likeness is something as arbitrary as our names, which we ourselves don't even choose, or a shared birthday, the date of which we had nothing to do with.

While Bob Zajonc showed that one way we unconsciously come to like something is by becoming familiar with it, another route to liking is that something is similar to you, even if those similarities are objectively meaningless. Remember back in Chapter 1, the story of Ötzi and the fact that human beings frequently killed each other in the ancient world. Our ancestors banded together as families in self-defense, and then as groups of families into tribes. Recognizing kin could well be a life-or-death example of evaluating whether to say yes or no. That someone was similar to you was a fundamentally good thing back then. Now flash forward to modern times. If someone, or something else, shares features of our self, our identity, we usually feel positively toward that person or thing. But this is a tendency that evolved long ago. We usually do not realize, at least at first, the actual reason why we have that positive feeling, and we certainly do not realize how strongly it might affect us regarding important choices, goals, and motivations. The researchers who discovered and documented the effect of this positive feeling call it *implicit egotism*: our liking, without knowing the actual reasons why, of people and things that are similar to us, even if only in superficial ways.

Through statistical examination of large public record databases such as the 2000 U.S. Census, the 1880 U.S. Census, and the 1911 English census (all now available online), as well as such other sources as Ancestry.com, psychologists Brett Pelham, John Jones, Maurice Carvallo, and their colleagues have discovered some quite startling patterns in human behavior.

First, there are disproportionately more Kens who live in Kentucky, Louises who live in Louisiana, Florences who live in Florida, and Georges who live in Georgia (these are just a few examples) than would be expected if determined by chance alone (by how prevalent the name is in general, compared to how many people live in these states). This is not because they were born there and thus more likely to be named after the state in some way. They *moved* there. They chose that state over all the other ones they could have chosen. Other studies have shown that men named Cal and Tex are disproportionately likely to move to states resembling their name. And people don't just choose states with names similar to their own; people also disproportionately live on streets that match their last names—such as Hill or Park, Washington or Jefferson.

Sharing name letters (especially initials) also affects choices of occupations: there are proportionally more Dennys who are dentists, and Larrys who are lawyers, than should happen by chance alone. Meanwhile, people whose names start with *H* tend to be more likely to own hardware stores, whereas people whose names begin with *F* are more likely to own furniture stores. Across eleven different lines of work, men are disproportionately more likely than chance to work in occupations whose titles match their surnames: for example, Barber, Baker, Foreman, Carpenter, Farmer, Mason, Porter. This effect was as true in 1911 England as it is in the modern-day United States. The name-letter effect held for all eleven occupations. For example, there were 187 Bakers who were actually bakers, compared to the 134 expected by chance (taking both frequency of name and frequency of occupation into account). For Painters, an actual 66 versus the 39 expected by chance, Farmers 1,423 versus 1,337. You can see by these numbers that these are not big effects, and there were certainly many Painters and Farmers who did something else entirely. That the names are significant influences *at all* is what is remarkable. And the effects are statistically reliable, and hold even when controlling for and ruling out some important alternative explanations generated by skeptics, such as gender, ethnicity, and level of education.

Now birthdays. Here, just as remarkably, one's birthday has a significant influence on a person's choice of spouse. People disproportionately marry someone who shares birth date numbers with them. Take Summit County, Ohio, where there were half a million marriages from 1840 to 1980. Looking at the birth-day number, regardless of month, a couple getting married was 6.5 percent more likely than chance to have the same birth day of the month. Looking at birth month, regardless of day, couples were 3.4 percent more likely than chance to be born in the same month. This effect was then found again when researchers consulted statewide Minnesota marriage records from 1958 to 2001. In Minnesota, couples were 6.2 percent more likely to share the same birth-day number, and 4.4 percent more likely to be born in the same month.

I have succumbed to this effect myself. As I've already made abundantly clear, I'm a die-hard Led Zeppelin fan, going back to the time I first heard "Heartbreaker" on the Chicago station WLS, in the fall of 1969, when I was fourteen years old. Since then I've always felt a kinship with their music, but especially with Jimmy Page, the lead guitarist. Why is this? What do we have in common? Not much. I could never play the guitar, while he was a child prodigy and then a genius at it, let's not even talk about looks, and he's British. The answer? We share the same birthday. I feel a strange and obviously undeserved pride about this. At least it's clear that I'm not alone in feeling such kinship!

A heartening, real-world demonstration of using unconscious affiliations for self-betterment occurred about ten years ago at a high school in my area. At the beginning of the school year, Yale researchers gave at-risk students who were struggling in math a fictitious *New York Times* article about a student from another school who had won a major math award. There was a little "bio box" at the top of the article. In that box, for half of the students in the class, the birthday given for the award winner was made to be the same as for the student, although no mention was made of this fact. For the other students, the award winner's birthday was a different month and date from theirs. That was all the experimenters did, just a small, invisible tweak to create a link to the student's own identity.

In May of the following year, at the end of that school term, the researchers looked at the final math grades for all the students in the study. And lo and behold, the students who had shared a birthday with the award winner had significantly higher final grades in math than the students who did not have the same birthday as the winner. Those who had the same birthday felt more similar to the award winner, and this carried over to their belief about their own math ability, with positive effects on their level of effort for the rest of the school year.

A few years ago, when my daughter was in third grade, the kids in her class played Secret Santa. They all wrote down the three things they liked the most, as guidance for choosing gifts, and each child picked a different child's list out of a box. For the student for whom my daughter played Secret Santa, his first love was Real Madrid soccer, and his second was "math." He was the only student in the class who put down "math" as one of the things he liked the most. This particular student even requested, on his form, that his present be math related.

His name? Why *Matthew*, of course.

Grumpy Cats and Competent Politicians

Remember the movie *Home Alone*? Remember Old Man Marley, the scary-looking next-door neighbor who turns out at the end to be kind and friendly after all?

Looks can be deceiving. My daughter had a librarian at her grade school who looked very crabby, and my daughter and all the other first graders were afraid of her. This continued until one day the librarian came up to her and said she liked her boots. Suddenly my daughter's opinion of the librarian completely changed for the better. It's a person's *behavior* that matters, not their face. We all know this at an intellectual level, of course, but it is very hard to shake the impression we get from a person's face, especially our first impressions. It is not so much that we think we know what a person is like based just on their face. It is that we feel absolutely certain we are *right* about what we think about them.

There is a social media star who weighs about fifteen pounds, never says or writes anything, and just has her picture taken all the time. And she has four legs. Grumpy Cat is funny to us because she looks so damn grumpy all the time. And it is funny because we know she is just a cat and doesn't realize how she looks to us, and most likely isn't really grumpy at all. She just looks that way. Grumpy Cat is relevant here because what we are doing when we judge a person's personality from just his face is treating it as if it were a window into his emotional state. A person we meet can have a chronic angry look to his face, but that does not mean he is always angry. (The same goes for cats.) Recently on social media I read a rant by a friend who was going off about a woman he had never met and knew nothing about, based just on this woman's photograph, saying what a bitch she must be. Another wise friend said, "Just because she has resting bitch face doesn't mean she isn't a nice person."

Darwin, you will recall, recognized the adaptive value, over evolutionary time, of communicating our emotions to others, mainly through our facial expressions. It was one of the first—perhaps *the* first—way that we humans communicated with each other. Evolutionary psychologists John Tooby and Leda Cosmides call our attention to the intriguing fact that the muscles of the face are the only ones in the entire human body that directly connect bone to skin. Why would this be? Because our bones are what we use to move parts of our body, this direct connection must exist so that we can move the skin of our face. Why only our face and not other parts of our body? Because the face is the part of us that other people look at the most, to see where we are looking, to watch our mouth to help them understand what we are saying, and so on. In other words, we have been specifically designed by evolution to display our emotions on our faces *so that others can see them.*

Are we born with the ability to read a person's emotional state from their facial expression, and are we born to trust unquestioningly what the other person's face is telling us? According to Darwin, we came to trust those facial expressions so much because we learned that emotions are difficult to fake; indeed, the facial muscles involved are hard to move voluntarily. Our ancestors had to trust what other faces were telling them because often their lives depended on quickly reading and assessing the people they encountered. Again, we are reminded of poor Ötzi, murdered thousands of years ago in that high mountain pass. As Tooby and Cosmides argued, "Given the homicidal nature of the ancient world, knowing someone was approachable and friendly would be a true life or death judgment." As you might expect, then, the facial expressions of the people around us are still today one of the most powerful signals our environment gives us about whether we should stay or go. Modern research has confirmed that we make very fast assessments of whether a person is a friend or foe (stay or go) within a split second of meeting them. Furthermore, these impressions are so powerful—we trust this flash assessment so much—they can even affect the outcome of important things such as political elections.

Alexander Todorov is a Princeton psychologist and neuroscientist specializing in people's immediate reaction to faces. In his early experiments, he asked participants to make personality judgments of people based only on their faces. They were shown a series of faces, taken from a database of seventy amateur actors, males and females between twenty and thirty years of age, and in different studies rated each person's attractiveness, likability, competence, trustworthiness, or aggressiveness. These studies confirmed what Darwin and Ekman had concluded: there was high agreement among the raters in these personality judgments across the five traits rated and across all the faces rated. Everyone was "reading" each face in pretty much the same way. Also, these personality assessments were computed by the participants' brains with lightning speed. How long the face was presented on the screen didn't affect the personality judgments—the raters had the same sense of competence or trustworthiness, for example, after seeing a face for just one-tenth of a second or for a full second, or with unlimited time to see it. And it was the trait of *trustworthiness* that showed the highest consensus agreement of all among the raters, even when the faces were shown for just a split second.

Todorov and his colleagues moved on to see if a political candidate's face influenced how competent voters thought he or she was. Their earlier research had shown that people believe competence to be the most important attribute for a politician to have. He and his team took photographs from actual governor and congressional candidates' websites, and then showed them to people from other voting districts, so that the study participants didn't know who the candidates were, or their policies, or political party—and they also only saw the pictures briefly, again for as little as a tenth of a second.

Remarkably—and somewhat disturbingly, when you think about it—those rapid judgments of competence based on the face alone correctly predicted the outcome of gubernatorial elections from 1995 to 2002. Princeton undergraduates who participated in the study saw the faces of the winner and the runner-up for eighty-nine gubernatorial races and were asked to decide who was more competent, "relying on their gut reactions." These predictions were just as accurate when the faces were shown for only 100 milliseconds as they were when the faces were on the screen for many seconds. Interestingly, when another group of participants was asked to think carefully and make a good judgment (instead of doing it fast based on their gut), this actually *reduced* the ability of the (now slow and deliberate) face ratings to predict the election outcome. That reminded me of the automatic-attitude research that Shelly Chaiken and I had conducted years earlier, in which we found stronger unconscious evaluation effects after removing the conscious, deliberate aspects of evaluation from the task as much as possible. It also suggests that the actual voters in these elections were more often going with their gut appraisals of the candidates' faces than making careful judgments about their characters.

In their second experiment, the researchers removed other important influences on competence judgments, such as cultural stereotypes, in order to gauge the pure effect of the face itself. They looked at only the fifty-five gubernatorial races for which the gender and ethnicity of the candidates were the same. Doing so increased the percentage of correctly predicted races from 57 percent to 69 percent, and the face judgments of competence now accounted for 10 percent of the candidates' vote shares in these elections. And it is how competent the face appears that is especially important to voters—in this experiment, no other personality trait judgments of the faces predicted the election outcomes. This effect has been found again and again in other elections, in the United States and other countries.

Obviously we as voters are putting way too much faith in these quick-and-dirty assessments based on faces alone. Our track record on electing trustworthy politicians is pretty bad. There have been far too many elected officials (including a string of governors in my home state of Illinois) who may have had a trustworthy face but were then indicted and convicted for corruption. So the real question is, why do we feel so sure about people when we quickly size them up based on their faces alone? I think Grumpy Cat has the answer to this one. We did not evolve to read a person (or a cat, for that matter) based on static photographs of their face; photography is only a very recent invention. We evolved to size up a person quickly based on seeing them (and not just their face) in action, if only for a brief period of time. Static photographs, frozen in time, fool us. When we look at a photograph, such as the stock photo of a candidate or politician in a newspaper article, we are mistaking the signs of a temporary emotional state (which is what we are wired to do) for a long-term, chronic personality trait. And that turns out to be a big mistake.

Seeing candidates or politicians on TV doesn't help much, either, if we mainly see them in stock, stage-managed situations (as in their campaign ads, speeches, or "photo opportunities"). Todorov's studies consistently show that the candidates' faces by themselves are influencing a lot of voters. What that suggests is that even seeing the candidates on TV, to the extent we do, doesn't add much to what we already conclude from their face alone.

While competence may be the important face trait determining who we vote for, other face traits have surprising amounts of influence on other important real-life outcomes. Take court cases, for example. Leslie Zebrowitz of Brandeis University has devoted much of her research career to the study of how our faces determine our treatment by society. She and her colleagues have shown that qualities of a defendant's face influence conviction rates and sentencing in actual court cases. Going into courtrooms during trials they have found that, when all other facts of the case are the same, "baby-faced" adults are more likely to be found innocent and given lower sentences than are other defendants. Racially prototypic faces cause the defendant to be treated differently as well. Shockingly but not surprisingly, black defendants who had darker skin received sentences that were on average three years longer than did black defendants with lighter skin who committed the same crime. Sam Sommers of Tufts University has similarly shown that among blacks on trial, those who had more of an African appearance received harsher sentences overall, and were more likely to receive the death penalty if convicted of murdering a white victim, than were those who had less prototypic African facial appearance. Prison is nothing if not society's method of avoidance.

In a classic social psychology study from the 1970s, Minnesota researchers showed that in a get-to-know-each-other phone conversation, participants were rated as being friendlier and having a more attractive personality if the person talking to them believed that they were an attractive versus a less attractive person. They obtained this belief at the beginning of the experiment when they were given a photo of the other person, which was not actually of the person they were talking to. Nonetheless, believing that the person was attractive brought out the friendlier and more attractive side of the participants' personalities. We all are guilty of treating attractive people more favorably and with greater friendliness than we treat less attractive people.

Even babies are biased toward attractive people in this way, which shows that the tendency is a hardwired aspect of human nature. Newborn infants, not even a day old, prefer to look at attractive compared to unattractive faces, and they look at attractive faces longer when given the choice. It takes us as adults just a quick glance to know whether a face is attractive or not. Neuroscience studies have revealed that for adults, eye contact with photographs of attractive people activates the reward centers of the brain. In one study, viewing attractive faces alone, without judging them in terms of attractiveness, caused the activation of the participants' medial orbitofrontal cortex (reward center). We naturally and unconsciously like to see attractive faces; they are rewarding and pleasurable to us. So we hire attractive people instead of less attractive but equally qualified people, pay them more money, go to see the movies they are in, and want to have relationships with them. Badly. We really want them to stay, and not to go.

As we stay or go in the ever-unfolding present, we have mental and muscular reactions that operate on a different, faster, and more instinctual plane than does conscious thought. Evolutionary forces field-tested and kept these unconscious mechanisms because they allowed us to survive, to be an exception to the fact that 99 percent of all species that ever existed became extinct. We could easily have been one of them. But for millions of years our instincts for survival caused us to approach and support and love our tribe, and to avoid and fight and hate the other tribes.

Darwin argued that banding together like this to protect ourselves from other humans conferred on us a significant evolutionary advantage, and so became an innate tendency quite early on.

So it went, down through the millions of years of our species. We attacked and killed "them" and they attacked and killed "us," at horrific rates by modern standards. Distinguishing us from them, distrusting "them," and helping the others in our own group became things we were born to do. Today, underneath the nuances of faces, and the sharing of birthdays and name letters, the primordial code still is, Us versus Them, friend or foe, with us or against us. There are domains in modern life where these powerful motors of action, which governed the lives of our hominid ancestors, still move us. North versus South. Germany versus France. White versus Black.

And even: Yankees versus Red Sox.

Cheering for the Clothes

On the night of October 2, 2010, Monte Freire was at the U.S.S. Chowder Pot III in Branford, Connecticut, watching the Yankees play the Red Sox on one of the restaurant's big-screen televisions. A family man and an employee of the Parks and Recreation Department in Nassau, New Hampshire, Freire was in town to compete in a weekend softball tournament with friends. After having played earlier in the day, he and his teammates were now kicking back at the quaint, nautically decorated restaurant, which boasted a giant red lobster on its roof. There was no reason to think anything bad would happen. Or was there?

As any baseball fan knows, the rivalry between the New York Yankees and the Boston Red Sox is legendary. The teams' home cities themselves were fierce competitors for cultural and economic dominance during the eighteenth and nineteenth centuries, but their baseball stadiums became their symbolic battlefields starting in 1919, when the Sox traded the great Babe Ruth to the Yankees: Boston then suffered an eighty-six-year dry spell, failing to win a single World Series championship. (Superstitious fans called this the Curse of the Bambino, after Ruth's nickname.) Over the years, the Yankees were clearly the stronger competitor, though there were many exciting showdowns between the two teams, and Boston fans never wavered in their support of the underdog Sox. In 2004 the "curse" was finally broken. The Red Sox first vanquished the hated Yankees in an epic comeback in the league championship and then went on to win that year's World Series. (And then to win a couple more since.) The long-standing rivalry was still passionately intact that fall night at the Chowder Pot.

The game up on the big screen that Freire and his friends were watching was a decisive one for the Yankees. If they won, they would take their division. The Red Sox, naturally, hoped to prevent this. The restaurant was crowded with fans. At some point during the game, Freire and his friends began trading words with a local man named John Mayor, a Yankees fan. As the game progressed on-screen, Mayor became increasingly agitated and aggressive, loudly letting the visitors know that they were in "Yankee territory." Freire and his friends alerted a nearby bartender, but no employee intervened. The tension continued to escalate, and before anyone knew what was happening, Mayor pulled out a knife, came over and stabbed Freire in the neck, twice, and ran out of the restaurant.

Freire collapsed, bleeding, while his friends chased Mayor outside behind the Chowder Pot. They apprehended him, assailing him in an onslaught of punches and kicks, until police officers arrived. Freire was taken to the hospital, where he technically died twice that night, though doctors revived him both times, and he somehow pulled through. Mayor was also taken to the hospital to recover from the blows he'd received; then he was arrested and charged with attempted manslaughter.

I live about ten miles from the Chowder Pot, and drive by it on U.S. 1 all the time. When she was very little my daughter was quite frightened of the giant lobster on top of the building and would hide her face in her hands when we approached. So, like many in the area, I followed the news about the incident as it developed, and two days later, an article in the *Branford Eagle* noted, "Police were at a loss Sunday to understand how a baseball rivalry could go so wrong." Now, sports fans know very well that rivalries are intense, and can sometimes turn violent, and as a psychologist, I knew that sports are just a ritualized modern-day replication of the tribal conditions in which our mind evolved. And in the sports world, Yankees versus Red Sox is about as "us" versus "them" as it gets.

But as the quote from the local police showed, this can all seem rather odd to sports outsiders; after all, these are grown men playing a boy's game, hardly something worth killing another person over. In a recent stand-up routine, Jerry Seinfeld played this role of the outsider with perfect pitch. He goes to a baseball game with a friend. He makes the mistake of cheering for a player they all cheered for the last time he was at a game. "What are you *doing?*" says his friend, glaring at him. "He's on the Phillies!" Jerry looks puzzled: "But you loved the guy last year." "That's when he was a Met!" says his friend, in near exasperation. "Ahhh, I get it," says Jerry, as everything becomes clear. "We're cheering for the *clothes*."

Until the 1970s, and the advent of free agency, players didn't change teams all that much, and baseball fans could grow up cheering for pretty much the same players their entire childhood. Today things are very different, and a "hated" player on a rival team could suddenly be forgiven by fans, who now cheer for him instead. Seinfeld was right. When it comes right down to it, these days we are really cheering for the clothes.

There are two psychology experiments, an old one and a new one, that show how transient and plastic these "us" versus "them" feelings can be, and they speak to the senseless violence that happened at the Chowder Pot that night. Yet these studies also show that there is hope that we can control hatred and hostility toward out-groups. If "they" become included in a new "us," then we can all be happy together. If former "theys" become part of "our" team, just as with traded baseball players, dislike suddenly changes to like.

The classic study was done seventy years ago at Robbers Cave State Park in eastern Oklahoma, right off of Highway 2. Nestled up in the foothills of the Ozark Mountains, Robbers Cave is a green, protected wilderness containing lakes, hiking and equestrian trails, and camping grounds with cabins. It was here in this tranquil place, in the summer of 1949, that Muzafer and Carolyn Sherif carried out one of the most famous experiments in the history of psychology.

The Sherifs invited a group of twelve-year-old boys—none of whom previously knew each other—to the Boy Scout area of the park for a multiday camplike experience. The boys were all white and came from Protestant, lower-middle-class families. They didn't know that they were part of an experiment. What the Sherifs hoped to learn about intergroup conflict and cooperation hinged on creating two groups of boys, not unlike fans of opposing sports teams. They divided the boys into these groups on arrival, keeping them separated so neither group even knew there was another. For several days, each group hiked and swam and bonded in their own part of the camp, becoming a team of sorts. They found who the natural leaders were, established a kind of hierarchy, and cohered into a unified collective. And as boys are wont to do, each group came up with a cool name for themselves—one was the Eagles; the other was the Rattlers.

Then came the twist. The Sherifs brought the two groups together. But that wasn't all. As the boys soon discovered, not only was there another "tribe" in their midst, but they would be competing with this new opponent (out-group) in games such as tug-of-war and—of course!—baseball.

The boys' lives at the camp abruptly changed. Their collective and individual behavior now passed through a dramatically simplified mental filter of us against them. The Rattlers rallied their team spirit *against* the Eagles, withdrawing into a tighter unit and antagonizing their perceived foe. They stuck their team flag into the ground of the playing field and menacingly warned the Eagles not to mess with it. The Eagles, naturally, found a way to burn the Rattlers' flag, then trashed their cabin. Soon enough, the tensions become so heated that the "counselors" finally had to intervene physically to ensure the boys didn't hurt each other.

The Sherifs' *Lord of the Flies*–like experiment at Robbers Cave was unsettling. How easily the boys' liking and disliking of each other was so manipulated, simply by their being divided into two groups, and how these attitudes so quickly turned into hostile acts was discouraging. It becomes easier to understand how the horrible incidents like the one that nearly killed Monte Freire can happen.

At the end of that strange, balkanized summer for the twelve-year-old boys, the experimenters tried to end the hostility and animosity between the two groups. They did this by giving all the boys some important common goals, which they could accomplish only if they all worked together. For example, on the way back from a distant part of the state park, the vehicles carrying the boys got stuck in some deep mud on the dirt road. Only by all of them pulling on ropes could they get the trucks unstuck and get back to their camp—which they did, to much cheering and pride. After a few more shared accomplishments, they were now all one team, laughing and having a great time with each other, the former bitter rivals now great friends. Their "us" identity had been changed by the common, shared goals—instead of Rattlers and Eagles, now they were all boys at the same summer camp together.

In a modern experiment on the same theme, psychologists Jay Van

Bavel and Wil Cunningham showed how unconscious racism can be "e-raced" when members of the racial out-group become members of the main group. By showing black faces to white participants and telling them these will be your teammates on the next task, the participants' initially negative implicit attitudes toward these same black faces (measured by the IAT) suddenly changed to be positive. This was even before they did anything on the team together. Just like those of the boys in the Robbers Cave study, our unconscious stay-or-go responses to social groups are not hardwired and unchangeable, not by any means. The participants in the Van Bavel experiment were not cheering for the skin color in that second IAT task. They were cheering for the clothes.

CHAPTER 6

When Can You Trust
Your Gut?

At 9:40 on a Monday morning in New York City, four days before Christmas in 1982, a twenty-nine-year-old man named Reginald Andrews stood on a subway platform in Greenwich Village, waiting for an uptown train. He had been unemployed for over a year and had just come from an interview at a nearby meatpacking plant. He wasn't especially optimistic about how it had gone. He calculated that he had applied to nearly one thousand jobs over the last year, but he was still jobless, and things were looking increasingly dire for him, his wife, and their eight children. The phone company had recently shut off his family's service, and they were only getting by thanks to the generosity of people they knew in their community.

The train arrived and Andrews stepped toward the doors along with the rest of the passengers. As he did so, he noticed something alarming: an elderly blind man who was also moving to board the train mistook the space between two cars for the doorway to the car with his cane—and he fell down onto the tracks.

There was no time to analyze the situation before the train started moving, only seconds to act. Frantically calling out to other passengers to alert them of the situation, Andrews dropped down onto the tracks with the man.

As the crushing wheels of the train began groaning into motion, Andrews pulled seventy-five-year-old David Schnair, who was injured, into a crawl space tucked under the lip of the platform above. Had Andrews known it was there? What had he planned to do when he jumped down?

It didn't matter. They were just barely out of the way of the train when it stopped. One of the other riders, a woman, had managed to get the conductor to halt. Subway workers cut the power to the train, and soon after, the two men were lifted up to safety. Schnair had survived his near-death accident on the tracks, and Andrews had survived his near-death act of heroism. And thankfully, the down-and-out family man was rewarded for his heroism—big-time.

The day that Reginald Andrews performed his staggeringly brave feat, I was just a few blocks away from that subway station, in my NYU apartment working hard on a chapter for a book that had to be finished in a couple of weeks. The subway rescue was all over the local news that evening and then network news also picked up the story. The national coverage attracted the attention of no less than President Ronald Reagan, who mentioned Andrews the next day at his church when he was fielding inquiries from the media and then phoned Andrews. At first Andrews thought it was a prank, but as the call continued and he listened to the voice, he realized it was no joke. It really was the president of the United States on the line. Reagan congratulated Andrews for his heroic actions and wished him a merry Christmas. Later, the president called the plant where Andrews had interviewed that Monday morning. Reagan spoke to the supervisor there and suggested that he hire Andrews. Of course, the supervisor did just that.

Andrews's gut decision had saved not only an innocent life, but his family's economic security, too. I remember watching Reagan's annual State of the Union address to Congress one month later and can vividly recall the moment when the president told his audience what Andrews had done and pointed to him up in the Capitol gallery, where Andrews sat as his invited guest, receiving a standing ovation from the senators, congressmen and congresswomen, and justices of the Supreme Court gathered there that evening.

Now fast-forward eighteen years, to May 11, 2010. It was a Thursday afternoon and Rose Mary Mankos stood on another Manhattan subway platform, on the Upper East Side, waiting for another train. The forty-eight-year-old lawyer from the Stuyvesant Town neighborhood a few miles south stood among the after-school crowd of students on their way home. She carried a black LeSportsac backpack, which she inadvertently let drop onto the tracks. What should she do? She jumped down to get the bag.

To many people, the distance from the floor of the tracks back up onto the platform looks easily scalable. But as transit authorities know all too well (and try to warn riders), it isn't. Climbing up and out is difficult. This was the horrible predicament in which Mankos now found herself—she didn't know how to get back up onto the platform—as she and the other people waiting in the station heard the ominous rumble of a train approaching the station.

Bystanders shouted for her to lie down between the tracks. They told her that the cars would pass over her, but she was too frightened to do so. The conductor of the oncoming train saw he was bearing down on a person in front of him and yanked the emergency brake while hammering hard on his horn, its earsplitting blast filling the station. It was no use. As the train slowed into the station, Mankos tried to squeeze herself against the platform, but she couldn't get out of the way. She was killed.

Two people who leapt down onto subway tracks, two life-threatening crises, and two radically different outcomes—each defined by a gut decision made in a moment. For one, his gut decision made him a hero and changed his life for the better; for the other, it led to a horrible and premature end to her life. In hindsight, it is easy to see Andrews made the right decision and Mankos did not—it is always easy after the fact to identify the times when it was good to trust our gut and the times when it was not so good. But we need to know what the right thing to do is before we do it, not afterward. Entire books—bestsellers—have appeared in recent years that seem to give completely conflicting advice on this question: can we trust our intuitions (*Blink*, by Malcolm Gladwell), or not (*Thinking, Fast and Slow*, by Daniel Kahneman)? The answer lies in between. There are times when you can and should, and times when you can't and shouldn't. I will provide eight simple rules, based on the accumulated research evidence, for when you should and when you should not trust your gut.

In general, we tend to trust our intuition. In one study by decision researchers Carey Morewedge and Michael Norton and their colleagues, people reported that their intuitions and gut feelings—such as when they have a hunch, when their mind wanders onto a topic while reading, when ideas seem to just pop into their heads—revealed more about their true feelings, their real selves, than did their normal conscious thoughts, as when they are deliberately thinking about something, trying to solve a problem, or making a plan. Participants rated how spontaneously each of a variety of mental experiences occurred for them, and separately rated how much each type of experience revealed about their true beliefs and feelings. These two ratings were highly related—the more spontaneous and less intentional a mental experience, such as a dream or a Freudian slip, the more that people trusted it as a revealing insight about themselves.

Why do we trust our intuition, even more than our careful thinking? Basically, we trust our intuition for the same reason we trust our senses. Information coming into our minds easily and naturally, without our trying to figure it out or spending any effort on it, seems "true" and "out there in the world" just like when we look at that very large plant in our yard and know, immediately and without having to think about it at all, that it is a tree. I can look out my window across the lake to a low ridge, which the sunrise is lighting up against the pale blue sky, and imagine the StayPuft Marshmallow man stomping along on top of that ridge. But I can only produce a weak image of this with my imagination alone, and I know I am working hard to imagine it, so I know it is not real. If Mr. StayPuft was really out there on the ridge, the visual experience would be much stronger and clearer, and I would not have to try at all to produce it. How much I have to try to see the image (using my imagination) is a very powerful cue to whether the thing I am "seeing" is real or not. We tend to trust our intuitions for similar reasons: the more easily a particular thought appears in the mind, without our trying to produce it, the more we trust its validity, and the less we doubt it is true. We are wired to trust our senses, without questioning them; the alternative, to not trust our senses and to question them, is to be psychotic, and that is a very frightening state to be in.

Rules for When to Trust Your Gut: 1–4

What if the information we encounter out in the world is not coming into our senses so clearly and easily? What if it is getting dark, say, and we aren't quite sure that's our friend walking toward us, or our dog in the bushes over there, and we have to look harder and think about who or what that is? Then we are not so confident about what we think we are seeing—and this is when gut responses come in. We have to wager on what the right move is, and hope betting on ourselves will pay off.

So while we do tend to trust our intuitions, we also recognize that they can be wrong or misleading. When I began work on this chapter, I created a thread on Reddit, the social media and discussion hub, asking users about times their gut reactions turned out to be totally wrong. I noticed that their responses fell into two main categories: fear when in fact none was necessary, and overconfidence when just the opposite was needed. In the first category, a woman wrote about how, after first meeting her current romantic partner, she was convinced he was a "player." She kept him at a distance, until she finally saw past her wary instincts and realized "he's the sweetest and most faithful of men." Other people wrote about times they thought someone was in danger (owing to a strange sound, or a sketchy-seeming dark street) and rushed to the rescue, only to discover a perfectly harmless situation. In the second category, of overconfidence, one man wrote that he always thought the girls he liked would come around and take notice of him, but they never did. Another Reddit user wrote about how he always thought he did well on the tests he ended up doing very poorly on. All the responses from my questions were fairly lighthearted, but they highlighted how it was not uncommon for our "blinks" to blind us.

Both of the subway jumpers, Andrews and Mankos, had to act under extreme time pressure. They had to act quickly or the blind man would have been killed or the backpack destroyed. They both took huge chances with their own lives. With the advantage of hindsight, because of the different outcomes, we know that Andrews made the right choice, and Mankos the wrong choice. But it could easily have been the other way around. Andrews and the blind man could have been killed if Andrews hadn't had the time to tuck them into the crawl space; Mankos might have been helped up onto the platform by other passengers or the train might have stopped in time. But Andrews would still have been a hero for his selfless attempt to save another person by risking his own life, and Mankos a tragic risk-taker because her backpack was not worth the chance she took. Even if she had managed to escape to safety, she'd made a bad choice. The difference in their outcomes, life versus death, happens to dovetail with the difference in what they stood to gain. In one case, an innocent, helpless person's life; in the other, a backpack. One is worth risking your life for; the other is not. But both Andrews and Mankos trusted their gut. What to make of this?

As with the tragic case of Rose Mary Mankos, our intuition can lead us astray if we are too quick to accept intuitive answers that would be proven wrong by just a moment's reflection. Decision researcher Shane Frederick has developed a simple three-item quiz to measure a person's tendency to make quick intuitive decisions without reflecting on them. For example: *If it takes 5 widget-making machines 5 minutes to make 5 widgets, how many minutes would it take 100 widget-making machines to make 100 widgets?* Many people quickly answer 100 because that so naturally follows the pattern of the example in the premise. It just feels right. The first one is 5, 5, 5 so the second one must be 100, 100, 100. But the correct answer is actually 5 minutes, which is the time for a single widget maker to produce a widget. No matter how many machines you have, each one will take 5 minutes, so 100 machines will make 100 in 5 minutes (one each). This reminds me of that old prank where a friend tells you to complete each sentence as fast as possible: "A funny story is a . . . ??" JOKE (you say). "To jab with your finger is a . . . ??" POKE. "A popular soft drink is a . . . ??" COKE. "The white of an egg is a . . . ??" YOLK. *Gotcha!*

Not questioning our gut can sometimes leave us with egg on our faces.

So right off the bat we have two basic rules for when to trust your gut. **Rule #1 is to supplement your gut impulse with at least a little conscious reflection, if you have the time to do so.** (Sometimes, as in Reginald Andrews's case, we do not, but in Mankos's case she did.) Conscious and unconscious thinking have different strengths, and different weaknesses, as we will see in a moment, and using both if you can is the best way to go. Check your work, if you can! **Rule # 2 is that when you don't have the time to think about it, don't take big chances for small gains going on your gut alone.** The blind man's life was worth it to Andrews, God bless him. But the backpack just wasn't worth it. Know the stakes. (Taking big risks for small rewards reminds me of all the tailgaters on the roads around where I live—right on my rear bumper at 50 mph or faster. Big risk, very small gain—I just don't get it.)

Decision researchers generally do not like intuition and tend to portray conscious reflection as a white knight that rides to the rescue of our error-prone gut. But knights can make mistakes as well. Yes, we can underthink, but we can also *over*think our choices, so that our conscious deliberations are the ones that lead us astray. Timothy Wilson and Jonathan Schooler discovered this by studying strawberry jam, college classes, and cat post-ers. (They did this one experiment at a time, not by focusing on all three things at once, which probably would've gotten messy.)

In their first study, they had participants judge the quality of different brands of jam, then compared their ratings with those of experts. They found that the participants who were asked to spend time consciously analyzing the jam had preferences that differed further from those of the experts, compared to those who responded with just the "gut" of their taste buds. In Wilson and Schooler's second study, they interviewed hundreds of college students about the quality of a class. Once again, those who were asked to think for a moment about their decisions were further from the experts' judgments than were those who just went with their initial feelings. And in their final study, participants got to choose a poster to take with them as a gift for being in the study. They could choose one of two types of posters: those of paintings such as Van Gogh's irises or Monet's water lilies, or silly posters with cartoons of cats. They either chose right away or were asked to first think about the reasons for their choice. In the "gut" reaction condition only 5 percent took the dumb cat poster, but in the "think first" condition 36 percent chose the dumb cat poster. Three weeks later the participants were contacted and asked how much they liked the poster on their wall. Those who had more spontaneously gone with their gut were happier with the gift they had chosen than were those who had decided after thinking about it first. The immediate snap judgment was a better predictor of future satisfaction than careful and patient consideration of the choice.

When this "strawberry jam" study was published in the early 1990s, Shelly Chaiken and I were in the middle of the automatic attitude research I described in Chapter 5. We found Wilson and Schooler's findings to be very much in synch with our own conclusions. The greater the involve-ment of conscious and intentional evaluation processes in our studies, the harder it was to detect the unconscious attitude effect, and the weaker those effects were. It was as if the conscious evaluation processes were *interfering* with the more natural unconscious appraisals of the objects in our studies. So too with the strawberry jam studies—the more that people thought about their feelings about the jam, the less their stated opinions reflected their true underlying attitudes.

The different strengths and weaknesses of conscious and unconscious decision-making were revealed in a groundbreaking series of studies by Dutch researchers Ap Dijksterhuis and Loran Nordgren and their colleagues when they tested their Unconscious Thought Theory (UTT). Dijksterhuis and Nordgren were the first to extend the study of unconscious mental processes to the domain of judgment and decision-making, one of the last bastions of psychological science to accept a role for the unconscious. Psychological science had long presumed that judgments and decisions were almost exclusively conscious activities. Of course, there have been many studies over the past half century, most famously by Daniel Kahneman and Amos Tversky, showing the irrational or heuristic shortcuts that people take when making conscious decisions, but in those studies the actual making of the judgment or decision was always a conscious, deliberate process. Dijksterhuis and Nordgren's UTT research showed that the judgments *themselves* could be made unconsciously, during a period of time when the conscious mind was distracted by doing something else entirely. Not only that, but also, more provocatively, they concluded that the results of the unconscious decision process were often *superior* to those of the consciously made judgments.

How did they test this? First, they gave participants the information needed to make a judgment such as which car was better to buy or which apartment was better to rent, out of four alternatives. They varied each of the four choices on relevant dimensions (gas mileage, price, reliability, luxury). So one car model might have the best gas mileage but a higher price and require a moderate amount of service at the garage; another might have poor mpg but need hardly any service; and so on. These four alternatives were deliberately constructed so that there was an actual objective right answer to the question of which car was the best one to buy, taking all four features into account. The same with the apartment choices: one might have the lowest rent but not the best location; another might have more space but not the best view; etc.

After the participants read all of this information about the cars or the apartments, some of them were then asked to think about which car or apartment was the best one, and others were prevented from thinking about the cars or apartments (consciously, that is) for the same period of time. Instead of being able to think about the cars or apartments, they had to do a difficult mental task that took up all of their available attention. (Imagine, for example, counting backward from 643 by sevens as fast as you can.) After this task was completed, the participants gave their decisions about the best apartment or car. Lo and behold, more of the participants in the unconscious thought condition made the best choice than did those in the conscious thought condition. The researchers then replicated this effect across many similar studies. While this was a quite surprising finding when it first appeared, it did bear out what Freud had written more than one hundred years earlier in *The Interpretation of Dreams:* "The most complicated achievements of thought are possible without the assistance of consciousness."

How did the participants in the unconscious judgment condition make the best choice? Again, neuroscience research has helped explain just what was happening to the unconscious deciders during the distraction period. When David Creswell and his fellow neuroscientists at Carnegie Mellon University imaged the brains of participants during the experiment, both when they were reading about the various cars or apartments, and then later during the "unconscious thinking" (gut) time, they found that the area of the brain that had been active while the participants were consciously learning all the features of the cars or apartments remained active during the time when they were distracted by the task (and were thinking unconsciously). Furthermore, the more active that same area of the brain during the later unconscious thought period, the better the quality of the decision the participant made. In other words, the same part of the brain that was first used to acquire the important information was then used by the unconscious "gut" processes in solving the problem, while the conscious mind was elsewhere.

Dijksterhuis, Nordgren, and their colleagues continued to research the conditions under which unconscious decisions were as good or better than consciously made decisions, and the times when conscious decisions were superior. Their conclusions are very relevant to our question of when can we trust our gut, and when we can't. Unconscious decisions tend to be better when the judgment is complex and many different dimensions or features have to be combined and integrated, as with the cars and apartments. Our conscious working memory is limited and can't hold as much information at any given time; we can handle up to three things at once comfortably, but more than that becomes a stretch. Because our conscious mind can focus on only a few features, as in the strawberry jam or cat poster studies, other relevant features are not taken into account, and don't have the influence they should. Conscious thought is powerful, but it is limited as to the complexity of what it can consider at any given moment. Still, conscious processes are better than unconscious ones if there is a rule to follow. For example, if you have to constrain your apartment or car choices because of your budget, and must exclude those that are too expensive, or if you have to walk to work and thus can't live more than a mile away from your job, then conscious judgments will be better at taking those constraints into account. A natural question here is, Can these different modes of thought work together?

In their most recent studies, the UTT researchers have shown how the best decisions are made via a combination of conscious and unconscious processes, and in this order: *conscious first, then unconscious.* For example, you should first consciously eliminate any options that fail to meet the necessary criteria, such as too expensive or too small, too far away, and so on. Only then should you give the unconscious judgment process the options that pass the first test by doing something else and not thinking (consciously) about the choice for a while, and then seeing how you feel about it later.

Our ability to solve complex problems unconsciously, without the aid of conscious thought, makes sense from an evolutionary standpoint, given that we developed our conscious thinking abilities late in our human history. With this in mind, it would make sense if unconscious thought mechanisms worked better for those types of problems we were more likely to encounter "back in the day" of our ancient past, like judging the fair treatment of others or detecting who was harming others in a group. The ability to make such distinctions was key to harmonious social life and group solidarity. Researchers Jaap Ham and Kees van den Bos and their colleagues have applied the UTT idea to such problems as they might appear in modern life, for example, in judging guilt or innocence in a complex legal case, and judging the fairness of a company's hiring procedures.

We are born sensitive to violations of fair treatment and with the ability to detect those who are causing harm to others, and assign blame and responsibility to them. Recent research has shown that even children three to five years old are quite sensitive to fairness in social exchanges. They preferred to throw an extra prize (an eraser) away than to give more to one child than another—even when that extra prize could have gone to themselves. Of course, the two concerns, of guilt and fairness, are related.

Witness the huge public and media scrutiny paid a few years ago to the seemingly trivial matter of whether Tom Brady, the New England Patriots' quarterback, was involved in the slight deflation of the footballs in a conference championship game. As far as world or national problems are concerned, this was a very insignificant matter, yet it consumed the American public's attention and dominated the news cycle for weeks and even months afterward. We are still very much like our long-forgotten toddler selves who shout "Cheater!" when we see injustice in a game.

Ham and Van den Bos used the standard UTT study procedure, with an immediate three-minute conscious thought period, and a three-minute distraction (unconscious thought) period condition to see if we solve these problems unconsciously. Participants made fairness judgments about complex job application procedures. There were four application procedures described; one was objectively the most fair and another the most unfair, with the other two in between. In the fairest procedure, for example, the application process was clearly explained and all of the requested information on the application was read and considered in the hiring decision. In the least fair procedure, the application process was not very clearly described and only one of the four tests given applicants was used in the hiring decision. Participants were divided into the immediate, conscious, and unconscious decision conditions, and once again, those in the unconscious decision condition were the best at saying which of the procedures was the most fair.

In another study, participants were given the many details of an actual legal case in the Netherlands, a complicated affair in which an underage girl took a horse and carriage for a drive without the permission of their owner or her parents. Entirely coincidentally, a neighbor chose that exact moment to set off explosives to scare birds away from their crops. The explosion caused the horse to bolt, and this caused the animal to get hurt and the carriage to be damaged. It was a tricky case because there were many contributing factors, and several parties at fault. A binding arbitrator ruled that each of the four parties involved (the neighbor, the girl, her parents, the owner of the horse and carriage) was responsible in varying degrees for the damage that occurred, but the study participants didn't know this. They had to assign guilt and responsibility on their own.

After all the evidence was presented, one group of participants made their judgments immediately, another was allowed to think about their justice judgments for three minutes before giving them, and another performed a distractor task for three minutes and then gave their judgments. How closely a participant's judgments matched the arbitrator's actual judgment was the measure of judgment accuracy, and the important question was what degree of responsibility each party had. Again it was the participants in the unconscious decision-making condition who made the most accurate judgment about the legal case. This finding has clear practical importance, since jurors (in the United States, at least) are not allowed to take notes or have any technological assistance when making a judgment. Often court cases are complex; many different pieces of information must be taken into consideration, different pieces of evidence point in different directions, and there can be extenuating circumstances to take into account as well. Unconscious decision processes are better at combining and integrating all this complexity.

However, for complex financial decisions or any decision to which actual quantified data is relevant, it is obviously better to use computers and the relevant data than to rely on a period of attention-distracted, unconscious thought. The bestseller *Moneyball,* by Michael Lewis, showed how better decisions about drafting and trading professional baseball players could be made by relying less on the intuition of scouts and more on quantifiable aspects of the game, such as an outfielder's speed in tracking down a fly ball.

I'm a big baseball fan and have played what used to be called rotisserie baseball for nearly twenty years now. It was the original "fantasy" sports game, in which players assume the role of a professional team's general manager and draft a starting lineup for a particular sport. Today millions of people play these games in a daily format. I play the season-long version. It is highly competitive, and one of the most important parts of the season comes well before the actual baseball season starts—the day that you and your competitors draft your teams. Preparation is the key. Starting in January, we pore over the many published guides with facts and figures on all the major-league players.

Technological advances have greatly increased the kinds of objective information available about all the players and removed much of the "gut" or intuitive aspects from the game—the fantasy game as well as the real-life general manager's job. Major League Baseball has installed radar and other sensitive devices in its stadiums so that companies such as StatCast can measure things like how hard a ball is hit—its "exit velocity" in miles per hour leaving the bat. Pitchers' curveballs can be measured in terms of number of spins per second. And although the fantasy leagues typically don't use it, there is plenty of data gathered on defensive plays, such as the speed of an outfielder in tracking a fly ball, and the efficiency of the route he took to catch it. In addition to this new data about players' performance, there are new ways of looking at the traditional kinds of data collected, such as fly ball rate, hard-contact rate, and percentage of hits after the ball is put in play (that is, not striking out), in order to develop more accurate indexes of a player's abilities in isolation from his teammates' performance, and also in isolation from the luck factor. (For example, a higher than average batting average on balls put into play on the field is usually just good luck, and can be expected to regress to the league average over time, predicting a lower batting average for that player in the near future.)

In the old days, before all of this technology and sophisticated data analysis, baseball teams relied on scouts—usually older scouts with much experience and a good "eye" for players. Successful scouts relied on cues that over the years had predicted major-league success. Scouting was an art form in many ways, because the scouts were relying in large part on their intuition, their fast and uncanny ability to appraise talent based often on little things that the untrained eye would never notice. The sound of the bat hitting the ball was often mentioned by scouts—a certain kind of *crack!* that signaled solid contact. Or, for pitchers, the *pop!* of the ball when it hits the catcher's mitt.

The scouts weren't "guessing," however. They would not have been successful for so many years if they were. They were able to pick up the important cues and put them together well. Their success at scouting was evident in their ability to predict which young players would become stars and which would not—the successful scouts had a better track record than the less successful ones. But the intuitive nature of their personal appraisal process made it difficult for them to justify or explain their gut reactions to younger, less experienced personnel. It was their years of experience, years of close observation, that gave them their expertise. In part, they were taking advantage of what modern cognitive science calls "statistical learning"—our ability, after a good deal of experience, to detect regularities in the world, to pick up reliable patterns and sequences to determine what predicts what—without necessarily being able to explain or even being aware what those predictors or patterns are. This comes naturally from close observation—keeping both the eyes and mind open—over extended periods of time.

When I am deciding which car to buy, I go to *Consumer Reports* and other relevant websites to gather reliable information about miles per gallon, how much service a car needs, and features necessary for where we live, such as good handling under icy road conditions and high clearance because of all the snow in the winter. But not all of life's important choices come with reliably measured data on the critical factors. In most aspects of our daily lives, we hardly have reliable data to use to make the best choices and decisions. Take Joe, for example. He is single and moving to a new town and wants to start dating—there are no *Consumer Reports* articles for that. Or for which career he is most suited and would find most fulfilling, whether he should live downtown or in the suburbs, or which of several suits or pairs of shoes he should buy. He may be able to get some objective information to help him make his decisions, but hardly a complete set of reliable data on each relevant feature or dimension. Few of our real-life choices come with the accurately measured, objective evidence, and tried-and-true predictive algorithms that investment bankers, and now baseball general managers use when deciding which stock to buy or which young baseball prospect to draft. (And even in those cases, prediction is far from perfect.)

The Unconscious Thought Theory research supports the fundamental point that evolution shaped our minds so that unconscious judgment processes produced reasonably accurate guidance for our behavior, especially for the millions of years before we had computers, algorithms, and spreadsheets (and baseball). So we come to **Rule #3: When you are faced with a complex decision involving many factors, and especially when you don't have objective measurements (reliable data) of those important factors, take your gut feelings seriously.** See how you feel after a period of distraction doing something very attention-demanding to get your (conscious) mind off the decision. Or sleep on it, because the unconscious never sleeps, as we'll see in Chapter 9.

There is one more important factor influencing our immediate gut reactions—our current goals and motivations—and that's the topic of Chapter 8. How we feel about the people we know, and the basics of our life such as food, cigarettes, and alcohol, can change dramatically depending on whether they help or hinder what we are trying to accomplish. There are studies that show, for example, that we tend to form new friendships with those who will help us reach our personal goals, and that we are less likely to become friends with people who are very similar but who would not help us reach those goals. Who we list as our best friends in our lives changes depending on what our current goal is. Smokers who want to stop smoking but haven't had a cigarette in many hours show implicit or automatic positive evaluations of cigarette-related items, such as an ashtray, but negative unconscious evaluations of those same items if they've just smoked and no longer have that need or craving.

Goals *change* the gut. Goals have a tremendous influence on our spontaneous appraisal of anything that is relevant to their pursuit; we have positive feelings toward something that helps us attain a goal and negative feelings toward things that do not. Like Seinfeld said, we are cheering for the clothes. A hated "dirty player" traded to our own team suddenly becomes a "wily veteran" who will do anything to help his team win. What was negative is now spun in a positive way—the gut feelings drive how the same behavior, the identical information, is spun. When we really crave a cigarette our gut says they are good (so good!); yet after we've had one and regret doing so, our gut reaction is that they are so bad (evil even). Your current goal changes your gut, and very often you aren't aware of the reason for those strong immediate reactions. This brings us to **Rule #4 for when you can trust your gut: Be careful what you wish for**, because your current goals and needs will color what you want and like in the present.

Rules for When to Trust Your Gut: 5–7

So far we have focused on our gut feelings about important choices and decisions we've been mulling over. But what about our initial, immediate gut reactions to entities we encounter, especially to people we meet? Can we trust these gut instincts?

Gut instincts are something all of us experience—without understanding how they function. In the 1980s, scientists finally began looking closely at the mechanics of intuition, and two decades later, pop culture followed, most notably in the form of Malcolm Gladwell's *Blink: The Power of Thinking Without Thinking*. The underlying premise of his book is that our first thought is usually our best thought, or that "blink" reactions—which don't require conscious reflection—are more reliable and useful than ones that arise from self-questioning and rumination. As we'll see, this is true, but only up to a point. Gladwell closed his book with a case where going with your gut was the wrong thing to do, the tragic story of Amadou Diallo, a victim of racial profiling who was shot dead by police in the South Bronx in a hail of bullets while entering his own apartment building unarmed. He was holding up his wallet to show police he had ID to prove he lived there, and in the dark night the police said they mistook the wallet in his hand for a gun. Diallo was black. Would the cops have mistaken the wallet for a gun if he had been white? For that matter, would they have even thought he was breaking into the apartment building in the first place? Such were the questions immediately raised in the public outcry that ensued.

One of the most important reasons the unconscious evolved was for "appraisal," in particular to evaluate other people. As we saw in the previous chapter, we evolved to make snap judgments and educated hunches about people and situations, to determine whether we should stay or go. Sometimes these instantaneous appraisals go very right, and sometimes they can go very wrong. When deciding whether we should trust someone or not, one important thing to keep in mind is that our modern world is quite different from the one in which our unconscious appraisal apparatus developed. Just as with unconscious decision-making, the more a current situation resembles the conditions we faced in our ancestral world, the more accurate a guide our gut will be. But if the situation differs—and there are indeed some very notable differences—our gut is more likely to lead us astray.

We have already seen how we quickly appraise others in terms of "us" versus "them." Even babies and young children have automatic, unconscious preferences for their own group and negative feelings for people in other social groups. In another one of our studies together, Mark Chen and I showed that subliminal presentation of smiling, attractive black faces (of models taken from popular magazines, but who were not famous) in the first part of the experiment caused greater hostility in white participants in the second part of the experiment—subliminal presentation of white faces did not. (Indeed, the officers involved in the Diallo episode certainly responded to an unarmed black man with a lot of hostility.)

As we've seen, our hardwired us-versus-them tendencies can even lead to attempted murder among rival baseball fans. While this kind of tribe-versus-tribe gut reaction was very helpful back in Ötzti's time, it is much less helpful today, in a world where people of various races and cultures mingle together in the same town or city. Unfortunately, it will be a long time before our innate wiring catches up with these seismic cultural shifts.

So this gives us another answer to the question of when can we trust our gut, which we will call **Rule #5: When our initial gut reaction to a person of a different race or ethnic group is negative, we should stifle it.** Our common negative initial gut reactions to people who are different from ourselves—and this can apply to religion or language as well as race and ethnicity—should not be trusted. These reactions are either a vestige of our evolutionary past, of Ötzti's time and earlier, or a product of our culture through very early socialization and the mass media, as we've already seen. Especially when it comes to people who are clearly different from us, we need to give people a chance, look beyond their superficial aspects, and base our appraisal of them on their actual behavior instead.

The experiment I did with Mark Chen with the subliminal black faces also points to a sixth answer to the trust-your-gut question, which we will call **Rule #6: We should not trust our appraisals of others based on their faces alone, or on photographs, before we've had any interaction with them.** This is for two reasons. First, the appraisal we make regarding static faces alone, as in photographs, is not diagnostic; it is not a valid predictor of that person's actual personality or behavior. Second, our unconscious reactions to people *after* we have had some experience with them, have seen them in action for even a little while, is a surprisingly *valid* predictor. As Mel Gibson's character in *Braveheart*, William Wallace, says to his troops facing an oncoming cavalry charge: "Wait for it . . . wait for it . . ." And it turns out that, like Mel's troops, we don't have to wait very long at all.

As we saw in Chapter 5, we clearly perceive several different and basic personality features directly from a person's face, in a photograph. This also happens when we first see someone in real life before even meeting her or seeing her interact with others. We read traits like competence and trustworthiness off a person's face with such confidence that a candidate's appearance in photographs can help determine the outcome of a political election. Even worse, studies in the courtroom have found that features of defendants' faces determine the likelihood of their being found guilty and the length of the jail sentences they receive. Recall that "baby-faced" adults are more likely to be found innocent, and defendants with more racially prototypic faces to receive harsher sentences. But we humans did not evolve to be able to read personality from static photographs, or from facial appearances alone. Rather, we evolved to be quite sensitive to a person's emotional expression—whether she looks sad, or disgusted, or panicky, for example—when she is *in action*, interacting with us or others. As Darwin was the first to point out, emotional expression is a more or less genuine marker of a person's internal emotional state that predicts, in turn, her likely behavior toward us. We can trust these expressions to give us accurate gut readings of a person's actual current state. However, the problem comes when we mistake a person's resting facial expression as an indicator of one of these short-term emotions.

You may have encountered an Internet video that went viral, called "Bitchy Resting Face," a parody of those ubiquitous pharmaceutical ads. The premise of the sketch was that there are women who aren't able to smile well and are perceived as bitchy or hostile. As cheesy, emotional music plays in the background, people who know women with Bitchy Resting Face tell how they've been hurt by women with this unpleasant facial expression. A man asks a woman to marry him, only to interpret her unintentional scowl as a rejection. A female customer insults a friendly clerk by sourly saying thanks. It's a hilarious concept, but also quite insightful. As one of the actors in the video says of women who suffer from Bitchy Resting Face, "They might not be bitchy at all." As we saw with Old Man Marley in *Home Alone* or my daughter's grade school librarian, appearances and first impressions based on faces alone can be, and are, deceiving.

Alexander Todorov, the Princeton scientist who showed how influential the faces of political candidates were to the outcome of elections, and his colleague Christopher Olivola, of University College London, looked into how accurate our fast personality assessments of a person are, based on their faces alone. Olivola and Todorov made use of an online website called "What's My Image?" on which people can post their own photographs and have other people rate their personalities, not knowing anything else about them. They were able to obtain data from more than one million appearance-based judgments—made by about nine hundred different people—as participants guessed about things such as: the pictured person's sexual orientation, whether they use drugs, if their parents are divorced, if they have ever been arrested or gotten into a fistfight, if they drink, if they're a virgin. The researchers could calculate how accurate these judgments were because the person posting the photograph provided the answers to these questions. And what they found was that the participants who saw the photographs actually produced *less* accurate predictions than did a separate group of participants who never saw the photographs, and instead just relied on how common or expected these behaviors were in general. If you had just guessed about a given person based only on how generally common it is to be heterosexual versus homosexual, a drug user, and so on, you would have done better than the one million responders who also had the photographs to go by. So from our eyes to our guts, things can go very wrong.

In a second study, more than 1,000 participants, recruited through a link on the *Scientific American* website, played a "Political Guessing Game," in which they guessed the political affiliation (Republican or Democrat) of each of nearly eight hundred political candidates, male and female, who ran in the 2002 and 2004 congressional elections—based just on photographs of the candidates' faces. The researchers varied the proportion of Democrats that a given participant saw, and told some of the participants beforehand what that proportion was, but again, seeing the photographs caused the participants to be less accurate overall than if they had just gone with the base rate proportion. When told that 30 percent of the photographs would be of Democrats, 3 out of every 10 photographs, the respondents thought they knew which were the Democrats better than they actually did, and going with their gut reaction to the face photographs decreased, rather than improved, their predictions.

But our intuition's dismal performance based on photographs is dramatically transformed, like a kissed frog into a prince, when it is based on the kind of information our evolutionary apparatus did have access to—a new person's *actual behavior.*

In 1992, Nalini Ambady and Robert Rosenthal coined an apt term to describe the brief input the unconscious uses to generate instinctual responses: *thin slices.* They were studying how accurately people could assess the abilities and personalities of others, based on just a fraction of that person's total behavior. For instance, you could sit in a classroom all day, all year, and then give your evaluation of the teacher's ability and performance. (That would be the whole ham.) Or you could sample an hour or so each of the five days of a given week. (That would be a nice fat slice of the ham.) Or you could push the edge of the envelope really far, as Ambady and Rosenthal did, and give people just a thirty-second video clip of the teacher in the classroom—nothing more. (That would be a thin slice of the ham, the kind you get piled high on a good deli sandwich.) Ambady and Rosenthal compared the assessments that people made based on that thin slice of thirty seconds to what experts said about that teacher based on hours of observation. And over many different studies of various occupations—teachers, therapists, CEOs—and abilities, they found that we are actually quite accurate, even with these thin slices, at assessing abilities and personalities, producing judgments not all that different from those of experts who have much more evidence at their disposal.

In one of their studies, Ambady and Rosenthal videotaped thirteen Harvard graduate fellows teaching classes, and spliced together three ten-second clips of each into a thirty-second reel that was a sort of sampler of their pedagogical prowess. Next, a group of participants watched the videos and rated how good the graduate fellows were as teachers according to thirteen categories. Then Ambady and Rosenthal waited until the end of the semester, when students in the fellows' classes filled out their usual end-of-course evaluations, and compared these "whole ham" ratings with the thin-slice ones from the experiment. Remarkably, they were highly correlated, showing a high degree of agreement between the thin-slice and whole-ham assessments. Ambady didn't stop there, though. She went on to make the slice even thinner—now we are talking 2nd Ave. or Katz's Deli thin—winnowing the video sampler down until it was just six fleeting seconds. Yet the participants seeing just this very short snippet of classroom performance still were able to accurately predict who the best teachers were in those semester-long classes. Ambady went on to produce other studies on thin slicing and found that humans can accurately assess other traits, such as sexual orientation, whether a CEO led a successful company, or if someone had a personality disorder. We are very lucky to have such an unconscious appraisal ability, and I have benefited firsthand from it.

After Christmas of 2012, I was in a McDonald's south of Indianapolis, just off the interstate, with my daughter Danielle. We were driving back east from a trip visiting family in Illinois, and I was a single parent at the time. It was getting to be lunchtime, so we pulled off to get gas and some lunch. Danielle, being six at the time, wanted a Happy Meal, so we went into the McDonald's next to the gas station. She was contentedly eating while playing with the coveted prize that she had found in the box with her hamburger and fries, when a younger child a few tables over from us started to cry, quite loudly, attracting the attention of most of us in that part of the restaurant. Danielle stopped playing and looked over at the child, too. Then she did something that I'll never forget. She picked up her toy, walked over to the crying child, and handed her the toy. The child looked at Danielle, took the proffered plastic toy, and immediately calmed down. It seemed as if the whole restaurant was watching this little scene unfold, and you can imagine how proud I was of my daughter. She came back over to our table, and all the other patrons went back to eating, except for one person.

That person came over to our table, apologized for interrupting us, and said she wanted to tell Danielle that what she had done to make the other child feel better was such a nice and generous thing to do. She was not speaking to me or looking at me, but from that "thin slice" of her behavior I felt I knew a great deal about her. Her kind words made both my daughter and me smile and we thanked her for coming over; after her order was ready at the counter she came back to sit down with us at our table. It turned out she was on her lunch break from a nearby hospital. We kept in touch until we were able to meet again during the summer, when my daughter and I made another driving trip to the Midwest, and the rest, as they say, is history—we were married a few years later. Now when all of us make the drive back to the Midwest we often pass that same McDonald's, which brings back memories of the day we met.

Not all first encounters with people are so positive, of course. How does our gut react to someone whose behavior shows we can't trust him? The answer: just like Dante thought it would. Yoona Kang, Jeremy Gray, Margaret Clark, and I conducted a neuroimaging study of the brain's immediate reactions to betrayal, back in 2011. In that study, the same insula brain region that became activated when the participant held something physically cold also became active when another participant betrayed them in an economics game, by greedily keeping all the money for themselves. That is a "cold" reaction based on actual experience with the person, and of course, because it is based on actual evidence about that person's trustworthiness, it should be trusted. And what is more, our brains also turn off the circuitry needed to produce mimicry responses (which signal bonding and friendship to the other person) when we encounter people who have shown by their behavior that they can't be trusted. In a study by Oriana Aragon, Michael Pineda, and myself, we measured the brain waves of participants while they played economics games with each other, and also while they watched each other's finger movements. Watching the other person's finger movements before the economics game caused the participants to immediately produce the brain waves associated with the start of the natural imitation process. However, after playing the economics game, if that other person had betrayed the participant—by keeping all the money for herself and not sharing any of it—then watching that other person's finger movements no longer produced those immediate brain waves associated with imitation (and bonding and friendship). **Rule #7 (it may be the most important one of all): You can trust your gut about other people—but only after you have seen them in action.**

Rules for When to Trust Your Gut: 8

Our instincts about other people evolved in quite different times, of course, eons before the advent of social media, so what about meeting people over the Internet? Social life on the Internet is like the Wild West of American history, uncharted, somewhat lawless, often dangerous, and constantly changing. Can we trust our gut when it comes to people we meet online? Can we know who someone really is before we meet him in person?

"Can you see the real me? Can you? Can you?" sings Roger Daltrey in one of my favorite songs by the Who, written long before the Internet was invented, much less something you carried in your pocket. We've always packaged ourselves for public consumption, putting our best foot forward and hiding or camouflaging our faults as best we can. And we do so today in spades. Anyone who has ever been on Facebook or Instagram or any other social media knows that people spend a great deal of time carefully presenting upgraded versions of themselves that project images of lives that appear more perfect than they are. Sometimes these public personas are outright fictions, as in the practice of "catfishing." Confiding our "real me," who we really are inside, to another person takes a lot of trust, because doing so makes us quite vulnerable, especially if some of those parts of the "real me" are looked down upon by society or those around us.

Back in the Stone Age of the Internet—meaning the 1990s—researchers in human communications and social psychologists started to study how this new electronic way of interacting with others was affecting social life. Katelyn McKenna was one of the pioneers. In one groundbreaking series of studies she went undercover, taking the role of "participant observer," gaining acceptance as a member of several electronic discussion boards, called newsgroups, covering a range of different topics. Back then it was not hard to participate in these anonymously, which enabled many people to join and participate in groups formed around topics that are called "stigmatized" interests. These could be political, like white supremacist groups, or sexual, such as cross-dressing or transvestism. But discussion groups also formed around more mundane specialized interests, like butterfly collecting, or Humphrey Bogart movies. People flocked to these forums because for many it was the first time they had found people who shared their interests. And especially for the stigmatized, socially frowned-upon interests—sexual proclivities such as cross-dressing or sadomasochism, political ones such as antigovernment militias or white supremacist groups—many of these people had spent their entire lives hiding that interest from not only their neighbors but in many cases also from their close friends and family, or even their spouse.

By infiltrating and participating in these groups, McKenna was able to gain the trust of the members. Then and only then, after many months and even years of participating, was she able to gather information from the members about how long they had been part of the group, how self-accepting they were of this interest—were they ashamed, okay with it, proud—and whether they had told their loved ones about it. She also kept track of whether the individuals actively participated in the group through posting and taking part in the electronic discussions, or "lurked" instead, just reading the other posts but not saying anything themselves.

What McKenna found was remarkable. In many cases, these newsgroup participants had been ashamed of or wanted desperately to keep their interest or behavior hidden. These were mainly older people—in their thirties, forties, or fifties—who had kept this part of themselves secret from others their entire lives. Many said that before they found that newsgroup, they had thought they were the only ones who had the interest. The truly remarkable effect of finding others with whom they could share their "real me" was that they came to no longer feel ashamed or bad about it. That first step of self-acceptance then, in many cases, led directly to their telling their close friends and family about it for the first time. Self-acceptance had to come first, but once that had happened, many people really wanted to come out and make that previously private part of themselves public. In some cases they did so after a lifetime, thirty or forty years, of keeping it a close secret.

I bring up McKenna's research to stress that being able to connect to the entire world of people enables us to find and interact with others who share very important aspects of ourselves, which we often would be unable to do in face-to-face, nondigital settings. Over social media we can develop relationships with people we might not have given a moment's notice to in real life. Over social media, those people can get by the "gating features," as we called them, such as attraction or the chronic features of their face, that we use to screen people in real-life, face-to-face encounters. These initial filters allow certain people past the gates but they block many others. Many potentially great romantic relationships don't get off the ground because of the importance we place on those gating features, mainly a person's physical attractiveness or general appearance. We should all keep in mind Nietzsche's advice to marry someone you can have conversations with, for most of your life together will be after the blush is off the rose.

Because many forms of social media (not all) enable us to bypass those gating features, then people who do not meet face-to-face, but instead through social media such as Internet discussion groups, email, blog sites, or chat rooms, might actually have just as stable and long-lasting relationships as those who meet in "real life." Back in the 1990s, there was a pungent stigma attached to meeting on the Internet and the common wisdom was that few of these relationships would survive a couple's first face-to-face encounter. But since then there has been a veritable explosion in online dating, and a recent national survey of nearly twenty thousand people who married between 2005 and 2012 found that fully 35 percent had first met online. About half of these people had met through online dating sites such as eHarmony and Match, the rest through their social networks (Facebook, Twitter), multiplayer game sites, chat rooms, or other online communities.

Social psychologist John Cacioppo and his colleagues, who collected and analyzed this data, reported that the couples who met online were, if anything, no more likely to have broken up than couples who had met in more traditional ways, and that they were just as satisfied in their marriages as well. Today, of course, unlike the Internet of the 1990s, you can see photos of the other person, as well as be "matched" on common interests (either by the dating platform or because you can read the content of their posts or are members of the same special interest group), so meeting online now has more gating features present than it used to. (Tinder, for example, is even more about initial attraction than are real-life encounters, involving quick yes-or-no, stay-or-go decisions based on photographs alone.) Still, meeting (and especially, getting to know) someone online can often afford you more important background information (values, political attitudes, and interests, for example) about a person than the traditional happenstance initial face-to-face meeting. And the emerging data on the quality and stability of Internet relationships is consistently disproving the initial (and somewhat snarky) skepticism of the 1990s regarding their likelihood of long-term success.

Don't get me wrong: attractiveness is important. It is a real feature of the person. As we've seen, attractive faces are a literal pleasure to look at; our brain's reward centers become active when we look at them. And, as we've seen, even babies prefer to look at attractive faces! It is just human nature to prefer attractive to unattractive people when it comes to close relationships. The problem comes when we use that attractiveness to make inaccurate assumptions about *other qualities* of the person. We tend to believe that what is beautiful is good and assume other good things, such as pleasant personality, competence, trustworthiness, when we see an attractive face. We have way too much confidence in these gut reactions based just on appearances. So that gives us **Rule #8: It is perfectly fine for attraction be one part of the romantic equation, but not so fine to let it be the only, or even the main, thing.** Not in the long run, anyway.

Our gut reactions served us well for many thousands, perhaps millions of years. If they had been misleading or counterproductive they would have been weeded out by natural selection. But our modern life is very different from what life was like over those thousands and millions of years. People of different races, who are different from our family and neighbors, are no longer enemies who can't be trusted. Modern technologies such as photographs of faces can fool our gut appraisal mechanisms that were developed instead for observing people in action, in the context of how they treat us and the others around us. Our gut reactions can be quite sophisticated at combining lots of information, and should be taken seriously, but here too we need to adjust for the conditions of modern life and make use of reliable data, if we have it, and the powerful ways of analyzing it now available, especially for important choices and decisions.

Today even experts disagree on whether intuitions are accurate, and whether we can trust our gut. Those who say we can't tend to study complex financial and business decisions, made with little or no time pressure, and based on reliable data, with powerful computers and software to analyze it. Those who say we can trust our instincts tend to be psychologists or evolutionary scientists, who study the mundane realities of daily life, where often we are under time pressure to make decisions and lack any relevant quantitative measures. So then, certainly, listen to what your gut, or heart, or other internal organ (including your brain) is telling you, take it seriously and don't dismiss it out of hand, but also *check your work*, and always remember to give the other person a chance.

CHAPTER 7

What You See
Is What You Do

In the early 1980s, while I was getting used to life in New York City and psychologists around the world were beginning to pay more attention to unconscious mechanisms, a neurologist at Salpêtrière Hospital in Paris was treating two older patients who had recently suffered strokes. The doctor's name was François Lhermitte. He was round-headed, balding, wore glasses, and sported a tie beneath his white lab coat—the image of medical expertise at the domed, four-hundred-year-old hospital where he worked. His patients, a man and a woman, were both acting strangely, and in the same way. Their behavior seemed to be entirely driven by cues in their environment, as if they no longer had independent control over what they did. "An excessive control of behavior by external stimuli at the expense of behavioral autonomy" is how Lhermitte described it. Naturally curious about what he might learn from their odd openness to outside influence, he decided to expose them to a variety of everyday contexts and observe what might happen.

Lhermitte started simply. Filling two glasses with water, he set them down in front of the patients, who promptly drank them right down. Nothing unusual there, of course. Except Lhermitte kept filling the glasses, and the patients kept drinking them all right down, glass after glass, even while complaining about being painfully full. They could not help but drink the full glasses of water placed in front of them. On a different occasion, the doctor took the man to his home, an apartment. He led the man out onto his balcony, which overlooked a nearby park, and they admired the view together. Right before reentering the apartment, Lhermitte softly

178

said "museum," and when back inside the patient proceeded to scrutinize the paintings and posters on the walls with great interest, also lavishing his attention on common objects that sat on the tables—plates and cups with little aesthetic interest—as if they too were actual works of art. On next being shown the bedroom, the man looked at the bed, proceeded to undress, and got into it. Soon he was asleep.

What was going on here? It certainly didn't seem like these two previously normal individuals were acting with conscious intent. As Lhermitte and other early neural psychologists knew (before brain scanning technology was invented), stroke victims often provide fascinating opportunities to understand the hidden operations of the mind, to part the curtain of behavior and peek into the backstage of its causes. The problems that people outwardly manifested after their strokes—in speech, vision, emotion, or memory—were important clues about the function and purpose of the region of the brain that had been damaged. So what did his two patients' bewildering suggestibility, a kind of blind obedience to their environment, reveal?

Lhermitte continued his experiments in new locales around Paris that seemed to bring out his two patients' bold and industrious nature. On the paths of the Tuileries Gardens, near the Louvre, they came across some gardening equipment: a watering hose and some rakes. Sure enough, both the man and woman grabbed the implements and spontaneously went to work, raking and watering, as if they themselves were gardeners. Despite their advanced years, they went on like this for hours, until the good doctor finally stopped them. On another occasion, in his medical office, the woman gave Lhermitte a physical exam, or at least her idea of what a medical exam was like. She went so far as ask him to lower his trousers for an injection, and, good sport that he was, Dr. Lhermitte complied (and even included a photograph of the scene when he published this research). Later, when he questioned them about their behavior, neither patient seemed to notice or find anything unusual or strange about it. They appeared unconsciously compelled by the naturally occurring primes in their environment, yet they had no trouble consciously justifying all these activities—their water-chugging, art appreciation, gardening, and practicing medicine without a license. Their strokes had fundamentally changed the nature of their behavior. The brain's fine-tuned responses learned in the past—or guided by the future, in relation to any plans or goals they might have had—had been replaced by a hypersensitivity to the present, and seemingly *only* the present.

Eventually, Lhermitte's two helplessly whimsical and hardworking stroke patients passed away. Careful examination of their brains revealed their strokes had damaged or destroyed the same location in both patients—areas of their prefrontal cortex that are critical for the planning and control of action. The patients were able to receive cues to behavior coming in from their environment through their five senses, but they lacked the complementary brain region that exerted intentional control over these impulses and their subsequent behavior. We more fortunate individuals have both of these, of course, but before Lhermitte's discovery (and Gazzaniga's, described earlier, at about the same time), scientists were only aware of the intentional control component. Lhermitte showed that we also have this second influence over our behavior, the outside environment, which suggests actions that are typical and appropriate for our current situation; without the conscious control component in place, those environmental cues can run the show all by themselves, with no conscious input or control necessary (but highly desirable, of course). Lhermitte humbly called this "environmental dependency syndrome," but it soon became more widely known in his honor as "Lhermitte's syndrome."

With the aid of brain imaging scanners that Lhermitte did not have in the 1980s, neuroscience research has subsequently confirmed his conclusions. A major review by neuroscientist Chris Frith and his colleagues at University College London concluded that our brains store our current behavioral intentions in the prefrontal and premotor cortex areas, but the areas that are actually used to guide that behavior are in an anatomically separate part of the brain, the parietal cortex. This discovery helps to explain how priming and other unconscious influences can affect our behavior, and how Lhermitte's patients could have been so influenced by their environments without having any intentional control over those influences. Priming and outside influences on our behavior can activate the guiding behavior in one part of the brain independent of the intention to perform that behavior, which is located somewhere else entirely.

Lhermitte's stroke patients were certainly behaving without consciously choosing or controlling their behavior, showing that the act of conscious choice is not necessary to produce sophisticated patterns of action. Rather, it seems that William James had it right (writing in 1890, he was remarkably prescient about many things) when, in his famous chapter on "The Will," he argued that our behavior actually springs from unconscious and unintentional sources, including behaviors appropriate to and suggested by what we are currently seeing and experiencing in our world. Our conscious acts of will, James said, are acts of control over these unconscious impulses, allowing some through but not others. The "control center" was exactly the part of the brain that was found damaged in Lhermitte's stroke patients. Every human mind, then, is a kind of mirror, generating potential behaviors that reflect back the situations and environments in which we find ourselves—a glass of water says "drink me," flower beds say "tend me," beds say "sleep in me," museums say "admire me." We are all programmed this way, to react to these external stimuli as much as Lhermitte's patients did. Before you know it, what you see is what you do.

Now, thirty years after the French doctor published his important observations, modern neuroscience has made remarkable advances in our knowledge of the brain and of the specializations of different brain regions, and how they interact with each other. Further research confirmed that, indeed, Lhermitte's patients were simply exhibiting in their behavior *uninhibited* unconscious impulses to action that all of us have. Fortunately for the rest of us, who have intact behavior control systems, we have those other operations in the brain, the *will* that William James described, which serves as a gatekeeper or filter on those constant impulses. So what does it mean that, deep down in our brains, we are always involuntarily generating responses that mirror not only what's directly going on around us, but also what's implied by the situation or context in which we find ourselves? At first glance, it might seem that we are mindless automatons, pack animals, following the rest of the herd. Aren't we, you might wonder, singular beings whose minds only express our unique nature as we think, talk, and do? Yes, and no—but with a lot more no.

We are much more like Lhermitte's patients than we realize or perhaps care to admit. Our hidden impulses shape how we act in the present in extensive and powerful ways. The behavior and emotions of others are contagious to us, not only when we witness them directly and in person, but even when we read about them, or see signs of them after the fact (that is, their visible consequences). The "suggestions" for how to act that come from what we are perceiving at the moment extend beyond the physical actions of others that we might unconsciously imitate, to rather complex and abstract forms of behavior that we have learned are appropriate for our particular environment (what people generally do when in a garden, a museum, or a bedroom). Subtle cues that drive us to behave both nobly and badly are continuously coming in through our senses to influence our mind as it navigates the present. And like Lhermitte's patients, we are unaware of these influences and so believe that we are acting autonomously.

The Chameleon Effect

We pay a lot of attention to the other people around us. Constantly, every day, we perceive other people doing things: their gestures or mannerisms, postures and emotional expressions, their tone of voice and speaking volume, and the content of what they say or write or post on social media. And what we see and hear has the natural effect of causing us to be more likely to do the same things ourselves—to *unconsciously* imitate them. We are not consciously aware of intending to do so. (As Darwin said was true of our emotional expressions, so too can we mimic and imitate intentionally as well as unintentionally, but mostly we do so without realizing it.) This adaptive tendency is not unique to humans, of course. We've all marveled at how schools of fish, and flocks of birds, seem to move as one, in unison. This does not happen because Fred Bird looks over at Susie Bird and decides, Hey, Susie is going that way, I think I will too! The movements are too fast and the synchrony too perfect to depend on a bunch of birdbrained intentional choices. Rather, the effect must be based on a hardwired connection between perception and behavior, an immediate impulse to action driven by the perception of the other birds' motion and direction. We humans have that same hardwired connection, the *perception-action link*; it's just that we have more intentional control over it if we become aware of its influence. In the late 1990s, I set out with my students to better understand this relatively unplumbed depth of the mind. We wanted to see whether people mimicked each other unintentionally, without meaning to or trying to.

In our experiment design, we strove to create a situation in which participants would not be focused on each other or on trying to make friends, since it was known that people intentionally mimic each other more when they are trying to establish a relationship. Would imitation and mimicry occur even without this motivation? Would the mimicry follow from merely seeing what the other person was doing? To test this in our lab at NYU, Tanya Chartrand and I told the unsuspecting participants that we were developing a new kind of projective personality test, like the old Rorschach test but with photographs instead of inkblots. They would just pick up a photograph from a stack on the table between them and say whatever came to mind when they looked at it. We wanted their interaction to be about each other as little as possible, and so we focused them instead on the photographs on the table.

Now, only one of the people at the table was an actual participant; the other was part of our experimental team, a confederate who exhibited one of two types of behaviors while working on the photograph task. We had two of these confederates, and the participant worked on the photographs with first one, then the other. The key was that one of the confederates posing as another participant would, by design, cross her legs and shake one of her feet in a kind of nervous manner. The other one would not shake her foot at all, but would touch her own head and face with her hand, tug her ear, rest her face in her hand, kind of like the famous Rodin sculpture, *The Thinker*. So the real participant and the first confederate took turns talking about the photographs, and after a while, we broke them up and the participant went into another room and did the same task with the second confederate. We predicted that the participants would act like human chameleons, changing their own behavior to match that of the person they were with, just as a real chameleon changes its color and spots to match the background of wherever it happens to be at the moment.

We secretly videotaped each of these interactions so that we could later measure how much face-touching and foot-shaking the actual participants did in each situation. The videotapes revealed that the participants indeed copied the behavior of the person they were with, and changed that behavior when moving on to be with a different person. They touched their faces and didn't shake their feet when with the face-touching confederate, and then they stopped touching their faces and shook their feet more when with the foot-shaking confederate. When questioned after the study, they showed no awareness of having imitated the two confederates during the experiment. The mirroring was entirely automatic and involuntary.

Examples of this *chameleon effect* abound in the world. All you have to do is look around. In fact, after our study was published, a CNN news crew that was doing a report on it went around New York's Central Park filming pairs and groups of people sitting on park benches, standing talking to each other, or walking in step—countless real-world examples of people unconsciously mimicking each other. The producer told us they had no trouble at all finding examples of the effect to film for their report.

So why do we have this link between what we see and what we do? The answer lies in our past and in our genes. Infants and babies imitate and mimic others just like adults do (even more so, in fact); it is not something we have to learn how to do, or try to do. If it is an innate tendency we are born with, then it most probably served us well over evolutionary time, producing adaptive advantages that aided our survival as a species. One benefit, concluded Andrew Meltzoff, one of the pioneers of research on imitation and mimicry in infants, is that young children learn much about how to react and behave in various situations just by imitating fellow children and their adult caretakers. Infants are wide open to such imitative tendencies because they haven't yet developed the ability to control those impulses (which starts around age three or four). In this way, they are much like Lhermitte's patients, with just the primitive imitative responses spurred by their surroundings (as well as internal impulses from being hungry or having gas), but not the ability to suppress or inhibit them. But what exactly is happening neurologically?

It turns out that our brains are wired to take in different streams of information from the eyes: one for purposes of understanding and knowing, and the other for the purpose of behaving appropriately. The first stream flows more or less into a conscious estuary, and the second one into a more automatic, unconscious one. These two visual streams were discovered in the 1990s by the neuropsychologists David Milner and Melvyn Goodale. Each stream comes out of the retina and then heads for the primary visual cortex of the brain for further analysis. One stream then goes to brain regions responsible for our *knowing*, such as identifying an object, and supplies the kind of information we use to answer questions about it. The other stream goes directly to a region responsible for *doing*, for how we respond. This *doing* stream of visual information operates mainly outside of conscious awareness, while the one for understanding and recognizing is normally accessible to consciousness.

Again, this discovery comes thanks to stroke patients who willingly allow themselves to be studied and thereby advance our understanding of brain regions and functions. Milner and Goodale noticed that a stroke patient who had brain damage in one small area could not tell correctly what it was that a researcher was holding (say, a book), but could nonetheless orient his hand correctly to take it (vertically or horizontally) when casually handed the object. But other patients could say correctly what the researcher was holding up, and yet were not able to orient their hands correctly when the object was passed to them. It turned out that different regions of the brain had been damaged in the two cases; damage in one region blocked the "knowing" visual stream but left the "doing" stream intact, while damage to the other region blocked the "doing" visual stream but left "knowing" intact. We are literally born mimics.

As a result of our neural structure, though, when we mimic, we usually don't know it. Information we perceive from another person's actions can affect our "doing" tendency separately from our knowing about it (and our conscious minds are usually focused on other things). The chameleon effect—together with Milner and Goodale's discovery of the two visual streams, and Lhermitte's discovery of environmental dependency syndrome—shows that *seeing* can lead directly to *doing* in the absence of *knowing*. Our brains and minds evolved not only to think and know, but especially to act, and to act quickly if need be. But besides supporting us in our infancy and toddlerhood as we learn how to behave appropriately—a huge benefit in itself, to be sure—what other beneficial consequences does the chameleon effect produce? The answer has many layers, but first and foremost it greatly helps us to collaborate and cooperate with each other.

The mirroring that we engage in is a form of social glue. It holds two or more people together. Unconscious mimicry promotes bonding. My lab saw this in action in a second study we did after the first "chameleon" one. We reversed the roles of the first study, and had the confederate try to mimic, in a subtle fashion, the body posture and body movements of the research participant while they both discussed the photographs on the table between them. In the control condition, the confederate did not try to mimic the participant. Afterward, the confederate left the room and we asked the participant various questions about the experiment, including how much they liked the other participant (actually the confederate) and how smoothly they felt their interaction had gone. If they had been in the condition in which the confederate had mimicked them while they discussed the photos together, the participants liked the confederate more, and also thought their interaction had gone more smoothly, compared to in the no-mimicry condition. When someone acts similarly to us, even in a subtle way, we pick it up and like the person more, and feel more of a bond with them; also, our interaction with them goes more smoothly, our actions seeming more coordinated and in synch. Our natural tendency to do what others are doing in the moment pays off in greater feelings of togetherness and friendliness. And, just like with Dante and his poetic coldness, this effect of behavioral synchrony and bonding is apparently something human cultures have been aware of for thousands of years—unconsciously, of course.

For millennia, we have known about the bonding force of ritualized behavior, when everyone does the same thing at the same time. For most of recorded time, military bands and drummers have marched with armies to keep them in step. The Romans dragged a band along with them while conquering Europe around 200 BC. Soldiers not only marched to the rhythm of the band's music but frequently used rousing songs to sustain them over long marches for days, weeks, and sometimes months. (During World War I, Belgian citizens were quoted as saying one of the worst parts of the German occupation of their country was having to listen to the soldiers' constant singing.) While military units no longer march into battle with their bands, there are still many aspects of public life that we perform in unison. In religious services, for example, we often stand, kneel, and sing or chant at the same time, in unison. Likewise, we all stand and sing our national anthem in unison before sporting events—secular religious events if there ever were any—in part to remind us that while we may cheer for different teams (and uniforms), we are all part of the same national community. We can even use the unconscious power of mimicry and affiliation to change the behaviors of others, including criminals from whom we need to extract information. By exploiting our unconscious urge to identify with others, law enforcement officials may be able to open new, noncoercive avenues for solving crimes. That is, if they so choose.

Unfortunately, the traditional and still most common approach of interrogators has been to create the exact opposite type of atmosphere—to threaten, bully, and even torture suspects in order to get important information out of them. One of the first things you see when taking a tour of the Tower of London, right inside the central "Bloody Tower," where enemies of the state were taken, is the rack on which prisoners were interrogated while their bones were slowly pulled apart and their bodies broken. And still today, five hundred years later, similar torture occurs.

In October 2002, a man named Abu Zubaydah was being held in a CIA "black site" detention center in Thailand. (Two months earlier, he had been captured in Pakistan by covert American forces. He was shot in the ensuing skirmish, then medical personnel tended to his wounds to ensure that he survived.) The CIA believed—erroneously—that he was a high-level Al Qaeda operative who possessed valuable information about 9/11, Osama bin Laden, and terrorist training camps in Afghanistan. To get this information, interrogators used what the government euphemistically called "enhanced interrogation techniques" to force the prisoner into a submissive, willing state. The CIA's enhanced technique was waterboarding—and they subjected Zubaydah to this medievally cruel practice on a staggering *eighty-three occasions*. It's painful even to imagine what his experience was like, but it's an important exercise to do so.

Likely already in an exhausted fragile state—Zubaydah had also somehow lost an eye since being detained—he would have felt interrogators fix his body to an inclined board, but he wouldn't have seen what happened next, since they put a piece of fabric over his face. Then his captors poured water through the fabric and into his mouth. This created a drowning sensation, as well as an accompanying state of physiological panic. Between Zubaydah's gasps and chokes, the CIA agents asked for information, then went on to pour more water over the fabric and into his mouth. The sounds were surely horrendous—gurgling, gasping, choking, moans. Then the agents increased the amount of water, blocking his airway until his body seized violently. After what must have seemed an eternity, Zubaydah would feel the board tilt up, allowing him to breathe again. Then came more demands for information that he didn't have. But the inhumane treatment he received didn't stop there.

In a truly upsetting 2016 article, the scholar Rebecca Gordon studied Zubaydah's case from its sinister beginning to its outrageous lack of an end.

Not only was he waterboarded; he was also deprived of sleep for days on end, slammed repeatedly against a supposedly soft wall, and forced to listen to loud sounds for psychosis-inducing lengths of time. The trauma of 9/11 had spurred the forces of the United States to inflict deep trauma on others in the name of what they believed was a higher cause. The ends justified the means, in their view. President George W. Bush used the information that they extracted from Zubaydah to justify the invasion of Iraq, and to justify the "enhanced techniques"—torture—used upon countless other prisoners during the so-called War on Terror. Except, as they later admitted, the information they got from Zubaydah using these methods was totally worthless. Everything about the interrogation approach was wrong.

We still live in a world in which terrorists kill innocent people, and in which the United States and other governments use various tactics to get information from people they detain, many of which continue to be quite inhumane. That's the (very) bad news. The good news is that new work by forensic scientists in the field of criminal justice has focused on the unconscious psychology of mimicry and imitation, and has begun to offer an alternative and much less cruel paradigm for how authorities conduct interrogations and extract information from suspects and enemies. This new approach, they report, also gains more valid and reliable information from the person being questioned than do the hard-line traditional methods, in which the suspect tends to tell the officials anything they want to hear, just to stop the unbearable pain and distress. Imitation and mimicry signal similarity, that I share your feelings and reactions to what is going on right now. It strengthens bonding and creates rapport between former strangers. As used in rituals by large social groups for thousands of years, it facilitates sharing and cooperation. So one would think that a good way to get someone who is uncooperative to be cooperative would be to try to establish rapport with them.

Mark Frank and his colleagues at the University of Buffalo looked at how that approach might play out in the arena of crime investigation and criminal interrogation. Cooperative witnesses are the primary sources of information for investigations. If a positive feeling is established between the person being questioned and the person asking the questions, the suspect or witness is more likely to cooperate. And if he is more cooperative, then he is more likely to provide valid and valuable information. Frank and his team conducted a study of the effect of such rapport on the accuracy and completeness of eyewitness reports. They used a video of a real-life event that all the participants saw, one time only, just as a real witness would see a key event only once. It was a vivid, minute-long color video in which a male bystander suddenly ran and dove into a burning car (apparently committing suicide), with agitated sounds from off-screen bystanders, and fire trucks arriving at the end. Then the participants were interviewed using one of three styles: either sympathetically to establish rapport, abruptly and coldly, or with the standard neutrality in which most law enforcement officials are trained.

In the first group, good rapport was established by the interviewer using a more relaxed body posture, a gentler tone, and referring to the participant by name. In the second group, the second style was employed—a harsher, staccato rhythm, stiff body posture, and the interviewer didn't refer to the participant by name. Then there was the traditional, neutral group. The results showed that being nice works.

Participants in the rapport condition talked longer and provided considerably more (50 percent more) correct bits of information about what happened in the tape than did the other groups. A mere five minutes of rapport building paid off in a significant gain in accurate information from the witness.

While that first study didn't specifically use imitation or mimicry to create the rapport, Frank's next one, with Paul Ekman and John D. Yarbrough, did just that. They developed what is called the IIE, "Improving Interpersonal Evaluations," for law enforcement and national security. The basic premise of the IIE is that good, effective interviewers create a more comfortable environment by building rapport with a subject. One technique they use to facilitate rapport is mimicry, in which the interviewer tries to match the behaviors of the interviewee. This involves the same kinds of behaviors that Chartrand and I had manipulated in our original chameleon studies—seating posture, resting a hand on the chin. Frank and his team added vernacular mimicry, the use of the same level of vocabulary as the witness. The stated goal of using mimicry in this interrogation technique is to establish synchrony of behavior between the interviewer and interviewee, because synchrony (as in group rituals) causes increased bonding and feelings of liking, which in turn lead to a sense of trust and to cooperation—a rapidly manufactured glue between two people. In fact, the instructions on using the IIE technique explicitly suggest periodically testing whether rapport remains established, by adjusting one's own position deliberately to see if the person being questioned follows suit (mimics back). The IIE is now widely used in the training of law enforcement officers because it is a proven improvement over traditional questioning techniques.

Interrogators are certainly not the only ones who are (or could be) making use of the positive effects of mimicry. In one Dutch study, waitresses were instructed either to repeat back their customers' orders (the mimicry condition) or not, without knowing why they were doing so (they did not know what the study was about). Those who mimicked the order back to the customer received significantly larger tips than those who didn't—the mimicry apparently increased the liking and bond between the waitress and customer and the more positive experience resulted in a bigger tip at the end. And in a study conducted in the home electronics section of a large French department store, four twenty-something male salesclerks took turns mimicking or not their customers' questions about the various MP3 players for sale. Which customers were mimicked and which were not was determined randomly. For example, "Can you help me choose an MP3 player for my grandson?" "Hello, yes, of course. *I can help you choose an MP3 player for your grandson.* How old is he?" These customers were later approached in the store parking lot and were asked to rate their store experience and liking for the clerk who helped them. They were also asked whether or not they had actually purchased the MP3 player. Nearly 80 percent had bought a player if they had been mimicked, compared to 62 percent of those who had not been mimicked; moreover, there was greater liking for the clerk and for the store itself in the mimicry than in the no-mimicry condition. These field studies demonstrate the power of mimicry in liking and bonding in our daily lives.

Contagious Behaviors

If what we see is what we do, then it follows that the more we see a certain person in our daily lives, the more opportunities we will have to do what they do. And who do we typically see more than anyone else? Our life partners.

Another consequence of our chameleonic nature has a fascinating physical effect in the context of long-term romantic relationships. Think of your typical middle-aged or elderly couple who has been married for twenty-five or thirty years or more. They see each other every day, they talk with each other, and they are constant witnesses, consciously or unconsciously, to each other's facial expressions and emotional reactions. If your partner is mainly smiling and happy, you likely will be, too; if they are sad and downcast, you will be more likely to be that way, too. As the two of you spend your lives together, you are unconsciously mimicking your loved one on a daily, even moment-to-moment basis. As a result, over the decades you will tend to use the same facial muscles in the same ways, sharing each other's emotions and expressions, so that eventually over many years you will come to develop the same muscle and line patterns on your face. In other words, in theory you should actually start to look more like each other, the longer you are together. But do you?

To test this prediction, my graduate school advisor Bob Zajonc and his colleagues at the University of Michigan analyzed photos of newlyweds—individual photos of each, not those showing them together as a couple—and then they analyzed photos of the same group of people after twenty-five years of marriage. The individual photos were paired both with the spouse's picture but also with pictures of strangers of the same age, and their similarities were rated by a group of people who did not know any of the subjects or that any of them were married to each other. The raters judged that members of a couple looked more alike than two people who were strangers to each other. But more important, the couple was rated as looking more alike after twenty-five years of marriage than when they had married. And consistent with the explanation that they looked more alike, they were happier because they paid more attention to each other and shared the same emotional reactions to their many life events. In addition, the more the two members of a couple were rated as looking alike, the happier the couple reported themselves as being. I tell the students in my classes to be careful who they marry, because they will end up looking like them! Imitation isn't just the highest form of flattery—it's a love potion, too.

However, our imitation and mimicry hardwiring does not cause us to reflexively trust and cooperate with just anyone. For example, what if a person has shown by her behavior that you can't trust her? Recall from Chapter 6 the study led by Oriana Aragon, in which the brain waves of participants were measured while they observed the finger movements of another person. The particular brain waves we measured were part of what is called the mirror neuron system, which is one of the brain's very first responses to our perception of other people's behaviors, and helps produce the tendency to make (mirror) those same movements. We found that this system normally became active when the participant observed the finger movements of another person, but it did not become active—this very first, immediate stage of imitation—when the participant watched the movements of someone who had just betrayed her in an economics game. Our brain's imitation mechanism is sensitive to who can and who cannot be trusted, and this happens on a level of which we aren't even aware. After all, it wasn't that the participant *chose* not to imitate that deceitful person. Rather, the unconscious machinery supporting that imitation shut down so early, the participant didn't even have a chance to do so.

We all want to have positive social relationships and to not be alone or isolated. But life doesn't always go the way we'd like it to, and in the school of hard knocks, sometimes we are excluded or rejected by others, like the poor kid on the playground at recess whom no one picks for their team. Or, as adults, when a group leaves after work to go get a drink together and no one thinks to ask us along. Now that's cold! Research has shown that when we find ourselves in such situations, we become more motivated than usual to try to form new bonds with people we meet, and at those times we are also more likely than usual to mimic and imitate others. It is as if our goal of making friends and getting others to like us already has the benefits of the chameleon effect wired into it. A similar dynamic comes into play during romantic pursuit, which, as we all know, often requires significant work in order for us to attain our goal. Evolution has also folded the chameleon effect into our instinctive bag of tricks for courtship. For our selfish genes, dating and mating are all about reproduction, getting those genes safely into the next generation. Thus it makes sense that in one experiment, men engaged in greater imitation and mimicry of a woman they were interacting with if, unbeknownst to the men the woman happened to be at the most fertile stage of her ovulation cycle at the time.

The other side of the same coin is that we will tend to resist these external influences on our behavior—both the chameleon effect of imitating others, and the Lhermitte effect of doing what the situation naturally calls for—if giving in to them conflicts with a goal or important motivation.

At one conference about twenty years ago, just after I'd presented our chameleon effect findings, the Scottish psychologist Neil Macrae went up to the podium for his own presentation. He asked everyone in the room to raise our hands if we'd seen the film *The Full Monty*. This was a popular movie at the time, about a group of downtrodden English men who decide to put on a striptease show. Many people in the audience had seen it and raised their hands. Then Macrae asked them to keep their hands up if, during the famous scene in the movie where the dancing male leads take off all of their clothes onstage—the proverbial "full monty"—they too had stood up in the theater and taken off all their clothes. The audience laughed and only a few jokers kept their hands up. But everyone got his point.

Behavioral contagion effects are not obligatory and uncontrollable, because, unlike Lhermitte's patients, we have a good deal of control over whether we do the same thing as the other person or not (if we realize we are doing it) and can also imitate intentionally if we want to. Recall that Darwin said the same thing about our emotional expressions. At receptions following talks I gave on the chameleon effect, I witnessed firsthand many attempts by people to control the effect, once they realized they were engaging in it themselves. Because I'd just been talking about the effect for the past hour or so, those at the reception were far more likely to notice themselves doing it, and it was fun to watch everyone trying very hard *not* to imitate each other. I would stand in front of a person chatting with my arms crossed on my chest. He would be doing the same, then realize it and suddenly jerk his arms into some other position! (And we'd both laugh at that point, knowing what was going on.) As Macrae's example suggested, chameleon effects will be less likely to occur when there are perceived *costs* to doing what others are doing. Remember as a child when you would pester your parents to let you do something, telling them all your friends were doing it? And remember their canned reply? *If your friends all jumped off a cliff, would you want to, too?*

Well, no, we wouldn't. Macrae and colleague Lucy Johnston demonstrated this limitation to behavior contagion effects in a two-part study. First, they primed participants with words related to helpfulness using the standard language test procedure, creating a Lhermitte-like impulse to help. The participants were then thanked and they left thinking the experiment was over. But on the elevator leaving the building, the real part of the experiment took place. A person on the elevator who was part of the experimental team dropped many pens on the floor, seemingly accidentally. What happened next? Those who had been primed with helpfulness words were more likely to bend down to help pick up the pens than were participants who had not been thus primed. The help-related words on the language test had their intended effect of increasing the participants' tendency to help—*except* when the pens were messy and leaking. In that condition, very few participants wanted to help pick them up even if they'd previously seen the helpfulness-related words on the language test. The cost or disincentives of "doing what others are doing" came into play and blocked the unconscious influence.

This "leaky pen" study also illustrates that at any given time, we can be receiving unconscious suggestions regarding more than one type of behavior, and it is possible for them to be in conflict with each other. Those pen-study participants primed with helpfulness had the impulse to help (as they were more likely to help than others in the non-leaky-pen condition), but they also had an even stronger impulse not to pick up the messy, leaky pens, as if they were transmitters of germs or disease. You may recall a cruel yet revealing hidden-camera stunt in which the producers of the show stuck a hundred-dollar bill to a piece of dog poop and left it on the sidewalk. Different people, it turns out, have different cost thresholds when faced with such a dilemma. (And different degrees of need for the money as well.) Some people grabbed the poopy Ben Franklin, while others didn't. Unfortunately, it is not only cooperation behaviors that can be increased by cues from the outside environment, but rudeness and antisocial behaviors as well.

Just as Macrae and Johnston showed that a subject's helpfulness could be increased in the elevator merely by having just seen and used words related to helpfulness, our lab showed that rudeness (as well as politeness) could be increased in the same fashion. Our participants were NYU students who came into our lab on Washington Place for an experiment on "language ability." They first completed a short scrambled-sentence test that featured words related to rudeness, words related to politeness, or, in the control condition, words related to neither concept. They were told that when they had completed that test they were to come down the hallway to find the experimenter, who would give them the second task of the study, after which they would be done.

When they had completed the language test and walked down the hall, however, the experimenter was busy talking to someone else, apparently another participant in the study. They could see the experimenter standing in a doorway talking into a room from which another person's voice could be heard. This other person (who was actually part of the experimental team) kept asking questions about the task she'd just been given, the experimenter would answer, and this conversation continued with the experimenter's attention focused entirely on this other person, while the actual participant was standing nearby. We wanted to see how long the participant would stand there waiting to get her second task before interrupting the conversation, how "polite" or "rude" her response would be. As soon as the participant had approached him in the hallway, the experimenter secretly started a silent stopwatch in his pocket.

While the participant stood there waiting to be given the second task, the experimenter kept talking. This went on until the participant finally interrupted him to ask for the second task—or until ten minutes had gone by, at which point he stopped the clock and gave her the second task. (As a matter of fact, when we first proposed the experiment to the university committee that screens and approves psychology studies, we did not include this ten-minute time limit, and they told us to put it in, since otherwise the participant might be standing there forever! That possibility had never occurred to us, because after all, New Yorkers are not generally known for their patience and politeness. We had just assumed everyone would interrupt in a matter of minutes, if not seconds. As it turned out, we were quite wrong about that.) The important measure was how long the participants in the rude and the polite conditions waited before interrupting. As we had predicted, those who had seen rude-related words on the first language task were both more likely to interrupt the experimenter (most of them did) and did so faster than those who had seen the polite words. But what surprised us was that most of those in the polite condition never interrupted at all, and just stood there patiently for the entire ten-minute maximum.

Researchers at the University of Florida have taken this rude priming effect out of the laboratory and into the business school classroom. They showed that in the workplace, the rudeness of others is "contagious." Like the common cold, it spreads from one person to another. In a negotiation class, the rudeness of a person's bargaining partner one week caused the recipient of the rudeness to be rude to a different person the next week.

The researchers also showed that witnessing a work team leader's very rude treatment of a team member had the same kind of effect that our "rude" language test had, to prime the concept of rudeness in their participants' minds. That is why reading rude-related words has the same kind of effect on behavior as witnessing actual rudeness in a real-world setting. Both of those activities cause the behavior concept (in this case, of rudeness) to become more active in your mind, and the more active it is, the more likely you will be to behave that way yourself.

The Florida studies showed how the chameleon effect can affect the workday climate for many people. The behavior of your colleagues and coworkers—and your own behavior as well, of course—can spread contagiously throughout the office. The researchers concluded that people may be largely unaware that the source of their own rude and aggressive behaviors is the rude behaviors of others that they witness—and that the phenomenon of negative behavioral contagion may be much larger and more consequential for organizations and society than we realize. Sometimes the contagious virus of antisocial behavior comes not from the behavior of other people, but from the visible consequences of their behavior that they leave behind. I'm talking broken windows, graffiti, litter, signs of disregard and even contempt for one's city and neighborhood. I'm talking New York City in the 1970s, '80s, and '90s.

Broken Windows and Status Updates

Ah yes, New York. It was 1995, and in my lab we had just completed the experiment on how rudeness or politeness primes caused people to interrupt or not. As with Lhermitte's stroke patients, the cues to their behavior had come in from the environment and influenced how they behaved in the ensuing situation. But isn't this what happens to us constantly, every day, while out on the streets of our cities, or the back roads of our farmlands, in the diners of our small towns? The cues as to what other people are doing, how they are acting, are constantly flowing in through our senses. New York is known for having some of the nerviest, brashest citizens in the world, yet if instead they were primed with politeness cues that had just streamed into their minds, they were capable of the utmost deference and decorum. (Temporarily, anyway; let's not get too carried away here.)

Deference and decorum were in short supply in New York City during the first fifteen years I lived there. The city had hit an all-time low. The Big Apple was infested with worms of a decline, and had become a wasteland of urban abandon. The U.S. economy was floundering, and the country's most iconic city was nearly bankrupt. The result was a place that was collapsing both physically and morally. Many landlords who tired of the financial strain of upkeep and management burned their buildings down to illegally collect insurance money, and there the ruins remained, haunting husks of displaced lives. Garbage fires burned and the homeless proliferated on the streets. Heroin addiction ravaged communities, and violence and crime were everywhere. There were constant muggings on the subway. Times Square was a neon kingdom for the sex trade, and prostitution spiked in all of the boroughs. Even the Statue of Liberty wasn't her same old beautiful self, as the water at her feet took on a greasy, iridescent sheen from oil contamination in New York Harbor. Many wondered how such a great city could have descended into such a dismal abyss.

By pure coincidence, we were conducting our rude-polite study at about the same time newly elected mayor Rudy Giuliani was enacting his plan of "enforcing the small stuff." In line with what is called broken windows theory, the idea publicly espoused by Mayor Giuliani was that if you crack down on the small but visible crimes such as vandalism, littering, and even jaywalking (cops really did start giving out tickets for people crossing big streets, like Fifth Avenue, in the middle of the block), then the larger, more serious crimes will also decrease. If people saw cleaner streets, intact buildings and storefronts, and fewer of their fellow citizens engaging in small-potatoes civil disobedience such as jaywalking, they would have greater respect for each other and for the laws in general. And Giuliani's plan, as pie-in-the-sky as it seemed to many at the time, was entirely consistent with the emerging psychological research on how external environmental cues can directly impact social behavior. Our mental representations of concepts such as politeness and rudeness, as well as innumerable other behaviors such as aggression and substance abuse, become activated by our direct perception of these forms of social behavior and emotion, and in this way are contagious. And people in New York were seeing a lot of hostility and addiction in the 1970s and '80s. And garbage.

Lots of garbage. There was garbage in the streets and graffiti covering walls and trains. But could this really and truly have affected how millions of New Yorkers behaved? More to the point, if all the garbage and detritus was cleaned up, would that actually help to decrease the rate of violent crimes? (If you had answered yes to this question in 1995 I would have told you about a certain bridge over the East River that I was willing to part with at a bargain price.)

But wait—maybe it could. Maybe it even did. Consider a study reported in *Science* magazine in 2007 by a group of Dutch researchers who changed the appearance of an actual city street so that the walls were either covered with graffiti or painted over so that there was no graffiti. After this setup, they placed advertising circulars around the handlebars of all the bicycles parked in the racks on that street. (The Dutch are big on riding bikes everywhere, so there were a lot of them.) Then the researchers just waited to see what the bike owners would do with the advertising circulars. Lo and behold, when there was lots of graffiti on the walls, the bike riders tossed more circulars down on the street, creating more litter. When there was no graffiti, there was also much less littering. No one saw anyone actually painting graffiti on the walls, so this wasn't a chameleon effect per se, but the signs or results of people having painted all over the walls were certainly there. The signs of others' antisocial behavior—the graffiti—primed another form of antisocial behavior in the bike riders, that of littering. It was a kind of Lhermitte effect.

The Dutch researchers then showed this same kind of effect in other ways, again out in the real-world city environment. They put the same circular flyers under the windshield wipers in a parking garage. If there were shopping carts scattered around the parked cars, clearly taken away from the nearby grocery store by the shoppers despite many signs asking people please not to do this, the shoppers again were more likely to litter, compared to when no shopping carts (no cues to antisocial behavior) were present.

In city dwellers' collective unconscious, one could say antisocial behavior spreads like a virus. What people saw is what they did themselves. But isn't this looking at the glass half-empty? One could just as well say it is half-full—that the bike riders who saw the graffiti-free wall littered *less,* and the drivers in the parking garage with no "taken" shopping carts littered *less,* in both cases because of the lack of antisocial behavior cues in those conditions of the study. So let's get back to Giuliani's grand experiment of the 1990s. How did it turn out?

I happened to be away from the city, on sabbatical leave in southern Germany, for a year in the middle 1990s. When I got back I was amazed by the change that had occurred just in that short time. I was expecting to have the same culture shock I'd experienced coming back from sabbaticals in the past—after becoming accustomed to the low crime and clean streets of small-town Germany, having to readjust to noisy, dangerous New York all over again. But this time the shock was the lack of culture shock. The streets seemed much cleaner, the people even a bit friendlier. The change was especially noticeable to me because I'd been away and hadn't experienced the citywide behavioral shift gradually, as my apartment building neighbors and psychology department colleagues had, but they had all noticed it, too.

The crime statistics from this period supported my impression. In the mid-1990s, New York City saw a dramatic decrease in serious crimes—assault and murder declined by an astounding *two-thirds*. There are of course other theories to explain this dramatic drop, and additional reasons for it, but it is also hard to argue with the positive consequences of a cleaner and more civil daily environment, with less visual evidence of the small crimes the broken windows theory was named after. And the Dutch research findings also support the idea that New York's low was so low at least partly because of behavior cues that "breaking windows" was okay, and that the city's resurgence in turn was a result of a new culture of cues for positive behavior being instituted instead.

As I've mentioned, I no longer live in New York City, or any city for that matter. I live in the farm country of central Connecticut, along with my family, our dogs and cats, and all the other animals that inhabit the area. Quite a change from twenty-plus years in Manhattan and Brooklyn, significantly reducing my exposure to the behavior of other people—in person, that is. Today, however, the Internet and social media reach everywhere, rural and urban areas alike, and new studies are showing that online moods, emotions, and behavior turn out to be just as contagious as offline, "real life" (in-person) behavior—maybe even more so. The unconscious mirroring of what other people do does not turn off just because the behavior we perceive is in digital instead of physical form. In fact, thanks to social media connecting us to one another far more widely than ever before, today there are many *more* opportunities for contagion effects than there used to be.

Birds in a flock move as one because they perceive each other's movements and speed, and there is a direct link in their brains between perception and action. We humans are similarly influenced by our peers' behavior, but unlike birds, we can see and hear what others do indirectly and virtually, in movies and videos and television, and through books and magazines and newspapers. Now these media have become enmeshed in our real lives in transformative new ways, as we are no longer just the passive consumers of images and texts, but constant creators of them as well. The media has *become* our real life. We can keep track of a very large group of our past and present friends on Facebook, Twitter, Instagram, or Snapchat, and they can keep track of us. And we can also follow the lives, musings, and behavior of celebrities as well. In "following" others we are exposed not only to their behavior and opinions but to their moods and emotions. As a result, the potential of the chameleon effect is in fact far greater today than it was when we first studied it in the 1990s.

Sociologists James Fowler and Nicholas Christakis have conducted several studies of behavior in large social networks. These demonstrate how many different forms of behavior and emotions spread over social connections on the Internet, so that you are often affected indirectly by people you don't even know. Say for example, you know Bob, Bob knows Dale, Dale knows Mary, Mary knows Wayne, but you don't happen to know either Mary or Wayne. All the same, because of their effect on the people you *do* know, whether Mary or Wayne is happy, cooperative, depressed, or obese makes it more likely you will be, too.

All of these emotions and behaviors have been found to spread and be more likely for a given person if people in their social network express those emotions, engage in those behaviors, or have those same qualities. The more you are in touch with people who are happy, the happier you are; with people who are overweight, the heavier you will tend to be. When people in your network cooperate with others, you are more likely to as well, and when they seem very sad, you become a bit sadder, too. The moods and behaviors of people to whom we are connected by friendship, family, or the same workplace are likely to "infect" us. The contagion is usually at least three people deep—three degrees of virtual separation—so that people you don't even know are affecting your behavior and emotions, because they know somebody who knows somebody that you know. Of course, it also works in the other direction.

The average person has more than three hundred Facebook friends, so there is a great capacity for our own moods and behaviors to affect a lot of people in return. Researchers at Facebook measured how positive or negative the posts in a given Facebook user's newsfeed were and showed that the more positive or negative the posts they read, the more positive or negative the user's own posts became—*up to three days later*. James is sad and depressed and this shows in his Facebook posts; the posts of his friend Mary are affected, but then yours will be, too, because you know Mary, even though you don't know James—and up to three days following James's sad post. Perhaps then we should become more mindful of the types of people we expose ourselves to on social media.

In a similar but more controversial study, Facebook researchers deliberately *manipulated* the positivity or negativity of the newsfeed for nearly 700,000 of their users. They did this not by creating fake posts but by filtering which of the many posts by the users' Facebook friends were put into their newsfeeds. (One thing I learned from this study was that most of us never see all of our friends' posts, because that would be an overwhelming number we couldn't possibly keep up with. Consequently, Facebook's programming filters all of those posts each day by certain criteria and only puts a subset into what you actually see.) For some users, their newsfeed was deliberately programmed to be a bit more negative than usual, and for others a bit more positive. Then the researchers measured how this change in the mood of the feed affected the recipient's own mood, as shown by the content and tone of their posts. They found that people indeed made more positive posts themselves if they were exposed to more positive posts of others, and people made more negative posts if they were in the group given more negative newsfeeds. Altogether, this research has shown that all types of behavior, including overeating and being cooperative, being rude or being polite, being a litterbug or not, are just as contagious over social networks as they are in person. Unconscious mimicry doesn't require physical proximity.

The same principle applies when we read material besides social media, such as novels, in which we lose ourselves in a different world, which we see from the perspective of the story's protagonist. Researchers at Cornell University had participants read a story in which the female protagonist goes on and stays on a diet to lose weight before a beach vacation in Cancún, and showed that this activated the readers' own dieting goals—unless in the story the protagonist was said to have achieved the weight-loss goal, in which case the readers' own dieting goal was not active. So the readers' own goals became active or not depending on whether the protagonist's goal was active or not. A second study found this same result again, but also that the more the reader identified with the protagonist, the more she wanted to lose weight. This happened, however, only when the character was successful in losing weight, not when she failed. Apparently, it is true not only that "what you see is what you do" but that "what you read is what you do."

The social setting we are in at any given moment also signals to us how we are supposed to behave, and these norms unconsciously guide us, effortlessly constraining our behavior to fit in and be appropriate (and not stand out and attract the disapproval of others). In a landmark 1950s sociological study by Roger Barker, drawing on many months of careful observation of the citizens of "Midwest" (which turned out to be Oskaloosa, Kansas), by far the largest determinant of how people behaved was not their individual personalities or character, but *where they were* at the time—in a church service, at the barbershop, at home, at a park, at a restaurant, on the highway. Everyone is quiet in church and stays put, runs around and is a bit noisy at the park, waits patiently for the meal to arrive at the restaurant, sits less patiently in traffic on the highway. The similarities in behavior across different people in the same setting are far greater than the similarity in behavior of the same individual across different settings. If you keep your eyes open to how your own and others' behavior clearly changes as you move from setting to setting, you can't help but observe this powerful influence on human behavior. You'll see what you do.

A clever demonstration of the unconscious nature of the setting effect comes from another Dutch study, this time at a university, involving the college library. As we all know, you are supposed to be quiet in libraries, since most people are there to read and study. In the experiment, college students were asked to take an envelope to another destination on campus. If the destination was the university library, they were quieter and spoke more softly to others on the way there than if they were heading to a different destination, such as the university cafeteria. The effect of having the destination "library" active in their minds (even though they were not in the library yet, but in busy hallways) was very similar to how "museum" or "doctor's office" or "garden" influenced the behavior of Lhermitte's stroke patients. Similarly, the behavioral norms when we are out on the street also influence our chameleonlike tendencies, causing us to do as others are doing.

For many of us, the most common settings in our life are home and work. We are often a very different person in these two places, because there are different sets of behavior appropriate for home but not appropriate for the office, and vice versa. And the different sets of people we interact with in the two settings have different expectations of us and we might even have distinctly different personalities in the two places. I know that as a dad at home I am the continual font of many awful jokes that I'd never dream of making at work. (But that's what dads do.) A 2014 set of studies by the Swiss economist Ernst Fehr and his colleagues examined how these different *situated identities* at home versus at work operate unconsciously to produce quite different behavior within the same person, even immoral behavior in one case and moral in the other. They studied a native figure—Swiss bankers.

Fehr and his colleagues did so via an online experiment conducted on the weekend while these investment bankers were at home, not at their place of business. Their theory was that the bankers had a situated identity at their workplace that was different from their identity when at home. For some of the bankers, their workplace identity was primed at the start of the experiment when they answered several questions about their office environment; the other group of bankers was not asked about their workplace. Then all of them played a coin-toss game where they won twenty dollars for each successful coin toss (either heads or tails each time), with the catch being that they themselves reported whether they'd been successful or not. No one but them would know if they were being honest. This made cheating to get more money a very easy thing to do. But the researchers could look at the overall percentage of successful coin tosses for the two experimental groups and compare it to the 50 percent expected by chance. It was significantly higher for the bankers who had first answered questions about their weekday workplace, suspiciously so, with many more successes than would have been likely to happen by chance alone. The nonprimed group, on the other hand, was actually quite honest in their self-reporting of the coin tosses, describing a success rate much closer to the 50 percent expected by chance. Remember that these participants were all investment bankers, the same type of people in both conditions of the experiment, just randomly assigned to first think about their workplace or not.

The moral behavior of the bankers was markedly different depending on which of their personal identities, corresponding to the two main settings of their lives, was currently active. Morally speaking, each was a different person at work than at home. In this way the Swiss bankers were like the Asian-American girls in the Harvard preschool—if you primed one identity, they behave one way (good at math, honest); if you primed the other identity, the same person behaved in a very different way (bad at math, dishonest). In both studies, these effects occurred without the participants being aware of or intending them. But identities can be primed for the better as well.

We've all gone into a grocery store and been offered recipe samples that encourage us to try a new dish or type of food. Dutch psychologist Esther Papies and colleagues went into Dutch grocery stores and handed out recipe flyers to obese shoppers when they first entered the store. For some of the shoppers, the flyer contained prime words related to dieting and healthy eating, and for other shoppers these words were not included. Then the researchers waited until the shoppers had done their shopping and gone through the checkout lines. They went up to each of them and asked to take a photograph of their cash register receipts, so they could see how many unhealthy snack foods, like potato chips, the shoppers had actually purchased. There was a remarkable drop in the purchase of snack foods caused by the primes in the recipe flyers, even though very few of the shoppers could remember what was on the flyers they'd looked at before they started shopping, and none believed that the flyers had influenced what they had bought in the store. (Imagine yourself in their situation—would you believe it?) But despite the shoppers being unaware of the influence of the flyers, if those handouts contained primes for healthy eating, they had a significant influence on the snack purchases of the obese customers.

In their next study, Papies and colleagues moved on to a local butcher shop permeated with the tantalizing smell of grilled chicken. When customers entered the shop, a poster attached to the glass door, visible from the outside, presented a weekly recipe from the butcher that was "good for a slim figure" and low in calories. On two mornings and two afternoons of the four days of the study, this poster was on the door, and the other mornings and afternoons it was not (that was the control condition). Papies and her colleagues observed the number of free meat snacks customers sampled from a tray in the store, after they had been primed with the dieting goal or not. When they were leaving the store one of the researchers asked them some background questions, including whether they were currently dieting and their current height and weight. As in the grocery store study, the poster—the dieting prime—caused restrained eaters (obese and currently on a diet) to eat about half as many snacks in this butcher's store, compared to restrained eaters when that poster was not on the front door. The poster did not affect how many snack items the nondieters ate in the store.

Obesity is a tremendous health and economic burden today in the United States and much of the developed world, so real-life priming interventions such as these are much needed. Yet a much more powerful and pervasive outside influence on what we do—advertising—does not always have our own best interests at heart. The makers of snack food and other unhealthy choices are trying hard to get you to eat their foods instead of eating healthily. Research proves that their ad campaigns work. Pictures of yummy advertised foods have been shown to directly activate eating-related areas of the brain associated with taste and reward. We showed the power of ads on eating behavior in a study led by Jennifer Harris of the Rudd Center for Food Policy & Obesity. Adults as well as a group of eight-year-old children participated one at a time, and watched a five-minute clip of a television comedy show, *Whose Line Is It Anyway?* A bowl of Goldfish crackers and a glass of water were set out for them while they watched. We edited the show so that it included food ads or not. After it was over we weighed the bowl of crackers to see how much the participant had eaten. Both the children and adults ate considerably more of the Goldfish when there were food ads in the show than when there were not. Food ads, then, act like unconscious behavioral suggestions and can influence our eating and other consumption, especially if we are not aware of their power over us.

The powerful link between television ads and our behavior was shown recently by a large national survey of more than one thousand young drinkers (they reported having had some alcohol in the past month), ages thirteen to twenty, conducted by researchers at Boston University's School of Medicine and Public Health. A strong relation was found between the number of alcohol ads these kids had seen on television and how much they themselves drank. Exposure to ads for sixty-one different alcohol brands was measured; these were the brands that advertised on the twenty most popular nonsports television programs watched by underage youth. (And of course there is a tremendous amount of alcohol advertising on sports broadcasts as well.) Underage drinkers who didn't see any alcohol ads had about 14 drinks per month on average, but those who saw the average amount of advertising drank about 33 drinks per month. And a separate study found that kids aged eleven to fourteen see between two and four of these ads every day, on average. The researchers concluded that the more alcohol ads the teenagers were exposed to, the more of that brand of alcohol they consumed.

Food and drink ads on TV and other media give us the idea or impulse to eat and drink, so we might want to second-guess the real reasons why we find ourselves heading to the refrigerator so often. And we also might want to monitor more closely the kinds of ads our children are being exposed to.

Even well-intentioned public service announcements to get us to stop smoking may have the opposite effect, because these contain cues about smoking. Many people are trying to stop smoking—for good reason, as worldwide more than five million deaths a year are caused by tobacco smoking. Yet attempts to help people quit or at least reduce their smoking often fail, not only because of the highly addictive components of tobacco smoke, but because the very intention to quit activates the same mental pathways and brain networks that are related to the craving for the cigarette. Neuroscientists have revealed this unintended consequence of the intention to stop smoking, through brain imaging research in which the same brain regions were found to become active in both cases—when people were craving a cigarette and when they were focusing on trying to quit smoking.

Dan Wegner and Robin Vallacher first discovered these "ironic" unintended consequences of trying not to do something. Perversely, when we try not to do something we have to keep in our minds the idea of what it is we do not want to do. But this keeps that unwanted behavior active in our minds, more so perhaps than if we were not actively trying not to do it. Our attempts to suppress the unwanted behavior work fine as long as we are paying attention to and actively trying to suppress that behavior, but if we are distracted, or our attention wavers (as when we are tired), then boom! You actually become more likely than usual to do exactly what you didn't want to do, because it is so active, accessible, and ready to go in your mind. Wegner and Vallacher showed this in many clever studies, such as telling their participants not to think about a white bear, and showing that with distraction they were much more likely to think about a white bear than if they'd never brought up a white bear in the first place. (Try this for yourself. Tell a friend to not think about a white bear, and see how much more often they do think of one compared to a different friend you'd never mentioned white bears to.)

The same thing happens with well-intentioned antismoking signs and antismoking television public service announcements (PSAs). Again, these are messages telling people not to do something. But in so doing, they remind people of that "something," which they might not have thought of otherwise. Often these PSAs show people smoking, which can have a "what you see is what you do" effect and increase instead of decrease smoking tendencies among viewers. Cigarette companies can no longer advertise their products, but the public service campaigns that they sponsor, featuring the words *smoking* and *cigarettes* and other visual and auditory cues to smoking, have been shown to actually increase smoking intentions and behavior among young people.

Seeking to understand this phenomenon more deeply, our lab experimentally demonstrated the perverse unintended effect of antismoking messages. In another study in our lab led by Jennifer Harris, fifty-six regular smokers watched a short segment of a television comedy show. For some of them, the commercial break halfway through the segment included an antismoking PSA (either from Philip Morris's QuitAssist campaign or from the American Legacy Foundation's "Truth" campaign); for others, it did not include an antismoking PSA. After they had watched the comedy show, all participants were given a five-minute break, and we watched to see how many of them would take this opportunity to go outside and smoke. We found that significantly more (42 percent and 33 percent for the Philip Morris and the "Truth" PSAs, respectively) of the smokers who saw the antismoking PSA went outside to smoke than did smokers who had not seen any antismoking PSA (11 percent). By presenting strong cues about cigarettes and smoking behavior, these antismoking messages had the unintended consequence of increasing smoking instead. What we see is what we do, especially when we are passively watching television or surfing the Web and not paying close attention to the messages bombarding us.

The mimicking nature of our mind isn't inherently good or bad—it depends on the suggestions we're receiving from the outside world in the present, like the cues that Lhermitte's eccentrically exuberant patients picked up on. Our chameleonlike nature makes us more likely to do what other people are currently doing. This effect extends to what we see people doing in advertisements, as well as to our knowledge of what people generally tend to do in standard settings and situations. Some situations induce us to be more polite and peaceful, others to be more rude and hostile. Some imitative behaviors, such as dishonesty, can lead to financial meltdown, as with greedy investment bankers, while others can lead to the renaissance of a city, as when Mayor Giuliani and his fellow New Yorkers "sweated the small stuff."

But the effect of our behavior on others, and theirs on us, *ultimately depends on us*. In practical terms, what you do really does influence the behavior of those around you and the general social climate. (This is especially true if you are a boss or a leader of others; they will take their cue for how to behave from how they see you behave.) You really can (and do) "pay it forward" by setting a good example, by performcing visible acts of kindness, such as holding the door for others, letting drivers trying to get out of a blocked lane of traffic merge in front of you, putting some change in a homeless person's proffered cap, or carrying your unwanted advertising flyer over to the corner trash can. Just as with voting, I suspect that many of us don't bother to do these small things because we don't think they really matter much. After all, each of us is just one person in a world of billions, one drop of water in a vast ocean. But the impact of just one person, the effect of just one act, multiplies and spreads to influence many other people. A single drop becomes a wave. The reverberations of a single act can be felt for days. Why not set that wave in motion whenever you get the chance?

PART 3

THE HIDDEN FUTURE

*The future is a world limited by ourselves;
in it we discover only what concerns us.*
—Maurice Maeterlinck

CHAPTER 8

Be Careful
What You Wish For

Hoy No Circula—Today You're Not Getting on the Road.

This was the name Mexico City gave its innovative "road-space rationing" program when it was instituted in 1989. The country's capital, a sprawling metropolis, stood in the top ranks of the dirtiest cities in the world. A friend who lived there at this time once mentioned that every time she blew her nose, her handkerchief would end up black. The main source of the heavy pollution and dangerously bad air quality was, of course, the abundance of cars. The city's traffic was notoriously dense, just as the great distances many had to traverse across the city for their commute to work were notoriously long. For the health of its millions of citizens, the city government created a program that would impose usage limitations on the car owners of the Distrito Federal. On certain days of the week they wouldn't be allowed to get on the road, which would gradually cause the smog to clear.

The plan was fairly simple, and was based on the last digit of a car's license plate number. One day a week, cars with the designated numbers were not allowed on the city's roads. On that day, the plan theorized, you would have to use public transportation or carpool with someone else. With decreased vehicle emissions fouling the air in the bowl-like valley of the city each day, people would suffer fewer contamination-related illnesses and early deaths. The newly improved collective health of the capital would make up for the individual annoyance. Sounds good, right?

Wrong. The well-intentioned program didn't take into account human nature, which tends to put one's own needs before the overall good of the group. (This is a classic problem in political science, called the "commons

211

dilemma," and plays a role in our global climate change problem as well.) People usually manage to find loopholes or ways around personal incon-venience. And in Mexico City, many people did indeed find a creative way to circumvent the new restrictions on road use, one that sabotaged the whole purpose of the reformist policy.

Drivers simply bought another car and obtained a different-ending license-plate number (even or odd) than that of their original car. This way, they could still drive into work every day—not only that, but the second car soon came to be used four days a week, not just one. So instead of reducing smog and road congestion, the new policy actually increased the number of cars, congestion, and smog. These second cars, of course, were by and large used cars, now pouring into Mexico City from the outlying regions to meet the demand—cars that were older and more polluting than the cars already in the city. Within six months after the new road use program began, the city's gasoline consumption had risen substantially, and pollution and road congestion had increased.

It is hard to predict or shape the future, especially where human behavior is concerned, even (or especially) when it is important to try to do so. This is especially true of policies that impose restrictions on individual freedoms to benefit the common good, as in Mexico City, or give incentives or rewards for desired behavior. In one famous example, which led to something called the cobra effect, the government of India put a bounty of hundreds of dollars on each cobra killed and brought in to the appropriate official, in order to help rid the country of these dangerous and too-common predators. But this new policy actually increased, rather than decreased, the cobra population. In fact, it led to an *explosion* of the cobra population! Why? Because many people started actively *breeding* cobras in order to bring them in and get the reward.

I bred my own cobras, you might say, in the first psychology experi-ment I ever participated in, back when I was taking Psych 101 in college. Introductory psychology classes typically require students to participate in five or ten experiments. In this experiment I was to do the "pursuit rotor task," an old-fashioned experimental task in which concentration and coordination are at a premium. You have to try to keep the metal rod in your hand in contact with a metal disc that is rapidly spinning on an old record turntable; doing so completes an electrical circuit that runs a timer that keeps track of how long you were able to keep the two in contact. The graduate student experimenter explained to me that I would do the task twice, and I would get paid up to ten dollars depending on how much better I did the second time than the first time. This was a lot of money to a college student in the 1970s. So he set the disc spinning and told me to begin, and went back into his control room. Naturally, I did really badly the first time around. For some reason, ahem, I just could not manage to keep the rod on the disc very long at all. The experimenter came in after the first part looking very concerned and asked whether I understood the task, what I was supposed to do. I said, yeah, but it was (ahem) so hard. He started the disc spinning the second time and went back to the control room. I was so much better the second time—almost perfect in fact. When he came back in the next time he looked very suspicious—and quite grudgingly counted out the nine dollars and change I had earned. Economists would say I behaved quite rationally. The incentives were such that to maximize my earnings I should do as poorly as possible the first time, and as well as I could the second time. But basic human motivations and the effect of rewards on behavior were apparently lost on the experimenter, who hadn't factored in the consequences beyond his scientific intentions—just like the policy makers in Mexico and India.

Like policies that seek to recast behaviors, our own personal desires and goals for the future can change us while we are pursuing them, often in unintended ways—hence, unconsciously. Pursuing a given goal can cause us to do things that go against our important values and self-concepts, things we'd normally consider immoral or unethical or unhealthy. It can cause us to be more open to outside influences, even subliminal advertising, than we normally are. It can cause us to spend our money in ways we will later think were silly and wasteful, when we get the bill. It can cause us to like people we'd otherwise not like, and also to like our friends less than we usually do. All because those changes will help us get to the goal we are currently trying for. Our current goals change us—our minds, hearts, and values. And without our being aware that these changes have taken place. This is why we must be careful what we wish for.

Goal-Colored Glasses

Because our goals and motivations are for desired *future* states, their influence resides in the third time zone of the hidden mind. What and who and where we want to be in the future, near or long term, shapes what we think, feel, and do in the present. What we want and need to get, where and who we want and need to be, all strongly influence what we like and don't like right now, at this moment. We become what we pursue and we start to see the world through goal-colored glasses. This is true whether the objective you're after is one you are consciously aware of or not.

Wishes wield great power over us. It is as if our goals reconfigure us, making us temporarily a different person with different values doing different things than we usually do. Unfortunately, we often recognize this only after the fact, after the goal has been reached or is no longer being pursued, and at that point we wonder what we were thinking. Dan Wegner used to tell the story of going through the cafeteria line with good intentions to eat a nice, healthy salad for lunch, and then sitting down and being surprised to see a hot, steaming plate of fries in front of him. ("How did that get there?") What he really wanted, and maybe usually got for lunch, won out because he wasn't paying enough attention to carrying out his good intention to do otherwise. (Overcoming our unconscious desires and breaking our bad habits is not easy but it can be done, as we'll see in Chapter 10.)

Our intentional goals, then, can have unintended consequences. But at least with a conscious desire, we have the chance to take off our goal lenses and think through the practical consequences of accomplishing it. But often, and for a variety of reasons, our motivations operate unconsciously, hidden in the background, influencing what we do before we know it. This is what the seventeenth-century Dutch philosopher Baruch Spinoza meant when he wrote that "men are usually ignorant of the causes of their desires—we are conscious of our actions and desires, but ignorant of the causes by which we are determined to desire anything." We may think we know why we are doing what we are doing, but often there is a deeper underlying reason.

I experienced this firsthand about fifteen years ago, driving back to New York from a Thanksgiving weekend with my sister's family in Tennessee. The trip was about nine hundred miles. I left at eight thirty in the morning and told everyone as I was getting in my car that I was going to make it back in twelve hours, as a kind of challenge, and all day I drove with this goal of making it back home by eight thirty at night. I did make it in time and was feeling quite pleased with myself as I walked out of the parking garage. But instead of heading to my nearby apartment building,

I found myself heading for the nearest liquor store, which at the time by state law closed at nine o'clock on Saturday, and would not be open on Sunday. It was at this point that I remembered that I didn't have anything to drink at home in my apartment. That night as I was having a glass of the wine I had just bought, it dawned on me why I had been so determined to get home by eight thirty. It had nothing to do with "the challenge" of driving nine hundred miles in twelve hours. It had everything to do with getting to the liquor store before it closed. When I realized the real reason I wanted to get back by eight thirty, the power of my need to have something to drink that weekend, I was somewhat shocked. It wasn't easy, but that glass of wine was the last drink I ever had. I had learned that what is good for our goals may not be good for our souls.

Do you remember the scene in the first *Lord of the Rings* movie where kindly Uncle Bilbo's face suddenly distorts into that of a ferocious beast, just because his nephew Frodo won't let him hold the Ring of Power? Just as Bilbo's need transformed him, goals can take us over and dramatically change our preferences and behavior. This is perhaps most clear in the case of strong addictions. In Chapter 5, we looked at a study of smokers trying to quit. Their unconscious attitudes toward smoking and cigarettes were negative, but when they had a strong need for a cigarette after not smoking for four hours, their unconscious attitudes toward smoking changed. Now, even though they very much wanted to quit, and knew all about the damage that smoking was doing to their bodies, that powerful need changed their unconscious feelings about smoking to positive. The strong goal *changed their minds.*

The decision researcher George Loewenstein, of Carnegie Mellon University, was the first to call our attention to how such powerful visceral needs can dramatically change our choices. Think of the alcoholic who in the morning swears (and believes it) that she will never touch the stuff again, and vows not to have anything to drink that evening. Yet when the clock rolls around and her body is expecting, nay, *demanding* the substance, her attitudes and behavior change drastically. At this point, she makes all sorts of rationalizations. "One more night won't make any difference," she says. "I'll quit tomorrow." But for too many addicts, that promise is never kept, and that tomorrow never comes.

We've already seen how another deep goal, the mating or reproduction motive, operates behind the scenes to guide behavior in its favor. Attractive female applicants, and to a lesser extent attractive male applicants, were considerably more likely to get called in for job interviews than less attractive applicants with the same qualifications. Attractive people activate the reward structures of our brains without our realizing or intending it. The mating motivation is unconsciously activated, regardless of the egalitarian, meritocratic values of the person who is doing the hiring.

Neuroscience research on the motivational circuits of the brain by Mathias Pessiglione and Chris Frith, of University College London, has confirmed that the perception of a reward activates the reward centers of the brain whether or not the person is consciously aware of the external reward. Participants squeezed harder on a handgrip task when a picture of a pound coin (the reward for doing well) was flashed subliminally before the task, compared to when a penny coin was subliminally flashed. Plus, the reward center of the brain, in the basal forebrain, was more active in the pound than in the penny coin condition.

Another study showed the unconscious operation of the mating motive. Male college students were primed, or not, with the goal to affiliate with women, through reading a short passage about a romantic encounter. Next they were given the choice of taking a short tutorial with another person, Jason or Jessica, on one of two topics, say geology and astronomy. Half the time Jason taught geology and Jessica taught astronomy, and half the time it was the other way around. But the actual topics they taught didn't matter— if the mating motive was operating unconsciously, the participants wanted to work with the female tutor more than they wanted to work with the male tutor. And at the end of the study, they really believed their choice was because of the topic she taught (geology or astronomy), that they had a genuine interest in that subject they had not known they had.

The problem with not knowing the real reasons for what you do is that we are all very good at coming up with positive reasons for our behavior after the fact. Bob didn't hire the woman because of her looks but (of course) because of her qualifications. Mary didn't have three shots of whiskey because she is addicted to alcohol but because she just wanted to—*deserved* to—relax after a long, hard day at work. Aziz didn't choose the tutorial topic because of the attractiveness of the tutor, but because he was genuinely interested in the topic. And I didn't race home at breakneck speed to get to the liquor store before it closed, but rather for the fun challenge of seeing if I could get home in under twelve hours. These are essentially *rationalizations* and our conscious mind is very good at coming up with them. In the 1980s movie *The Big Chill,* Jeff Goldblum's character says that rationalizations were more important to him than sex, because he'd often gone many months without sex, but he couldn't go one morning without a good rationalization.

When the mating goal is operating it can cause us to rationalize doing things we'd normally avoid because of the health risks involved. Take tanning salons and diet pills, for instance. They can help us achieve a mating goal because they can help make us feel more attractive to others— slimmer, with a healthy, sun-kissed, if sometimes orangey, look. But they can be bad for our health and physical safety; tanning salons damage our skin and elevate the chances of skin cancer; and diet pills increase blood pressure, hurt our heart, worsen sleep, and can lead to addiction. The negatives clearly outweigh the positives, which is likely why most people don't use diet pills or tanning beds.

Indeed, researchers at a large American state university found that a group of several hundred female undergraduates had generally negative opinions about using either one. They reported little if any interest in using a free tanning salon membership or in taking a diet pill known to cause heart problems later in life. But all that changed when their mating motive, their desire for a close romantic relationship, became active, after they had rated many photographs of highly desirable "local" men and women on a dating website. Now the female students' opinions about using tanning salons and diet pills became more positive. They expressed greater willingness to engage in these risky behaviors, and indeed, rated these behaviors as less risky than did the control group. The active mating goal caused them to *downplay* the negative aspect of the tanning salons and diet pills to themselves because those negative aspects interfered with the active goal of becoming more attractive. That goal was now overriding the students' usual beliefs and values, *changing their minds* so that they could more effectively pursue the objective of attracting a mate.

Attracting a mate, or preparing ourselves to do so, is something we often do during our leisure time, but during these free hours our mind seeks to satisfy other goals, too. Research by Shira Gabriel and her colleagues at the University of Buffalo has shown that much of our leisure time activity is devoted to meeting our deeper social needs to belong and to socialize, but mostly without our realizing it. According to the U.S.

Department of Labor, from 2003 to 2014 most of adults' leisure time was spent on solitary activities—watching TV and movies (56 percent), reading books (7 percent), and being on the Internet (9 percent). Only 13 percent, on average, was devoted to actual socializing—spending time with friends and coworkers (outside the office). How can this overwhelming preference for solitary activities be reconciled with the notion that we humans are a fundamentally social species?

It's because, as their many studies show, the seemingly nonsocial, solitary activities are actually social in nature. Down deep we feel we are spending time with the people we see on TV, and so they satisfy the need for real social contact that drives us. And very often we are not aware of how our "sneaky social self," as the researchers called it, meets its needs through these other, solitary activities. For example, when we are feeling lonely, we tend to watch more of our favorite shows, with characters we know better and are more familiar with, and indeed doing so causes us to feel less lonely. When we are not feeling lonely, on the other hand, we tend to just watch whatever happens to be on TV at the time.

Gabriel and her colleagues note that people often bemoan the fact that they watch too much TV, and when giving the reasons for why they do, they rarely give social reasons. Instead they say that they watch TV because they find the plot interesting, or they are bored. When challenged on this point, they are quite skeptical that the deeper reason is actually that these activities help fill important social needs. But they do. That's in large part why watching TV is such a popular activity, and pets are an excellent "substitute" as well. When one of my childhood heroes, Walter Cronkite, passed away, his family was at his bedside, but his several cats, to whom he was very close, were also there on the bed with him, too. Research has shown that just the presence of a dog, not even your own dog, helps reduce a person's distress after being socially excluded. Our best friends, indeed.

Hunger is another powerful unconscious motivator, like physical safety and reproduction, driving behavior in surprising ways. Most of us have learned, through our own experience, not to go grocery shopping when hungry. But some recent research has shown that being hungry makes you buy more of anything, not just food. Satisfying hunger is a deep evolutionary motivation that existed long before we had department stores and Targets and Best Buys, and it influences forms of consumption besides food. Alison

Jing Xu and her colleagues studied shoppers coming out of a large mall in Minneapolis–St. Paul, and by checking their cash register receipts and also asking them to rate how hungry they currently were, found that hungry shoppers bought more non-food-related items such as clothes, cosmetics, and electronics. In another study, they found that hungry people also took more of free items such as binders and paper clips, showing that it was not that they wanted to spend more money, but that they just wanted to acquire things, a desire influenced by the underlying need for food.

So, not only is it a bad idea to go grocery shopping when you are hungry, but it's a bad idea to go shopping for *anything* while hungry. If you are about to do any online shopping, you might want to head to the fridge first to grab a sandwich.

Our goals and needs also make us more sensitive to information we encounter that is relevant to our meeting those goals and needs. Sixty years ago, Harvard psychologist Jerome Bruner introduced the concept of "perceptual readiness," a theory that linked a person's current motivational state and desires with increased sensitivity to goal-relevant people and objects in one's environment. You unconsciously tune your attention to things that will help you satisfy your goals and needs. So in another study, Xu and her colleagues showed how hungry people become temporarily more sensitive to words related to hunger and to wanting, gaining, and acquiring, so much so that they are even able to see and identify those words when they were presented subliminally, for only 50 milliseconds, or one-twentieth of a second each. This was so fast that people who were not currently hungry could not identify those words. But the state of hunger *changed* the participant so that they were able to see things related to the goal that normally they could not see.

This greater sensitivity to goal-related information has implications for our degree of vulnerability to outside influences. We will be more influenced by ads, for example, when we already have the need or goal suggested by the ad. Recall the obese shoppers in the recipe-priming study from the previous chapter. Words related to healthy eating and dieting in a recipe flyer they saw when entering the store significantly decreased how much snack food they subsequently bought. But this recipe priming effect only worked for the obese or restrained eaters who had the dieting goal already—not for the other shoppers who did not have that goal.

Again, the message is that we should be careful what we wish for, because we will be more open to outside influence than we otherwise would be. Many of us are concerned about subliminal advertising, because we do not want to be manipulated by large corporations or governments to buy or do things we'd otherwise not want to. There is an urban myth from the 1950s about a movie theater in Fort Lee, New Jersey, that purportedly flashed "Drink Coke" and other subliminal messages during a movie, which caused people to flock like thirsty zombies out to the concession stands. This never actually happened. It was a hoax perpetrated by a public relations firm that was presented as fact in a bestselling book of the time, *The Hidden Persuaders,* by Vance Packard. Not only did the technology to present these messages during a movie not exist at the time, but the movie theater where it was said to have happened never existed, either! Nevertheless, the story did lead to many people becoming afraid of being manipulated in order to further a company's interests rather than their own, and without their consent.

In the past twenty years, research has shown that subliminal advertising can in fact influence your choices and behavior, but only if you already *have* the goal. If you are thirsty, it can affect what you choose to drink. If you are hungry, it can affect what you choose to eat. What is important about these outside influences is not so much whether they are subliminal or not, but whether you realize they can affect you or not. They weren't subliminal to the dieters in the grocery store, and the hungry shoppers at the department store could probably tell you they were hungry, yet in neither case were they aware that their dieting or eating goals influenced what and how much they bought.

External influences have more of an impact on you the more the goal matters to you. This basic principle was borne out in a recent review of hundreds of goal-priming studies, which found a reliable and robust goal-priming effect on behavior in general, but an even bigger effect when the goal was personally important to the participant. The stronger the need, and the more important the desire, the stronger the outside influence can be. This is very important when it comes to wishes for our career and our personal lives, since being motivated is good—but we should also know the secondary effects. Your current goal changes the information you are influenced by, and it also changes what you pay attention to and can later remember.

Take a couple who are in the front seat of a car driving on a highway.

The driver is focused on the traffic, the other cars around her, the road signs, and also on her car's own speed and maybe the air-conditioning. The passenger, sitting right next to her, is enjoying the fall foliage, reading the billboards, noticing the odd and funny license plates and bumper stickers. They will have very different memories of the trip when they reach their destination even though they were in the same place for several hours. This is because what we look at and pay attention to depends on its relevance to our current goal, which in this case is quite different for the driver and the passenger.

In 1978, Richard Anderson and J. W. Pichert performed a classic experiment on how we reconstruct memories of a situation in strikingly distinct ways depending on the goal we have in that situation. The experimenters had asked participants to watch a videotaped tour of a residential home. Everyone watched the same videotape. Some were told to watch the video as if they were a burglar who was planning on robbing the home; others were told to watch the video as if they were a potential home buyer. Afterward, the two groups had quite different memories of the video. The "home buyers" remembered how large the rooms were, the condition of the major appliances (such as the hot water heater and gas stove), and the number of bedrooms. The "burglars," on the other hand, remembered if there were basement windows that were accessible, valuable but portable consumer products such as televisions and stereos, as well as other belongings that could be sold. And because our attention is limited at any given moment, the "home buyers" missed a lot of the details the "burglars" picked up on, and vice versa. The participants' memories of the video were not an accurate copy of the tape (many people think memory works this way) but a version of it filtered and edited by the particular goal they had while watching.

Another risk of focusing on a goal for a long time is that your unconscious can continue to notice things and evaluate them when you no longer mean to be pursuing that goal at all. A great illustration and comical metaphor for this effect comes at the opening of the movie *Modern Times,* starring Charlie Chaplin. Chaplin's famous Tramp has been working long and hard in a factory where his one job is to tighten large bolts on giant moving gears all day. Finally the quitting-time whistle blows and everyone puts down their tools and files toward the exit. Charlie is so crazed from countless hours spent tightening these bolts that he can't quite control himself and leaves with his wrenches still in his hands. Uh-oh, out in the street is a buxom woman in a large coat with, you guessed it, very large buttons going down the front. To Charlie's goal-crazed mind, these look just like those bolts in the factory, and he jumps at the woman, trying to tighten those buttons, and chases her down the street as she tries to get away.

Players of the game *Tetris* might know what I'm talking about. People who play *Tetris* for prolonged periods of time report that they start seeing the real world as though it were a larger version of the game itself. Jeffrey Goldsmith wrote about such an experience in a *Wired* magazine article in 1994. He stayed for a week in Tokyo with a friend who had a Game Boy: "Tetris enslaved my brain. At night, geometric shapes fell in the darkness as I lay on loaned tatami floor space. Days, I sat on a lavender suede sofa and played Tetris furiously. During rare jaunts from the house, I visually fit cars and trees and people together." When we devote so much time and attention to a pursuit, it begins to pattern our thoughts, mental images, and even dreams in entirely unintended ways. The *Tetris* player viewed the world in terms of the shapes it includes, and the mental operations of the game occurred unbidden, with the player unconsciously fitting things together, rotating them to make a good fit—everything processing through the filter of a game played so much it had become hyperaccessible in his mind. Dream researchers have even found that people who played *Tetris* all day, even amnesiacs with no memory of having played, reported having dreams of different shapes falling from the sky, rotating and fitting into the pattern of spaces below.

I had the same experience in my office in the late 1980s when I became addicted to playing *Pac-Man*, the monochromatic version available for the very primitive desktop PCs of the time. My fingers would fly over the left, right, up, and down arrow keys and I got very good at evading the ghosties and racking up huge totals of points. One day after spending too long playing the game when I should have been getting work done, I looked up and noticed it was time to go down the hallway for a lunch-time brown-bag talk. To my surprise, when I went out into the hallway I immediately looked left down that hall, and then straight ahead down that other hall, to make sure they were clear before heading down to the talk. Our floor of the NYU Psychology Building was a maze of corridors (visitors often got lost) and when I got to the next juncture, I again found myself stopping to peer around the corner to make sure the way was clear before proceeding. To my *Pac-Man*–crazed mind it was as if our office floor had become the game maze, causing me to react to other people in the hallways as if they were Blinky, Pinky, Inky, and Clyde.

A Little Help from Your Friends

One of the most important mental operations your goals influence is the evaluation of things and people as good or bad, depending not on your personal values or long experience with them so much as on whether they help or hinder that goal. Your current goal can even unconsciously change who you consider your best friends to be. Most of us have diverse friendships; we don't do the same kinds of things with all of our friends. We like to confide in some and talk about serious things, with others we like to do activities like hiking or playing golf, with others the focus is on our kids. In college, that intense formative period of our young adulthood in which we create friendships that often last for the rest of our lives, the main activities we engage in are studying, or hanging out and relaxing. With this in mind, researchers used the shifting contexts of college to examine how goals might recast our close friendships. Could we feel closer to certain friends instead of others depending on the goal—studying versus relaxing—we have at the time?

Gráinne Fitzsimons and her research team asked a group of college students who their best friends were and what kinds of activities they did with them. The participants completed a short language test with words (primes) related to achievement and high performance, or to relaxation and enjoyment. Next, they completed a task designed to prime the achievement goal or the "relax and have fun" goal, without their realizing it. Then came the crucial measure: all of the students were asked to rank their set of friends, the ones they'd listed at the start of the study, from best friend to least-close friend. If the achievement goal had been triggered, the student listed people they typically studied with as being their best friends, but if the fun-party goal had been primed, now the student listed their party pals as being their best friends. The goal reordered the students' pecking order of best friends to reflect which ones were of more help in attaining it.

Not only does our current goal affect how we feel about our current friends, but it influences who we become friends with in the first place.

Students at Northwestern University first had their goal for academic success, or for physical fitness, primed so that it was operating unconsciously in the background. If their academic achievement goal had been primed, the students wanted to be friends with people whom they could study with, but if their fitness goal had been primed instead, they wanted to be friends with others they could work out with. They were not aware of the influence of their active goals on their friendship choices.

This effect works both ways. Not only do your goals affect how you think about your friends and other close relationships, but merely thinking about a close personal relationship can influence how effectively or vigorously you pursue your goal. Thinking about your mom, for example, brings to mind (often unconsciously) the goals that you associate with her, such as making her proud of you. Fitzsimons and I brought in college student participants who had said on a questionnaire a few months earlier that they had the goal of making their mother proud of them, and we also brought in a second group of participants who had other goals regarding their mother, such as helping her or being good friends with her (but not making her proud). Next, we had some of them think about their mothers, but just in a very incidental way, such as writing down what she did on a typical Saturday, drawing a map of her neighborhood, listing her hobbies, and so on. In the control group, the participants just answered questions about themselves, none about their mothers.

Did thinking about their moms trigger the goal of making her proud—that is, achievement motivation? After the "mom" priming part of the experiment, all of the participants then worked on a short verbal task, taken from the board game Scrabble. We gave each of them the same seven wooden letter tiles, and their job was to come up with as many different words as they could in five minutes using just those letters. As we had predicted, the students who had the goal of making their mothers proud of them *and* who had just thought about their mom before the Scrabble task outperformed all of the other participants. Thinking about Mom was not enough if you did not associate her with the goal of high performance and achievement; also, wanting to make your mom proud of you was not enough if you had not just thought about her and so primed, or "woken up," that goal. Merely thinking about an important person in your life therefore makes it more likely you will then immediately pursue the goal you typically associate with them. Importantly, this effect can occur even when the person is not there—she may not be physically present, but she is *psychologically* present. It doesn't matter if she is actually thousands of miles away from you.

So our current goal influences what we like and dislike; it can cause us to like some people more than others depending on whether they are a help or a hindrance to our achieving a goal. Your current goal can even cause you to like someone you'd normally not like at all. For instance, that goal can change how you'd normally react to negative, rude behavior, and if that rudeness is good for your current goal, you can actually end up liking that rude person.

Take a scenario in which a personnel director is interviewing candidates for a job opening, a situation that our lab simulated by making a realistic videotape of a job interview. The camera was positioned behind the interviewer at his desk, so you only saw him from behind, but you could see the person being interviewed seated in front of the desk. Everyone who participated in the study saw the same tape, with one exception. The exception had nothing to do with the job interview itself. Rather, in this fairly busy office, with secretaries and others coming in and out during the interview, a coworker named Mike suddenly appeared in the doorway and reminded the job interviewer that it was noon and they had planned to go out to lunch that day. The key difference between the two tapes was how Mike acted. In one version, Mike was very polite and even deferential, apologizing for interrupting the interview and saying he would wait outside the door. In the other version, Mike was instead very rude, angrily pointing out that they had made plans to go out to lunch that day and it was time to go.

The participants had not been told to judge Mike at all, only to evaluate the job candidate on whom the camera was focused, in terms of how suitable he was for the job. Here is where the goals come in. One group of our participants was told that the job interview was to be a waiter at a nearby restaurant. We knew that most people think that waiters are supposed to be polite and deferential—with a "the customer is always right" kind of attitude. The other group of participants was told the interview was for a very different kind of job—that of a reporter at the *New York Daily News*, assigned to cover organized crime. The ideal qualities for the crime reporter were the exact opposite of those for the waiter—the crime reporter had to be tough, aggressive, and persistent—rude, if need be.

The job candidate was the same in both videotapes, and the questions asked by the interviewer during the videotape were generic and vague enough to apply to both positions, and regarded things such as employment history, motivation to do well, and so on. But after the participants watched the tape, we asked them—surprise!—not about the actual job candidate, but about Mike, who had interrupted. We asked how much they liked Mike and also to rate him on several personality traits, such as politeness and rudeness.

As you would expect, in a control condition where no job was mentioned, the participants liked polite nice Mike significantly more than rude nasty Mike. This tendency was even stronger in the waiter condition. People usually like polite and kind people more than rude and nasty people; no surprise there. But here is the kicker: in the crime reporter condition, participants actually liked *rude* Mike more than they liked polite Mike. This occurred even though they clearly recognized he was rude and aggressive. What changed here was that these traits, while normally not a good thing, *were* a good thing for the participants' current goal of evaluating the job candidate for a crime reporter condition. While that goal was active and operating, they happened also to encounter Mike, and even though they had no conscious intentions or instructions to evaluate Mike at all, their active goal reacted positively to his rudeness. The active goal, consciously focused on someone else entirely, caused them to like a person whom, without that goal operating at the time, they would have clearly disliked instead.

The implications for real life are considerable. The personal traits and values we might value in people in one domain of our life, say at work, may well not be the ones we'd value in a romantic relationship. And vice versa. Imagine a personnel director who in her off hours is actively dating and looking for that special someone. If that goal becomes strong enough over time, as with Charlie Chaplin's compulsion to tighten bolts, she might like and even hire people who are more suited for romantic relationships than for a position in the company. And she may not realize she is applying the wrong criteria, just like the Italian job employers who overwhelmingly favored attractive over unattractive applicants. Flip it around and one can see an investment banker or a police lieutenant liking and choosing to date people who are greedy and competitive, or efficient and emotionless. And would grade school teachers who value quiet, obedient, studious children then also prefer the same kind of person as a friend or date?

Cheating Ourselves

On April 21, 1980, a woman with short dark hair crossed the finish line of the Boston Marathon wearing a yellow Adidas running shirt with her race number pinned to it. Rosie Ruiz had taken first place in the women's category, beating 448 other runners. The crowd swirled nearby, and they had reason to be excited. Not only had an unassuming, twenty-six-year-old Cuban-born woman with very little previous marathon experience won one of the world's most famous athletic competitions—but she had come in with the third-best women's time in history, a stunning 2 hours, 31 minutes, and 56 seconds. She was an office assistant in everyday life, suddenly transformed into a running champion. It was the perfect Cinderella story.

Except that it wasn't. Not even four hours after declaring her the winner, the race organizers began receiving reports that threw the veracity of Ruiz's sensational performance into doubt. For one thing, the women who finished after her, world-class competitors who had been in the lead before the twentieth mile, had no memory of Ruiz overtaking them. In spite of the mounting suspicion, she stuck to her story, offering to take a lie detector test. The next day came the proverbial smoking gun: two Harvard students who had been watching the marathon had seen Ruiz pop out of the crowd and join other runners late in the race. Soon after, it also came out that when she had qualified to compete in Boston, in the New York City Marathon, she had done so only by riding the subway and using the same technique of slipping into the final stretch of the race. On April 29, eight days after her false victory, officials stripped Ruiz of her title.

Forms of cheating and deception, much less extreme than Rosie Ruiz's, of course, are commonplace in sports, as in "flopping" in basketball to trick the referee into calling a personal foul on your opponent (who didn't actually hit you very hard). We've all seen soccer players writhe on the ground in apparent agony, clutching their shins after a hard tackle, while viewers at home watch replays showing no contact even occurred. These spectacular and obvious sports examples highlight what researchers have shown to be a general human tendency: when the goal of achievement and high performance is active, people are more likely to bend the rules in ways they'd normally consider dishonest and immoral, if doing so helps them attain their performance goal.

Over my many years of teaching, I've found that very few students obediently put down their pens or pencils when I announce "time's up" on a test. Sometimes after asking them several times to hand in their test, and waiting many minutes, I've had to finally pull the test out of their hands while they are still furiously writing! (One even called me rude for doing so.) Experimentally, along with my NYU colleagues Peter Gollwit-zer and Annette Lee-Chai, my lab re-created this effect by first priming the achievement goal in our participants using the scrambled-sentence technique, with words such as *achieve, strive,* and *succeed* embedded in the test. Then we gave them a set of Scrabble letter tiles and three minutes in which to write down as many words using just those letters as they could. Then the experimenter said she had to leave the room to start another experiment, and if she did not get back in time she would announce "Stop" over the intercom when time was up, at which point they were to put down their pencils and stop working.

What our participants did not know was that we had a video camera hidden in the front of the room, and so could check later whether they had actually put their pens down when told to over the intercom, or whether they continued to write down words until the experimenter reappeared (after about five minutes). For those participants in which the achievement goal was operating, thanks to the prime, more than 50 percent of them "cheated" by continuing to write down words long after the Stop command; in the control condition only about 20 percent did so. If the active achievement goal can cause a person to bend the rules like this on a relatively unimportant task—with no prizes, no recognition, no possibility of anyone noticing; just a psychology experiment—it is easy to understand its power over our moral judgments and behavior when actual money or athletic victories are on the line.

Rosie Ruiz wanted to win the Boston Marathon so badly that she quite literally took shortcuts to do so. She cheated, in an outrageous and quite public manner. Her fervent desire to win the famous and prestigious race had convinced her that cheating to do so was somehow okay. Ruiz is an extreme example of a tendency we all have, to do things that help us achieve our strong goals that we would not do in the absence of that goal.

Our goals are such a powerful influence over us that they can override even our long-term values and beliefs. What if I told you that seminary students, wanting to spend their lifetimes as priests and ministers, and with strong personal values and self-concepts about helping others and behaving morally, would walk right by a sick person lying by the side of the road, just because their current goal was to get to their next class quickly because they were running late? But that is exactly what happened in the famous "Good Samaritan" study done at Princeton University in the 1970s.

In this experiment, conducted by John Darley and Daniel Batson, seminary students were asked to give a speech on either vocational careers for people studying to be members of the clergy, or the Good Samaritan parable in the Bible, in which one man helps a stranger who is in need after everyone else has passed him by. In order to give this speech, all participants had to walk from one building to another. Importantly, some participants were told that they were running late and had to hurry to reach the other building, while others were not. On the way to the other building, in a covered walkway, all of the students passed a shabbily dressed person slumped on the ground and in apparent distress. This person was actually part of the experimental team. The point of the study was to see who would help, and what situational and personality factors made a difference in helping.

It turned out that the only thing that predicted how likely a student was to stop and help was whether they were in a hurry or not. The type of speech they were to give, and how religious they were (as measured on a personality scale), made no difference. All that mattered was whether they had to get to the next classroom quickly. Stopping and helping someone would cost them time, and this was valued negatively by the "get there fast" goal. This objective was such a strong unconscious influence that it short-circuited their own moral beliefs, and even the very relevant moral principle that was currently on some of their minds—the Good Samaritan parable itself!

What's important to appreciate here is that the seminary students didn't somehow transform into bad people. Rather, their active goal directed their attention away from the person in need, made it less likely they'd feel that the person needed their help, devalued the notion of their stopping to help, and guided the seminary students' behavior toward getting to the next class as quickly as possible. Based on their discussions with the participants after the study was over, Darley and Batson believed that the students who were in a hurry did not interpret the person as being in distress, needing help. The researchers concluded that "because they were hurrying" the seminary students were so focused on getting to the next class on time that they did not have their normal empathic reactions to seeing a person in distress. Stopping to help meant being late for class, and so the goal placed a *negative* value on helping a person in distress, changing the students' minds from the positive value of helping someone in distress—which, ironically, is the entire point of the Good Samaritan parable they were in such a hurry to discuss in their next class.

A Dangerous Aphrodisiac

One factor that has tremendous power to change our goals and thus transform our values and behavior is power itself. The power of power is legendary: as the saying goes, power corrupts, and absolute power corrupts absolutely. Cases of power abuse and corruption among government officials are unfortunately all too commonplace; my home state of Illinois has almost a tradition now of sending politicians first to the Governor's Mansion and then to prison, because of their abuse of power for personal gain.

Often the power abuser seems entirely oblivious to how his or her behavior must seem to the public, as if they are somehow unaware of it being a misuse of power at all. But for anyone else, it doesn't pass the "smell test." George H. W. Bush's librarian of Congress sealed all materials related to the Iran-Contra arms scandal (in which Bush was involved as vice president) for fifty years, on Bush's last day in office in 1993; a few weeks later, that same person was named the librarian of the Bush Presidential Library at Texas A&M at the quite princely salary (especially at the time) of $400,000 a year. No connection between the two events, of course. And not that long ago, South Carolina's governor had to resign because he flew down to South America to see his mistress, hardly bothering to hide the fact. Examples of this are surprisingly easy to find, and you just have to shake your head in wonderment that the corruption was so out in the open—as if the power abuser were blind to the unconscious influence of power, unlike everyone around them.

There are several theories as to why power has this corrupting effect, but the one I'd like to focus on here is that power has the natural effect of activating one's own important, personal goals—the ones that are usually constrained or suppressed because of social disapproval or expected punishments for pursuing them. These are often selfish goals that are achieved at the expense of other people. Power gives you the ability to get what you want despite others' objections or lack of consent. What our lab's research has shown, in fact, is that giving a person power reveals what those deep wants actually are. And we can quote my home state's all-time hero, Abraham Lincoln, on this point: "Anyone can do the right thing when they are made to," he wrote. "If you really want to judge a man's character, give him power."

In the 2016 U.S. presidential campaign, more than a dozen women came forward to level accusations against Donald Trump for abusing his power and status to inappropriately touch or kiss them—for example, contestants reported that as owner of the Miss Universe and Miss Teen USA beauty pageants, he felt entitled to walk into their dressing rooms while many were naked or half-naked, and Trump had been caught on tape by *Access Hollywood* ten years earlier bragging about walking up to women he didn't know and kissing and fondling them. Quite discouragingly, such heinous behavior by the powerful is not unusual, and even tolerated by some, although scientists have been studying it for a while.

Our lab became interested in the issue of sexual harassment in the 1990s after a Supreme Court nominee, Clarence Thomas, was accused of inappropriate advances by a former employee, Anita Hill. In the years since, our country has made gains in addressing this systemic problem, but there is clearly much progress still to be made. Sexual harassment is the sexual objectification of subordinates (or less powerful coworkers), the act of treating them as sex objects instead of with respect as a colleague or work teammate. There are several forms that sexual harassment can take, but one of the most egregious is the quid pro quo variety, as in, *I'll give you this in exchange for that.* This can be explicit or implicit. To give a real-life example, in one case a male boss in Tennessee actually said to his female subordinate, in front of a roomful of employees, "Let's go discuss your raise at the Holiday Inn."

In 1993, Louise Fitzgerald, a law professor at the University of Illinois, examined the body of Supreme Court cases of quid pro quo sexual harassment, especially the testimony of the accused (usually male) harassers. She concluded from her study that fully 75 percent of the accused harassers *did not know or realize they were doing anything wrong.* Their usual story was that 1) they were genuinely attracted to the woman, and 2) they behaved toward her just like we all do toward someone we are attracted to: we smile at them, ask them out, court them, behave amorously toward them. In other words, they believed—apparently sincerely, according to Fitzgerald's analysis—that they were genuinely attracted to the victim of their harassment *solely* because of her qualities (looks, demeanor, personality), and that it had nothing to do with their power over her.

Fitzgerald's conclusions tipped us off that power might be having an unconscious influence over the harassers, in unconsciously activating their strong personal goal of having sexual relations with women, causing them to be attracted to women they have power over and to behave toward them in inappropriate ways. In its extreme or quid pro quo form, the powerful boss uses that power inappropriately to pursue the objective of having sex with women he has power over, in the form of hiring or firing them, and doling out raises and promotions.

At the time, the mid-1990s, other researchers had developed personality scales that distinguished between men who were likely to sexually harass and those who were not. What seemed to separate those with the tendency from those without it was the willingness to use leverage or power over a woman to get sexual favors from her. Another important determinant was what the person admitted he would do *if it was guaranteed he would not get caught*—that is, if nothing bad would happen to him. We and other researchers were astonished and dismayed by the large percentages of men who said they would probably commit rape and sexual assault under such circumstances.

In one study, we had men who scored high on these tendencies and those who scored low come into our NYU lab for a study purportedly on visual illusions. Before they worked on the illusions, we first primed them using the scrambled-sentence method with words related to power, such as *boss, authority, status,* and *power.* In the control condition no power words were presented. We expected that unconsciously activating the idea of power would then trigger the goal of sex in the high-sexual-harasser group, and that this would in turn cause them to become more attracted than otherwise to a female confederate also taking part in the visual illusion study. So after the two of them viewed and made ratings of several standard visual illusions, we took them into separate rooms and asked the male participants several innocuous questions about their experience in the experiment. One of those concerned the "other participant" and how pleasant and attractive she was. We could then see how the power-priming manipulation influenced how attracted the male participant had been to the female student who took part in the study with him.

First, the good news—the male participants who had scored low on sexual harassment and aggression tendencies found the woman to be equally attractive whether they were in the power priming or control priming group. For these men, power made absolutely no difference in how attracted they were to the woman. But it was a very different case for the men who were high in these harassment and aggression tendencies. For those in the control condition, without the idea of power being active, they actually found the woman to be unattractive—below the midpoint of the unattractive-to-attractive rating scale. It was only when the idea of power was active in their minds that they considered the woman to be attractive, as attractive as the nonharasser men had rated her to be. In other words, when the idea of power was triggered in their minds, exerting an unconscious influence on their feelings, the woman became more attractive to them. So what this study suggests for real-life power situations, quite alarmingly, is that sexual harassers are attracted to women *because* of the power they have over them.

Because these effects of power were shown to operate unconsciously, without our participants' awareness, it is easier to see how real-life bosses, such as those in the sexual harassment case studies reviewed by Louise Fitzgerald, could sincerely report they did not know they were doing anything wrong or unethical. To them they were behaving as they believed all of us do when we are attracted to someone. But what they missed was the effect of their own power over the person whom they found attractive. It is for this reason—that power itself can be an aphrodisiac, in the words of Henry Kissinger—that many universities and businesses have made it a matter of policy to forbid dating and romantic relationships between students and professors, bosses and subordinates, or anyone holding potential power over the other person's outcomes. The high-profile case of Yale philosophy professor Thomas Pogge, accused of quid pro quo sexual harassment of many of his students, highlights the continuing need for enforcement of such a policy. While Pogge's behavior, occurring as it did over many years, was especially egregious, the goal of such blanket policies is to prevent even the unintentional influences of power on attraction, which our studies as well as the actual legal cases show often occurs. For while the power holder may (consciously) believe that it is all innocent and aboveboard, the relatively powerless person may well feel uncomfortable and worry about real consequences for their career if they do not return the interest.

Still, there is a "good news" or "half-full" summary of our study, in that power did not corrupt everybody. For our participants who did not have the personal goal of sex connected with the idea of having power, there was no unconscious effect of power over their attraction to the woman. My Yale colleague Margaret Clark was the first to show that not everyone has selfish, exploitative goals regarding other people; there are also those of us who are more *communally* oriented toward their fellow humans and actually put the other person's interests above those of their own. Think parents, in this regard. Parents—good ones, at least—typically put the interests of their children above their own, even though the parents have the power in the household and not so much their children. How would such communally oriented people react to having power over others? We decided to examine this in our lab with . . . a desk.

At NYU, my colleagues Serena Chen and Annette Lee-Chai and I reasoned that people with communal orientations or goals toward other people would react to power differently than the rest of us. We used a personality scale that Margaret Clark had developed that distinguished those people, and selected a communal and a control group of participants for our studies. In the first experiment, we had participants come into my actual professor's office for the study, saying that all of the usual lab rooms were busy at the time. They were casually asked to sit in one of the two chairs in the office: either in my big, leather chair (which I still have, and am sitting in right now, in my office at home) behind my desk, or in the student's small, wooden chair in front of the desk. We did this to prime the idea of power in a naturalistic way. For the students in the study, sitting behind my desk was the power position, sitting in front of it the low-power position.

Then we gave the participants some questionnaires that measured how concerned they were with what others thought of them, and also fairly explicitly measured racism. If you weren't that concerned about what others thought of you—a hallmark of having power, because others can't do harm to you—then you would have lower scores on the "caring what others thought" scale and higher scores on the racism measure. Indeed, that is what we found in the control condition: Participants were less concerned about what others thought when they sat in the powerful professor's chair than when they sat in the relatively lower-power student chair in front of the desk. But the opposite effect happened for the students who had communal goals toward other people, who generally put others' interests above their own. For them, sitting in the "power chair" caused them to care *more* than usual about what others thought, and they became *less* racist when in the power chair, not more.

In a further study, power-primed participants, given the choice, took the easy tasks in the experiment for themselves and left the harder ones for the other person to do. Unless, again, they were communally oriented individuals. When those participants were primed with power-related words, they subsequently took more of the harder tasks and left the easy ones for the other person to do. When the idea of having power was active in their minds, they became more concerned about the other person, and less about themselves. The unconscious effect of power on our participants depended on their own important goals, and unconsciously activating the idea of power revealed clear differences in their selfishness and their degree of concern for other people. In other words, it revealed their character.

Lincoln was more right than he knew.

What we wish for, our desired futures in the short term as well as the long, has considerable and mainly hidden effects on our minds and behavior. More than we may realize, our current goal is in control, and often overrides our core beliefs and personal values, making us de facto a different person while that goal is operating. This is why we have to be careful what we wish for, because these wishes and desires can take over our minds in ways we are not aware of. We are delegating control to that goal, and while we may not be aware of or even approve of what that goal is up to, we are nonetheless personally responsible for it.

We need to be especially careful when it comes to our own important and possibly selfish goals that, if satisfied, would come at the expense of others. This is why it is so important to cultivate a genuine care and concern for others, because those tendencies will reveal themselves to others, even unconsciously on our part, when we get the chance to act on them, as in our power studies. Above all, never wish for bad outcomes for yourself or anyone else, as you might do when you're angry at them, because to your mind a goal is a goal, and that spiteful wish might come back to bite you. On the other hand, wishing for positive things, such as setting an important goal for yourself, can help make your dreams come true—because while you're dreaming, your unconscious never sleeps.

CHAPTER 9

The Unconscious
Never Sleeps

"Over the years, I've found one rule. It is the only one I give on those occasions when I talk about writing," explains the larger-than-life American author Norman Mailer in *The Spooky Art,* his book on being a writer. "A simple rule. If you tell yourself you are going to be at your desk tomorrow, you are by that declaration asking your unconscious to prepare the material. You are, in effect, contracting to pick up such valuables at a given time. Count on me, you are saying to a few forces below: I will be there to write."

Mailer's strategy clearly worked for him. Over the course of his lengthy career, he wrote more than thirty books and became one of the most celebrated—and controversial—writers in the United States. In 1948, he published his first novel, *The Naked and the Dead,* about his experiences as a soldier in World War II, which catapulted him into the literary firmament at the precocious age of twenty-five. While many writers of his era would see their future creative output blocked or severely delayed after the success of a first novel—notably, Ralph Ellison's *Invisible Man,* Harper Lee's *To Kill a Mockingbird,* or Joseph Heller's *Catch-22,* all magnificent books—Mailer kept writing away. He threw his wild energy at nearly every genre, refusing to limit himself just to fiction: essays, reportage, biography, creative nonfiction, plays—he tried it all. While Mailer may have failed to write the Great American Novel, he was undoubtedly a Great American Writer.

Where does such artistic fecundity come from?

Mailer considered his unconscious a full partner in his writing projects—and a partner to be treated with respect. He believed that he had to establish a reliable trusting relationship with his hidden mind. If you give your unconscious such an assignment, he said, then you'd better fulfill your part of the bargain and be there the next morning to write, on schedule, and not decide to sleep in, or take the day off. Otherwise, and especially if this kept happening, your unconscious would not take you seriously the next time you made such a request, and would not prepare the material you wouldn't be there to work on anyway.

Your unconscious knows what your important goals are by how much you think about them consciously and how much time and effort you put into them. As we saw in the last chapter, for important goals especially, your values and feelings and choices become slanted in the direction that best helps you to accomplish those goals, literally changing your mind for the sake of that goal. In this chapter the pervasive influence of the future on the hidden workings of the mind will become even more apparent. We are unconsciously working on our important goals behind the scenes: making use of *downtime* during the day when the conscious mind is not currently engaged on some task, and while we are at sleep at night; always *vigilant* like a sentinel, on the lookout for information relevant to that goal and noticing events and objects that might be helpful, which we'd otherwise miss; and trying to *find answers* that we are having difficulty coming up with consciously. My alligator dream was a perfect example of how my mind unconsciously came up with a solution to a problem I'd been racking my brain over for many years.

Behind the scenes, your mind is working on your future, constantly. Indeed, neuroscience has shown this is the mind's default mode, what it spends its time doing when nothing else is going on. It is working on important problems that have not yet been solved in the past or the present, those that are still to *be* solved in the future. It is guiding us in every way possible toward a future in which our important goals will have been achieved, our important needs met, and our important problems solved. The research on Unconscious Thought Theory described in Chapter 6 showed how periods of unconscious thought are superior in combining and integrating many different relevant features and pieces of information. Early research on creativity, on coming up with "out of the box" solutions to seemingly unsolvable problems and dilemmas, also showed that these solutions are often produced by unconscious insights, the solution fully formed when it is delivered to consciousness.

By a very strange coincidence, the insightful problem-solving capacities of the unconscious mind were discovered in the 1930s by an American psychologist with a name eerily similar to that of the famous author of *The Naked and the Dead*, who had independently championed the role of unconscious thought in creative work.

Norman Mailer, meet Norman Maier.

Revelations in the Bathtub

The coincidences do not end with the nearly identical names. It turns out that Norman Maier has several connections to this book. One of his students was T. C. Schneirla, later to became the curator of the American Museum of Natural History and the author of the classic paper on "should I stay or should I go" approach-avoidance motivations, which was featured in chapter 5. Maier's mentor while at the University of Chicago from 1929 to 1931, where he performed his famous creativity experiments, was Professor Karl Lashley, the original thinker who, as we described in Chapter 4, was the first to discover priming and mental readiness effects. Maier went from Chicago to the University of Michigan, where he served on the Psychology Department faculty for more than forty years and, in another eerie coincidence, passed away in September 1977—the very month I began my graduate work there.

Maier was a maverick, interested in reasoning and problem-solving in the era of behaviorism. His early work at Chicago under Lashley identified one major problem with conscious problem-solving, called *functional fixedness*, in which we dwell too much on the usual use of an object and miss other, more creative ways it might be used. This happens even more when we are under time pressure or stress. Maier discovered that unconscious mechanisms working on the problem, because they are not as bound as conscious thought by a limited focus of attention, can come up with these novel solutions where conscious reasoning can't, and deliver them to us as sudden "aha!" moments.

In his famous experiment, Maier filled a large empty room in the Psychology Laboratory of the University of Chicago with normal, everyday objects such as extension cords, tables and chairs, poles, and pliers and clamps. Of particular importance were two long ropes that he hung from the ceiling so that they reached all the way to the floor. One rope was hung over by a wall, and the other was in the center of the room. Into this unusual and cluttered space he brought his sixty-one participants. Each of them, one at a time, was asked to solve many problems involving the various objects in the room. Some had rather simple solutions and some not so simple. But the real focus of the study was the problem involving the two ropes. Maier told each participant that his task was to tie the ends of the two cords together. The catch was that they were too far away from each other for anyone just to take one end and walk over to the other cord and tie them together. Maier started the stopwatch in his pocket without the participant knowing he did so, just as we would do sixty years later in our rude-or-polite interruption study at NYU.

The creative solution was to tie one of the heavy tools (pliers or clamps) to the end of one rope, put it in motion so it swung toward the other rope, then bring the other rope and, when it was in range, tie the two ends together. Thirty-nine percent of the participants solved the problem on their own, not needing any hints. The rest had not solved it after ten minutes had passed. At this point, they were given the first of two hints; if after another couple of minutes the first hint didn't produce the solution, the second hint was given. Thirty-eight percent of the participants were able to solve the problem after one or more of the hints had been given—this was half of the total number of participants who eventually solved the problem, and the group that Maier was particularly interested in. The remainder of the participants, 23 percent, never solved the problem even after the second hint and additional time.

The first hint was the priming hint. Maier walked over to the window and incidentally brushed the nearby rope with his body, putting it in slight motion. (If this subtle clue did not work after a few minutes, Maier resorted to a not-so-subtle one—he just handed the participants the pliers and told them the solution involved using it.) There were sixteen participants who solved the problem after the hint involving the accidentally swaying rope. They had been puzzling over the problem for ten full minutes, but after Maier had casually put one of the ropes in motion, most of them came up with the solution, which involved tying the pliers to one of the ropes and putting it into motion, in less than forty seconds. But when asked afterward how they solved the problem, only one of the sixteen said that this event had aided them with the solution. The other fifteen participants did not mention the swaying of the cord in describing how they came up with the answer; in fact, none of them remembered having seen the cord move. According to Maier, "They insisted that if the suggestion aided them, they were certainly unconscious of it."

Maier concluded that the most plausible explanation was that the motion hint played an important part in bringing about the solution but was not *consciously* experienced by the participant. He was struck also by how the solution appeared in the participants' consciousness in a complete form: "suddenly and no development could be noted." It was not as if steps along the way were experienced and then conscious reasoning guided the process and put together the solution. Rather, the new way of understanding the problem—seeing the ropes not as ropes but as part of a pendulum—is suddenly there in its complete form, having been produced by unconscious means.

At around the same time, another famous creativity problem was being developed by Karl Duncker, a German psychologist exiled by the Nazis in 1935. It was published posthumously in 1945. The problem involves the following material: a book of matches, a box of tacks, and a candle. You are given these items and the task of fixing the candle to the wall so that it won't drip wax on the floor when it is lit. This is similar to Maier's rope problem because the solution involves thinking outside the box (literally, in this case) to see the box the tacks are in as not just a box but as a potential platform for the candle. Once you see it this way, it is a simple matter to use one of the tacks to fix the box to the wall, set the candle upright inside the open box, and light it with the matches. The key to the puzzle is to think of the box as a separate item from the tacks it holds, not just as a container for the tacks, but as something useful in its own right.

One way to unconsciously induce this kind of insight is to subtly emphasize the box and tacks as being two separate things. E. Tory Higgins of Columbia University and his colleagues came up with a way to do this, using words to prime the insight, instead of a behavior—brushing against the rope—as Maier had done. The key was to emphasize, or prime, either the word *and* or the word *of* before the participant ever worked on the candle problem. Thirty male undergraduates were first presented slides of ten objects described by the experimenter using *and* instead of *of*; for example, a "bottle and water" instead of a "bottle of water," a "crate and plates" instead of a "crate of plates." Then they were assigned the candle problem.

Just like in Maier's study after the rope-in-motion hint, a greater number of participants solved the problem in the *and* condition than in either the *of* condition or the control condition (with just the slides and no verbal description of them). Eight out of ten students solved the problem after the *and* hint, but only two out of ten did so in each of the other two conditions. Again, the interesting part was when the participants were asked afterward how they solved the problem, and in particular, whether anything in the early part of the study might have affected their ability—either positively or negatively—to solve it. Just as in Maier's rope study, none of the participants in the candle study reported any relation between the tasks. They expressed no awareness of any influence of the slide task (*and* versus *of*) on their ability to solve the candle problem. The prime was used by the unconscious to solve the problem, and participants were unaware of its help.

Researcher Janet Metcalfe, also of Columbia University, has studied these "insight" problems, difficult puzzles wherein it is just as hard to figure out how to solve the problem as it is to figure out the answer. These are problems such as "Describe how to put 27 animals in four pens in such a way that there is an odd number of animals in each pen," or "Describe how to cut a hole in a three-by-five inch index card that is big enough for you to put your head through." For these types of problems, your predictions about whether or not you will eventually be able to find the answer do not at all predict whether you do eventually solve the problem or not. It is as if we do not have conscious access to the answer *or* to the way in which it will be solved. Metcalfe concluded that for these kinds of problems, too, the solution, when it came, appeared with a sudden, unforeseen flash of illumination. This is because the solver was working on the problem unconsciously, and when she reached a solution, it was delivered to her fully formed and ready for use.

How exactly is this seemingly magical feat accomplished? As we saw in Chapter 6, Dijksterhuis and colleagues in their Unconscious Thought Theory research showed that a better, or at least equally good, choice among alternatives is made when the person makes the choice after a period of unconscious thought rather than conscious thought. A key component of this theory is that when one is distracted or prevented from consciously considering the alternatives, neural reactivation occurs, in which the same brain regions used when acquiring the information on which the decision is to be based are now active unconsciously. And recall that this finding was later confirmed by David Creswell and colleagues at Carnegie Mellon University when they showed that the unconscious problem-solving process was making use of the same brain regions that had been active when consciously learning about the problem and all the relevant information. And the more those regions were active while conscious attention was elsewhere, the better the resulting solution to the problem.

This might remind you of the famous story of the old Greek in his bathtub. You know, the one who yelled "Eureka!" These insight problems studied by Maier and Duncker, Metcalfe and Higgins are being solved in the same way Archimedes suddenly solved a physics problem he'd long been puzzling over, when the answer came to him out of the blue while he was relaxing in a public bath. According to the Greek historian Plutarch, after the solution dawned on him Archimedes shouted "Eureka!" several times and then ran off naked down the streets of Syracuse without explaining himself to anyone. Indeed, there are many examples of scientific and other intellectual and artistic breakthroughs that occurred when the person least expected it and was thinking about something else—such as to Einstein while shaving, and Archimedes while bathing. And even when the person was not thinking at all, but was fast asleep.

Ah yes—dreams! The wonderful, muggy, Floridian swamp of the mind, where strange journeys occur, and breakthroughs sometimes take place. At least *I* think of dreams this way, since in such a place I discovered my miraculous alligator.

Benzene. An organic compound made of only two elements from the periodic table—hydrogen and carbon, six atoms of each. Colorless and toxic, it holds together many important compounds like a fantastic glue. Raw petroleum exists thanks to benzene, making it very important to modern civilization. Yet in spite of its clear importance, in the nineteenth century it was still shrouded in mystery. After the English scientific genius Michael Faraday discovered its existence in 1825, more than thirty-five years passed and chemists still didn't understand the structure underlying its gummy molecular core. This was troubling, since it limited science's ability to play with its full potential.

The German organic chemist August Kekulé was one of the scientists trying to unlock the secret of benzene in the 1860s. He was no newbie to the business of pondering hidden chemical truths—a few years earlier he had brilliantly theorized how carbon atoms in a sense linked arms to stay together—and he had the perfect look of the scholarly scientist: white rabbinical beard and furrowed brow. But his mind, both its conscious and unconscious components, as well as the minds of many other chemists, had been working on the problem of benzene to no avail. When might the crucial insight come?

Around this time, Kekulé was putting together a new chemistry textbook. One night at home, immersed in this project, he got sleepy. (Can you blame him?) Here is his account of what happened next:

I turned the chair to the fireplace and sank into a half sleep. The atoms flitted before my eyes . . . wriggling and turning like snakes. And see, what was that? One of the snakes seized its own tail and the image whirled scornfully before my eyes. As though from a flash of lightning I awoke. I occupied the rest of the night in working out the consequence of the hypothesis.

Another revelatory, creepy reptile—an alligator in my case, a snake in Kekulé's. The meaning of the dream with its momentous implications for chemical theory was immediately evident to him. It directly delivered to his conscious mind the insight that he needed. The snake eating its own tail—a mythical symbol known as the ourobouros—was the key that unlocked the cabinet with the secret: the benzene *ring*. Like the snakes in that fiery circle, benzene's hydrogen and carbon molecules linked themselves together in a cyclical fashion that alternated single and double bonds. Kekulé had solved the problem and his vision became as famous, or even more famous, than the discovery itself, which established him forever as one of the founding fathers of organic chemistry. But Kekulé's dream was not a miracle or supernatural event, because the dream was made possible by a mind well prepared, from extensive conscious thought and struggle with the problem. The amount of effort he had consciously put into solving this problem was understood by his mind to reflect how important it was to him to come up with a solution to the problem. In retrospect, his future was assured.

In all of these cases, genius and creativity were the result of unconscious problem-solving capabilities. In Mailer's case, he deliberately made use of downtime by giving his mind tasks to work on while he consciously did other things. In Maier's and Duncker's "think outside the box" creativity studies, unconscious solutions were produced for problems that conscious thought could not solve. The solution popped into the participants' conscious mind fully formed, ready to go, just like it did for Archimedes and Kekulé, when they were doing something else entirely. In all of these cases, the lightbulb creativity came from unconscious mental processes working on the same problem as the person's conscious mind. They were *teammates* working toward the same goal.

Be Like Mike

Frederic Myers was one of the first psychological scientists, a contemporary of William James, Pierre Janet, and Alfred Binet—all of whom are today much better known. It is actually a bit odd that Myers is not better known, because he was greatly respected and later eulogized by nearly every prominent psychologist of his era, and collaborated with Janet on the landmark research at the Salpêtrière Hospital in Paris. Among Myers's many intellectual quests was his lifelong study of genius and creativity. Myers's definition of *genius* anticipated the studies of creativity by Maier and Duncker, as well as the advice given by Norman Mailer to aspiring writers in *The Spooky Art*. Genius, said Myers, is the ability to make use of subliminal (unconscious) thought more than most people do or can. He said the inspiration of genius or creative breakthroughs comes from a rush of subliminal ideas into the conscious stream of ideas that the person is intentionally manipulating. Brilliant insights come from making more use of the unconscious powers of the mind than most people do.

There are people of genius in all walks of life, not only science and literature but inventors such as Thomas Edison and Steve Jobs, and songwriters and musicians such as Bob Dylan, who won the Nobel Prize in Literature in 2016 for lyrics that the Swedish Academy compared favorably to the work of the ancient Greek poets Homer and Sappho. Dylan, however, often seemed unaware of where these lyrics came from, or what they meant. When he was finally reached for his reaction to winning the Nobel Prize and was told of the comparisons made between his lyrics and the poetry of the ancient Greeks, he said he would leave such analysis to the academics, because he did not feel qualified to explain his lyrics. And guitar legend Eric Clapton recalled the time in 1975 when, on the beach at Malibu, Dylan offered him a song, "Sign Language," for Clapton's new album. "He told me he had written the whole song down at one sitting, without even understanding what it was about. I said I didn't care what it was about. I just loved the words and the melody. All in all it's my favorite track on the album."

In the sports world geniuses proliferate as well, and once in a while there comes along an athlete who "changes the game" by being so consistently different and creative that entrenched, established ways of playing cannot constrain them. Conventions become outmoded just because of that one person. In my lifetime no athlete seemed to be playing this "different game" as much as Chicago Bulls NBA star Michael Jordan.

It was Game Two of the first round of the 1986 Eastern Conference NBA playoffs, featuring the Boston Celtics against the Chicago Bulls, on a Sunday afternoon at Boston Garden. The Celtics, along with the Los Angeles Lakers, dominated the league in the 1980s and were at the pinnacle of their powers that year. Five future Hall of Famers played for Boston that season, including their awesome front three of Larry Bird, Robert Parish, and Kevin McHale. They were the number-one playoff seed in their conference, and were playing the number-eight seed, the Bulls, in the first round.

I watched that game from a rather unusual location—the paddock area behind Belmont Park race track in Elmont, New York. It was a beautiful spring afternoon and I had taken a train called the Belmont Special from Manhattan's Penn Station directly to the track out on Long Island. It was a great way to get out of the city and enjoy a beautiful park and fresh air and have fun watching—and placing some small bets on—the horse races.

I didn't go there to watch the Bulls-Celtics game, but after putting down my two-dollar bet on the fourth race of the day I noticed a crowd gathered around a large TV set on the wall. The sound was up so I could see and hear it was the playoff game. Celtics fans, I concluded, and went to watch the race.

When I came back after that race to put my money down for the fifth race, however, the crowd had grown exponentially. Now hundreds of people were gathered to watch. Someone had put the sound up as high as it would go, so I stopped to see what was going on. And then I stayed for the rest of the game and forgot all about the horses.

It was late in the game, and the score was much closer than most people had expected, but that wasn't the reason for the crowd. A rising star in the league named Michael Jordan was performing explosive alchemies on the court, driving through the vaunted Celtics defense—one of the best teams of all time, remember—like it wasn't even there, going to the basket or pulling up suddenly for a soft midrange jumper. He had scored 30 points, then 40, then over 50—he was going to break the record for the most points in a playoff game at this point (which he did, with 63 points, a record that still stands today). The Celtics could not stop him, and he was single-handedly keeping his team in the game. How was he doing this?

What remains in my memory is a kind of blur of improbable and beautiful baskets, a highlight reel of a virtuosic Jordan as he flashed and soared, darted and levitated. He was going where these very experienced defenders were not expecting him to go, pulling up for his jumper when they thought he was driving to the basket. The Celtics' instincts were just wrong, over and over again. Clearly Jordan was doing the unexpected, the creative and unusual, time and time again, and even when the Celtics made adjustments, he adjusted, too. Double- and triple-teaming him didn't work. The crowd around the TV at Belmont was gasping and cheering his every move.

His teammates later said that before the game, Jordan was especially focused. This was a nationally televised game on a Sunday afternoon in an era of just a few networks or TV coverage; the entire NBA-loving country was watching. He knew that and he put on a show. This was the day that Michael Jordan the phenomenon, His Airness, No. 23, officially arrived. He and his Bulls would go on to win six championships in the next twelve years—but that Sunday afternoon was when the legend was born.

The outmanned Bulls finally lost the game, in double overtime, and the Celtics would go on to win yet another NBA championship that year, but what remains as a luminous moment in sports history wasn't the Celtics' win, but Jordan's performance in the Bulls' loss. Larry Bird captured this best himself in his summary of the game to reporters afterward. "I think he's God disguised as Michael Jordan," said Bird. "He is the most awesome player in the NBA. Today in Boston Garden, on national TV, in the playoffs, he put on one of the greatest shows of all time. I couldn't believe anybody could do that against the Boston Celtics."

There is no way Jordan could have done what he did against the mighty

Celtics, playing as hard as they could in a playoff game in front of their home crowd on national television, by constantly *consciously* thinking and deciding what to do, what move to make, what shot to make, all through that game. Deliberate conscious thought is too slow, and the NBA game too fast, for that. He saw patterns of players and anticipated where they would go, well before anyone else did, and he constantly took advantage of that foresight. Think about it. A thousand tiny little things were happening on the court at every moment: this player moving there, that one there, an ever-whirling kaleidoscope of bodies and opportunities and risks—all of which required constant analysis and advantageous responses. Jordan's "instincts"—which is just another word for unconscious processes—were guiding him unerringly, and no one else had such instincts. His performance that day—and over the next twelve seasons— fit Frederic Myers's definition of a genius as someone who makes more and better use of their subliminal thought processes than do the rest of us. Because of the limits of the conscious mind in terms of how much information it can handle at any one time, and its relative slowness in dealing with that information, Jordan's unconscious delivered strategies he needed to counter the Celtics' increasingly desperate defenses against him fully formed, to his conscious mind, focused on the goal of winning that game. He had to be doing things this very experienced defense did *not* expect, that were not usual—that, in other words, were very creative. The amount of analysis and work being done unconsciously had the added benefit of freeing Jordan's conscious mind from those details, giving him more capacity for higher-level strategy and planning. Jordan was in "the zone"—that mythic state achieved when the unconscious clicks into its highest gear and the conscious mind tranquilly adds its own special contributions. Sports announcers in fact often describe a basketball player on a hot streak, who seemingly can't miss, as "unconscious," implying a level of performance higher than what can typically be attained through fallible, slow, limited conscious means.

Of course, as much as we want to "Be Like Mike" (as the Gatorade advertising slogan had it), all the unconscious problem-solving in the world won't give us his experience, physique, and skills from years of dedication and practice. To take such full advantage of unconscious help we have to first do the conscious work—as had Mailer, Archimedes, and Kekulé, in their own domains. Jordan certainly did his conscious homework: he was known to say that during his career he took more shots in his mind than he ever did on the court. And I didn't have my own little dream about the alligator until I'd first spent years of thinking and reading about my own personal puzzle.

But Michael Jordan's unbelievable outburst that April afternoon in Boston does show what fruits can be harvested if you follow Norman Mailer's advice and give your unconscious assignments as if it were your partner, and begin work on important tasks and goals early enough to reap the benefits of creativity and problem-solving while your conscious mind is on other things. In writing this book I have made frequent use of this advice—reading and starting to think about the next chapter a day or two before I'd actually have the time to work on it. What I have discovered is that ideas will come to me, and I will notice stories in the news or remember examples from the past that I would not have had or noticed otherwise. And I give this advice to my students as well: not to wait until a week before a paper is due, or a job talk is to be given, before starting to work on it, but instead to start early just to get that goal running and working for them—and in doing so glean the insights and advantages of that goal working in the background while they are consciously taking care of other things.

When the mind is not busy dealing with the present, it tends to focus on the future, working on goals and simulating different solutions. Thinking is "expensive" in terms of how much energy it requires—the human brain constitutes on average 2 percent of a person's total body weight but consumes about 20 percent of the energy a person expends while awake—and over evolutionary time we did not always have stores of food so readily available, and often had to spend a lot of our energy just finding our next meal. In other words, making efficient use of our mind's capacities by doing things more cheaply in the background makes a lot of adaptive and calorie-saving sense.

This arrangement reminds me of a project launched in 1999 to make use of downtime on thousands of PCs in order to search through massive sets of radio wave data recorded from different places in the universe. The point of doing so was to assist the search for extraterrestrial intelligence, or SETI. SETI@home was conceived by David Gedye along with Craig Kasnoff at the University of California, Berkeley, and is still a popular volunteer-distributed computing project. Proposed government funding for SETI was ridiculed by members of the U.S. Congress, most famously by Senator William Proxmire and his "Golden Fleece" awards, as wasteful and frivolous. So Gedye and Kasnoff looked to alternative, much cheaper ways to analyze the massive amounts of radio wave data. They did so by having volunteers (I was one of the early ones) download sets of the radio data that would then be analyzed on our own PCs when we weren't using them, with the results sent back automatically to SETI headquarters. In the same way, your mind is using downtime to work on your important goals and current concerns, and sending the results back to your consciousness—especially when solutions are discovered, as in the occasional spectacular dreams that culminate a great deal of intense, and expensive, conscious thought.

Sometimes our mind grabs on to downtime a bit too eagerly, such as when we are studying something for a test that we are not all that interested in, or a boring section of a book or newspaper that we are generally interested in. Our mind can wander away, and we find ourselves staring at the page, and even turning the page mechanically, without really reading what is on it. Our mind is thinking about something else entirely. What are those other things and why does the mind wander to them so much?

Motivational scientist Eric Klinger has studied these questions his entire career. On the average, we are awake and conscious sixteen hours of the day, and having conscious thoughts all that time. Klinger estimates that we have about four thousand discrete thought segments (thoughts on one topic before they switch to a different one) every day. His research has shown that fully one-third to *one-half* of all your waking thoughts are not focused on what you are doing or seeing right now, but are instead your mind wandering around to other topics. Evidently, these are topics it finds more interesting than whatever it is you are doing right then. (This is why I am sure this has never happened to you *not even once* while reading this book.) Students reading textbook chapters, and even people relaxing with a good book with less-than-engaging passages, turn instead to other thoughts: *Why didn't my boyfriend call, where do I want to go for dinner, will I ever get a job, am I ready for tomorrow's lecture, how am I going to afford that car I promised my son for his high school graduation?*

When our mind wanders, its wandering is being directed. It has a purpose, and it isn't random—it is all about our future, our important, unmet, still-standing goals, the things we are worried about and the things we need to get done pretty soon. The mind is making productive use of its downtime, much like the way your PC schedules updates and virus checking for the downtimes when you aren't using it.

Thoughts That Go Bump in the Night

Let's return to the mysterious "messages" of dreams. Modern psychological science research on this area, much of it by motivation expert Klinger, has shown that our currently important goals occupy not only our waking mental downtime but our sleeping minds as well. Klinger and his team studied people while their subjects were asleep, and when they showed the signs of being in the dreaming state (that is, when they displayed REM, or rapid eye movement, activity), he played words and phrases to them though headphones. These were designed to be relevant to the current life goals of the sleeping person—important goals such as "want to join a helping profession" or "be friends with my son again." In a control condition, words and phrases relevant to another sleeper's goals, but not their own, were played to the person. After a few minutes, the dreamers were woken up and asked to report what they had just been dreaming about. The dreamers were three times more likely to have dreamed about topics and themes related to the words and phrases if those words were related to their important goals than if they were not. During the night, the unconscious mind was clearly wide awake.

So even while we are dreaming, our mind is unconsciously working on our important goals and concerns, and is more sensitive than usual to incoming information relevant to those goals. It works on goals such as how to fix an important relationship that has gone sour, solving a problem at work, finding the right birthday present for your spouse or child, and even larger life goals related to your career. Klinger and his colleagues concluded that the priority your mind gives to your important goals continues to operate in your dreams while you sleep.

The influence of the future on the unconscious mind can also seem unpleasant at times. There are some objectives we can't just let go of when we want or even need to, like a looming term paper deadline or a painful conversation we know we should have with someone. We might procrastinate and put off those unpleasant but necessary activities for another day, going out drinking instead of studying, or telling ourselves we'll have that conversation later on in the week. In these cases, unresolved goals can continue to operate unconsciously even when we are actively *avoiding* working on them consciously. As Norman Mailer put it, "Rule of thumb: Restlessness of mind can be measured by the number of promises that remain unkept." Remember, your future-oriented mind is not all about making you feel relaxed and happy; it is all about getting your important goals and tasks completed. And if that means nagging you with worries and anxiety, so be it. Such stubbornness often leads to one's mind going bump in the night. In other words, it can lead to bad sleep.

A commonly reported problem in sleep studies is that when people wake during the night, worries and anxieties spontaneously pop into mind that prevent them from going back to sleep. While we are sleeping, the same areas of the brain that were consciously working on problems are continuing to try to solve them unconsciously. The unconscious is not very good at making specific plans for the future—good at finding solutions to problems, and pursuing a goal in general, yes, but not so good at formulating concrete plans for specific sequences of actions—so it punts the problem to the conscious mind, saying, "Here, you deal with it." If these worries are significant—like a test or presentation or whether to break up with our boyfriend or girlfriend—they come up as spontaneous thoughts once we awaken. One of my favorite Talking Heads songs put it best: it's the middle of the night and everyone else is asleep, but "I'm wide awake on memories—these memories can't wait."

In a study of insomnia that compared good and poor sleepers, of the people who reported having difficulty sleeping, more than 80 percent had difficulty getting back to sleep after waking in the nighttime. This is a problem people can have their entire lives. On the average these people had trouble getting back to sleep for more than seventeen years—one person had the problem for sixty years. The researchers found that by far, the most common type of thought that kept them awake, nearly 50 percent of them, was about the future, the short-term events coming up in the next day or week. Their thoughts were about what they needed to get done the following day, or in the next few days. Even the relatively positive thoughts of the night were about uncompleted tasks for the next day, such as getting a birthday present for a loved one. In short, the main cause of not being able to get back to sleep at night was negative, anxiety-provoking thoughts about the near future, about things they had to get done, problems they needed to solve.

Why did the mind, working unconsciously on these problems while the person slept, have to nag and bother them about the problem as soon as they woke up? Because the problems were important and time-sensitive ones that could not be solved unconsciously. They needed conscious problem-solving help. So as soon as the person woke up, as soon as their conscious mind was online again, these pressing goals and concerns were waiting for them in their mental in-box. In particular, what the unconscious process was asking for was a concrete plan. This is the specialty of conscious thought processes, and not something that can be done unconsciously, so the unconscious process nags. Once the plan is in place, the nagging tends to stop. You even might be able to get back to sleep.

Imagine you wake up and start to worry that maybe you left the oven on last night, or forgot to lock your door. You can lie there and worry, or you can get up and check. Then you can get back to sleep because the problem is taken care of. But other problems causing troubling thoughts in the night are not so easily fixed at three in the morning. Perhaps you have a health issue that you've been meaning to get checked but haven't yet, and you wake up worrying about that. You can't take care of it right then, but you can make a firm plan and commitment that the next morning when the doctor's office is open, you will call and make an appointment. Making that plan is all the unconscious goal is asking you to do, and you should be able to get back to sleep again.

Researchers have experimentally demonstrated how these plans can turn off the distracting, pestering influences of incomplete goals. Ezequiel Morsella and I and our colleagues showed how unfulfilled goals intrude on your conscious thoughts. Some participants in the study were told in advance that they were later going to take a geography quiz, in which they would be asked to name every state in the U.S.; the other participants were told they would be speed-counting the number of letters in state names presented to them (for example, WISCONSIN = 9). The key difference between these two future tasks was that one of them would be easier to do if one thought about it beforehand (naming all the states) and the other one would not (counting the number of letters in a state name). So we expected that having the state-naming goal would cause more intrusive thoughts (because the person would be unconsciously working on that goal in advance) compared to the letter-counting goal. The important part of the study came before the participants actually did their assigned task—we asked them to do an eight-minute meditation-like exercise requiring one to clear the mind of excess thought and to focus on breathing only. During this time they wrote down any intrusive thoughts they might have. Those participants who expected to name all fifty states reported having seven times more intrusive thoughts (thinking of all the state names they could) than did the participants who were expecting to do the letter-counting task. This shows the first part of the "nagging unconscious" effect, especially during downtime.

What about the second part? Would making a concrete plan for how to complete that incomplete goal cut down on the nagging thoughts? To examine this, researchers E. J. Masicampo and Roy Baumeister first had their participants write about two important tasks they needed to finish, such as a term paper that was due soon, and then gave them a passage from a mystery novel to read—*The Case of the Velvet Claws*, by Erle Stanley Gardner, featuring the infallible defense attorney Perry Mason. After they read about the exploits of the intrepid Mr. Mason, they were asked how often their mind had wandered while they were reading, and also how much they had thought about that unfinished task. As you might expect, participants reported many thoughts about the looming term paper, as their mind wandered away from the mystery novel. However, a different group of participants, before they read the book passage, had been instructed to make a plan for exactly how they were going to complete the unfinished task. These participants reported having significantly fewer intrusive thoughts about the incomplete goal during their reading.

In a further experiment, participants were told that later on in the study they would be asked to list as many sea creatures as they could. But first they had to complete a task having nothing to do with sea creatures. Nonetheless, names of various sea creatures popped into their heads uncontrollably during this first task, distracting them from doing well on it. Not so for another group of participants who were given a good plan for how later to come up with a lot of sea creature names—by going through the alphabet and coming up with a name for each letter. With that helpful plan in place, thoughts about the upcoming task intruded much less on their first task. Having a concrete plan to complete a pressing, upcoming goal really cuts down on the unconscious goal's pestering. Finally, Masicampo and Baumeister also showed that making concrete plans cut down on the nervousness and anxiety we feel about deadlines and important but incomplete projects.

As Mailer admonished us, a good relationship between unconscious and conscious mental states isn't free. It is based on trust, so for it to work you have to live up to your part of the bargain. If you fulfill your part of the deal, and really do follow through, then the next time you try the middle-of-the-night trick of making a plan to get those nagging thoughts to stop, it will continue to work. But if you don't carry out that plan, maybe the next time the nagging will continue because you have shown that you really don't mean what you say when you make those plans. The nagging might not stop in fact until you actually do, say, call the doctor, or solve the problem, meaning you might well be up all night with thoughts that can't wait.

A few months after my sister in California had her first child, we had a mini family reunion in Illinois so we could all meet the new arrival. Her baby was the first of the next generation of our nuclear family, so we siblings gathered round the new mom in the living room to hear all about it, after she had settled the baby in a back bedroom for a nap. After fifteen minutes or so, she was midsentence in a really interesting story when she suddenly stopped talking, just stopped cold, and I saw her eyes shift hard right like she was trying to look behind her down the hallway. Puzzled, we asked what was wrong, and after a pause she explained she thought she'd heard something. None of the rest of us had heard anything at all. The back bedroom where her daughter was sleeping was more than sixty feet away. We stayed quiet for a while so that she could make sure there weren't any cries or sounds of distress, and then she continued her story.

Our most important goals and motivations are on the job 24/7, constant, vigilant sentinels for anything going on that is relevant to them. They are active in the background when we are engrossed in other activities or even when we are asleep. Sleeping parents can become instantly awake at the sound of a baby's whimper yet sleep contentedly through a raging thunderstorm. To make this possible the sleeping human brain continuously processes sensory signals, even when we are literally unconscious during sleep, and then triggers full awakening to important, critical stimuli in less than a second. It's amazing.

There is a classic experimental task in psychology that shows how attention-grabbing our goals are, even when we are trying to ignore them and pay attention to something else. It is called the Stroop task, invented in 1935 by one John Ridley Stroop of George Peabody College in Nashville,

Tennessee. In this task, all you have to do is to name the colors in which words are printed when presented to you one at a time. You don't have to name the words; actually the word itself is not relevant to your assigned chore of just saying what its color is. The interesting part of the Stroop task is that we can't help but read the words; it is an automatic and uncontrollable response. And then because we are reading the words, if they are relevant to our important goals then the goal will cause us to pay attention to them even when we are trying not to—because doing so distracts us from what we are supposed to be doing, which is to name the *color* of the word as fast as we can. The more the meaning of the word distracts us, the longer we take to say the color.

You can use how long a person takes to name the colors of particular categories or types of words as a measure of how interested they are in that category, or if those words correspond to an important goal or need for them. The longer they take to name the color, the more distracting and the more motivationally relevant that category of words. For example, in one such study, frequent drinkers of alcohol were slower to name the colors of alcohol-related words such as *beer, cocktail,* and *liquor* than were those who did not drink as much. What is more, the amount of this distraction, the degree to which the alcohol-relatedness of the words slowed down the color naming, was a function of how much that person usually drank in a week. The more important the goal, the more grabby were words related to it, and the more distraction caused by those words when the person was just trying to name their color as fast as possible. The distraction, caused by the automatic attention given to goal-relevant words, happened even though the person was not currently thinking about that goal at all, and when thinking about it would hurt their performance on what they were trying to do at the time, and even when, as in this experiment, there is no forewarning that anything related to the goal was about to happen—for the alcohol-related words to be distracting, it had to be because the goal of drinking was constantly vigilant in the background.

This is why cell phones are so dangerously distracting while you are driving. Texts or phone calls from those you are closest to, friends and family, are highly relevant to your important social relationship goals. Those central goals are constantly vigilant, ready to distract you by directing your attention toward your friends and loved ones. By now we all realize how dangerous texting while driving is, because you have to look away from the road to look at your device, then read it, and then (worst of all) type in your response. Of course, these instinctual reactions take your conscious attention away from the crucial demands of safely navigating your car through traffic.

And it is not just texting—today there are many other apps that drivers engage with while they are on the road. Navigational aids (which help with your current goal to get to where you're going); Snapchat, on which you can post photos while you are driving that show the speed of your vehicle (that meet your social goals of interacting with friends and being noticed by and popular with many others); and (even worse) Pokémon Go, which has drivers looking for game creatures out on the highways (with the goal of competing against friends and others). No wonder we in the United States are now recording the highest-percentage increases in highway fatalities in fifty years. This is after four decades of steady decline. The rate jumped in 2015 and increased even more sharply in 2016—there were 17,775 highway deaths in just the first six months of the year. And state police and other authorities blame this sudden increase on cell phones and phone apps. For example, one accident near Tampa, Florida, killed five people, and right before the crash a teenager in one of the cars had posted a Snapchat video showing the car in excess of 100 mph.

In response to this crisis, automakers say that new hands-free phone systems solve the problem because they keep the hands on the wheel and eyes on the road even while a driver is using the smartphone. But what they (and probably most people) don't appreciate is just how attention-demanding and distracting talking on the phone can be while you are driving. Even when it is "hands-free" (though often it is not even that), and even though you don't take your eyes off the road, the conversation itself can strongly distract your limited conscious attention, taking it away from where it needs to be—on your driving and your readiness to react to sudden unexpected moves of the other drivers. Conversations regarding issues at work, or problems at home, or, God forbid, arguments with your children or spouse are highly relevant to your very important goals regarding your close relationships, your career and job pressures, your chores, and other family tasks. Even pleasant conversations while driving can be distracting, when they are full of news or new developments or feelings being expressed. After all, we only have a limited amount of attention, and when it is taken away by something else, it leaves less for all that is involved in driving safely.

Have you ever been stuck behind a really slow driver, and when you finally get to pass him, you see that he's been on the phone the whole time? Distractions slow us, slow down our reaction times to sudden emergency situations, and take our attention away from monitoring the complex road or highway situation. One way that we compensate is to drive ever more slowly, often without realizing it, because at that lower speed we gain back the time we need to be able to react. This happened to me once, when I had come home from New York to visit my family up in northern Michigan and my mom had picked me up at the airport. While I was driving the forty-five miles on local roads to our cabin, she was filling me in on all the family news. I remember being very engrossed in all that she was telling me. But suddenly she went completely silent and looked over at me quizzically. "You do realize you've completely stopped, don't you?" And there we were, in the middle of state highway M-72, slowed down to almost a complete standstill.

Your important goals never sleep. They operate unconsciously in the background, without your needing to guide them or even being aware of them, vigilantly monitoring your environment for things that might help meet that need. Answers to problems can then pop into your mind out of seemingly nowhere. Sleep is a big chunk of downtime when conscious activities are at a minimum, and your mind uses that time unconsciously to continue to work on problems. The good news is that sometimes it is successful, providing a breakthrough answer or solution to a problem or puzzle you've worked on consciously for quite a while. The bad news is that if it is not making enough progress and time is short, your mind will nag at you and cause worries and anxiety. Your mind is not trying to torture you, no matter how it may seem. Rather, it has reached an impasse that can only be broken by a bit of conscious work—conscious work in the form of making a concrete plan for how to solve that problem in the near future.

Conscious and unconscious processes interact with and help each other. In this chapter we've described many ways that the unconscious takes the baton from conscious efforts and continues to work on the problem even after we've given up on it or moved on to other things we need to do. Like close colleagues or teammates working together to get something done, unconscious processes point your conscious attention to important information; they communicate honestly with your conscious mind

258

about whether they are having any success or not. Sometimes for very difficult problems the answer will even come to us in a dream, but usually only after a lot of conscious struggle with the problem. Creativity often relies on these unconscious activities—whether you're Michael Jordan, Norman Mailer, or plain old me.

It is okay to "sleep on it" or take your mind off a problem after giving it a lot of thought. In fact it could be very beneficial to do so. For one thing, conscious effortful cogitation is limited and tiring and so it is a good idea to refresh it by doing something else for a while. I've learned to trust myself when I want to get up from the desk and take a break, to make some coffee or walk out in the yard for a few minutes; this usually occurs when I have a vague but not fully formed idea of what I want to write next. The break usually helps; it gives unconscious processes a crack at it in a mini-Mailer way and I sit down again with a clearer notion of where to go. Many writers and thinkers espouse walks or exercise as a powerfully renewing practice for the mind. I used to do a lot of long runs in the countryside and would often have insights and research ideas that I would write down as soon as I got back home. While you are engaged in such exercise activities, your goals and unconscious problem solvers can take advantage of the downtime and often accomplish things you are having trouble doing consciously.

Talking to yourself as Mailer advises, giving yourself assignments, may sound a little weird. When I first moved to New York, there were "talkers" who were having conversations with themselves out loud while walking alone, and we knew they were a bit off and gave them their space. (Today there are many more "talkers" than there used to be, but now they have headsets and smartphones.) But if you think about it, isn't our normal conscious thought just internal talking to ourselves? And in fact this internal speech to ourselves actually starts out in young children as talking out loud to themselves, having a little conversation with themselves, and even telling themselves what they are going to do next. This short stage of development, around age three, was first noticed by the Russian developmental psychologist Lev Vygotsky in the 1930s. As they are developing the ability to think consciously, children first talk out loud to themselves, and only after doing so become able to "talk" silently, mentally, to themselves.

So what Mailer practiced and suggested to aspiring writers was actually a quite natural way of operating our mental machinery, one that takes more complete advantage of the cooperative nature of our conscious and unconscious modes of thinking and problem-solving. Our abilities to control ourselves, to *self-regulate,* actually depend on this ability to talk to ourselves—only after we are able to do so does self-control begin (around age four). And this ability to control our own minds and actions, to more effectively attain our important goals by making use of unconscious as well as conscious means to those ends, is the focus of the final chapter.

CHAPTER 10

You Have Mind Control

For thousands of years, we were special, as special as special could be. Not only the earth, but the entire universe revolved around us. In Western thought, the earth was the center of the universe, and human beings were the center of the earth. It was all created and existed solely for our benefit. And our conscious mind was at the core—our soul, the center of each of us, our supernatural link to God and eternity.

Then began hundreds of years of relentless dethronement. First came Copernicus and Galileo, with the theory and then, when the telescope was invented, the evidence that the earth was not in fact the center of the universe. It was not even the center of the solar system, since we revolved around the sun, not the other way around. Then came an even more devastating blow. Darwin showed that humans were not the center of life on earth—that all creatures great and small were not created in the form we saw them today, but became so only gradually over eons of time and through entirely natural processes, and this applied to us as well. Reading the writing on the wall, Nietzsche famously declared that God was dead. Whatever we were, we were all alone in the cosmos. But at least we still had our conscious mind, our superpower, our free will. At least within our own bodies, we were still the masters of ourselves, in control of what we did and what we thought.

Then came Freud and Skinner to deliver the final blows. Not only is your planet, the big rock you sit on, just a speck in a remote corner of the universe, and not only are you not especially different from all the other plants and animals in being shaped and molded by natural forces over great spans of time—you are not even in control of your own mind, your own feelings, or your own actions. Hidden forces operating inside you are in control, said Freud; you just don't realize it. And then Skinner took away even that modicum of agency. Nothing inside *you* matters at all, he insisted. Your environment, the outside world, is playing you like a violin—but you think you're Mozart.

The earth was no longer the center of the universe. Human beings were no longer the center of the earth, and our conscious minds were no longer the center of us. We've certainly been put in our place. In Greek mythology, the concept of hubris applied to mortals who believed they had godlike traits and abilities. Nemesis was the Greek god who punished such hubris, who put mortals in their place. We enjoyed our long period of hubris, up to the time of Copernicus, but then Nemesis showed up with the bill. This book has probably not helped matters in that regard, but my aim has been to reveal the true nature of the human mind, so that we can reclaim real agency.

Over and over again, deep influences from our past, present, and future have been shown to influence our behavior, our choices, our likes and dislikes, before we know it. Life lingers—experiences carry over from one situation to the next, and influence us later without our realizing it. We naturally mimic and imitate what others are doing and "catch" like a common cold their emotions and behaviors, even smoking and drinking more just because we see people do so on TV. Temporary goals and needs color what and whom we like and dislike, what we pay attention to and later remember, and affect what and how much we buy at a store. We are cocksure we have the true measure of a person just by looking at her face, but we don't. So many different unconscious influences operating just below the surface—how do I control them? Or am I at their mercy?

Do I have free will?

In this final chapter we will describe the most effective ways to control these influences—when they are unwanted—and to use these unconscious processes—when they are helpful—to your advantage. This is a two-way street: you can use conscious and intentional processes to counter or control unwanted unconscious influences, but you can also use unconscious mechanisms to help you where the usual conscious methods have not been enough to get the job done. I will make three main points that I hope you will take with you, to apply to your life outside the pages of this book.

Point #1: *Your conscious thoughts matter. This means, according to what psychologists mean by the term, you have "free will." But it is not as complete and all-powerful as you might have believed.*

If you've read up to this point in the book, you know about the many influences on us of which we are not generally aware, and thus do not control. As the legendary Cleveland Indians pitcher Bob Feller said of his fastball, "You can't hit what you can't see." So seeing—being more aware of—these hidden influences is the first step to controlling them, or using them for your benefit. Pretending they don't exist, and insisting that yes, you do have complete free will and control, will cause you to miss out.

Point #2: *Acknowledging that you do not have complete free will, or complete conscious control, actually* increases *the amount of free will and control you truly have.*

How can this be? People who insist that advertising or persuasive attempts by other people do not influence them are the ones who are most susceptible to being controlled by other people; insisting that what others do plays no role in what they do leaves them open to contagion effects; they are also more likely to bring their work life home with them. As it turns out, they will be less able to effectively control themselves, too, because they believe they can do it all through acts of conscious willpower, and so won't make use of unconscious means of self-control, which turn out to be the most effective (see Point 3).

We are captains of our souls, certainly, and it sounds great to be a captain, but as in any other path of life, there are bad captains as well as good ones. The wise captain takes the winds and currents into account, adjusts for them when they go against the ship's course, and takes advantage of them when they are heading the same way. The bad captain insists that only the steering wheel matters, and so crashes into the rocks, or ends up adrift at sea.

By acknowledging the operation of these hidden influences, you now have the chance to do something about them, to regain real control where you actually did not have it before. That's a net gain. But it gets even better. By delegating control to these unconscious forces, you become better able to accomplish your conscious and intentional goals. You put them in service of working on those important goals when your conscious mind is elsewhere and take advantage of their problem-solving and creative abilities. *You put them to work for you.* That's an even bigger gain.

Point #3: *The most effective self-control is not through willpower and exerting effort to stifle impulses and unwanted behaviors. It comes from effectively harnessing the unconscious powers of the mind to much more easily do the self-control for you.*
Now that turns the old wisdom on its head, doesn't it?

As it happens, people who are better able to self-control—who get better grades, are healthier and exercise more, are less overweight, don't smoke, make more money, have happier personal relationships—are *not* the ones who exert willpower more than the rest of us do. It is just the opposite. Those sainted, seemingly blessed individuals who regulate their lives so well are the ones who do the good things *less* consciously, more automatically, and more habitually. And you can certainly do the same.

So that is what we will cover in this final chapter. For now, put your mind at ease about all the things we've talked about in this book that are going on "upstairs" without your consciously guiding and monitoring them 24/7. Think of yourself as a CEO with a great staff. They all work for You Inc. and are dedicated and committed to your happiness and achievement. Relax and let them do their jobs.

Implement Your Intentions

Your conscious thoughts matter. They are *causal,* meaning that they have the power to change how you feel and what you do. This may seem rather obvious to you, but in fact, one hundred years ago mainstream scientific psychology declared exactly the opposite. At the start of the book, I noted how in 1913, the American psychologist John Watson, the founder of behaviorism, published a landmark paper that shook and transformed the nascent field of scientific psychology—especially the study of the mind. It was the psychological equivalent of Nietzsche's shattering announcement of God's death. Watson wrote and argued, in effect, "Consciousness is dead." Why? Because at the time he wrote, there were no reliable methods to measure or study conscious thought. This was well before the advent of computers and electronic timers and monitor screens that contemporary cognitive psychology uses to perform controlled studies of perception, attention, and judgment. All Watson had were the introspective reports of volunteer participants about what they were seeing and thinking, and these did not prove very reliable. The different participants didn't agree with each other on what they were seeing, even though they were looking at and judging the same things; they were thinking and feeling in different ways about those same things, and the same person didn't even see or think the same way at different points in time. Psychology was just getting started back then, and researchers were doing the best they could with the tools they did have, like pioneers out in the wild country on their own. But it was a mess. In modern phraseology, the results did not replicate. This bothered scientists deeply. Where were the generalizable conclusions? Where was the certainty?

Because the method of introspection did not produce reliable results, Watson concluded that a scientific psychology should not use introspection or study consciousness at all. Rather, research should focus only on the external Stimulus properties, and the organism's actual behavioral Responses, and not bother with such notions as internal thoughts and experiences. This came to be known as S-R psychology. What's more, because consciousness did not matter anymore, animals could be studied instead, as if they were nearly equivalent to humans in behavior. They did not have consciousness like we did, but consciousness no longer mattered. Watson and the behaviorists thus effectively banned the study of human consciousness from the realm of scientific psychology. Of course, this now seems absurd—what is more central to human experience *than* consciousness?

Watson held that consciousness should not be part of scientific psychology because there were no reliable methods to assess it, but his successor B. F. Skinner and his fellow "neobehaviorists" took this hard-line stance even further: because they could not measure it, and thus it could not be included in their laboratory models of animal (including human) behavior, Skinner and company concluded that consciousness played no causal role in real life, either. Because they were not able to study it as rigorously as they might want to, and because it did not exist as a variable to study in their lab, human consciousness therefore must not exist in the world outside the lab, either. Instead it was said to be an *epiphenomenon,* which simply means a spurious side effect of some other phenomenon, but not important or causal in its own right. Somehow, the lack of reliable methods to study conscious thought *at that time* was transmuted into the principle that conscious thought *did not exist* as an influential force in people's lives.

Behaviorists were focused on the present environment only, to the exclusion of the other time zones our minds live in—influences of our deep and recent pasts, and of our future goals and aspirations. To them it was as if we were all Lhermitte's patients, controlled only by the cues in the outside environment and nothing more. But this was only because the behaviorists themselves, at this point in the history of psychology, could only see the outside environment; they could not see the inner workings of the mind. Their logic was that if they could not see it, then it didn't exist. This attitude reminds me of nothing so much as two-year-olds playing hide-and-seek by covering their own eyes.

Once again, hubris was showing its arrogant head. The behaviorists went far beyond the reasonable desire for reliable methods; they assumed that because there were no reliable methods *yet* to study internal thought and judgment, there never would be. As far as the science of psychology went, they believed that they were the end of history—that the current state of their science was the pinnacle that could never be surpassed and improved upon by new technology or methods. But as we know, soon came transistors and computers and television monitors and electronic measurement devices, which did enable the scientific study of the mind. The resulting cognitive revolution, which was driven by these new methods, ousted behaviorism for good.

Psychology's version of the free will argument dates back to Watson's 1913 paper. The question was not about free will per se, but about whether conscious thought mattered, whether it played a causal role or not. Skinner and the behaviorists contended it did not, and based on his studies of pigeons and rats, Skinner wrote several popular books arguing human free will was an illusion. This is what most of us want to know when we ask, Does free will exist? We are asking, Are my own private thoughts and decisions vital and effective, does what I think about and decide change what I do, and do I thus have control over my judgments and decisions and, by extension, my life? And the answer to that question, based on decades of psychological research is a resounding yes.

Benjamin Franklin, in his *Autobiography,* wrote about how he did not eat meat, or "animals," including fish, because they hadn't done anything to us to "deserve the slaughter." But he used to love fish and also thought "they smelt very good coming hot out of the pan."

I balanc'd some time between principle and inclination, till I recollected that, when the fish were opened, I saw smaller fish taken out of their stomach; then thought I, "If you eat one another, I don't see why we mayn't eat you." So I dined upon cod very heartily. *So convenient a thing it is to be a reasonable creature, since it enables one to find or make a reason for everything one has a mind to do.* (My emphasis)

Franklin had used his conscious reasoning to justify the change in his principles about eating animals that he had wanted all along. We call this a *rationalization,* and in his case, this conscious reasoning was causal. It effected a change in his behavior (and moral stance regarding eating fish). The conscious mind is very good at spinning whatever we do, or want to do, in some positive way, or at least making it more justified and defensible. We mentally transform the setbacks and tragedies in our lives to make them seem lesser, in order to better cope with them emotionally. One of our favorite tricks is called *downward social comparison,* and we all do it. Discontented with something in our lives, we remind ourselves that there is always someone worse off, in worse shape than we are, and we count our blessings that at least our situation is better than theirs. Again, our conscious thoughts are causal here, because they have effectively changed (reduced) our level of emotional distress. Mentally transforming the situation into something different, and easier to handle, is a major way we control both our emotions and our impulses—thinking of the double chocolate cake as five zillion calories instead of how yummy it will taste.

One theme of this book has been how you can use unconscious mechanisms to help reach your conscious goals. Want to make friends and bond with a new acquaintance? Look at them, pay attention to them, and let the natural, unconscious mimicry effect happen on its own, with the nice consequence of increasing liking and bonding between you. Have a difficult or time-consuming task ahead? Start working on that goal earlier than usual so unconscious goal pursuit processes naturally help to solve the problem, come up with creative outside-the-box solutions, alert you to relevant and helpful information, and work on the problem during your mind's downtime.

Likewise, it turns out that the best way to effectively exert self-control is to turn as much of the workload over to unconscious, automatic mechanisms as you can. There are two main forms of unconscious self-control that research has shown to be tremendously helpful in everyday life. One is short-term and tactical, the other is long term and strategic.

In the short term (think: remembering to do something you keep forgetting to do, or starting to exercise), the most effective way to carry out your difficult intentions is through the use of *implementation intentions.* My longtime colleague Peter Gollwitzer discovered and developed the powerful technique of implementation intentions as the most effective way of carrying out difficult intentions and desired behavior. These are concrete plans you make as to *when, where,* and *how* you will carry out the intention. Using them, you can overpower many of the unconscious influences we've described in this book.

In the long term as well (think: dieting, exercising, or studying on a regular basis), the best way to keep on track and avoid temptations and get your goals accomplished is not by exerting willpower in some titanic struggle of mind over matter, but by *establishing good habits* through regular routines of place and time.

Both of these methods of self-control are more effective than conscious and effortful methods because they make use of the natural and automatic ways that our environment cues our behavior. Implementation intentions work by specifying a precise future place and time at which you will perform the intended behavior. Habits work also by specifying a routine, daily place and time that you will carry out the desired behavior. This removes the need for remembering to perform that behavior, which we often have trouble doing with so much else going on in our lives; it also removes the chance for us to weasel our way out of it (as in the case of exercise or dieting, or cutting down on drinking), which, as Benjamin Franklin pointed out, our conscious powers of reason are quite adept at doing. In both cases, doing the useful, needed thing *without thinking* makes a more reliable and effective self-control method.

Skinner, like Freud, was not completely wrong. It is definitely true that stimulus events in our environment can often automatically trigger behavioral responses. As we saw with Lhermitte's patients, and Roger Barker's research on the power of settings on our behavior, cues in our environment can be direct and powerful determinants of what we do and how we do it. In one of his early studies, Gollwitzer and his students asked students at a Munich university what they wanted to accomplish while they were home on Christmas vacation. For example, did they want to finish an important course assignment, or perform an important personal task such as, for the male students especially, telling their father they loved him? All of the students wanted to get these goals accomplished. The researchers instructed some of them to make firm and strong goal commitments, such as "I will tell my father I love him!" But another group was instructed to make a concrete plan as to where, when, and how they would actually do this, such as: "When my father picks me up at the train station, and I get into the car, I will tell him I love him!" When the students came back after vacation, the researchers asked if they had completed their vacation-time goals. This early study showed that the students who made the implementation intention—the time and place they would actually carry out the desired behavior—were far more successful in carrying out their intentions than the other students, even the ones who had committed themselves to completing their goals.

Soon after learning about implementation intentions, I decided to try it out myself, because I'd borrowed a book from a colleague at NYU and kept forgetting to bring it into work, like the typical absentminded professor. My colleague was getting a bit impatient since he really needed his book for a paper he was working on. So after yet another failure and unpleasant scene in my office, I told myself, When I walk in my apartment door this evening, I will go straight to my desk and put that book in my briefcase! Later on, when I got home, I found myself walking to my bedroom instead of the kitchen as I usually did, in the dark, before even turning on any lights. I remember being puzzled a bit by where my legs were taking me, until I found myself at my desk and looking right at that book. As I still had my briefcase in my hand it was an easy matter to put the book inside, and I didn't have to give it another moment's thought. Done: intention implemented.

Brain imaging studies have shown how these implementation intentions work. Basically, when an implementation intention is formed, control over behavior shifts from one brain region to another. When you have the goal and desire to do something, a region associated with self-initiated actions, part of what is known as the Brodmann area, becomes active. This would be the case for a goal such as "I want to go to the store today to pick up milk and something for dinner." But when implementation intentions are formed, such as "When I finish typing up this report, I will get up from my desk and head out to the store," a different part of that region becomes active, the part that is associated with environmentally driven behavior. So the brain scanning studies have shown that intentions in general are controlled by internal thought (remembering to do something you want to do) but implementation intentions—which are more reliable and effective—shift the control of behavior from your self-generated internal thoughts to a stimulus from the outside environment, so that when X happens, you will do Y, without having to remember or stop and think about it at the time. It will happen before you know it.

Once implementation intentions began gaining scientific currency, health psychologists applied the technique to cases where people were having trouble following complex medication regimens, when missing a medication might mean the difference between life and death. In one early study, Pascal Sheeran and Susan Orbell had elderly nursing home patients form implementation intentions for when, where, and how they would take each of their several daily pills. This was not as easy as it sounds for them, because some pills need to be taken with food and others on an empty stomach, some in the morning and some in the evening, and each time they would have to remember to take the pill, which was itself problematic. In the control condition, over a several-month period, the elderly patients were successful only 25 percent of the time in taking their pills at the right time each day. But a separate group of patients formed implementation intentions. Here the patient would say, "Right after I finish breakfast and get back to my room I will take Pill 1." And: "At bedtime right before I turn the light out I will take Pill 4." The key is to specify future events that are highly likely to happen, on a routine basis. This group, over a several-month period, had a remarkable 100 percent adherence rate. Of course, not all studies find such perfect outcomes, but it was pretty clear that these elderly patients were helped greatly by delegating the control over taking their medications away from their conscious willpower and to regular routine environmental events.

A major reason why people don't carry through on their good intentions is that they simply forget to do what they intended. In a survey of women who wanted to but had not performed breast self-examinations, 70 percent reported that they'd just forgotten to. Making implementation intentions to perform the self-exam or to make a doctor's appointment for routine screening would help not only the individual reduce their chances of serious illness, but also society at large in reducing the cost of health care for everyone. A health insurance company sent mailings to twelve thousand employees who were overdue for a regular colonoscopy, asking them to make an implementation intention—a specific plan—for where, when, and how they would make the appointment for the procedure. The rate of making the appointment increased from 6.2 percent for those who got the reminder only, to 7.2 percent for those who got the reminder plus the instructions to make a concrete plan. This increase of 1 percent may sound small, but researchers at the Memorial Sloan Kettering Cancer Center report that increasing the rate of routine colonoscopies by just this amount saves 271 years of life for every 100,000 people in the at-risk group.

As we have seen in several very close U.S. presidential elections in the twenty-first century, the total number of people who vote affects the outcome. Political scientists have started using implementation intentions to increase voter turnout at primary and regular elections. For example, in a field study conducted during the 2008 Pennsylvania Democratic primary contest between Barack Obama and Hillary Clinton, nearly 300,000 voters were contacted by phone by a professional company that placed millions of calls that year for the various campaigns. There were two groups in the study. In one the potential voters were asked to make an implementation intention regarding where, when, and how they would vote on Election Day, and the other group received just the standard encouragement-to-vote message. Election Days are often on Tuesdays, when people have be at work, get their kids to school, and pick them up—in other words a regular busy day on which it can be hard to find the time to go vote. Often people do not know in advance even where their polling place is, so figuring this out ahead of time and making a concrete plan can make a big difference. And indeed, in this large study of an actual state primary election, there was a 4 percent higher turnout in the implementation intention group than in the standard encouragement call group. Political campaigns spend millions of dollars (on mailings, door-to-door canvassing, TV advertisements) for even a 1 percent increase in turnout, so to them this is a very large effect.

Implementation intentions don't just help us do things; they help us *not* do things—like give in to unwanted unconscious impulses and influences. For example, if we truly want to not be racist, our unconscious will help us express this desire not just in thoughts but acts. In one of Gollwitzer's early studies, students committed to equality were more likely to effectively jump into a fast-moving conversation and disagree with racist comments than were students who didn't have the same active goal of not being racist. In other studies on racism, participants were instructed to assume the role of police officer, and to shoot as soon as they could when a photograph appeared on the screen of a person holding a gun. The person in the photograph was always holding something, and half the time he was unarmed and holding something else entirely, such as his wallet. Half the time the person in the photo was white and the other times they were black. In the control condition as in several previous studies, white participants were more likely to mistakenly shoot an unarmed black person than unarmed white person, and less likely to correctly shoot an armed white than an armed black person. But in the implementation intention condition, where participants first told themselves, "If I see a person, then I will ignore his race!," this bias was significantly reduced. The implications here for law enforcement are obvious.

We saw in Chapter 6 that mimicking another person increases bonding and liking in a very natural way. In a French department store study, salespeople who mimicked their customers were more successful at persuading those customers to buy expensive electronic devices compared to salespeople who did not mimic. Can implementation intentions shield you from these unconscious influences? Recently Gollwitzer and his colleagues showed that implementation intentions to be thrifty were able to block these subtle effects of being mimicked by someone else. Participants first told themselves, "If I am tempted to buy something, then I will tell myself I will save my money for important investments!" Later, when the study seemed to be over, the experimenter tried to get the participants to take their payments for being in the experiment in the form of chocolates or coffee, instead of in cash. The experimenter mimicked some of the participants' body language, as we had done in one of our chameleon studies. In a control condition the participants had the same goal of being thrifty but did not form specific implementation intentions about saving money. Those who did not form the intention were more susceptible to the mimicking and accepted more chocolates and coffee—three times more, in fact. But not those in the implementation intention condition. They showed no increase in acceptance of chocolate or coffee caused by the mimicry. Implementation intentions—delegating control over your future behavior to reliable cues—appear to be a very practical way to avoid sales pressure and the tendency to buy more than you want to, causing later regret.

Temptations come in many forms, and you can apply this simple formula to your own particular weaknesses: "If I am tempted to [eat a big dessert/go out with my friends/talk back to my boss/buy more new clothes] then I will tell myself [I need to eat healthy/I must finish my class assignment/be polite and respectful/ save my money for the future]." In one Dutch study of more than two hundred unsuccessful dieters, those who used implementation intentions to avoid yielding to their particular temptations (chocolate, pizza, or french fries) were then successful in decreasing how much unhealthy food they ate over the following two weeks. For example, dieters who wanted to stop eating so much chocolate, they would tell themselves, "The next time I am tempted to eat chocolate, I will think of dieting!" This worked better than the "don't do it" or "don't eat it" ("The next time I am tempted to eat chocolate, I will not eat it!") intention conditions, which only served to keep the dieters' attention focused on the temptation.

I have used this technique myself to block the carryover effects of the day at work to the evening at home. The reliable situation on which I pin my implementation intention is "when I get out of my car in the driveway." I can pretty much count on that happening each day after work, unless I want to sit in my car in the driveway all night. The problem that provoked this desire for change was finding out the hard way that bad moods from work were lingering over and affecting how I acted at home. So when I was having a rough time at the office several years ago—as a result of the common pressures of too much to do, with too little time to do it—my mood and stresses and feelings about people there would carry over to how I interpreted and reacted to quite benign events at home. I would come inside, very tired, and my little girl, about three at the time, would come running to the door, excited to see me. I would sit down and she would naturally want all of my attention, to look at something she had drawn or want to play. On several occasions I found myself being impatient with her as if she were someone at work—yet another person wanting something from me, wanting my time when I just wanted to relax and do something that *I* wanted to do. But seeing her disappointed face caused me great remorse and I resolved to take steps to stop that from ever happening again. I needed a way to control this unconscious carryover effect—to prevent my automatic interpretation of my daughter's wish to do things with me as "yet another person demanding my time."

Because I already knew about the power of implementation intentions, I hit on this strategy. It was to link (a) my intention to show happiness at seeing my family and talk with them when I got home, to appreciate their being glad I was there and wanting to be with me, to (b) a routine and reliable environmental cue—getting out of my car and standing in my driveway, before going into the house. So I made an implementation intention, something like: "When I get out of my car and stand in the driveway, I will be happy to be home and greet my family warmly!" And I did this often enough for it to become a regular habit, cued by the regular situation of getting out of my car. There may have been a few lapses over the years since, but not many, and this tactic has been effective for me in blocking unwanted carryover effects from work to home.

Implementation intentions are not magic spells, though. You need to do your part—to be really committed to this new goal and intention, and honestly want to carry it out. Too many times our good intentions fail because down deep, we really don't want to change—we really want to keep smoking, drinking, and being lazy. Implementation intentions, like any goal you might have, only work if you are truly committed to carrying them out.

The power of using external cues to help you control unwanted impulses and behavior extends beyond once-in-a-while occasions and can drive significant lifestyle changes. Actually, research is demonstrating that forming good habits that delegate control of your behavior to routine daily situations and events is the most effective way we can regulate ourselves in the long run—to get better grades, better jobs, and healthier diets and ways of living. This is great news, but you still have to develop those good habits to begin with. And that can be hard. So here is another occasion where implementation intentions can get you started on the better path. Maybe a heart patient takes a walk each day as soon as she returns home from work, as soon as she get out of her car in the driveway, before even going into the house. Or maybe she goes upstairs to change out of her work clothes and immediately puts on exercise clothes, like shorts, a T-shirt, and running shoes. Those small steps will lead to bigger and better things.

Once this new desired behavior is in place, after several successful days of using the implementation intentions, then it will become the new habit, your new routine, and situational cues (arriving in one's driveway, undressing after work in one's bedroom) become the unconscious triggers of this new complex behavior. The first few weeks are the hardest, but then it just becomes part of your routine and something you do without thinking. Even something you want to do. When I was doing a lot of long-distance running, training for the New York City Marathon back in the 1990s, I relied on a great guidebook many runners use, *Galloway's Book on Running*. In it, the pioneer running guru Dr. George Sheehan is quoted as saying that "the body wants to do what it did yesterday. If you ran yesterday, it wants to run today. If you didn't, then it doesn't want to." So the important thing is to stick to your routine and not take days off if you can avoid it, because that will just make it harder to get going again and you will lose the momentum you worked so hard to gain.

If you think about it, habits already "run" your life. Roger Barker showed back in the 1950s that by far the main cause of how we behave is the particular situation or setting we are in. We are quiet and respectful in church, relaxed and conversational when we go out to dinner, louder and more boisterous when out among tens of thousands of fellow fans at a college football game. And we know what to do and how to behave appropriately in each of these situations, without a moment's thought. In a fast-food restaurant, for example, we first order the food and then wait for it, and then take it, sit down, and eat. But in a fancy restaurant we would never order the food first. We instead wait to be seated, wait for our menus, place our order, then wait for the food to be brought out. It all feels very simple because it is familiar. Imagine if we were from some-where with no fast-food restaurants, only the fancier sit-down type—we would go into McDonald's, sit down at a table, and wait a very long time for someone to come take our order!

We all experience this kind of "culture shock" when we travel to a new country. There, many of our assumptions are wrong and we don't know so easily what is the right thing to do. Even the simplest of activities can require a lot of conscious effort: translating the signs, learning the local norms and customs of behavior, and trying not to do anything offensive out of one's ignorance. It can be very tiring! Or worse, it can be danger-ous—many people from the United States get hit by cars when walking in London because they are looking the wrong way, without thinking, when they cross a street. Visiting a place where the norms and rules are different shows us how much of our daily lives back home are actually under the control of unconscious habitual processes that relieve these constant, draining demands on our conscious mind to such a great extent.

The good news is that we can exploit this mechanism of habit to change our lives for the better. Many if not most of us believe it takes a lot of will-power and internal strength to stifle and suppress strong temptations and impulses—that doing so is a titanic, ongoing struggle that can last throughout the day or throughout one's life. But new research shows it is actually the opposite. People who effectively self-control are *less* beset by temptations and spend *less* effort stifling impulses than do people with lower self-control.

Yes, you read that right. People with good self-control manage their lives in advance. By using *unconscious* means to self-regulate, making "necessary evils" such as healthy eating and exercising and studying a routine part of their lives, they make the positive activities a routine habit so that they don't need to fight to get started, or overcome the disinclination to do them. Conscious and effortful self-control is too taxing and too unreliable, and as we know, vulnerable to rationalizations ("just one piece of cake won't hurt anything") and excuses ("I've had a hard day and just need to relax tonight").

In a series of studies, Brian Galla and Angela Duckworth of the University of Pennsylvania looked at people who scored high on a standard measure of self-control ability. They used a ten-item questionnaire with statements such as "I am good at resisting temptation," "I do things that feel good in the moment but regret later on," and "Sometimes I can't stop myself from doing something, even if I know it is wrong," and asked participants to agree or disagree on a 1–5 scale. In their first study, they found that people who scored highly on that scale were more likely than other people to report that they did a beneficial behavior, such as exercise, "without having to consciously remember"; it was "something I do automatically." They were more likely than others to exercise at the same regular time and place every day—linking that place and time, the external cues, to their desired behavior. And they made the behavior routine and habitual by being more likely to do it every day than occasionally. As a result, the effective self-regulators reported needing less effort and struggle to do the activities and reported having less difficulty in doing them, compared to people with less self-control. In other words, actual and effective self-control was associated with using *less* willpower and effort to do the desired activity, not more.

Galla and Duckworth performed a number of studies to confirm this basic principle. In one, for example, people with high self-control were more likely to report being able to study under difficult circumstances, such as when they just did not feel like it, when they were in a bad mood, when they were stressed out, and when they were tempted to do something else. The regular routine of studying helped them to overcome these obstacles but did not help those low in self-control.

Recent studies of people who are good at self-control have revealed that they experience fewer temptations than the rest of us and less often need to control themselves at all. In one German study, more than two hundred people were tracked throughout each day for one week, using Black-Berrys that would beep them at random intervals and ask questions about their experiences at that moment—about their temptations, desires, and about the self-control they were exerting. And those who were the best at self-control, measured by a standard questionnaire with questions such as "I am good at resisting temptations," reported having fewer of those temptations during that week. In a different study done at McGill University in Montreal, students who reported exerting more self-control over temptations and impulses were not the ones who were the most successful at attaining their important goals. Instead, when the researchers checked back on them at the end of the semester, those who had the most success at achieving their goals were the ones who experienced fewer temptations in the first place. The researchers concluded that "in the long term exerting self-control is not beneficial."

You might gather from this that people who are good at self-control just don't have the same strong desires as the rest of us—the poet William Blake certainly thought so, when he said, "Those who restrain desire do so because theirs is weak enough to be restrained." But it appears Blake was wrong about this. What is really going on is that effective self-controllers set up their environment so that those tempting cues and opportunities are not present in the first place. When they go to the store, they do not buy the unhealthy snacks, and if they want to cut down on how much they drink, they don't stock their liquor cabinet. This is the other side of the coin of using external cues to promote desired behavior (which is how implementation intentions and good habits operate); here the trick is to remove the unwanted external cues instead. Kentaro Fujita, a self-control and motivation researcher at Ohio State University, explains that "the really good dieter wouldn't buy a cupcake. They wouldn't have passed in front of a bakery; when they saw the cupcake, they would have figured out a way to say yuck instead of yum."

Wendy Wood, of the University of Southern California, a leading expert on habits and self-control, told me that over the past twenty-five years, "the successful campaign to reduce smoking was achieved mainly by changing the environments in which people live. Smoking has been reduced largely due to smoking bans, taxes, eliminating cigarette and tobacco ads from television and magazines, and removing cigarette displays and ads in stores. These were environmental changes that made it more difficult to smoke and thus helped to break the habitual behavioral patterns." Wood's own research program has shown that habitual behaviors are grounded in a person's regular daily environment—they are cued and maintained automatically and unconsciously by it. In short, we are learning that the best way to change a behavior is to change the person's environment. In the case of the good habits you desire to have, tie them to a regular place and time; for the bad habits you want to get rid of, remove from your surroundings the cues and opportunities that support them.

The unconscious mind powerfully and often invisibly affects our behavior, sometimes even frighteningly so. It shapes not only the people we are in the moment, but also the people we become and the goals we will—or won't—achieve. Yet, as we have seen in this chapter, our conscious mind can also be an instrument we play—a Fender Stratocaster, say, or a Gibson Les Paul (Jimmy Page's favorite), iconic guitars of the era of classic rock. Science has revealed that our unconscious mind evolved to respond to our conscious messages as long as we know how to effectively communicate those messages. By tuning the strings of our mind with our intentions, we can radically improve our health, our mental peace, our career, and our relationships. We can exercise and even increase the free will we do have, and enjoy the ways in which our species is indeed so very special.

CONCLUSION

You Are the DJ

When I had my life-changing alligator dream in the fall of 2006, my daughter was just a few months old. She was a tiny, gurgling, love-inducing promise—a promise of a future life. I hoped the life that lay in front of her would be full of joy and peace, of aspirations and deep satisfaction, though I also knew hardships and disappointments would periodically appear, and I fervently hoped that I had the skills, the ability, and the patience to help her confront and overcome these challenges. As I fell asleep that afternoon and my unconscious sent me a message that would so sharply recast how I saw the human mind, her own mind was rapidly developing. Unbeknownst to her, her brain was already guiding her to have in-group preferences that would divide the world into us and them. Within a few years, as she began to understand that she existed and shared qualities with other people, she would be vulnerable to sabotage of her own performance as a girl because of her society's prejudices toward women. And as she grew and found that she liked certain things and aspired to others, these preferences and drives would shape who became her friends and how she acted toward them. As you might imagine, knowing what I did about the hidden trapdoors of the mind considerably increased my already numerous worries—but it also helped me know what to watch out for. My research, then, became as much about being a father as being a scientist.

During the ten years it took me to plan and write this book, I have watched my daughter grow up. We've gone through a lot together. She has transformed from a noisy and adorable teething infant into a remark-

279

ably poised and witty eleven-year-old, complete with braces, who now stands at the doors of adolescence. Along the way she has been my real-life superhero on more than one occasion, and I've dedicated this book to her. All parents want to leave their children something valuable that will help them lead happy lives when we are gone. This book, in a certain sense, is that inheritance I hope to give to her—my life's work, the wisdom and insight I've toiled to accumulate during my time on this amazing planet of ours. (That said, I am aware that few children thrill to the idea of reading a book by one of their parents, or even of listening to him talk for more than a minute at a time.) However, this legacy of sorts isn't just for my daughter. My aim is for it to be useful to anyone and everyone interested in learning how understanding your mind can help you understand yourself better, and thereby better yourself.

Why would we want to better ourselves? From an individualistic standpoint, the answer is obvious: so we can be happier, healthier, and more successful. But no person exists in isolation; no benefit accrues in a vacuum. We send ripples in all directions, just as we receive the ripples of others, and just as our social networks both digital and nondigital tremble with the interactions of friends, family, acquaintances, and strangers. If we truly better ourselves, we have a chance at bettering our community, and by extension, our world. But this process requires something that often seems like it's in short supply: *humility*. The humility to accept that we don't fully understand why we do what we do all of the time. I'm not saying that accepting this is easy; it's not. But once you let that self-doubt in, as uncomfortable as this can be, other things follow: curiosity, surprise, new ideas, examination of unquestioned assumptions, perhaps hard but important realizations, and finally—miraculously—change. The possibility of leaving behind a better world for our children, even if they don't read the books we write for them.

Conscious and unconscious mental processes do different things well. If they both did the same things well and the same things not so well, then they'd be redundant, and we would not have evolved both of them. So it is not that one is bad and the other good. It is that each is good but in its own domain. They work together, usually in harmony, and dynamically: one causes the other and vice versa. For example, conscious experiences in one situation linger into the next situation without our realizing it and become the unconscious influences in that subsequent setting. Unconscious processes work on our important problems and goals, and pop answers and solutions into our conscious minds. Unconscious goals direct our conscious attention to things relevant to our goals and cause us to notice and then make use of those things. *Both* forms of thought are part of you, not only the conscious part. Together they comprise your real, inner self. This is why you need to be careful what you wish for. Those conscious wishes can manifest themselves in unconscious ways when you least expect it and perhaps cause you to do things you'd rather not have done. Your strong needs can have unintended consequences, such as when you shop when hungry, or race a thousand miles home on the interstate to get home before the liquor store closes.

I learned a lot about human motivation from my colleague Peter Gollwitzer, and especially how people can consciously take control over the automatic and unconscious effects that the outside world can have on them before they know it. Peter and I first met in Munich in 1989, when he asked me to his institute to give a talk and do a workshop with his students. My area was social cognition, and his was social motivation, and it was a perfect fit. Before he taught me about motivation, though, he taught me some German. As it was my first time visiting Germany, I didn't know much, and so one day during my visit I asked him what the German word for consciousness was. "Bewusstein," he informed me. *Bewusstein,* I said to myself. Then a few moments later I asked, "And what is the word for unconscious?" He gave me a bemused look and rolled his eyes. "*Un*bewusstein," he said. (As in: *You dummy.* Come to think of it, that alligator in my dream gave me the very same look . . .)

Gollwitzer's research in the late 1980s was literally decades ahead of its time, and unlike the German word for unconscious, it was nothing I could have figured out for myself. His lab was demonstrating a kind of combination of unconscious and conscious mental effect—the intentional turning-over of control of your behavior to external environmental cues, to future events—a weird mixture of free will and not-free-will. Making conscious use of your unconscious powers. And it was just my good dumb luck to be living in Germany at that time and for him to invite me to Munich to learn all about what he was doing in his lab. Put his research of the 1980s together with my work back then on automatic, unconscious influences of the outside world, and here's what you get, and what you can do with it:

Your environment is composed of cues that can prompt your behavior, and also primes that might influence you without your realizing it. So why not take control over that environment? After all, if primes are like reminders, we use sticky notes and other means to remind ourselves to do something important, when otherwise we'd have forgotten all about it. So we already make use of the basic idea of priming ourselves, kind of like how the farmers and ranchers of Darwin's time used the principle of natural selection to breed fatter cows and larger ears of corn, without knowing how it worked. Shape your surroundings to be a more helpful, beneficent influence. There is no reason that you have to permit unwanted influences to continue. Let's take something simple, such as the photographs on your desk at work, or your teenager's posters on her wall. What kinds of goals are associated with these? What do you think about, what comes to mind when you look at them? For some of us, a photo of our spouse might not be such a good idea, if it triggers thoughts of romance and attraction in our work setting, where we would rather not have those temptations, or behave toward others in inappropriate ways. But if it instead triggers thoughts of our family, and the goal of working hard to provide for them, then it would be a positive influence. I'm reminded of the famous episode of *The Simpsons* where Homer has photos of baby Maggie on the wall in front of him at the Springfield nuclear power plant, along with the slogan "Do it for her." You just have to ask yourself those questions and be honest with yourself about the answers, and take the potential future unconscious influences of those photos seriously.

Some researchers have insightfully pointed out that posters of such luminaries as Einstein and Superman might actually be counterproductive. If we cannot realistically be like them, then those posters might cause lower self-esteem and be demoralizing, not the intended higher self-esteem and motivation. I'll never be as smart as Einstein, you think, and consequently feel smaller; I'll never be as strong or fast or brave as Superman, you sadly admit, and feel diminished. So choose your role model prime wisely—someone you look up to but whom you can actually emulate in your life. Lincoln, for example, who was honest and did the hard thing even though it was unpopular. Or Martin Luther King Jr., who preached (and practiced) nonviolence and reconciliation between the races, and inspired millions of people by his example and his words. Remember that the outside world can only prime things inside you that are already inside you—all the Superman priming in the world can't make you fly, and healthy-eating priming won't work if you don't already want it to. *But the outside world* can *activate the goals and qualities you do possess, and the behaviors that are within your realm of possibilities.*

Over the years I've heard from many people wanting to know if they can prime themselves, or teachers who want to prime their students to achieve more and get higher test grades. This is a great idea but has two main problems. The first we've just mentioned: outside primes can only activate what is already inside you. The second problem is that you would be aware that you are doing it—it is no longer an unconscious, passively operating influence if you are doing it consciously and intentionally. It is similar to why you can't tickle yourself—you are aware of it and are in control over it. But all is not lost. It may well be that for the first few days or weeks after you hang the photograph of Lincoln or MLK on your wall, you are aware of why it is up there. But eventually it will become part of the background—you will stop noticing and paying conscious attention to it. You might even come to forget why you put it up there in the first place. It is after that point, when it is there in front of you but you are no longer paying conscious notice to it, when it has become part of the woodwork, that the priming effects can occur. Do it for yourself, but do it for the long term, and then, as New Yorkers say, *fuhgedaboudit!*

That's the beauty of using unconscious influences to your advantage. Because they are natural and happen on their own, you only have to start the process and then relax and let it work for you. Take the chameleon effect, in which just paying attention to a new acquaintance leads naturally to imitation and mimicry, which in turn leads to liking and bonding. All you have to do is pay attention to the other person—look at him and listen to what he is saying. The rest happens on its own. Maybe you want to set an important goal for yourself, to get something done or solve a problem. You need to give your goal some conscious thought in order to "set" it as an important goal, and then you will find yourself working on it unconsciously and reaping the benefits—as though you the CEO delegated the task for a while to a trusted and very capable member of your staff.

Priming does have its unwanted influences, such as through television ads. Kelly Wallace, the CNN correspondent, wrote about the strong effect of beer and alcohol TV ads on underage drinking. She had preteen children of her own at home, so she made the decision to record the football games she (and her kids) wanted to watch, so that she could then fast-forward through the commercials. That's a great idea, and it was prompted by her taking "what you see is what you do" effects seriously. People who deny that ads influence them certainly have the right to that opinion, and hence may not do anything to stop the influence of those ads, but they should keep in mind that their children might also be watching and thus exposed to those influences—and the evidence is quite clear that they *will* be influenced.

For other unconscious influences, such as when life lingers from one setting into another, when they create problems in your life you can use implementation intentions to break the spell—"when I get out of my car in the driveway, then I will remind myself to be happy to be home and with my family!" When meeting new people, try to see through the superficial drivers of your impressions, such as their races and faces and their attractiveness, and focus instead on their personality and how they treat you and others. Base your opinions, and your trust, on what they do and not just how they appear.

And you should probably choose your Facebook "friends" more wisely, and take more control over your newsfeed and your social networks in general, because people out there whom you don't even know are influencing your mood, your weight, your tendencies to help and cooperate— so many things—before you know it. How they act and what they feel and think seep into you through your social networks and become an actual part of you, of who you are inside as well as outwardly to others. You don't have to be at their mercy; you can control whom you come in contact with, at least much more than most of us do now.

Develop good habits to be the person you want to be. If you want to be less racist and sexist, then use implementation intentions such as "When I see a person of color, I will remind myself to be fair!" See people who are different from yourself as opportunities to practice egalitarianism and fairness. Start to exercise at the same time and place every day and do not excuse yourself for any reason (except actual emergencies); buy healthier foods at the store and snack less. The more you practice these positive behaviors, the more habitual and easier they will become the next time, and the next time, till they become second nature, the new "real you." And remember that other people see what you do and are influenced by it, just as you see what they do and are influenced by them. Your good deeds and prosocial acts multiply because they are literally contagious to others—but so is the effect of your bad and antisocial behaviors. Set a positive example and it will spread out from you like a wave.

It has been a long road of discovery since I started graduate school in the 1970s, parsing out those operations of our mind that we are aware of from those that we are not. This book is a record of how much we do know our own minds, as well as how much of its workings we are not usually aware of. What our lab has been up to most recently, while I've been writing this book, in fact, is extending this fundamental question to how well we know the minds of *others*. While we are not consciously aware of much that goes on in our own minds, we certainly know even less about what goes on in the minds of other people. And the relatively greater degree to which we know our own conscious thoughts, compared to theirs, leads to some important consequences in how we think about other people, and what they are up to, and even how good and moral they are compared to ourselves.

There has already been insightful research on this issue by Emily Pronin of Princeton and David Dunning of Cornell University and their colleagues. What they have shown is that we don't know what other people's thoughts or intentions are, but we do know ours, and so we often give ourselves credit for having good intentions even if we don't carry them out. Well, we say, I meant to give money to that charity, I just forgot to, so I'm still a good person. But because we don't have the same access to the good intentions of others, we don't give other people that same benefit of the doubt and consequently grade them more harshly when they fail to give to a charity or donate their time to a good cause. Even though we didn't give to the charity either, we see other people as stingy or selfish or uncaring for not doing so, while we meant to but "just forgot." Hardly seems fair, does it?

But our special access to our own conscious thoughts, combined with our complete lack of access to those of others, has some surprising implications for how we feel special, and even somewhat alone and isolated, in the social world. My Yale colleagues Erica Boothby and Margaret Clark and I have shown that people—all or at least most of us—believe we are (somehow) relatively invisible to others in public settings. Each of knows that we commonly "check out" other people on the train or in the waiting room with us, or sitting in the classroom or on the other park benches. We do this surreptitiously, of course, avoiding eye contact, and we don't think anyone notices when we do it. But we also do not think anyone is checking us out in turn. Our surveys show that each of us thinks he or she is pretty much the only one doing this—that we are checking others out but not being looked at by anyone else. My colleagues and I called this the "invisibility cloak illusion," after the Harry Potter stories. But if you think about it, of course we are being looked at and checked out as much as we are doing the same to others. After all, you are my "other person" and I am yours. And you think you are watching me but I am not watching you, and I think you are not watching me but I am watching you, and logically we both can't be right. In reality, we are both checking each other out and thinking (erroneously) we are the only ones doing it.

In a sense, what we are doing as individuals is making the same logical error that John Watson and the behaviorists did one hundred years ago. Recall that they concluded that because they did not have methods to reliably measure conscious thoughts, therefore conscious thoughts did not matter, and played no important causal role in human emotions or behavior. It is a logical fallacy to conclude that just because you don't have direct evidence that other people are observing you, they are not doing so. Of course you don't have evidence of their thoughts and surreptitious attention, any more than they have this evidence about yours. And you don't have direct evidence of their having good intentions, either, and you (and I, and everyone) therefore conclude they don't have them. And they conclude that you don't have them, leading to you (and me, and everyone) protesting that yes, you did intend to do the good thing; how dare they suggest otherwise. This has profound implications for how we judge and form opinions about each other, especially those in out-groups, such as other political parties, and how we can quite easily assume their malevolent intent.

Now take this basic duality between our access to our own mind versus our lack of access to other people's minds into another domain, not of how much we and others are looking at each other, but of how much we and others are *thinking* about each other. And the same thing happens. Each of us believes we are thinking, during random moments throughout the day, of the other people in our life—family, children, coworkers—but that those other people are not in turn thinking about us. (Maybe sometimes, but not at all as much as we are thinking about them.) Why not? Well, again, we have no evidence that they are, and why should they, anyway? That would be somewhat egotistical of us, wouldn't it, to assume that others are thinking about us when we are not around? Yet, again, we know *we* do this about the other people *we* know. And when you start to ask people about it, once again, everyone acknowledges thinking about the other people in their lives several times a day, but at the same time believes that those others are thinking about them far less often. (We call this the *mind gap*, in a play on the famous and ubiquitous sign in the London Underground reminding riders to "mind the gap" between the train and the platform.)

What a boon it would be, especially for people who feel lonely, or unloved and unappreciated, to know that others are indeed thinking about them during the day. How easy it would be for people to keep track, just jot down when it happens, when they have thoughts about the others in their life and then get people together to show each other, that yes, I do think about you, and wow—really—you think about me, too? I bet there would be a lot of happy faces when they found that out.

This is a rewarding new direction for our lab's research because it extends the question of how aware we are of what is going on in our own minds, with all the important implications and consequences we've described in this book, to that of how aware we are of what is going on in the minds of others—and there do seem to be very important implications and consequences for that degree of awareness (and especially, lack of awareness) as well. We certainly seem to base some rather important conclusions about other people, relative to ourselves, on our naked inability to know what is going on in their heads, as if our not being *aware* of what is going on means nothing *is* going on. And like many of the negative consequences of the hidden mind operations we've described in this book, these mistaken conclusions and logical fallacies about the minds of others seem quite fixable, with even just a moment's reflection. But most of all, this emerging research reminds us how interconnected we all are, not just through our visible actions, but through our invisible thoughts as well. We are as dependent on other people as our conscious mind is dependent on our unconscious, and welcoming this truth into our outlook can help us better support the people in our lives, and receive their support as well.

* * *

When I first started DJing as a high school student at the college radio station in my town, I was a bit of a disaster. I choked on the weather forecast the first time I spoke into the mic, those fades from one song to the next were trickier than I thought they would be, and I once went to the bathroom while a long song was playing and managed to lock myself out of the control room.

As the DJs of our own lives, things don't always go smoothly. We can get flustered under pressure, have trouble learning new things (remember when you first started to drive?), and when things really get bad, lose control. (Just ask the racehorse owner Steve Coburn.) But we do learn from those times, we avoid those same mistakes, and things get easier. Our presents, and especially our futures, can be better than our pasts. After a month or two on the air I was actually pretty darn good at segues and mixing songs together, and I learned to not talk so much and get out of the way of the music, which, after all, was what my listeners were tuning in for. What those listeners may not have realized was that I was just as into the music that was currently playing as they were. Sure, I was busy putting the newscast together or getting the next song ready on the second turntable, but I was with them in the present moment, too. My mind was in the future getting ready for what would come on the air next, but my real reason for being a DJ was to experience and have control over the music playing right then in the present.

And today, if you check out my iPhone playlists, you'll find mostly the same music I was playing back then—a lot of Zeppelin, of course, but also Traffic, Cream, and Lynyrd Skynyrd, plus more obscure bands like Spooky Tooth and Savoy Brown, which I only discovered thanks to the station's music library. And the 1980s and '90s are represented, too, with a lot of Talking Heads and a bit of Nirvana and Pearl Jam. Music still has the same power over me it always has. While my mind is being infused with what is blasting through my headphones, a lot of the old emotions and feelings and memories flood back in, too. We can't help but live in all three time zones simultaneously, remembering and reliving the past, the roots of who we are now, and planning and worrying about what we have to get done for tomorrow and next week, what we hope to get done this year, and what we want our life to be like five years from now. The past and the future constantly shape our present.

The present moments of 1970s Led Zeppelin contained the indelible past of American blues, just as in the present mind of a 1970s Illinois psychology major were the titanic voices of Skinner and Freud. Since then, most of my present moments have been with an eye toward the future goal of understanding just how much free will and control we actually have over what we think, feel, and do. But all of this has been experienced with the soundtrack of my past playing in my head—not just those incredible years at the radio station, but also my wide-eyed wonder as a child, the trees I climbed and the baseball I played, my crazy high school band buddies, and memories of my father. At the radio station, my initially clumsy DJ skills eventually became second nature, and getting used to the routine allowed me to have fun, feel cool, and bring some joy to my late-night listeners. My hope with this book is that you now feel more at home in the DJ booth of your own mind, and can take even better control over the soundtrack of your life.

Acknowledgments

This book would not exist without two people. It is the brainchild of my agent Doug Abrams, of Idea Architects. Doug first approached me ten years ago and then kept after me, patiently but persistently, until my life had settled down enough for me to be able to take on the task. Without Doug's unwavering belief in the message and value of this book, his experience and expertise, and most of all his unflagging support and encouragement, you'd be sitting there holding nothing in your hands right now. (And maybe wishing there was a book to explain why you were doing such a strange thing.) Since this was my first attempt at a more mainstream, nonacademic book and style of writing, Doug's colleagues Aaron Shulman and Lara Love Hardin were invaluable in shaping my prose to be less technical and more accessible, as well as in discovering fascinating stories that illuminated key points.

But even so, no progress would have been possible without the practical and emotional support of my wife, Monica, which enabled me to buckle down and get writing. She took so much at home onto her shoulders, and off mine, giving me the uninterrupted time and space I needed, nearly every morning without exception for several years in a row. She read drafts of chapters and gave it to me straight when things weren't clear or if one chapter wasn't as interesting as another. Her constant love, support, and encouragement—and no small amount of patience—were essential. Just as water doesn't exist without both hydrogen and oxygen, this book doesn't exist without both Doug and Monica.

Our daughters, Danielle and Lexie, also gave a lot of support and encouragement even though I was working on the book through several summer vacations in a row. I look forward to making it up to them in the

291

near future. And while they may not have realized it at the time, I was paying close attention to them and learned a lot about human nature in general and childhood in particular watching them both grow up.

Great thanks also to my colleagues who have stuck with me through thin as well as thick over the past decade (and in several cases much longer): Margaret Clark, Ran Hassin, Ezequiel Morsella, Gary Latham, Norbert Schwarz, Dan Gilbert, Sandra Murray, Marcia Johnson, June Gruber, Todd Heatherton, Gene Borgida, Tim Wilson, Roy Baumeister, Peter Gollwitzer, Gabriele Oettingen, Simone Schnall, and Ap Dijksterhuis. And several others generously gave of their time and expertise to help with specific topics and issues covered in the book: Harry Reis, Wendy Wood, Benjamin Karney, Margaret Shih, and Shira Gabriel.

My editor at Simon & Schuster/Touchstone, Trish Todd, and her incredible colleagues and staff also bolstered me with enthusiasm and cogent guidance, improving the initial manuscript in significant ways throughout the editorial and publication process. From start to finish, I could not have been in better hands. I'm very fortunate that they believed in this project and devoted so much time and energy to bring the book to you.

There are of course many other people to whom I am indebted for their guidance, support, and partnership over the course of my academic career—and because this book covers much of that career, which in turn was influenced by my childhood and adolescence, I would be remiss not to acknowledge their significant contributions. But there are so many to thank over that long span of time that I can only do so here through a blanket statement of my deep appreciation for all that they have done, along with making a firm implementation intention to give them specific thanks and recognition when future opportunities arise. So to my sisters and mother, the memory of my father, my fellow students at the Universities of Illinois and Michigan, my colleagues and graduate students at NYU and Yale—thank you all. It won't be the last time you hear that from me.

Notes

Introduction: Let's Do the Time Warp Again

p. 2 or even created our thoughts and actions: Nisbett & Wilson (1977), Zajonc (1980).

p. 2 around New England in a twenty-six-foot: Gazzaniga (1985, p. 64).

p. 3 but it moved nonetheless: Penfield (1961).

p. 4 "the Cocktail Party Effect": Cherry (1953), also Moray (1959).

p. 6 existed long before Freud: Whyte (1960).

p. 6 "tumbling ground for whimsies": James (1890).

p. 7 his work was the future of psychology: Perry & Laurence (1984).

p. 7 and knowledge about how our mind works: See Nisbett & Wilson (1977), Wilson & Brekke (1994).

p. 7 were making tremendous advances: Koestler (1967).

p. 8 the energy we use while awake: Raichle & Mintun (2006).

p. 9 get out of bed in the morning: Miller, Galanter, & Pribram (1960).

p. 10 disapproval of tanning salons and diet pills: Hill & Durante (2011).

p. 11 originated in the physical mind: Perry & Laurence (1984), Crabtree (1993).

p. 11 as Jung then proceeded to do anyway: This encounter occurred in 1909 while they were sailing across the Atlantic together to a conference in Massachusetts (where they met William James for the first and only time), and was a major reason for the rift that developed between them, which lasted the rest of their lives (see Rosenzweig, 1994).

p. 12 only through psychotherapy: Freud (1915); also Jones (1953, 1957).

p. 12 even in some branches of scientific psychology: Bargh (2016).

p. 13 playing by its own rules: This point was originally made by Ulric Neisser in a prescient 1963 paper seeking to reconceptualize Freudian psychodynamic concepts in terms of the emerging principles of cognitive science.

p. 13 major mental and emotional problems: Modern psychoanalysis is still based on Freud's theories and writings, largely independent of the findings and theories of scientific psychology, so there remains today a legacy of Freud's "separate mind" model of the unconscious, not only in psychoanalytic theory and practice but in domains traditionally influenced by psychoanalysis, such as psychi-

293

atry. Medical science of the mind (psychiatry) is much more influenced today by growing knowledge of brain structure and function and the chemical pathways involved, for which psycho-pharmaceutical drugs (such as antidepressants) are developed as solutions or palliatives. Still, the Freudian notion of the unconscious as a separate and inaccessible mind within us is still very present in popular culture, as in the 2015 Pixar movie *Inside Out,* an animation feature about emotions and the mind, in which "the unconscious" is depicted as a dark locked room within the mind's central control center.

p. 17   the adaptive unconscious: See Wilson (2002).

Chapter 1: The Past Is Always Present

p. 23   during our species' long evolution: Ötzi's story is drawn from information presented by the South Tyrol Museum of Archaeology: http://www.iceman.it/en/oetzi-the-iceman.

p. 23   "during ancient savage times?": Darwin (1877).

p. 24   laboratory studies of the time: Langer (1978).

p. 26   In one of our first experiments: Bargh & Thein (1985).

p. 27   how intelligent that person is: Higgins, King, & Mavin (1982).

p. 29   to those we were originally born with: Donald (2001).

p. 30   "where it is no longer needed": James (1890).

p. 32   intentional use of those systems: See Bargh & Morsella (2010), also Koestler (1967).

p. 33   in some symbolic way: Ghiselin (1952), Hadfield (1954).

p. 33   modern evolutionary biology and psychology: See Dawkins (1976), Mayr (1976), Deacon (1997), Donald (1991), Jaynes (1976).

p. 33   the old unconscious machinery that was still there: Bargh & Morsella (2008), Jaynes (1976, Chapter 1); this was also one of the central arguments of Arthur Koestler's devastating and characteristically brave attack on the then dominant behaviorist school of psychology, *The Ghost in the Machine* (1967).

p. 34   as Darwin himself argued: Darwin (1872).

p. 34   just don't want to have: Wolf (1994).

p. 34   that ever existed are now extinct: Dawkins (1976).

p. 35   one out of every three men were murdered: Chagnon (1988), LeBlanc (2003).

p. 35   was about 1 out of 4: LeBlanc (2003), Chagnon (1988).

p. 35   is about 1 in 100,000: LeBlanc (2003); see also Pinker (2011).

p. 35   Obama echoed Roosevelt's words: Obama's final State of the Union address, January 13, 2016.

p. 35   the process of economic recovery: Roosevelt (1933/1938).

p. 36   imagine in detail their own death: Nail et al. (2009).

p. 36   who had not been threatened: Skitka et al. (2002).

p. 36   University of California researchers followed: Block & Block (2006).

p. 36   but not to pleasant images, presented to them: Oxley et al. (2008), also Dodd et al. (2012). Adult conservatives also show higher sensitivity to threats (for example, disgust or danger) as compared to liberals (Duckitt et al., 2002; Inbar, Pizarro, & Bloom, 2009) and are more attentionally vigilant to potentially threatening stimuli (Carraro, Castelli, & Macchiella, 2011; Hibbing et al., 2014).

p. 37 compared to those who don't: Kanai et al. (2011).

p. 37 We conducted two experiments: Napier et al. (2017).

p. 40 "who come to his rallies": Johnson (November 7, 2016).

p. 40 as "disgusting" as well: http://abcnews.go.com/politics/wirestory/talk-sex-tapes-presidential-campaign-sordid-turn-42491738 and https://www.washingtonpost.com/news/post-politics/wp/2015/12/21/donald-trump-calls-hillary-clinton-disgusting-for-using-the-restroom-during-a-debate/.

p. 41 but from infections: Gilchrist (1998).

p. 41 such as Adolf Hitler: Kershaw (2000), pp. 13, 582-583.

p. 42 get preventative flu shots: Huang et al. (2011).

p. 43 in a clean room: Schnall et al. (2008), see also Chapman et al. (2009), Denke et al. (2016).

p. 44 of our larger human nature: See Frank & Shaw (2016).

p. 44 Darwin had been exchanging letters: Snyder et al. (2010).

p. 44 Paul Ekman and his colleagues: Ekman et al. (1969); see also Ekman (2003).

p. 46 "and activities with others": Kirschner & Tomasello (2004).

p. 46 Harriet Over and Malinda Carpenter: Over & Carpenter (2009).

p. 47 cooperation goal operate unconsciously: The cooperation motive can be primed and then operate unconsciously in adults as well as children: Neuberg (1988), Bargh et al. (2001), Storey & Workman (2013).

p. 48 carried out an intriguing experiment: Busetta et al. (2013); see Maestripieri et al. (2016).

p. 49 Workers of above-average looks: Maestripieri et al. (2016).

p. 50 performance on the task: Karremans et al. (2009).

p. 50 operate through the nose: Miller & Maner (2010, 2011).

p. 50 aware of this influence at all: For other demonstrations of the unconscious effects of odors and scents, see Holland et al. (2005) and Arzi et al. (2014).

p. 51 but your harm: See, for example, Derlega et al. (1993).

Chapter 2: Some Assembly Required

p. 53 "three sets of eyes": *Inferno 34:*53-57.

p. 54 "straw in glass": *Inferno 34:*10-15.

p. 54 tried to do to him?: *Inferno 33:* 109.

p. 54 "they would not be warmed": Gardiner (1989).

p. 55 trust between two people: Derlega et al. (1993).

p. 55 this trust breaks down: Holmes & Rempel (1989).

p. 55 called "suckers": Dawkins (1976).

p. 57 for more than twenty years: Simpson et al. (2007, 2011, 2014).

p. 58 that occur in close relationships: Simpson et al. (2007, 2011, 2014).

p. 61 in their given location: Emlen (1967).

p. 61 studies by Harry Harlow: Harlow (1958).

p. 62 100-watt lightbulb: Harlow & Suomi (1970).

p. 63 feelings of insecurity: Bowlby (1969).

p. 63 performed a simple experiment: Asch (1946).

p. 64 read about the person: Williams & Bargh (2008).

p. 65 just held a cold beverage: IJzerman & Semin (2009).

p. 65 in a warm, prosocial way: Storey & Workman (2013), Williams & Bargh (2008, Study 2).

p. 65 texting family and friends: Inagaki & Eisenberger (2013).

p. 66 in an economics game: Kang et al. (2011).

p. 66 or a cold father: Our comprehension of the meaning of other metaphors as well, such as a "rough" day or "driving a hard bargain," involves activation of the brain's somatosensory cortex, which is primarily involved in processing the physical sensations themselves (roughness, hardness, etc.). See Lacy et al (2012), Denke et al. (2013), Schaefer et al. (2014, 2015, 2017), and Puvermueller & Fadiga (2010).

p. 66 from four to six years of age: IJzerman et al. (2013).

p. 66 insecurely attached children: See also Chen et al. (2015).

p. 67 members of their own group: Kelly et al. (2005); also Bar-Haim et al. (2006).

p. 68 don't yet understand a word!: Kinzler et al. (2007).

p. 69 toward the other: Tajfel et al. (1971).

p. 69 the same automatic negative effect: Perdue et al. (1990).

p. 69 people in their society: Fiske et al. (2007).

p. 69 racial and social groups: Dunham et al. (2008).

p. 71 implicit racial preferences: There is currently some debate among psychological scientists regarding the stability or reliability of the IAT as a measure of stable individual differences in implicit racial attitudes—for example, can and should it be used as a diagnostic screening device by employers who prefer not to hire people with unconscious negative racial attitudes? However, there is much less doubt that the IAT reveals positive or negative implicit attitudes at the time of measurement, and all of the IAT research discussed in this book concerns the latter and not the former case. See Banaji & Greenwald (2013) and Singal (2017) for opposing viewpoints on the individual difference issue.

p. 71 as do White adults: An *implicit* measure is one that reveals a person's attitude indirectly, without asking their opinion directly. For example, the greater difficulty (resulting in longer response times) of using the same button to say both Black and Good compared to the same button to stand for White and Good implies something about the person's racial attitudes. On the other hand, an *explicit* measure of racial attitudes is the traditional kind of questionnaire or survey question, which just asks people directly how much they like/dislike blacks and how much they like/dislike whites, and they typically answer on a scale, such as from 1 (not at all) to 7 (very much so).

Chapter 3: Prime Time

p. 73 in the first place: Pinker (1994).

p. 74 for being like a villainous country: http://www.dailymail.co.uk/news/article -3609562/Sons-American-GI-defected-North-Korea-1960s-country-s-latest -propaganda-stars-one-captain-imperial-army.html and http://www.cbsnews .com/news/joe-dresnok-an-american-in-north-korea/.

p. 75 choices, opinions, and actions: Cohen (2015).

p. 76 The story begins: Uhlmann et al. (2009).

p. 77 When they were graduate students: Uhlmann et al. (2009).

p. 78 a person's judgments and behavior: Cohen (2015).

p. 78 something she was aware of: Bargh & Chartrand (2000).

p. 78 back to the 1950s: See Bargh & Chartrand (2000).

p. 79 perhaps even suicidal: Higgins et al. (1977).

p. 79 aware of the reminding or not: Rogers & Milkman (2016).

p. 83 had not checked off that box: Steele & Aronson (1995).

p. 83 are slow and have bad memories: Meisner (2012).

p. 83 *White Men Can't Jump?*: See Stone et al. (1999).

p. 84 no-identity primed control group: Ambady et al. (2001).

p. 86 "that sexually objectifies the female body": Fredrickson et al. (1998).

p. 86 under controlled laboratory conditions: Fredrickson et al. (1998).

p. 88 Ambady and her colleagues: Weisbuch et al. (2009).

p. 89 featuring each character: More details on the study and the clips used can be found at www.sciencemag.org/cgi/content/full/326/5960/1711/DC1.

p. 91 evening news broadcasts: Gilens (1996).

p. 92 "images of blacks are at work": Gilens (1996, p. 537).

Chapter 4: Life Lingers

p. 96 the heavy holiday traffic: In fact, studies have found that the more fast-food restaurants there are in a particular area (zip code), the faster and more impatient people who live in that zip code area are in making financial decisions (Zhong & DeVoe, 2010).

p. 97 "as no other woman could": http://dangerousminds.net/comments/marianne_ faithfull_is_naked_under_leather_in_girl_a_motorcycle.

p. 97 can affect conscious, rational thoughts: Cantor et al. (1975).

p. 99 while crossing a much safer bridge: Dutton & Aron (1974).

p. 99 focused on anger and aggression: Zillmann et al. (1974).

p. 99 early theory of emotion: Schachter & Singer (1964).

p. 100 on an unconscious level: For example, Gilbert & Gill (2000).

p. 101 William James understood: James (1890, Volume 1, p. 82).

p. 102 my hometown of Champaign: Schwarz & Clore (1983).

p. 103 a comprehensive study: Hirschleifer & Shumway (2003).

p. 104   and her colleagues: Zaval et al. (2014).

p. 105   a computer simulation called Cyberball: Williams & Jarvis (2006).

p. 106   the socially warm, "included" participants: Zhong & Leonardelli (2008, Study 1).

p. 106   or .68 Fahrenheit: IJzerman et al. (2012).

p. 106   using an oral thermometer: Inagaki et al. (2016).

p. 107   than cold food and drinks: Zhong & Leonardelli (2008, Study 2).

p. 108   a full week later: See also Koltyn et al. (1992). Beever (2010) reported similar success with a thermal therapy for type 2 diabetes patients.

p. 108   do not receive any treatment: Nutt (2016).

p. 108   lonely or homesick: Troisi & Gabriel (2011).

p. 108   could pay big dividends: Shalev & Bargh (2011).

p. 109   availability heuristic was discovered: Tversky & Kahneman (1974).

p. 109   become famous overnight: Jacoby et al. (1989).

p. 110   or walking the dog: Ross & Sicoly (1979).

p. 111   in a 2003 research article: Eibach et al. (2003).

p. 113   of a strong emotion: Phelps (2009, 2012).

p. 113   on TV after the race: https://www.youtube.com/watch?v=zZRSg-yabP0.

p. 114   hoarding is a significant problem: Black et al. (1998), Christianson et al. (1994).

p. 114   according to *Scientific American:* https://www.scientificamerican.com/article/real-world-hoarding/.

p. 115   Jennifer Lerner and her colleagues: Lerner & Keltner (2001), Lerner et al. (2004).

p. 115   the "endowment effect": Kahneman et al. (1991).

p. 117   are effective in reducing: Black et al. (1998), Christenson et al. (1994), Faber & Christenson (1996).

p. 118   "begun to drive employees crazy": https://www.washingtonpost.com/news/business/wp/2015/06/03/why-wal-mart-is-ditching-its-celine-dion-soundtrack-and-getting-a-deejay/.

p. 119   called the *visual buffer:* Sperling (1960).

p. 120   a form of priming effect called anchoring: Kahneman (2011, Chapter 11).

p. 120   "and they are wrong": Kahneman (2011, p. 127).

Chapter 5: Should I Stay or Should I Go?

p. 126   wouldn't shake his hand: Sadler-Smith (2012, p. 126).

p. 126   patients with Korsakoff's syndrome: Johnson et al. (1985).

p. 127   Then he used a sophisticated data technique: Osgood (1949).

p. 128   his major book on this research: Osgood (1949).

p. 128   published an influential paper: Schneirla (1959).

p. 129   the more often we encounter them: Zajonc (1968, 1980).

p. 130   overrides the mere exposure effect: See LeDoux (1996).

p. 131   more important than others: Fazio et al. (1986).

p. 133   more general than it was before: Bargh et al. (1992, 1996).

p. 134   have confirmed our findings: Herring et al. (2003).

p. 134　in response to those things: Solarz (1960).

p. 135　computerized displays and timing: Chen & Bargh (1999).

p. 136　had white participants make: Kawakami et al. (2007).

p. 137　and other addictions: Wiers et al. (2011).

p. 139　a life-or-death example: LeBlanc (2003).

p. 139　some quite startling patterns in human behavior: Pelham et al. (2003), Jones et al. (2002, 2004), Beggan (1991), Pelham & Carvallo (2015).

p. 139　Washington or Jefferson: Pelham et al. (2003).

p. 140　and level of education: Pelham & Carvallo (2015).

p. 141　won a major math award: Walton et al. (2012).

p. 142　our emotions to others: Darwin (1872).

p. 142　directly connect bone to skin: Tooby & Cosmides (2005, pp. 49-50).

p. 143　the people they encountered: Tooby & Cosmides (1990).

p. 143　based only on their faces: Willis & Todorov (2006).

p. 143　people believe competence: Todorov et al. (2005).

p. 144　and other countries: See also Ballew & Todorov (2007).

p. 145　our treatment by society: See Zebrowitz & Montepare (2014).

p. 146　prototypic African facial appearance: Sommers (2006).

p. 146　and more attractive side: Snyder et al. (1977).

p. 146　when given the choice: Langlois et al. (1987), Slater et al. (2000).

p. 146　a face is attractive or not: Olson & Marschuetz (2005).

p. 146　reward centers of the brain: Papies & Barsalou (2015).

p. 146　medial orbitofrontal cortex: O'Doherty et al. (2003).

p. 146　that ever existed became extinct: Dawkins (1976).

p. 147　innate tendency quite early on: Darwin (1872, p. 132).

p. 148　"rivalry could go so wrong": http://www.newhavenindependent.org/index.php/branford/entry/yankee_fan_stabs_red_sox_fan_/.

p. 149　one of the most famous experiments: Sherif et al. (1954).

p. 151　how unconscious racism can be "e-raced": Van Bavel & Cunningham (2009).

Chapter 6: When Can You Trust Your Gut?

p. 155　or making a plan: Morewedge & Norton (2009), Morewedge et al. (2014).

p. 156　to blind us: See Inbar, Cone, & Gilovich (2010) for an insightful analysis of when people tend to trust and when they don't trust their gut intuitions.

p. 157　if we are too quick: Kahneman & Frederick (2002).

p. 157　without reflecting on them: Frederick (2005).

p. 157　our error-prone gut: For example, Frederick (2005), Morewedge & Kahneman (2010).

p. 158　a gift for being in the study: Wilson & Schooler (1991).

p. 159　Unconscious Thought Theory: Dijksterhuis & Nordgren (2006).

p. 160　"without the assistance of consciousness": Freud (1899, p. 593).

p. 160　the decision the participant made: Creswell et al. (2013).

p. 161   *conscious first, then unconscious:* Nordgren et al. (2011).

p. 161   assign blame and responsibility to them: Ham & van den Bos (2009, 2010a, 2010b).

p. 161   to fairness in social exchanges: Shaw & Olson (2012), Shaw et al. (2012).

p. 164   in isolation from the luck factor: See, for example, Ron Shandler's annual *Baseball Forecaster.*

p. 164   to pick up reliable patterns and sequences: Turk-Browne et al. (2005, 2009, 2010).

p. 167   to evaluate other people: Lazarus (1991).

p. 167   presentation of white faces did not: Bargh et al. (1996, Experiment 3).

p. 169   website called "What's My Image?": Olivola & Todorov (2010).

p. 170   coined an apt term: Ambady & Rosenthal (1992).

p. 170   just a fraction of that person's total behavior: Ambady et al. (2001).

p. 171   videotaped thirteen Harvard graduate fellows: Ambady & Rosenthal (1993).

p. 172   immediate reactions to betrayal: Kang et al. (2011).

p. 173   participants while they played economics games: Aragon et al. (2014).

p. 174   groundbreaking series of studies: McKenna & Bargh (1998).

p. 175   private part of themselves public: Wicklund & Gollwitzer (1982).

p. 175   had first met online: Cacioppo et al. (2013), see also Finkel et al. (2012).

p. 176   what is beautiful is good: Eagly et al. (1991).

Chapter 7: What You See Is What You Do

p. 178   is how Lhermitte described it: Lhermitte (1986, p. 342).

p. 180   the parietal cortex: Frith et al. (2000).

p. 182   the *perception-action link:* Dijksterhuis & Bargh (2001).

p. 183   with photographs instead of inkblots: Chartrand & Bargh (1999).

p. 184   imitation and mimicry in infants: Meltzoff (2002).

p. 184   David Milner and Melvyn Goodale: Goodale et al. (1991).

p. 185   usually focused on other things: See Hommel (2013).

p. 185   but especially to act: Bargh & Morsella (2010).

p. 186   around 200 BC: Wiltermuth & Heath (2009).

p. 186   the soldiers' constant singing: Tuchman (1962, pp. 201-202).

p. 187   a truly upsetting 2016 article: https://www.thenation.com/article/the-cia-waterboarded-the-wrong-man-83-times-in-1-month/.

p. 188   crime investigation and criminal interrogation: Collins et al (2002).

p. 189   did just that: Frank et al. (2006).

p. 190   significantly larger tips: Van Baaren et al. (2003).

p. 190   large French department store: Jacob et al. (2011).

p. 192   form new bonds with people we meet: Lakin et al. (2008).

p. 192   chameleon effect wired into it: See Chartrand & Lakin (2013).

p. 192   men engaged in greater imitation and mimicry: Miller & Maner (2011).

p. 193   in a two-part study: Macrae & Johnston (1998).

p. 194   in the same fashion: Bargh et al. (1996, Study 1).

NOTES

p. 195   the rudeness of others is "contagious": Foulk et al. (2016).

p. 198   a group of Dutch researchers: Keizer et al. (2008).

p. 200   more likely you will be, too: Christakis & Fowler (2009), Fowler & Christakis (2008), Rosenquist et al. (2011).

p. 201   Researchers at Facebook: Kramer (2012).

p. 201   more controversial study: Hill (2014).

p. 201   Facebook researchers: Kramer et al. (2014).

p. 201   before a beach vacation in Cancún: Lee & Shapiro (2016).

p. 202   study by Roger Barker: Barker & Wright (1954).

p. 203   A 2014 set of studies: Cohn et al. (2014); see also Cohn et al. (2015) for similar findings produced by priming the criminal identities of prisoners.

p. 204   being aware or intending them: See also Welsh & Ordonez (2014) for another demonstration of unconscious influences on ethical behavior in the workplace.

p. 204   went into Dutch grocery stores: Papies et al. (2014).

p. 204   tantalizing smell of grilled chicken: Papies & Hamstra (2010).

p. 205   and much of the developed world: Wang et al. (2011).

p. 205   instead of eating healthily: Williams & Poehlman (2017).

p. 205   associated with taste and reward: Simmons et al. (2005).

p. 205   led by Jennifer Harris: Harris et al. (2009).

p. 205   not aware of their power over us: Television commercials can have positive effects on eating behavior as well; see Anschutz et al. (2008).

p. 205   of more than one thousand young drinkers: Naimi et al. (2016); Wallace (2016).

p. 206   between two and four of these ads every day: Collins et al. (2016).

p. 206   heading to the refrigerator so often: See Chandon & Wansink (2011).

p. 206   Neuroscientists have revealed: Tang et al. (2013).

p. 206   trying not to do something: Wegner (1994).

p. 207   well-intentioned antismoking signs: Earp et al. (2013).

p. 207   fifty-six regular smokers watched: Harris et al. (2014).

p. 208   how they see you behave: Zdaniuk & Bobocel (2013).

Chapter 8: Be Careful What You Wish For

p. 212   climate change problem as well: Hardin (1968).

p. 213   changes have taken place: Huang & Bargh (2014).

p. 214   "ignorant of the causes of their desires": Quoted in Ratner (1927, p. 253).

p. 215   attitudes and behavior change drastically: Loewenstein (1996).

p. 216   person who is doing the hiring: Maestripieri et al. (2016, p. 44).

p. 216   aware of the external reward: Pessiglione et al. (2007).

p. 216   about a romantic encounter: Bar-Anan et al. (2010).

p. 216   after the fact: Parks-Stamm et al. (2010).

p. 217   at a large American state university: Hill & Durante (2011).

p. 217   without our realizing it: Gabriel et al. (2016).

p. 218   there on the bed with him: Brinkley (2012).

p. 218   helps reduce a person's distress: Aydin et al. (2012).

p. 219   how hungry they currently were: Xu et al. (2015).

p. 219   the concept of "perceptual readiness": Bruner (1957).

p. 220   concerned about subliminal advertising: See Wilson & Brekke (1994).

p. 220   never existed, either!: Pratkanis (1992), Moore (1982).

p. 220   important to the participant: Weingarten et al. (2016).

p. 222   wrote about such an experience: Goldsmith (1994).

p. 222   pattern of spaces below: Stickgold et al. (2000), Goldsmith (1994), Leutwyler (2000).

p. 223   activities they did with them: Fitzsimons & Shah (2008).

p. 224   unconsciously in the background: Slotter & Gardner (2010).

p. 224   the goal of making their mother proud of them: Fitzsimons & Bargh (2003).

p. 225   videotape of a job interview: Bargh et al. (2008).

p. 228   priming the achievement goal: Bargh et al. (2001); see also Bargh & Gollwitzer (1994).

p. 228   athletic victories are on the line: See Mazur et al. (2008).

p. 229   seminary students were asked to give a speech: Darley & Batson (1973).

p. 230   to seeing a person in distress: Darley & Batson (1973, pp. 107-108).

p. 230   in their next class: In general, religious primes and thoughts do increase prosocial behavior, unconsciously as well as consciously (see meta-analytic review by Shariff et al., 2016), so the findings of the Good Samaritan study demonstrate just how powerful an important temporary goal can be in overriding other, conflicting influences on a person's behavior.

p. 230   surprisingly easy to find: See Bargh & Raymond (1995) for many contemporary examples; almost every day there are news stories about people in power making policies or using their official authority for their personal, family, or friends' advantage, often quite blatantly and publicly. (Just off the top of my head, the White House recently encouraged us to buy clothes from the president's daughter's clothing line. It is remarkable how obvious and commonplace this misuse of power is. Sad!)

p. 231   have been studying it for a while: See Gruenfeld et al. (2008).

p. 231   still to be made: See the official government reports by the U.S. Centers for Disease Control and Prevention (2012) and Department of Defense (2013).

p. 231   "discuss your raise at the Holiday Inn": Fitzgerald (1993).

p. 232   nothing bad would happen to him: Pryor (1987), Malamuth (1989a, 1989b).

p. 232   purportedly on visual illusions: Bargh et al. (1995).

p. 233   of such a policy: https://www.buzzfeed.com/katiejmbaker/yale-ethics-professor and https://sites.google.com/site/thomaspoggeopenletter/.

p. 234   do not return the interest: New studies show that the effects of power on sexual harassment and aggression may be particularly strong in those who are usually low in power over others and for whom having power is a new thing—see Williams et al. (2016).

p. 234   above those of their own: Clark & Mills (1979).

p. 234   than the rest of us: Chen et al. (2001).

NOTES

Chapter 9: The Unconscious Never Sleeps

p. 237 "I will be there to write": Mailer (2003, pp. 142-144).

p. 239 In his famous experiment: Maier (1931).

p. 241 published posthumously: Duncker (1945).

p. 241 using words to prime the insight: Higgins & Chaires (1980).

p. 242 to figure out the answer: Metcalfe (1986), Metcalfe & Wiebe (1987).

p. 242 this finding was later confirmed: Creswell et al. (2013).

p. 243 other intellectual and artistic breakthroughs: See the compendium *The Creative Process*, published by Brewster Ghiselin in 1952.

p. 244 "consequence of the hypothesis": Hadfield (1954, p. 113).

p. 245 Myers's definition of genius: Myers (1892), see Crabtree (1993, pp. 327-350).

p. 245 Homer and Sappho: Gunderson (2016).

p. 246 "favorite track on the album": Clapton (2007).

p. 246 against the Boston Celtics: http://www.espn.com/blog/statsinfo/post/_/id/116844/a-closer-look-at-michael-jordans-63-point-game.

p. 249 and simulating different solutions: Gilbert & Wilson (2007), Raichle et al. (2001), Buckner & Carroll (2007).

p. 249 of the energy a person expends while awake: Buckner & Carroll (2007), Raichle & Mintun (2006).

p. 250 about four thousand discrete thought segments every day: Klinger (1978).

p. 250 to get done pretty soon: Klinger et al. (1980).

p. 251 studied people while asleep: Hoelscher et al. (1981).

p. 251 while you sleep: Klinger (2013, p. 4).

p. 252 "promises that remain unkept": Mailer (2003, p. 144).

p. 252 specific sequences of actions: See Chapter 10, also Gollwitzer (1999).

p. 252 compared good and poor sleepers: Fichten et al. (2001).

p. 253 intrude on your conscious thoughts: Morsella et al. (2010).

p. 254 they needed to finish: Masicampo & Baumeister (2011).

p. 254 defense attorney Perry Mason: Not completely infallible, actually. After several years and many episodes of the show, Perry did finally lose a case. This was so unexpected and such a shock to the audience that several members of my family screamed when the jury announced their verdict and I think one of my sisters fainted.

p. 255 through a raging thunderstorm: Siegel (2009).

p. 255 in Nashville, Tennessee: Stroop (1935).

p. 256 were trying to do at the time: Fadardi & Cox (2009).

p. 257 has drivers looking for game creatures: Boudette (2016).

p. 257 cell phones and phone apps: http://www.stltoday.com/news/local/metro/why-are-traffic-fatalities-rising-in-missouri-illinois/article_4f3608bf-64a6-550d-9bc0-7924dc0d6429.html.

p. 257 and eyes on the road: Boudette (2016).

p. 259 in the 1930s: Vygotsky (1934).

NOTES

Chapter 10: You Have Mind Control

p. 261 famously declared God was dead: A century later, popular culture is still reacting to this statement. In one of my favorite episodes of *The Simpsons,* Lisa gets Homer to go outside to see a meteor shower. Awestruck by the spectacle, Homer quietly says, "I wish God were alive to see this."

p. 262 what we see people do on TV: See Williams & Poehlman (2017).

p. 264 have happier personal relationships: Tangney et al. (2004).

p. 264 especially the study of the mind: Watson (1913).

p. 266 free will was an illusion: For example, Skinner (1971).

p. 266 a resounding yes: Baumeister et al. (2011).

p. 267 how yummy it will taste: Lazarus (1991), Mischel (2014).

p. 268 intentions and desired behavior: Gollwitzer (1993, 1999), Gollwitzer & Brandstaetter, (1997), Gollwitzer & Sheeran (2006).

p. 268 routines of place and time: Wood & Ruenger (2016).

p. 269 Brain imaging studies: Gilbert et al. (2009), Burgess et al. (2007).

p. 270 several daily pills: Sheeran & Orbell (1999), see also Gollwitzer (1999).

p. 270 they'd just forgotten to: Orbell et al. (1997).

p. 271 in the at-risk group: Rogers et al. (2015).

p. 271 that year for the various campaigns: Nickerson & Rogers (2010).

p. 272 this bias was significantly reduced: Stewart & Payne (2008), Mendoza et al. (2010).

p. 272 mimicked by someone else: Wieber et al. (2014); see also Gollwitzer et al. (2011).

p. 273 more than two hundred unsuccessful dieters: Van Koningsbruggen et al. (2011).

p. 275 *Galloway's Book on Running:* Galloway (1984).

p. 276 a ten-item questionnaire: http://www.sas.upenn.edu/~duckwort/images/upperdarbypd/01092013_briefscc.pdf.

p. 277 confirm this basic principle: Galla & Duckworth (2015).

p. 277 who are good at self-control: Hofmann et al. (2012).

p. 277 who reported exerting more self-control: Milyavskaya & Inzlicht (2017).

p. 277 "is not beneficial": Quoted in Resnick (2016).

p. 278 "instead of yum": Quoted in Resnick (2016).

p. 278 "changing the environments in which people live": W. Wood, personal communication, August 2016.

p. 278 change the person's environment: Papies & Hamstra (2010).

Conclusion: You Are the DJ

p. 282 forgotten all about it: Rogers & Milkman (2016).

p. 282 larger ears of corn: Darwin (1859).

p. 282 Einstein and Superman: Nelson & Norton (2005).

p. 284 through the commercials: Wallace (2016).

p. 285 as stingy or selfish or uncaring: Pronin (2009), Epley & Dunning (1999).

p. 286 Harry Potter stories: Boothby et al. (2017a).

p. 287 the *mind gap*: Boothby et al. (2017b).

References

Ambady, N., LaPlante, D., & Johnson, E. (2001). Thin-slice judgments as a measure of interpersonal sensitivity. In J. A. Hall & F. J. Bernieri (Eds.), *Interpersonal sensitivity: Theory and measurement* (pp. 89–101). Mahwah, NJ: Erlbaum.

Ambady, N., & Rosenthal, R. (1992). Thin slices of behavior as predictors of interpersonal consequences: A meta-analysis. *Psychological Bulletin, 111*, 256–274.

Ambady, N., Shih, M., Kim, A., & Pittinsky, T. L. (2001). Stereotype susceptibility in children: Effects of identity activation on quantitative performance. *Psychological Science, 12*, 385–390.

Anderson, R. C., & Pichert, J. W. (1978). Recall of previously unrecallable information following a shift in perspective. *Journal of Verbal Learning and Verbal Behavior, 17*, 1–12.

Anschutz, D. J., van Strien, T. V., & Engels, R. C. (2008). Exposure to slim images in mass media: Television commercials as reminders of restriction in restrained eaters. *Health Psychology, 27*, 401–408.

Aragón, O. R., Sharer, E. A., Bargh, J. A., & Pineda, J. A. (2014). Modulations of mirroring activity by desire for social connection and relevance of movement. *Social Cognitive and Affective Neuroscience, 9*, 1762–1769.

Archer, R. L. (1987). Commentary: Self-disclosure, a very useful behavior. In V. L. Derlega & J. H. Berg (Eds.), *Self-disclosure: Theory, research, and therapy* (pp. 329–342). New York: Plenum.

Arzi, A., Rozenkrantz, L., Holtzman, Y., Secundo, L., & Sobel, N. (2014). Sniffing patterns uncover implicit memory for undetected odors. *Current Biology, 24*, R263–R264.

Asch, S. E. (1946). Forming impressions of personality. *Journal of Abnormal and Social Psychology, 41*, 258–290.

Aydin, N., Krueger, J., Fischer, J., Hahn, D., Kastenmuller, A., Frey, D., et al. (2012). "Man's best friend": How the presence of a dog reduces mental distress after social exclusion. *Journal of Experimental Social Psychology, 48*, 446–449.

Banaji, M. R., & Greenwald, A. G. (2013). *Blindspot: Hidden biases of good people.* New York: Random House.

Bar-Anan, Y., Wilson, T. D., & Hassin, R. R. (2010). Inaccurate self-knowledge formation as a result of automatic behavior. *Journal of Experimental Social Psychology, 46*, 884–894.

Bargh, J. A. (2016). The devil made me do it. In A. Miller (Ed.), *The social psychology of good and evil* (2nd ed.). New York: Guilford.

Bargh, J. A., Chaiken, S., Govender, R., & Pratto, F. (1992). The generality of the automatic attitude activation effect. *Journal of Personality and Social Psychology, 62*, 893–912.

Bargh, J. A., Chaiken, S., Raymond, P., & Hymes, C. (1996). The automatic evaluation effect: Unconditional automatic attitude activation with a pronunciation task. *Journal of Experimental Social Psychology, 32*, 185–210.

Bargh, J. A., & Chartrand, T. L. (2000). A practical guide to priming and automaticity research. In H. Reis & C. Judd (Eds.), *Handbook of research methods in social psychology* (pp. 253–285). New York: Cambridge University Press.

Bargh, J. A., Chen, M., & Burrows, L. (1996). Automaticity of social behavior: Direct effects of trait construct and stereotype priming on action. *Journal of Personality and Social Psychology, 71*, 230–244.

Bargh, J. A., Green, M. L., & Fitzsimons, G. M. (2008). The selfish goal: Unintended consequences of intended goal pursuits. *Social Cognition, 26*, 520–540.

Bargh, J. A., & Gollwitzer, P. M. (1994). Environmental control of goal-directed action: Automatic and strategic contingencies between situations and behavior. In W. D. Spaulding (Ed.), *Integrative views of motivation, cognition, and emotion: Nebraska symposium on motivation* (Vol. 41, pp. 71–124). Lincoln, NE: University of Nebraska Press.

Bargh, J. A., Gollwitzer, P. M., Lee-Chai, A. Y., Barndollar, K., & Troetschel, R. (2001). The automated will: Nonconscious activation and pursuit of behavioral goals. *Journal of Personality and Social Psychology, 81*, 1014–1027.

Bargh, J. A., & McKenna, K. Y. A. (2004). The Internet and social life. *Annual Review of Psychology, 55*, 573–590.

Ballew, C. C., & Todorov, A. (2007). Predicting political elections from rapid and unreflective face judgments. *Proceedings of the National Academy of Sciences, 104*, 17948–17953.

Bargh, J. A., & Morsella, E. (2008). The unconscious mind. *Perspectives on Psychological Science, 3*, 73–79.

Bargh, J. A., & Morsella, E. (2010). Unconscious behavioral guidance systems. In C. R. Agnew, D. E. Carlston, W. G. Graziano, & J. R. Kelly (Eds.), *Then a miracle occurs: Focusing on behavior in social psychological theory and research* (pp. 89–118). New York: Oxford University Press.

Bargh, J. A., & Raymond, P. (1995). The naive misuse of power: Nonconscious sources of sexual harassment. *Journal of Social Issues, 26*, 168–185.

Bargh, J. A., Raymond, P., Pryor, J., & Strack, F. (1995). Attractiveness of the underling: An automatic power → sex association and its consequences for sexual harassment and aggression. *Journal of Personality and Social Psychology, 68*, 768–781.

Bargh, J. A., & Thein, R. D. (1985). Individual construct accessibility, person memory, and the recall-judgment link: The case of information overload. *Journal of Personality and Social Psychology, 49*, 1129–1146.

REFERENCES

Bar-Haim, Y., et al. (2006). Nature and nurture in own-race face processing. *Psychological Science, 17,* 159–163.

Barker, R. G., & Wright, H. F. (1954). *Midwest and its children: The psychological ecology of an American town.* New York: Row, Peterson & Company.

Baumeister, R. F., Masicampo, E. J., & Vohs, K. D. (2011). Do conscious thoughts cause behavior? *Annual Review of Psychology, 62,* 331–361.

Beever, R. (2010). The effects of repeated thermal therapy on quality of life in patients with type II diabetes mellitus. *Journal of Alternative Complementary Medicine, 16,* 677–681.

Beggan, J. K. (1991). On the social nature of nonsocial perception: The mere ownership effect. *Journal of Personality and Social Psychology, 62,* 229–237.

Black, D. W., Repertinger, S., Gaffney, G. R., & Gabel, J. (1998). Family history of psychiatric comorbidity in persons with compulsive buying: Preliminary findings. *American Journal of Psychiatry, 155,* 960–963.

Block, J., & Block, J. H. (2006). Nursery school personality and political orientation two decades later. *Journal of Research in Personality, 40,* 734–749.

Boothby, E. J., Clark, M. S., & Bargh, J. A. (2017a). The invisibility cloak illusion: People (incorrectly) believe they observe others more than others observe them. *Journal of Personality and Social Psychology, 112,* 589–606.

Boothby, E. J., Clark, M. S., & Bargh, J. A. (2017b). *The mind gap: People (incorrectly) believe that they think more about others than others think about them.* Manuscript under review, Yale University.

Boudette, N. E. (2016, November 15). Biggest spike in traffic deaths in 50 years? Blame apps. *The New York Times,* online edition.

Bowlby, J. (1969). *Attachment and loss* (Vol. I: Attachment). London: Hogarth Press and the Institute of Psycho-Analysis.

Brinkley, D. (2012). *Cronkite.* New York: Harper.

Bruner, J. (1957). On perceptual readiness. *Psychological Review, 64,* 123–152.

Buckner, R. L., & Carroll, D. C. (2007). Self-projection and the brain. *Trends in Cognitive Sciences, 11,* 49–57.

Burgess, P. W., Dumontheil, I., & Gilbert, S. J. (2007). The gateway hypothesis of rostral prefrontal cortex (area 10) function. *Trends in Cognitive Sciences, 11,* 290–298.

Busetta, G., Fiorillo, F., & Visalli, E. (2013). Searching for a job is a beauty contest. MPRA (Munich Personal RePEc Archive) paper No. 49382. Available online at http://mpra.ub.uni-muenchen.de/49392/.

Cacioppo, J. T., Cacioppo, S., Gonzaga, G. C., Ogburn, E. L., & VanderWeele, T. J. (2013). Marital satisfaction and break-ups differ across on-line and off-line meeting venues. *Proceedings of the National Academy of Sciences, 110,* 10135–10140.

Cantor, J. R., Zillmann, D., & Bryant, J. (1975). Enhancement of experienced sexual arousal in response to erotic stimuli through misattribution of unrelated residual excitation. *Journal of Personality and Social Psychology, 32,* 69–75.

Carraro, L., Castelli, L., & Macchiella, C. (2011). The automatic conservative: Ideology-based attentional asymmetries in the processing of valenced information. *PLOS-One, 6:* e26456. doi: 10.1371/journal.pone.0026456.

Centers for Disease Control (USA). (2012). *Sexual violence.* Atlanta, GA: Author.

REFERENCES

Chagnon, N. A. (1988, February 26). Life histories, blood revenge, and warfare in a tribal population. *Science, 239,* 985–992.

Chandon, P., & Wansink, B. (2011). Is food marketing making us fat? A multi-disciplinary review. *Foundations and Trends in Marketing, 5,* 113–196.

Chapman, H. A., Kim, D. A., Susskind, J. M., & Anderson, A. K. (2009). In bad taste: Evidence for the oral origins of moral disgust. *Science, 323,* 1222–1226.

Chartrand, T. L., & Bargh, J. A. (1999). The chameleon effect: The perception-behavior link and social interaction. *Journal of Personality and Social Psychology, 76,* 893–910.

Chartrand, T. L., & Lakin, J. (2013). Antecedents and consequences of human behavioral mimicry. *Annual Review of Psychology, 64,* 285–308.

Chen, M., & Bargh, J. A. (1999). Consequences of automatic evaluation: Immediate behavioral predispositions to approach or avoid the stimulus. *Personality and Social Psychology Bulletin, 25,* 215–224.

Chen, S., Lee-Chai, A. Y., & Bargh, J. A. (2001). Relationship orientation as a moderator of the effects of social power. *Journal of Personality and Social Psychology, 80,* 173–187.

Chen, Z., Poon, K.-T., & DeWall, C. N. (2015). Cold thermal temperature threatens belonging: The moderating role of perceived social support. *Social Psychological and Personality Science, 6,* 439–446. doi:10.1177/1948550614562843.

Cherry, E. C. (1953). Some experiments on the recognition of speech, with one and two ears. *Journal of the Acoustical Society of America, 25,* 975–979.

Christakis, N., & Fowler, J. (2009). *Connected: The amazing power of social networks and how they shape our lives.* New York: Little, Brown.

Christenson, G. A., et al. (1994). Compulsive buying: Descriptive characteristics and psychiatric comorbidity. *Journal of Clinical Psychiatry, 55,* 5–11.

Clapton, E. (2007). *Clapton: The autobiography.* New York: Broadway Books.

Clark, M. S., & Mills, J. (1979). Interpersonal attraction in exchange and communal relationships. *Journal of Personality and Social Psychology, 37,* 12–24.

Cohen, D. (2015). Cultural psychology. In G. Borgida & J. Bargh (Eds.), *Handbook of Personality and Social Psychology: Attitudes and Social Cognition* (pp. 415–456). Washington, DC: American Psychological Association.

Cohn, A., Fehr, E., & Marechal, M. A. (2014). Business culture and dishonesty in the banking industry. *Nature, 516,* 86–89. doi: 10.1038/nature13977.

Cohn, A., Marechal, M. A., & Noll, T. (2015). Bad boys: How criminal identity salience affects rule violation. *Review of Economic Studies, 82,* 1289–1308.

Collins, R., Lincoln, R., & Frank, M. G. (2002). The effect of rapport in forensic interviewing. *Psychiatry, Psychology, and Law, 9,* 69–78.

Collins, R. L., Martino, S. C., Kovalchuk, S. A., Becker, K. M., Shadel, W. G., & d'Amico, E. J. (2016). Alcohol advertising exposure among middle school-age youth: An assessment across all media and venues. *Journal of Studies on Alcohol and Drugs, 77,* 384–392.

Crabtree, A. (1993). *From Mesmer to Freud: Magnetic sleep and the roots of psychological healing.* New Haven, CT: Yale University Press.

Cresswell, J. D., Bursley, J. K., & Satpute, A. B. (2013). Neural reactivation links unconscious thought to decision-making performance. *Social Cognitive and Affective Neuroscience, 8,* 863–869.

Darley, J. M., & Batson, C. D. (1973). From Jerusalem to Jericho: A study of situational and dispositional variables in helping behavior. *Journal of Personality and Social Psychology, 27,* 100–119.

Darwin, C. (1859). *On the origin of species.* London: John Murray.

Darwin, C. (1872). *The expression of the emotions in man and animals.* London: John Murray.

Darwin, C. (1877). A biographical sketch of an infant. *Mind, 2,* 285–294.

Dawkins, R. (1976). *The selfish gene.* New York: Oxford University Press.

Deacon, T. W. (1997). *The symbolic species: The co-evolution of language and the brain.* New York: Norton.

Denke, C., Rotte, M., Heinze, J-J, & Schaefer, M. (2016). Lying and the subsequent desire for toothpaste: Activity in the somatosensory cortex predicts embodiment of the moral-purity metaphor. *Cerebral Cortex, 26,* 477–484. doi: 10.1093/cercor/bhu170.

Derlega, V. J., Metts, S., Petronio, S., & Margulis, S. T (1993). *Self-disclosure.* London: Sage.

Dijksterhuis, A., & Bargh, J. A. (2001). The perception-behavior expressway: Automatic effects of social perception on social behavior. In M. P. Zanna (Ed.), *Advances in experimental social psychology* (Vol. 33, pp. 1–40). San Diego: Academic Press.

Dijksterhuis, A., & Nordgren, L. F. (2006). A theory of unconscious thought. *Perspectives on Psychological Science, 1,* 95–109.

Donald, M. (1991). *Origins of the modern mind: Three stages in the evolution of culture and cognition.* Cambridge, MA: Harvard University Press.

Donald, M. (2001). *A mind so rare: The evolution of human consciousness.* New York: Norton.

Duncker, K. (1945). On problem solving. *Psychological Monographs, 58* (Whole No. 270).

Dunham, Y., Baron, A. S., & Banaji, M. R. (2008). The development of implicit intergroup cognition. *Trends in Cognitive Sciences, 12,* 248–253.

Dutton, D. G., & Aron, A. P. (1974). Some evidence for heightened sexual attraction under conditions of high anxiety. *Journal of Personality and Social Psychology, 30,* 510–517.

Eagly, A. H., Ashmore, R. D., Makhijani, M. G., & Longo, L. C. (1991). What is beautiful is good, but . . . : A meta-analysis review of research on the physical attractiveness stereotype. *Psychological Bulletin, 110,* 109–128.

Earp, B. D., Dill, B., Harris, J. L., Ackerman, J. M., & Bargh, J. A. (2013). No sign of quitting: Incidental exposure to no-smoking signs ironically boosts cigarette-approach tendencies in smokers. *Journal of Applied Social Psychology, 43,* 2158–2162.

Eibach, R. P., Libby, L. K., & Gilovich, T. D. (2003). When change in the self is mistaken for change in the world. *Journal of Personality and Social Psychology, 84,* 917–931.

REFERENCES

Ekman, P. (2003). *Emotions revealed*. New York: Henry Holt.

Ekman, P., Sorenson, E. R., & Friesen, W. V. (1969). Pan-cultural elements in facial display of emotions. *Science, 164*, 86–88.

Emlen, S. T. (1967). Migratory orientation in the indigo bunting, *Passerina cyanea*. Part II: Mechanism of celestial orientation. *The Auk, 84*, 463–489.

Epley, N., & Dunning, D. (1999). Feeling "holier than thou": Are self-serving assessments produced by errors in self- or social prediction? *Journal of Personality and Social Psychology, 79*, 861–875.

Faber, R. J., & Christenson, G. A. (1996). In the mood to buy: Differences in the mood states experienced by compulsive buyers and other consumers. *Psychology and Marketing, 13*, 803–819.

Fadardi, J. S., & Cox, W. M. (2009). Reversing the sequence: Reducing alcohol consumption by overcoming alcohol attentional bias. *Drug and Alcohol Dependence, 101*, 137–145.

Fazio, R. H., Sanbonmatsu, D. M., Powell, M. C, & Kardes, F. R. (1986). On the automatic activation of attitudes. *Journal of Personality and Social Psychology, 50*, 229–238.

Fichten, C. S., Libman, E., Creti, L., Amsel, R., Sabourin, S. Brender, W., et al. (2001). Role of thoughts during nocturnal awake times in the insomnia experience of older adults. *Cognitive Therapy and Research, 25*, 665–692.

Finkel, E. J., Eastwick, P. W., Karney, B. R., Reis, H. T., & Sprecher, S. (2012). Online dating: A critical analysis from the perspective of psychological science. *Psychological Science in the Public Interest, 13*, 3–66.

Fiske, S. T., Cuddy, A., & Glick, P. (2007). Universal dimensions of social cognition: Warmth and competence. *Trends in Cognitive Sciences, 11*, 77–83.

Fitzgerald, L. F. (1993). Sexual harassment: Violence against women in the workplace. *American Psychologist, 48*, 1070–1076.

Fitzsimons, G. M., & Bargh, J. A. (2003). Thinking of you: Nonconscious pursuit of interpersonal goals associated with relationship partners. *Journal of Personality and Social Psychology, 84*, 148–164.

Fitzsimons, G., & Shah, J. (2008). How goal instrumentality shapes relationship evaluations. *Journal of Personality and Social Psychology, 95*, 319–337.

Foulk, T., Woolum, A., & Erez, A. (2016). Catching rudeness is like catching a cold: The contagion effects of low-intensity negative behaviors. *Journal of Applied Psychology, 101*, 50–67.

Fowler, J. H., & Christakis, N. A. (2008). Dynamic spread of happiness in a large social network: Longitudinal analysis over 20 years in the Framingham Heart Study. *British Medical Journal, 337*, a2338.

Frank, M. G., & Shaw, A. Z. (2016). Evolution and nonverbal communication. In D. Matsumoto, H. C. Hwang, & M. G. Frank (Eds.), *American Psychological Association handbook of nonverbal communication* (pp. 45–76). Washington, DC: American Psychological Association.

Frank, M. G., Yarbrough, J. D., & Ekman, P. (2006). Investigative interviewing and the detection of deception. In T. Williamson (Ed.), *Investigative interviewing: Rights, research, and regulation* (pp. 229–255). Portland, OR: Willan.

Frederick, S. (2005). Cognitive reflection and decision making. *Journal of Economic Perspectives, 19*, 25–42.

Fredrickson, B. L., Roberts, T-A, Noll, S. M., Quinn, D. M., & Twenge, J. M. (1998). That swimsuit becomes you: Sex differences in self-objectification, restrained eating, and math performance. *Journal of Personality and Social Psychology, 75*, 269–284.

Freud, S. (1899). *The interpretation of dreams*. Translated by James Strachey. New York: Basic Books.

Freud, S. (1915). The unconscious. In *The Standard Edition of Sigmund Freud* (Vol. 14) pp. 159–215. London: Hogarth.

Frith, C. D., Blakemore, S.-J., & Wolpert, D. M. (2000). Abnormalities in the awareness and control of action. *Philosophical Transactions of the Royal Society of London, 355*, 1771–1788.

Gabriel, S., Valenti, J., & Young, A. F. (2016). Social surrogates, social motivations, and everyday activities: The case for a strong, subtle, and sneaky social self. In J. M. Olson & M. P. Zanna (Eds.), *Advances in experimental social psychology, 53*, 189–243.

Galla, B. M., & Duckworth, A. L. (2015). More than resisting temptation: Beneficial habits mediate the relationships between self-control and positive life outcomes. *Journal of Personality and Social Psychology, 109*, 508–525.

Galloway, J. (1984). *Galloway's book on running*. Bolinas, CA: Shelter.

Gardiner, E. (Ed., 1989). *Visions of heaven and hell before Dante*. New York: Italica Press.

Ghiselin, B. (Ed., 1952). *The creative process: Reflections on invention in the arts and sciences*. Berkeley: University of California Press.

Gilbert, D. T., & Gill, M. J. (2000). The momentary realist. *Psychological Science, 11*, 394–398.

Gilbert, D. T., & Wilson, T. D. (2007). Prospection: Experiencing the future. *Science, 317*, 1351–1354.

Gilbert, S. J., Gollwitzer, P. M., Cohen, A. L., Oettingen, G., & Burgess, P. W. (2009). Separable brain systems supporting cued versus self-initiated realization of delayed intentions. *Journal of Experimental Psychology: Learning, Memory, and Cognition, 35*, 905–915.

Gilchrist, M. R. (1998). Disease and infection in the American Civil War. *American Biology Teacher, 60*, 258–262.

Gilens, M. (1996). Race and poverty in America: Public misperceptions and the American news media. *Public Opinion Quarterly, 60*, 515–541.

Gladwell, M. (2004). *Blink: The power of thinking without thinking*. New York: Little, Brown.

Goldsmith, J. (1994, May 1). This is your brain on Tetris. *Wired*. https://www.wired.com/1994/05/tetris-2/.

Gollwitzer, P. M. (1993). Goal achievement: The role of intentions. *European Review of Social Psychology, 4*, 141–185.

Gollwitzer, P. M. (1999). Implementation intentions: Strong effects of simple plans. *American Psychologist, 5*, 493–503.

REFERENCES

Gollwitzer, P. M., & Brandstätter, V. (1997). Implementation intentions and effective goal pursuit. *Journal of Personality and Social Psychology, 73*, 186–199.

Gollwitzer, P. M., & Sheeran, P. (2006). Implementation intentions and goal achievement: A meta-analysis of effects and processes. *Advances in Experimental Social Psychology, 38*, 69–119.

Gollwitzer, P. M., Sheeran, P., Troetschel, R., & Webb, T. L. (2011). Self-regulation of priming effects on behavior. *Psychological Science, 22*, 901–907.

Goodale, M. A., Milner, A. D., Jakobsen, L. S., & Carey, D. P. (1991). Perceiving the world and grasping it: A neurological dissociation. *Nature, 349*, 154–156.

Gruenfeld, D. H., Inesi, M. E., Magee, J. C., & Galinsky, A. D. (2008). Power and the objectification of social targets. *Journal of Personality and Social Psychology, 85*, 111–127.

Gundersen, E. (2016, October 29). World exclusive: Bob Dylan—"I'll be at the Nobel Prize Ceremony . . . if I can." *The Telegraph.*

Hadfield, J. A. (1954). *Dreams and nightmares.* Harmondsworth, England: Penguin.

Ham, J., & Van den Bos, K. (2009). Lady Justice thinks unconsciously: Unconscious thought can lead to more accurate justice judgments. *Social Cognition, 27*, 509–521.

Ham, J., & Van den Bos, K. (2010a). The merits of unconscious processing of directly and indirectly obtained information about social justice. *Social Cognition, 28*, 180–190.

Ham, J., & Van den Bos, K. (2010b). On unconscious morality: The effects of unconscious thinking on moral decision-making. *Social Cognition, 28*, 74–83.

Hanusch, K. U., Janssen, C. H., Billheimer, D., Jenkins, I., Spurgeon, E., Lowry, C. A., et al. (2013). Whole-body hyperthermia for the treatment of major depression: Associations with thermoregulatory cooling. *American Journal of Psychiatry, 170*, 802–804.

Hardin, G. (1968). The tragedy of the commons. *Science, 162*, 1243–1248.

Harlow, H. F. (1958). The nature of love. *American Psychologist, 13*, 673–685.

Harlow, H. F., & Suomi, S. J. (1970). The nature of love—simplified. *American Psychologist, 25*, 161–168.

Harris, J. L., Bargh, J. A., & Brownell, K. D. (2009). Priming effects of television food advertising on eating behavior. *Health Psychology, 28*, 404–413.

Harris, J. L., Pierce, M., & Bargh, J. A. (2014). Priming effect of antismoking PSAs on smoking behaviour: A pilot study. *Tobacco Control, 23*, 285–290.

Herring, D. R., White, K. R., Jabeen, L. N., Hinojos, M., Terrazas, G., Reyes, S. M., Taylor, J. H., & Crites Jr., S. L. (2013). On the automatic activation of attitudes: A quarter century of evaluative priming research. *Psychological Bulletin, 139*, 1062–1089.

Hibbing, J. R., Smith, K. B., & Alford, J. R. (2014). Differences in negativity bias underlie variations in political ideology. *Behavioral and Brain Sciences, 37*, 297–307.

Higgins, E. T., & Chaires, W. M. (1980). Accessibility of interrelational constructs: Implications for stimulus encoding and creativity. *Journal of Experimental Social Psychology, 16*, 348–361.

Higgins, E. T., King, G. A., & Mavin, G. H. (1982). Individual construct accessibility and subjective impressions and recall. *Journal of Personality and Social Psychology, 43*, 35–47.

Higgins, E. T., Rholes, W. S., & Jones, C. R. (1977). Category accessibility and impression formation. *Journal of Experimental Social Psychology, 13*, 141–154.

Hill, K. (2014, June 28). Facebook manipulated 689,003 users' emotions for science. *Forbes* online blog: http://www.forbes.com/sites/kashmirhill/2014/06/28/facebook-manipulated-689003-users-emotions-for-science/#1a5b8624704d.

Hill, S. E., & Durante, K. M. (2011). Courtship, competition, and the pursuit of attractiveness: Mating goals facilitate health-related risk taking and strategic risk suppression in women. *Personality and Social Psychology Bulletin, 37*, 383–394.

Hirschleifer, D. A., & Shumway, T. (2003). Good day sunshine: Stock returns and the weather. *Journal of Finance, 58*, 1009–1032.

Hoelscher, T. J., Klinger, E., Barta, S. G. (1981). Incorporation of concern- and nonconcern-related verbal stimuli into dream content. *Journal of Abnormal Psychology, 49*, 88–91.

Hofmann, W., Baumeister, R. F., Foerster, G., & Vohs, K. D. (2012). Everyday temptations: An experience sampling study of desire, conflict, and self-control. *Journal of Personality and Social Psychology, 102*, 1318–1335.

Holland, R. W., Hendriks, M., & Aarts, H. (2005). Smells like clean spirit: Nonconscious effects of scent on cognition and behavior. *Psychological Science, 16*, 689–693.

Holmes, J. G., & Rempel, J. K. (1989). Trust in close relationships. In C. Hendrick (Ed.), *Review of personality and social psychology* (Vol. 10, pp. 187–220). London: Sage.

Hommel, B. (2013). Ideomotor action control: On the perceptual grounding of voluntary actions and agents. In W. Prinz, M. Beisert, & A. Herwig (Eds.), *Action science: Foundations of an emerging discipline* (pp. 113–136). Cambridge, MA: MIT Press.

Huang, J. Y., Sedlovskaya, A., Ackerman, J. M., & Bargh, J. A. (2011). Immunizing against prejudice: Effects of disease protection on attitudes toward out-groups. *Psychological Science, 22*, 1550–1556.

IJzerman, H., Gallucci, M., Pouw, W. T., Weissgerber, S. C., Van Doesum, N. J., & Williams, K. D. (2012). Cold-blooded loneliness: Social exclusion leads to lower skin temperatures. *Acta Psychologica, 140*, 283–288.

IJzerman, H., Karremans, J. C., Thomsen, L., & Schubert, T. W. (2013). Caring for sharing: How attachment styles modulate communal cues of physical warmth. *Social Psychology, 44*, 161–167.

IJzerman, H., & Semin, G. (2009). The thermometer of social relations: Mapping social proximity on temperature. *Psychological Science, 20*, 1214–1220.

Inagaki, T. K., & Eisenberger, N. I. (2013). Shared neural mechanisms underlying social warmth and physical warmth. *Psychological Science, 24*, 2272–2280.

Inagaki, T. K., Irwin, M. R., & Eisenberger, N. I. (2015). Blocking opioids attenuates physical warmth-induced feelings of social connection. *Emotion, 15*, 494–500.

Inagaki, T. K., Irwin, M. R., Moieni, M., Jevtic, I., & Eisenberger, N. I. (2016). A pilot study examining physical and social warmth: Higher (non-febrile) oral temperature is associated with greater feelings of social connection. *PLoS-One, 11(8):* e0160865.

Inbar, Y., Cone, J., & Gilovich, T. (2010). People's intuitions about intuitive insight and intuitive choice. *Journal of Personality and Social Psychology, 99,* 232–247.

Inbar, Y., Pizarro, D. A., & Bloom, P. (2009). Conservatives are more easily disgusted than liberals. *Cognition and Emotion, 23,* 714–725.

Jacob, C., Gueguen, N., Martin, A., & Boulbry, G. (2011). Retail salespeople's mimicry of customers: Effects on consumer behavior. *Journal of Retailing and Consumer Services, 18,* 381–388.

Jacoby, L. L., Kelley, C., Brown, J., & Jasechko, J. (1989). Becoming famous overnight: Limits on the ability to avoid unconscious influences of the past. *Journal of Personality and Social Psychology, 56,* 326–338.

James, W. (1890). *Principles of psychology.* New York: Henry Holt.

James, W. (1912/1938). Does consciousness exist? In *Essays in radical empiricism* (pp. 1–38). New York: Longmans, Green.

Jaynes, J. (1976). *The origin of consciousness in the breakdown of the bicameral mind.* New York: Houghton Mifflin.

Johnson, J. (2016, November 7). "Something is happening that is amazing," Trump said. He was right. *Washington Post.* Available online at www.washingtonpost. com/politics/something-is-happening-that-is-amazing-trump-said-he-was-right/2016/11/06/ab9c0b48-a0ef-11e6-8832-23a007c77bb4_story.html.

Johnson, M. K., Kim, J. K., & Risse, G. (1985). Do alcoholic Korsakoff's syndrome patients acquire affective reactions? *Journal of Experimental Psychology: Learning, Memory, and Cognition, 11,* 22–36.

Jones, E. (1953, 1957). *The life and work of Sigmund Freud* (Vols. I and III). New York: Basic Books.

Jones, J. T., Pelham, B. W., Carvallo, M., & Mirenberg, M. C. (2004). How do I love thee? Let me count the Js: Implicit egotism and interpersonal attraction. *Journal of Personality and Social Psychology, 87,* 665–683.

Jones, J. T., Pelham, B. W., Mirenberg, M. C., & Hetts, J. J. (2002). Name letter preferences are not merely mere exposure: Implicit egotism as self-regulation. *Journal of Experimental Social Psychology, 38,* 170–177.

Kahneman, D. (2011). *Thinking, fast and slow.* New York: Farrar, Straus & Giroux.

Kahneman, D., & Frederick, S. (2002). Representativeness revisited: Attribute substitution in intuitive judgment. In T. Gilovich, D. W. Griffin, & D. Kahneman (Eds.), *Heuristics and biases: The psychology of intuitive judgment* (pp. 49–81). New York: Cambridge University Press.

Kahneman, D., Knetsch, J. L., & Thaler, R. H. (1991). Anomalies: The endowment effect, loss aversion, and status quo bias. *Journal of Economic Perspectives, 5,* 193–206.

Kanai, R., Feilden, T., Firth, C., & Rees, G. (2011). Political orientations are correlated with brain structure in young adults. *Current Biology, 21,* 677–680.

Kang, Y., Williams, L., Clark, M., Gray, J., & Bargh, J. A. (2011). Physical temperature effects on trust behavior: The role of insula. *Social Cognitive and Affective Neuroscience, 6,* 507–515.

Karremans, J. C., Verwijmeren, T., Pronk, T. M., & Reitsma, M. (2009). Interacting with women can impair men's cognitive functioning. *Journal of Experimental Social Psychology, 45,* 1041–1044.

Kawakami, K., Phills, C. E., Steele, J. R., & Dovidio, J. F. (2007). (Close) distance makes the heart grow fonder: The impact of approach orientation on attitudes towards Blacks. *Journal of Personality and Social Psychology, 92,* 957–971.

Keizer, K., Lindenberg, S., & Steg, L. (2008). The spreading of disorder. *Science, 322,* 1681–1685.

Kelly, D. J., Quinn, P. C., Slater, A. M., Lee, K., Gibson, A., Smith, M., Ge, L., & Pascalis, O. (2005). Three-month-olds, but not newborns, prefer own-race faces. *Developmental Science 8,* F31–F36.

Kershaw, I. (2000). *Hitler 1936–1945: Nemesis.* New York: Norton.

Kinzler, K. D., et al. (2007). The native language of social cognition. *Proceedings of the National Academy of Sciences USA, 104,* 12577–12580.

Kirschner, S., & Tomasello, M. (2004). Joint music making promotes prosocial behavior in 4-year-old children. *Evolution and Human Behavior, 31,* 354–364.

Klinger, E. (1978). Modes of normal conscious flow. In K. S. Pope & J. L. Singer (Eds.), *The stream of consciousness: Scientific investigations into the flow of human experience.* New York: Plenum.

Klinger, E. (2013). Goal commitments and the content of thoughts and dreams: Basic principles. *Frontiers in Psychology, 4,* 415. doi: 10.3389/fpsyg.2013.00415.

Klinger, E., Barta, S. G., & Maxeiner, M. E. (1980). Motivational correlates of thought content frequency and commitment. *Journal of Personality and Social Psychology, 39,* 1222–1237.

Koestler, A. (1967). *The ghost in the machine.* London: Hutchinson.

Koltyn, K. F., Robins, H. I., Schmitt, C. L., Cohen, J. D., & Morgan, W. P. (1992). Changes in mood state following whole-body hyperthermia. *International Journal of Hyperthermia, 8,* 305–307.

Kramer, A. D. I. (2012). The spread of emotion via Facebook. *Proceedings of the Computer-Human Interaction Society* (CHI: Association for Computing Machinery, New York), pp. 767–770.

Kramer, A. D. I., Guillory, J. E., & Hancock, J. T. (2014). Experimental evidence of massive-scale emotional contagion through social networks. *Proceedings of the National Academy of Sciences, 111,* 8788–8790.

Lacey, S., Stilla, R., & Sathian, K. (2012). Metaphorically feeling: Comprehending textural metaphors activates somatosensory cortex. *Brain and Language, 120,* 416–421.

Lakin, J. L., Chartrand, T. L., & Arkin, R. M. (2008). I am too just like you: Nonconscious mimicry as an automatic behavioral response to social exclusion. *Psychological Science, 19,* 816–822.

Langer, E. J. (1978). Rethinking the role of thought in social interaction. In J. H. Harvey, W. J. Ickes, & R. F. Kidd (Eds.), *New directions in attribution research* (Vol. 2, pp. 25–35). Hillsdale, NJ: Erlbaum.

REFERENCES

Langlois, J. H., Roggman, L. A., Casey, R. J., Ritter, J. M., Rieser-Danner, L. A., & Jenkins, V. Y. (1987). Infant preferences for attractive faces: Rudiments of a stereotype. *Developmental Psychology, 23,* 363–369.

Lazarus, R. S. (1991). *Emotion and adaptation.* New York: Oxford University Press.

LeBlanc, S. A. (2003). *Constant battles: The myth of the peaceful, noble savage.* New York: St. Martin's Press.

LeDoux, J. (1996). *The emotional brain.* New York: Simon & Schuster.

Lee, T. K., & Shapiro, M. A. (2016). Effects of a story character's goal achievement: Modeling a story character's diet behaviors and activating/deactivating a character's diet goal. *Communication Research, 43,* 863–891.

Leutwyler, K. (2000, October). Tetris dreams. *Scientific American.* Available online at https://www.scientificamerican.com/article/tetris-dreams/.

Lhermitte, F. (1986). Human anatomy and the frontal lobes. Part II: Patient behavior in complex and social situations: The "environmental dependency syndrome." *Annals of Neurology, 19,* 335–343.

Lieberman, M. D., Ochsner, K. N., Gilbert, D. T., & Schacter, D. L. (2001). Do amnesics exhibit cognitive dissonance reduction? The role of explicit memory and attention in attitude change. *Psychological Science, 12,* 135–140.

Loewenstein, G. (1996). Out of control: Visceral influences on behavior. *Organizational Behavior and Human Decision Processes, 65,* 272–292.

Macrae, C. N., & Johnston, L. (1998). Help, I need somebody: Automatic action and inaction. *Social Cognition, 16,* 400–417.

Maestripieri, D., Henry, A., & Nickels, N. (2016, in press). Explaining financial and prosocial biases in favor of attractive people: Interdisciplinary perspectives from economics, social psychology, and evolutionary psychology. *Behavioral and Brain Sciences.* doi: 10.1017/S0140525X16000340.

Maier, N. R. F. (1931). Reasoning in humans: II. The solution of a problem and its appearance in consciousness. *Journal of Comparative and Physiological Psychology, 12,* 181–194.

Mailer, N. (2003). *The spooky art: Some thoughts on writing.* New York: Random House.

Malamuth, N. M. (1989a). The attraction to sexual aggression scale: Part One. *Journal of Sex Research, 26,* 26–49.

Malamuth, N. M. (1989b). The attraction to sexual aggression scale: Part Two. *Journal of Sex Research, 26,* 324–354.

Masicampo, E. J., & Baumeister, R. F. (2011). Consider it done! Plan making can eliminate the cognitive effects of unfulfilled goals. *Journal of Personality and Social Psychology, 101,* 667–683.

Mazur, N., Amir, O., & Ariely, D. (2008). The dishonesty of honest people: A theory of self-concept maintenance. *Journal of Marketing Research, 45,* 633–644.

McKenna, K. Y. A., & Bargh, J. A. (1998). Coming out in the age of the Internet: Identity "demarginalization" from virtual group participation. *Journal of Personality and Social Psychology, 75,* 681–694.

Meisner, B. A. (2012). A meta-analysis of positive and negative age stereotype priming effects on behavior among older adults. *Journals of Gerontology Series B: Psychological Sciences and Social Sciences, 67,* 13–17.

REFERENCES

Meltzoff, A. N. (2002). Elements of a developmental theory of imitation. In A. N. Meltzoff & W. Prinz (Eds.), *The imitative mind: Development, evolution, and brain bases* (pp. 19–41). Cambridge: Cambridge University Press.

Mendoza, S. A., Gollwitzer, P. M., & Amodio, D. M. (2010). Reducing the expression of implicit stereotypes: Reflexive control through implementation intentions. *Personality and Social Psychology Bulletin, 36,* 512–523.

Metcalfe, J. (1986). Feeling of knowing in memory and problem solving. *Journal of Experimental Psychology: Learning, Memory, and Cognition, 12,* 288–294.

Metcalfe, J., & Wiebe, D. (1987). Intuition in insight and noninsight problem solving. *Memory & Cognition, 15,* 238–246.

Miller, G. A., Galanter, E., & Pribram, K. A. (1960). *Plans and the structure of behavior.* New York: Holt, Rinehart, & Winston.

Miller, S. L., & Maner, J. K. (2010). Scent of a woman: Men's testosterone responses to olfactory ovulation cues. *Psychological Science, 21,* 276–283.

Miller, S. L., & Maner, J. K. (2011). Ovulation as a male mating prime: Subtle signs of women's fertility influence men's mating cognition and behavior. *Journal of Personality and Social Psychology, 100,* 295–308.

Milyavskaya, M., & Inzlicht, M. (in press). What's so great about self-control? Examining the importance of effortful self-control and temptation in predicting real-life depletion and goal attainment. *Social Psychological and Personality Science.*

Mischel, W. (2014). *The marshmallow test: Mastering self-control.* New York: Little, Brown.

Moore, T. E. (1982). Subliminal advertising: What you see is what you get. *Journal of Marketing, 46,* 38–47.

Moray, N. (1959). Attention in dichotic listening: Affective cues and the influence of instructions. *Quarterly Journal of Experimental Psychology, 11,* 56–60.

Morewedge, C. K., & Norton, M. I. (2009). When dreaming is believing: The (motivated) interpretation of dreams. *Journal of Personality and Social Psychology, 96,* 249–264.

Morewedge, C. K., Giblin, C. E., & Norton, M. I. (2014). The (perceived) meaning of spontaneous thoughts. *Journal of Experimental Psychology: General, 143,* 1742–1754.

Morewedge, C. K., & Kahneman, D. (2010). Associative processes in intuitive judgment. *Trends in Cognitive Sciences, 14,* 435–440.

Morsella, E., Ben-Zeev, A., Lanska, M., & Bargh, J. A. (2010). The spontaneous thoughts of the night: How future tasks breed intrusive cognitions. *Social Cognition, 28,* 640–649.

Myers, F. W. H. (1892). The subliminal consciousness. *Proceedings of the Society for Psychical Research, 7:*298–355, *8:*333–404, 436–535.

Nail, P. R., McGregor, I., Drinkwater, A. E., Steele, G. M., & Thompson, A. W. (2009). Threat causes liberals to think like conservatives. *Journal of Experimental Social Psychology, 45,* 901–907.

Naimi, T. S., Ross, C. S., Siegel, M. B., deJong, W., & Jernigan, D. H. (2016). Amount of televised alcohol advertising exposure and the quantity of alcohol consumed by youth. *Journal of Studies on Alcohol and Drugs, 77,* 723–729.

REFERENCES

Napier, J. L., Huang, J., Vonasch, A., & Bargh, J. A. (2017). Superheroes for change: Physical safety promotes social (but not economic) liberalism. *European Journal of Social Psychology*.

Neisser, U. (1963). The multiplicity of thought. *British Journal of Psychology, 54*, 1–14.

Nelson, L. D., & Norton, M. I. (2005). From student to superhero: Situational primes shape future helping. *Journal of Experimental Social Psychology, 41*, 423–430.

Neuberg, S. (1988). Behavioral implications of information presented outside of conscious awareness: The effect of subliminal presentation of trait information on behavior in the Prisoner's Dilemma Game. *Social Cognition, 6*, 207–230.

Nickerson, D. W., & Rogers, T. (2010). Do you have a voting plan? Implementation intentions, voter turnout, and organic plan making. *Psychological Science, 21*, 194–199.

Nisbett, R. E., & Wilson, T. D. (1977). Telling more than we can know: Verbal reports on mental processes. *Psychological Review, 84*, 231–259.

Nordgren, L. F., Bos, M. W., & Dijksterhuis, A. (2011). The best of both worlds: Integrating conscious and unconscious thought best solves complex decisions. *Journal of Experimental Social Psychology, 47*, 509–511.

Nutt, A. E. (2016, October 19). Report: More than half of mentally ill U.S. adults get no treatment. *Washington Post*, online edition. Available at https://www.washingtonpost.com/news/to-your-health/wp/2016/10/19/report-more-than-half-of-mentally-ill-u-s-adults-get-no-treatment/?utm_term=.64aff6703167.

O'Doherty, J., Winston, J., Critchley, H., Perrett, D., Burt, D. M, & Dolan, R. J. (2003). Beauty in a smile: The role of medial orbitofrontal cortex in facial attractiveness. *Neuropsychologia, 41*, 147–155.

Olson, I. R., & Marshuetz, C. (2005). Facial attractiveness is appraised in a glance. *Emotion, 5*, 498–502.

Orbell, S., Hodgkins, S., & Sheeran, P. (1997). Implementation intentions and the theory of planned behavior. *Personality and Social Psychology Bulletin, 23*, 945–954.

Osgood, C. E. (1949). *The measurement of meaning*. Urbana, IL: University of Illinois Press.

Over, H., & Carpenter, M. (2009). Eighteen-month old infants show increased helping following priming with affiliation. *Psychological Science, 20*, 1189–1193.

Oxley, D. R., et al. (2008). Political attitudes vary with physiological traits. *Science, 321*, 1667–1670.

Papies, E. K., & Barsalou, L. W. (2015). Grounding desire and motivated behavior: A theoretical framework and empirical evidence. In W. Hofmann & L. F. Nordgren (Eds.), *The psychology of desire* (pp. 36–60). New York: Guilford.

Papies, E. K, & Hamstra, P. (2010). Goal priming and eating behavior: Enhancing self-regulation by environmental cues. *Health Psychology, 29*, 384–388.

Papies, E. K., Potjes, I., Keesman, M., Schwinghammer, S., & van Koningsbruggen, G. M. (2014). Using health primes to reduce unhealthy snack purchases among overweight consumers in a grocery store. *International Journal of Obesity, 38*, 597–602.

Papies, E. K., & Veling, H. (2013). Healthy dining: subtle diet reminders at the point of purchase increase low-calorie food choices among both chronic and current dieters. *Appetite, 61*, 1–7.

Parks-Stamm, E. J., Oettingen, G., & Gollwitzer, P. M. (2010). Making sense of one's actions in an explanatory vacuum: The interpretation of nonconscious goal striving. *Journal of Experimental Social Psychology, 46,* 531–542.

Pelham, B. W., Carvallo, M., DeHart, T., & Jones, J. T. (2003). Assessing the validity of implicit egotism: A reply to Gallucci (2003). *Journal of Personality and Social Psychology, 85,* 800–807.

Pelham, B., & Carvallo, M. (2015). When Tex and Tess Carpenter build houses in Texas: Moderators of implicit egotism. *Self and Identity, 14,* 692–723.

Penfield, W. (1961). Activation of the record of human experience. *Annual Reports of the College of Surgeons England, 29,* 77–84.

Perdue, C. W., Dovidio, J. F., Gurtman, M. B., & Tyler, R. B. (1990). Us and them: Social categorization and the process of intergroup bias. *Journal of Personality and Social Psychology, 59,* 475–486.

Perry, C., & Laurence, J.-R. (1984). Mental processing outside of awareness: The contributions of Freud and Janet. In K. S. Bowers & D. Meichenbaum (Eds.), *The unconscious reconsidered* (pp. 9–48). New York: Wiley.

Pessiglione, M., Schmidt, L., Draganski, B., Kalisch, R., Lau, H., Dolan, R., & Frith, C. (2007). How the brain translates money into force: A neuroimaging study of subliminal motivation. *Science, 316,* 904–906.

Phelps, E. A. (2009). Emotion's influence on attention and memory. In L. Squire, T. Albright, F. Bloom, F. Gage, & N. Spitzer (Eds.), *New encyclopedia of neuroscience* (pp. 941–946). Oxford, UK: Elsevier.

Phelps, E.A. (2012). Emotion and memory. In L. Nadel & W. Sinnott-Armstrong (Eds.), *Memory and law.* New York: Oxford University Press.

Pinker, S. (1994). *The language instinct.* New York: William Morrow.

Pinker, S. (2011). *The better angels of our nature: Why violence has declined.* New York: Viking.

Pratkanis, A. (1992). The cargo cult science of subliminal persuasion. *Skeptical Inquirer, 16,* 260–272.

Pronin, E. (2009). The introspection illusion. In M. P. Zanna (Ed.), *Advances in experimental social psychology, 41,* 1–67.

Pryor, J. B. (1987). Sexual harassment proclivities in men. *Sex Roles, 77,* 269–290.

Pulvermueller, F, & Fadiga, L. (2010). Active perception: Sensorimotor circuits as a cortical basis for language. *Nature Reviews: Neuroscience, 11,* 351–360.

Raichle, M. E., et al. (2001). A default mode of brain function. *Proceedings of the National Academy of Sciences USA, 98,* 676–682.

Raichle, M. E., & Mintun, M. A. (2006). Brain work and brain imaging. *Annual Review of Neuroscience, 29,* 449–476.

Raison, C. L., Hale, M. W., Williams, L. E., Wager, T. D., & Lowry, C. A. (2015). Somatic influences on subjective well-being and affective disorders: The convergence of thermosensory and central serotonergic systems. *Frontiers of Psychology, 5,* 1580.

Ratner, J. (Ed., 1927). *The philosophy of Spinoza—Selected from his chief works.* New York: Random House.

Reinhard, M.-A., Greifender, R., & Scharmach, M. (2013). Unconscious processes improve lie detection. *Journal of Personality and Social Psychology, 105,* 721–739.

Resnick, B. (2016, November 3). *The myth of self-control.* Vox.com. Available online

REFERENCES

at http://www.vox.com/science-and-health/2016/11/3/13486940/self-control -psychology-myth.

Rogers, T., & Milkman, K. L. (2016). Reminders through association. *Psychological Science, 27,* 973–986.

Rogers, T., Milkman, K. L., John, L. K., & Norton, M. I. (2015). Beyond good intentions: Prompting people to make plans improves follow-through on important tasks. *Behavioral Science & Policy, 1,* 33–41.

Roosevelt, F. D. (1933, March 4/1938). Inaugural address. In S. Rosenman (Ed.) (1938), *The public papers of Franklin D. Roosevelt* (Vol. 2, pp. 11–16). New York: Random House.

Rosenquist, J. N., Fowler, J. H., & Christakis, N. A. (2011). Social network determinants of depression. *Molecular Psychiatry, 16,* 273–281.

Rosenzweig, S. (1994). *The historic expedition to America (1909): Freud, Jung and Hall the king-maker.* St. Louis: Rana House.

Ross, M., & Sicoly, F. (1979). Egocentric biases in availability and attribution. *Journal of Personality and Social Psychology, 32,* 880–892.

Sadler-Smith, E. (2012). *Inside intuition.* New York: Routledge.

Schaefer, M., Charkasskiy, L., Denke, C., Spies, C., Heinz, A., Stroehle, A., Song, H., & Bargh, J. A. (2017). *Incidental haptic sensations influence judgment of crimes: Neural underpinnings of embodied cognitions.* Paper presented at the annual meetings of the Cognitive Neuroscience Society, San Francisco, March 2017.

Schaefer, M., Heinze, H.-J., & Rotte, M. (2014). Rough primes and rough conversations: Evidence for a modality-specific basis to mental metaphors. *Social Cognitive and Affective Neuroscience, 9,* 1653–1659.

Schaefer, M., Rotte, M., Heinze, H.-J., & Denke, C. (2015). Dirty deeds and dirty bodies: Embodiment of the Macbeth effect is mapped topographically onto the somatosensory cortex. *Scientific Reports, 5,* 1–11.

Schnall, S., Haidt, J., Clore, G. L., & Jordan, A. H. (2008). Disgust as embodied moral judgment. *Personality and Social Psychology Bulletin, 34,* 1096–1109.

Schneirla, T. C. (1959). An evolutionary and developmental theory of biphasic processes underlying approach and withdrawal. In M. R. Jones (Ed.), *Nebraska Symposium on Motivation* (pp. 1–42). Lincoln, NE: University of Nebraska Press.

Schwarz, N., & Clore, G. (1983). Mood, misattribution, and judgments of well-being: Informative and directive functions of affective states. *Journal of Personality and Social Psychology, 45,* 513–523.

Shalev, I., & Bargh, J. A. (2011). Use of priming-based interventions to facilitate psychological health: Commentary on Kazdin & Blase (2011). *Perspectives on Psychological Science, 6,* 488–492.

Shariff, A. F., Willard, A. K., Andersen, T., & Norenzayan, A. (2016). Religious priming: A meta-analysis with a focus on prosociality. *Personality and Social Psychology Review, 20,* 27–48.

Shaw, A., DeScioli, P., & Olson, K. R. (2012). Fairness versus favoritism in children. *Evolution in Human Behavior, 33,* 736–745.

Shaw, A., & Olson, K. R. (2012). Children discard a resource to avoid inequity. *Journal of Experimental Psychology: General, 141,* 382–395.

REFERENCES

Sheeran, P., & Orbell, S. (1999). Implementation intentions and repeated behaviors: Augmenting the predictive validity of the theory of planned behavior. *European Journal of Social Psychology, 29*, 349–370.

Sherif, M., Harvey, O. J., White, B. J., Hood, W. R., & Sherif, C. W. (1954/1961). *Intergroup conflict and cooperation: The Robbers Cave experiment.* Manuscript available online at https://www.free-ebooks.net/ebook/Intergroup-Conflict-and-Cooperation-The-Robbers-Cave-Experiment/pdf?dl&preview.

Shook, N. J., & Clay, R. (2011). Valence asymmetry in attitude formation: A correlate of political ideology. *Social Psychological and Personality Science, 2*, 650–655.

Siegel, J. M. (2009). Sleep viewed as a state of adaptive inactivity. *Nature Reviews Neuroscience, 10*, 747–753.

Simmons, W. K., Martin, A., & Barsalou, L. W. (2005). Pictures of appetizing foods activate gustatory cortices for taste and reward. *Cerebral Cortex, 15*, 1602–1608.

Simpson, J. A., Collins, W. A., & Salvatore, J. E. (2011). The impact of early interpersonal experience on adult romantic relationship functioning: Recent findings from the Minnesota Longitudinal Study of Risk and Adaptation. *Current Directions in Psychological Science, 20*, 355–359.

Simpson, J. A., Collins, W. A., Salvatore, J. E., & Sung, S. (2014). The impact of early personal experience on adult romantic relationship functioning. In M. Mikulincer & P. R. Shaver (Eds.), *Mechanisms of social connection: From brain to group* (pp. 221–234). Washington, DC: American Psychological Association.

Simpson, J. A., Collins, W. A., Tran, S., & Haydon, K. C. (2007). Attachment and the experience and expression of emotions in adult romantic relationships: A developmental perspective. *Journal of Personality and Social Psychology, 92*, 355–367.

Singal, J. (2017). Psychology's racism measuring tool isn't up to the job [Blog post]. Retrieved from http://nymag.com/scienceofus/2017/01/psychologys-racism-measuring-tool-isnt-up-to-the-job.html.

Skinner, B. F. (1971). *Beyond freedom and dignity.* New York: Knopf.

Skitka, L. J., Mullen, E., Griffin, T., Hutchinson, S., & Chamberlin, B. (2002). Dispositions, ideological scripts, or motivated correction? Understanding ideological differences in attributions for social problems. *Journal of Personality and Social Psychology, 83*, 470–487.

Slater, A., Bremner, G., Johnson, S. P., Sherwood, P., Hayes, R., & Brown, E. (2000). Newborn infants' preference for attractive faces: The role of internal and external facial features. *Infancy, 1*, 265–274.

Slepian, M. L., Young, S. G., Rule, N. O., Weisbuch, M., & Ambady, N. (2012). Embodied impression formation: Trust judgments and motor cues to approach and avoidance. *Social Cognition, 30*, 232–240.

Slotter, E. B., & Gardner, W. L. (2010). Can you help me become the "me" I want to be? The role of goal pursuit in friendship formation. *Self and Identity, 10*, 231–247.

Snyder, P. J., Kaufman, R., Harrison, J., & Maruff, P. (2010). Charles Darwin's emotional expression "experiment" and his contribution to modern neuropharmacology. *Journal of the History of the Neurosciences, 19*, 158–170.

Snyder, M., Tanke, E. D., & Berscheid, E. (1977). Social perception and interpersonal

REFERENCES

behavior: On the self-fulfilling nature of social stereotypes. *Journal of Personality and Social Psychology, 35,* 656–666.

Solarz, A. (1960). Latency of instrumental responses as a function of compatibility with the meaning of eliciting verbal signs. *Journal of Experimental Psychology, 59,* 239–245.

Sommers, S. R. (2006). On racial diversity and group decision-making: Identifying multiple effects of racial composition on jury deliberations. *Journal of Personality and Social Psychology, 90,* 597–612.

Sperling, G. (1960). The information available in brief visual presentations. *Psychological Monographs: General and Applied, 74,* 1–29.

Steele, C. M., & Aronson, J. (1995). Stereotype threat and the intellectual test performance of African Americans. *Journal of Personality and Social Psychology, 69,* 797–811.

Stewart, B. D., & Payne, B. K. (2008). Bringing automatic stereotyping under control: Implementation intentions as efficient means of thought control. *Personality and Social Psychology Bulletin, 34,* 1332–1345.

Stickgold, R., Malia, A., Maguire, D., Roddenberry, D., & O'Connor, M. (2000, October 13). Replaying the game: Hypnagogic images in normal and amnesics. *Science, 290,* 350–353.

Stone, J., Lynch, C. I., Sjomeling, M., & Darley, J. M. (1999). Stereotype threat effects on Black and White athletic performance. *Journal of Personality and Social Psychology, 77,* 1213–1227.

Storey, S., & Workman, L. (2013). The effects of temperature priming on cooperation in the iterated prisoner's dilemma. *Evolutionary Psychology, 11,* 52–67.

Stroop, J. R. (1935). Studies of interference in serial verbal reactions. *Journal of Experimental Psychology, 18,* 643–662.

Tajfel, H., Billig, M. G., Bundy, R. P., & Flament, C. (1971). Social categorization and intergroup behavior. *European Journal of Social Psychology, 1,* 149–177.

Tang, Y.-Y., Tang, R., & Posner, M. I. (2013). Brief meditation training induces smoking reduction. *Proceedings of the National Academy of Sciences, 110,* 13971–13975.

Tangney, J. P., Baumeister, R. F., & Boone, A. L. (2004). High self-control predicts good adjustment, less pathology, better grades, and interpersonal success. *Journal of Personality, 72,* 271–324.

Todorov, A., Mandisodza, A. N., Goren, A., & Hall, C. C. (2005). Inferences of competence from faces predict election outcomes. *Science, 308,* 1623–1626.

Tooby, J., & Cosmides, L. (1990). The past explains the present: Emotional adaptations and the structure of ancestral environments. *Ethology and Sociobiology, 11,* 375–424.

Tooby, J., & Cosmides, L. (2005). Conceptual foundations of evolutionary psychology. In D. Buss (Ed.), *The handbook of evolutionary psychology* (pp. 5–67). Hoboken, NJ: Wiley.

Troisi, J. D., & Gabriel, S. (2011). Chicken soup really is good for the soul: "Comfort food" fulfills the need to belong. *Psychological Science, 22,* 747–753.

Tuchman, B. (1962). *The guns of August.* New York: Random House.

REFERENCES

Turk-Browne, N. B., Jungé, J. A., & Scholl, B. J. (2005). The automaticity of visual statistical learning. *Journal of Experimental Psychology: General, 134,* 552–564.

Turk-Browne, N. B., Scholl, B. J., Chun, M. M., & Johnson, M. K. (2009). Neural evidence of statistical learning: Efficient detection of visual regularities without awareness. *Journal of Cognitive Neuroscience, 21,* 1934–1945.

Turk-Browne, N. B., Scholl, B. J., Johnson, M. K., & Chun, M. M. (2010). Implicit perceptual anticipation triggered by statistical learning. *Journal of Neuroscience, 30,* 11177–11187.

Tversky, A., & Kahneman, D. (1974). Judgment under uncertainty: Heuristics and biases. *Science, 184,* 1124–1131.

Uhlmann, E. L., Poehlman, T. A., & Bargh, J. A. (2009). American moral exceptionalism. In J. Jost, A. Kay, & H. Thorisdottir (Eds.), *Social and psychological bases of ideology and system justification* (pp. 27–52). New York: Oxford.

U.S. Department of Defense. (2013). *2012 workplace and gender relations survey of active duty members.* (Note No. 2013–007). Washington, D. C.: Retrieved from http://www.sapr.mil/public/docs/research/2012_Workplace_and_Gender_Relations_Survey_of_Active_Duty_Members-Survey_Note_and_Briefing.pdf.

Van Baaren, R. B., Holland, R. W., Steenaert, B., & van Knippenberg, A. (2003). Mimicry for money: Behavioral consequences of imitation. *Journal of Experimental Social Psychology, 39,* 393–398.

Van Bavel, J. J., & Cunningham, W. A. (2009). Self-categorization with a novel mixed-race group moderates automatic social and racial biases. *Personality and Social Psychology Bulletin, 35,* 321–335.

Van Koningsbruggen, G. M., Stroebe, W., Papies, E. K., & Aarts, H. (2011). Implementation intentions as goal primes: Boosting self-control in tempting environments. *European Journal of Social Psychology, 41,* 551–557.

Von Hartmann, E. (1884/1931). *Philosophy of the unconscious—Speculative results according to the inductive method of physical science.* Translated by W. C. Coupland (based on the 9th German edition of 1884). New York: Harcourt, Brace.

Vygotsky, L. S. (1934/1962). *Thought and language* (E. Hanfmann & G. Vakar, Trans.). Cambridge, MA: MIT Press. (Original work published 1934.)

Wallace, K. (2016, September 9). The more alcohol ads kids see, the more alcohol they consume. CNN. http://www.cnn.com/2016/09/07/health/kids-alcohol-ads-impact-underage-drinking/index.html.

Walton, G., Cohen, G., Cwir, D., & Spencer, S. J. (2012). Mere belonging: The power of social connections. *Journal of Personality and Social Psychology, 102,* 513–532.

Wang, Y. C., McPherson, K., Marsh, T., Gortmaker, S. L, & Brown, M. (2011, August 27). Health and economic burden of the projected obesity trends in the USA and the UK. *Lancet, 378,* 815–825.

Watson, J. B. (1913). Psychology as the behaviorist views it. *Psychological Review, 20,* 158–177.

Wegner, D. M. (1994). Ironic processes of mental control. *Psychological Review, 101,* 34–52.

Weingarten, E., Chen, Q., McAdams, M., Yi , J., Hepler, J., & Albarracin, D. (2016).

REFERENCES

From primed concepts to action: A meta-analysis of the behavioral effects of incidentally-presented words. *Psychological Bulletin, 142,* 472–497.

Wiers, R. W., Eberl, C., Rinck, M., Becker, E., & Lindenmeyer, J. (2011). Re-training automatic action tendencies changes alcoholic patients' approach bias for alcohol and improves treatment outcome. *Psychological Science, 22,* 490–497.

Weisbuch, M., Pauker, K., & Ambady, N. (2009). The subtle transmission of race bias via televised nonverbal behavior. *Science, 326,* 1711–1714.

Welsh, D. T., & Ordonez, L. D. (2014). Conscience without cognition: The effects of subconscious priming on ethical behavior. *Academy of Management Journal, 57,* 723–742.

Whyte, L. L. (1960). *The unconscious before Freud.* New York: Basic Books.

Wicklund, R. A., & Gollwitzer, P. M. (1982). *Symbolic self-completion theory.* Hillsdale, NJ: Erlbaum.

Wieber, F., Gollwitzer, P. M., & Sheeran, P. (2014). Strategic regulation of mimicry effects by implementation intentions. *Journal of Experimental Social Psychology, 53,* 31–39.

Williams, K. D., & Jarvis, B. (2006). Cyberball: A program for use in research on interpersonal ostracism and acceptance. *Behavioral Research Methods, 38,* 174–180.

Williams, L. E., & Bargh, J. A. (2008). Experiencing physical warmth influences interpersonal warmth. *Science, 322,* 606–607.

Williams, L. E., & Poehlman, T. A. (2017). Conceptualizing consciousness in consumer research. *Journal of Consumer Research.* Digitally published August 2016. doi: 10.1093/jcr/ucw043.

Williams, M. J., Gruenfeld, D. H., & Guillory, L. E. (2016, in press). Sexual aggression when power is new: The effects of acute high power on chronically low-power individuals. *Journal of Personality and Social Psychology.*

Willis, J., & Todorov, A. (2006). First impressions: Making up your mind after 100 ms exposure to a face. *Psychological Science, 17,* 592–598.

Wilson, T. D. (2002). *Strangers to Ourselves: Discovering the Adaptive Unconscious.* Cambridge, MA: Harvard University Press.

Wilson, T. D., & Brekke, N. (1994). Mental contamination and mental correction: Unwanted influences on judgments and evaluations. *Psychological Bulletin, 116,* 117–142.

Wilson, T. D., & Schooler, J. W. (1991). Thinking too much: Introspection can reduce the quality of preferences and decisions. *Journal of Personality and Social Psychology, 60,* 181–192.

Wiltermuth, S. S., & Heath, C. (2009). Synchrony and cooperation. *Psychological Science, 20,* 1–5.

Wolf, S. (1994). *Freedom within reason.* New York: Oxford University Press.

Wood, W., & Ruenger, D. (2016). Psychology of habit. *Annual Review of Psychology, 67,* 280–314.

Xu, A. J., Schwarz, N., & Wyer Jr., R. S. (2015). Hunger promotes acquisition of nonfood objects. *Proceedings of the National Academy of Sciences, 112,* 2688–2692.

Zajonc, R. B. (1968). The attitudinal effects of mere exposure. *Journal of Personality and Social Psychology, 9,* Monograph Supplement 2, part 2, pp. 1–27.

REFERENCES

Zajonc, R. B. (1980). Feeling and thinking: Preferences need no inferences. *American Psychologist, 35,* 151–175.

Zajonc, R. B., Adelmann, P. K., Murphy, S. T., & Niedenthal, P. M. (1987). Convergence in the physical appearance of spouses. *Motivation and Emotion, 11,* 335–346.

Zaval, L., Keenan, E. A., Johnson, E. J., & Weber, E. U. (2014). How warm days increase belief in global warming. *Nature: Climate Change, 4,* 143–147.

Zdaniuk, A., & Bobocel, D. R. (2013). The automatic activation of (un)fairness behavior in organizations. *Human Resource and Management Review, 23,* 254–265.

Zebrowitz, L., & Montepare, J. (2015). Faces and first impressions. In G. Borgida & J. Bargh (Eds.), *Handbook of Personality and Social Psychology* (Vol. 1, Attitudes and Social Cognition). Washington, DC: American Psychological Association.

Zhong, C.-B., & DeVoe, S. E. (2010). You are how you eat: Fast food and impatience. *Psychological Science, 21,* 619–622.

Zhong, C.-B., & Leonardelli, G. J. (2008). Cold and lonely: Does social exclusion literally feel cold? *Psychological Science, 19,* 838–842.

Zhong, C.-B., & Liljenquist, K. (2006). Washing away your sins: Threatened morality and physical cleansing. *Science, 313,* 1451–1452.

Zillmann, D., Johnson, R. C., & Day, K. D. (1974). Attribution of apparent arousal and proficiency of recovery from sympathetic activation affecting excitation transfer to aggressive behavior. *Journal of Experimental Social Psychology, 10,* 503–515.

Index

INDEX

INDEX